more
Quips
Quotes
&Anecdotes
for Preachers and Teachers

ANTHONY CASTLE

TWENTY-THIRD PUBLICATIONS
A Division of Bayard   MYSTIC, CT 06355

First published in the United Kingdom in 1994 under the title
Quotes and Anecdotes by
KEVIN MAYHEW LTD
Maypole Farm
Rectory Road
Buxhall
Stowmarket
Suffolk, IP14 3BW, U.K.

Reprinted under license in the USA by
TWENTY-THIRD PUBLICATIONS
A DIVISION OF BAYARD
185 Willow Street
P.O. Box 180
Mystic, CT 06355
(860) 536-2611
(800) 321-0411

ISBN:1-58595-136-6
Library of Congress Catalog Card Number: 00-135471
Printed in the U.S.A.

CONTENTS

More Quips, Quotes, & Anecdotes
for Preachers and Teachers

Dedicated to
my wife, Liz

PREFACE

Fourteen years ago, when the first edition of this book was published, I never dreamt that it would be so well received by ministers, teachers and general readers in countries as far apart as Australia, India and the USA. This present revision of a book which began life, in my student days, as a simple exercise book for my own personal use, is intended to make a pastoral aid more relevant and suitable for widespread use. That is all the book has ever claimed to be, a pastoral aid, for those who have the privilege of proclaiming and promoting the Good News of the Kingdom. Besides its obvious use in the preparation of sermons and school assemblies, it has provided fillers for parish newsletters, stimulation for prayer groups and bedside reading for the retiring Christian.

During its lifetime *Quotes and Anecdotes* has prompted the writing of several books and inspired a series of posters, but most important of all, I know it has been an appreciated aid to countless hard-working ministers and teachers; I hope and pray that this revised edition will give as much help and support.

ANTHONY P. CASTLE

A1
THE VALUE OF TIME

'You know *the time* has come.' *Romans 13:11*

QUOTATIONS

Time is full of eternity. As we use it so shall we be.
(Henry Manning)

It is the wisest who grieve most at loss of time. *(Dante)*

He who neglects the present moment throws away all he has.
(Schiller)

Time deals gently with those who take it gently.
(Anatole France)

One always has time enough if one will apply it. *(Goethe)*

Time is a circus, always packing up and moving away.
(Ben Hecht)

Time is a threefold present: the present as we experience it, the past as a present memory and the future as a present expectation. *(St Augustine of Hippo)*

In rivers the water that you touch is the last of what has passed and the first of that which comes; so with present time.
(Leonardo da Vinci)

Dost thou love life? Then do not squander Time, for that's the stuff life is made of. *(Benjamin Franklin)*

Come what, come may, time and the hour run through the roughest day. *(Shakespeare)*

The great rule of moral conduct is, next to God, to respect time. *(Lavater)*

You will find rest from vain fancies if you do every act in life as though it were your last. *(Marcus Aurelius)*

(Today) is a gift from God which holds out immense opportunities for us. It is the first day of the rest of our lives; whatever yesterday was like, today is wholly new and the future lies ahead. *(David Hope)*

PROVERB

All the treasures of earth cannot bring back one lost moment. *(French proverb)*

HUMOUR

Teacher Jimmy, name a great time saver.

Jimmy Love at first sight!

Professor Mr Jones, will you tell me why you keep looking at your watch?

Jones Yes, Sir, I was frightened that you might not have time to finish your interesting lecture!

WORD PICTURES

'What of all things in the world, is the longest and the shortest, the swiftest and the slowest, the most divisible and the most extended, the most neglected and the most regretted, without which nothing can be done, which devours all that is little, and enlivens all that is great?' Question put to Zadig in Voltaire's *Zadig – a Mystery of Fate.* Zadig replied: 'Time'.

When a man sits with a pretty girl for an hour, it seems like a minute. But let him sit on a hot stove for a minute – and it's longer than any hour. That's relativity. *(Albert Einstein)*

In a garden next to Gloucester Cathedral there is a sundial which bears this inscription:
   'Give God thy heart, thy service and thy gold;
   The day wears on and time is waxing old.'

A hunter in India with a sling had come to the end of his stones and wanted one to sling at a bird in a tree. He saw some fine stones lying near, and took up a handful to hurl one by one with his sling. Without very much success, however, for the bird flew gaily off, and the stones fell into the river, only one remaining of the handful he had taken. He was going to throw it away, but seeing it was pretty, he saved it as a plaything for his little daughter.

   On the way home, he met a diamond merchant, and showed him the stone. The merchant saw at once that it was a diamond, and offered a large sum for it. The hunter started lamenting his bad fortune, and on being asked why he was so disconsolate, he explained that it was because he had not realised the value of the stones he had thrown into the river. Had he but saved them, a fortune might have been his. They were now lost to him for ever. So is every day of life precious – it can never be recovered. (*Anon*)

Time is:
   too slow for those who wait,
   too swift for those who fear,
   too long for those who grieve,
   too short for those who rejoice; but for those who love,
   time is eternity. (*Henry Van Dyke*)

Take Time to *THINK* . . . It is the source of power.
Take Time to *PLAY* . . . It is the secret of perpetual youth.
Take Time to *READ* . . . It is the fountain of wisdom.
Take Time to *PRAY* . . . It is the greatest power on earth.
Take Time to *LOVE* and *BE LOVED* . . . It is a
                                  God-given privilege.
Take Time to *BE FRIENDLY* . . . It is the road to happiness.
Take Time to *LAUGH* . . . It is the music of the soul.

Take Time to *GIVE* . . . It is too short a day to be selfish.
Take Time to *WORK* . . . It is the price of success.
Take Time to *DO CHARITY* . . . It is the key to heaven.
(Anon)

USEFUL TEXTS

Time:
Appropriate, for different events, *Eccles. 3:1-8*
Of Christ's return, *Matt. 24:36*
Right, to respond to the Gospel, *Mark 1:15*
Should be carefully used, *Eph. 5:16*

See also: A19 Patience
B25 Quiet-time for prayer
C34 The value of little things

A2
INTEGRITY

'Integrity is the loincloth round his waist.' *Isaiah 11:5*

QUOTATIONS

A man or woman of integrity, sincerity and good nature can never be concealed, for his or her character is wrought into their countenance. *(Marcus Aurelius)*

The measure of a person's real character is what he would do if he knew he would never be found out.
(Thomas Macaulay)

Integrity without knowledge is weak and useless, and knowledge without integrity is dangerous and dreadful.
(Samuel Johnson)

Some people are likeable in spite of their unswerving integrity!
(Don Marquis)

It is a fine thing to be honest but it is also very important to be right. *(Winston Churchill)*

I am not bound to win,
    but I am bound to be true.
I am not bound to succeed,
    but I am bound to live up to the light I have.
I must stand with anybody that stands right,
    stand with him while he is right,
and part with him when he goes wrong.
(Abraham Lincoln)

PROVERBS

An honest man does not make himself a dog for the sake of a bone. *(Danish proverb)*

They are all honest men, but my cloak is not to be found. *(Spanish proverb)*

HUMOUR

An honest fisherman is a pretty uninteresting person. *(Anon)*

'My boy,' said the businessman to his son, 'there are two things that are essential if you are to succeed in business.'
'What are they, Dad?' asked the boy.
'Integrity and sagacity.'
'What is integrity?'
'Always, no matter what, always keep your word.'
'And sagacity?'
'Never give your word!'

Make yourself an honest man, and then you may be sure that there is one rascal less in the world. *(Carlyle)*

WORD PICTURES

In Napoleon's expedition to Russia, a Russian peasant was captured, forced into Napoleon's service and branded on the arm with the letter 'N'. When he understood what it meant, he chopped off the arm that had been branded, rather than serve his country's enemy. *(Anon)*

I once knew a village joiner who was also undertaker when need arose. His language and manners were crude and as far as I know he only entered a church when his professional duties required him to do so. Yet there was an occasion after a funeral when he heard a group of bystanders saying how sorry they were for the widow who had been left with a young family. Roughly he pushed his way in. 'How much sorry are you?' he demanded, adding 'I'm sorry five pounds!' And he took the money from his pocket there and then to start a collection. *(Edmund Banyard)*

While women weep as they do now, I'll fight; while little children go hungry as they do now, I'll fight; while men go to prison, in and out, in and out, I'll fight; while there is a poor lost girl upon the street, I'll fight; while there yet remains one dark soul without the light of God, I'll fight – I'll fight to the very end. *(General William Booth)*
1

Some years ago, a young businessman, who had risen to a position of importance, fell in love with a well-known and highly respected actress. For many months he was constantly in her company, escorting her to all 'the right places'. Eventually he decided to marry the young lady. Before doing so, however, he hired a private detective to investigate her. The task was assigned to a special agent, who had no knowledge of the identity of his client.

Finally, the agent's report was sent to him. It read:

'Miss – has an excellent reputation. Her past is spotless, her associates beyond reproach. The only hint of scandal is that in recent months she has been seen in the company of a businessman of doubtful reputation.' *(Anon)*

USEFUL TEXTS

Integrity:
In trials, *Job 2:9*
As guide, *Prov. 11:3*
As protection, *Ps. 25:21*

See also: B19 Conscience
B20 Growth to maturity
B26 The whole man
C23 Zeal for what is right

A3

PERSEVERANCE

'Happy is the man who does not lose faith in me.'
Matthew 11:6

QUOTATIONS

By perseverance the snail reached the ark.
(Charles H. Spurgeon)

Go bravely on doing the daily duties and trusting that as our
day is, so shall our strength be. *(Edward King)*

Every noble work is at first impossible. *(Carlyle)*

The falling drops will at last wear the stone. *(Lucretius)*

Perseverance is not a long race; it is many short races one after
another. *(Walter Elliott)*

Though perseverance does not come from our power, yet it
comes within our power. *(St Francis de Sales)*

He greatly deceives himself who thinks that prayer perfects one
without perseverance and obedience. *(St Francis de Sales)*

We cannot command our final perseverance, but must ask it
from God. *(St Thomas Aquinas)*

He said not, 'Thou shalt not be tempested, thou shalt not be
travailed, thou shalt not be afflicted,' but he said, 'Thou shalt
not be overcome.' *(Julian of Norwich)*

PROVERBS

What can't be cured must be endured. *(English proverb)*

The man who removed the mountain began by carrying away small stones. *(Chinese proverb)*

HUMOUR

Consider the postage stamp: its usefulness consists in the ability to stick to one thing till it gets there. *(Josh Billings)*

Even the woodpecker owes his success to the fact that he uses his head and keeps pecking away until he finishes the job he starts. *(Coleman Cox)*

A great oak is only a little nut that held his ground.
(L & N Magazine)

Teacher   'Johnny, what is the difference between perseverance and obstinacy?'

Pupil   'One is a strong will and the other is a strong won't.'

'My boy,' said the wealthy man, 'when I was your age, I used to carry bricks for bricklayers.'
'I'm mighty proud of you, Dad. If it hadn't been for your perseverance I might have had to do something like that myself!'

STATEMENTS

If any one saith that he will for certain, of an absolute and infallible certainty, have that great gift of perseverance unto the end, unless he have learned this by special revelation; let him be anathema. *(Council of Trent, Session 6)*

If any man saith that the justified either is able to persevere without the special help of God in the justice received; or that with that help he is not able; let him be anathema.
(Council of Trent, Session 6)

WORD PICTURES

After Sir Walter Raleigh's introduction to the favour of Queen Elizabeth I, he wrote with a diamond on a window pane:
'Fain would I climb, but that I fear to fall.'
The Queen, seeing the words, wrote underneath with a diamond:
'If thy heart fail thee, do not climb at all.' *(Anon)*

An old coloured preacher was asked to define Christian perseverance. He answered: 'It means, firstly, to take hold; secondly, to hold on; thirdly and lastly, to nebber leave go.'

M. Louis Blériot, the famous airman who was first to cross the Channel in an aeroplane of his own designing, only achieved his object through marvellous perseverance. Ten machines were built and wrecked, but still he did not give up; it was with his eleventh aeroplane that he finally, on 25 July 1909, flew the Channel in 37 minutes. And even then he was badly lame with a scalded foot, which would have prevented most men from attempting the adventure. *(Anon)*

This is the romantic story of the father and mother of Thomas Becket, as told by Charles Dickens in his *Child's History of England*:

Gilbert Becket, Thomas' father, made a pilgrimage to the Holy Land and was taken prisoner by a Saracen who had one fair daughter. She fell in love with Gilbert and told him she wanted to marry him, and was willing to become a Christian if they could escape to a Christian country. He returned her love until he found an opportunity to escape with his servant, Richard. When he returned to England, he forgot the Saracen girl.

But she had not forgotten Gilbert. She left her father's home in disguise and made her way to the coast. The merchant had taught her two English words, 'London' and 'Gilbert'. She went among the ships, saying again and again the same word, 'London'. Sailors showed her a ship bound for London, and she paid her passage with some of her jewels and arrived in London.

As the merchant was sitting one day in his office, his servant came running in, saying, 'Master! The Saracen lady is here. As I live, she is going up and down the street calling out, "Gilbert, Gilbert".' The merchant hurried to find her. When she saw him, she fainted in his arms. Soon after they were married. *(Anon)*

The Rev Dr Francis Xavier Chu Shih-de SJ received his doctorate in France. He returned to China, was jailed in 1953 and died in jail in 1983. He wrote this letter to his brother in 1949 before boarding the plane for Shanghai.

Every day many people are escaping from China to Hong Kong. Yet I cannot find any one, apart from myself, who is preparing to leave Hong Kong for China. Everyone laughs at me for being a fool. In the eyes of the world I am indeed the biggest fool ever born! When a merchant cannot make a profit in one place, he will move somewhere else. Yet I am a priest, and the life of a priest is to serve his flock.

As long as there are Christians left in Shanghai, I must return there. Even if there is not a single Christian left in Shanghai, I must still return there. Because I am a priest. I represent Christ and his Church. Wherever I am, the Church is. I am willing to stay in Shanghai, to let the Communist Party know that the Catholic faith is still alive. *(Thoughts of Chinese Christians)*

Nevertheless, whatever the particular objective may be, it is far better to start with the knowledge that we are human and as a consequence limited in what we can do, and that at the end of the day, for all our efforts, the results may not be very spectacular. I know of no substitute in any field of human endeavour for hard work, for clear and realistic thinking and planning, and, most important of all, for perseverance. The person who ferrets away, who never lets go, who when faced with an impasse or just cannot see what he should do next, is content to wait and relax until something happens to give him an opening, is the one who will usually achieve the most.

Without in any way renouncing the need to set our sights high, to be satisfied with nothing less than the best, and to commit ourselves totally and unreservedly to participating in the struggle to build a more liveable world, I have come to believe that the important thing is to keep going and to appreciate that even one small improvement is infinitely worth making. It is the multiplication of many people, each working in their own chosen field and in their own individual way, that brings about genuine change. *(Leonard Cheshire)*

USEFUL TEXTS

Perseverance:
In practising forgiveness, *Matt. 18:21-22*
Until the end, *Mark 13:13*
In doing good, *Gal. 6:9*
In prayer, *Eph. 6:18*

See also: A19 Patience
B49 Coping with doubt
C30 Increase our faith
C35 Hope

A4

EMMANUEL – MARY'S CHILD

'The maiden is with child and will give birth
to a son whom she will call Emmanuel.'
Isaiah, 7:14

QUOTATIONS

He became what we are that he might make us what he is.
(St Athanasius of Alexandria)

The Word of God became man that you also may learn from a
man how a man becomes a God. *(St Clement of Alexandria)*

It is the general rule, that all superior men inherit the elements
of superiority from their mothers. *(Nichelet)*

God's presence is not discerned at the time when it is upon us,
but afterwards, when we look back upon what is gone and over.
(Cardinal Newman)

There is only one way of being faithful to the Incarnation and
that is to become an embodied testimony to the living God.
Perhaps the core of the apologetic task in every age is to be
created in lives rather than in arguments. *(Gabriel Marcel)*

The eternal logos of God has a human heart, he risked the
adventure of a human heart, until pierced by the sin of the
world, it had flowed out, until it had suffered to the end on the
cross. *(Karl Rahner)*

PROVERB

God often visits us, but most of the time we are not at home.
(French proverb)

HUMOUR

A Nativity play was to be performed in the church hall and a country vicar went to town to get a streamer for display. Unfortunately he forgot the measurements so he wired his wife for details. The telegraph clerk at the other end nearly had a fit when the reply message was received. It read: 'Unto us a Child is Born – seven feet six by one foot three.'

A kindly British family had made contact with a Romanian middle class family who were struggling to cope in the severe economic situation in their country. The British couple decided to send their new Romanian friends a Christmas parcel and thought it a good idea to include a traditional Christmas pudding. For good measure they added a fresh sprig of holly on the top.

Some weeks later they received a thankyou letter for the parcel, which included the following line: 'thank you too for the plant, we watered it every day but sadly it died'.
(BBC Radio 4)

WORD PICTURE

One Christmas, Santa Claus brought me a toy engine. I took it with me to the convent, and played with it while mother and the nuns discussed old times. But it was a young nun who brought us in to see the crib. When I saw the Holy Child in the manger, I was distressed because little as I had, he had nothing at all. For me it was fresh proof of the incompetence of Santa Claus.

I asked the young nun politely if the Holy Child didn't like toys, and she replied composedly enough, 'Oh, he does but his mother is too poor to afford them'. That settled it. My mother was poor too, but at Christmas she at least managed to buy me something even if it was only a box of crayons. I distinctly remember getting into the crib and putting the engine between his outstretched arms. I probably showed him how to wind it as well, because a small baby like that would not be clever enough to know. I remember too the tearful feeling of reckless generosity with which I left him there in the nightly darkness of the chapel, clutching my toy engine to his chest.
(Frank O'Connor)

No one can celebrate a genuine Christmas without being truly poor. The self-sufficient, the proud, those who have no need even of God – for them there will be no Christmas. Only the poor, the hungry, those who need someone to come on their behalf, will have that someone. That someone is God, Emmanuel, God-with-us. Without poverty of spirit there can be no abundance of God. *(Oscar Romero)*

On this night, as we Christians have done every year for 20 centuries, we recall that God's reign is now in this world and that Christ has inaugurated the fullness of time. His birth attests that God is now marching with us in history, that we do not go alone, and that our aspiration for peace, for justice, for a reign of divine law, for something holy, is far from earth's realities. We can hope for it, not because we humans are able to construct that realm of happiness which God's holy words proclaim, but because the builder of a reign of justice, of love, and of peace is already in the midst of us. *(Oscar Romero)*

USEFUL TEXTS
Emmanuel:
Observance of God's coming in flesh, *1 Tim. 3:16*
Observance of Christ's birth, *Matt. 1:18-21*

See also: A37 Christ the King
B4 Mary – Handmaid of God
B8 The Word
B46 Christ the Sacrament of God
C45 The Divinity of Christ

A5

MAN FOR OTHERS – UNSELFISHNESS

'You are my servant in whom I shall be glorified.'
Isaiah, 49:3

QUOTATIONS

The secret of being loved is in being lovely; and the secret of being lovely is in being unselfish. *(Josiah Holland)*

The most satisfying thing in life is to have been able to give a large part of oneself to others. *(Teilhard de Chardin)*

The love of liberty is the love of others; the love of power is the love of ourselves. *(William Hazlitt)*

We are more troublesome to ourselves than anyone else is to us. *(St Francis de Sales)*

Self-sacrifice is good in its way, but we must take care that we don't sacrifice to the detriment of others. *(Kathleen Hinkson)*

Man's highest life does not consist in self-expression, but in self-sacrifice. *(R. H. Benson)*

Oysters are more beautiful than any religion . . . there's nothing in Christianity or Buddhism that quite matches the sympathetic unselfishness of an oyster. *(Siki)*

HUMOUR

If people knew how much ill-feeling Unselfishness occasions, it would not be so often recommended from the pulpit.
(C. S. Lewis)

Teacher	'Unselfishness means going without something you need voluntarily. Can you give me an example, Jimmy?'
Jimmy	'Yes, sometimes I go without a bath when I need one!'

WORD PICTURES

Two-year-old Sharon and her friend Michael, who was nearly four, were playing happily in the garden. Suddenly their mums, who were enjoying a quiet cup of coffee in the kitchen, were disturbed by a great commotion. Rushing to the window they saw both children trying to jam themselves, at the same time, on the seat of the one and only tricycle. After much shouting and screeching both managed to squeeze on, but neither could move! When their mums got to them Sharon was sobbing and Michael was stoutly and loudly proclaiming, 'If one of us got off I could ride it properly.'

It was resolved that they would take turns. Michael had the first short ride up the concrete garden path, pursued after less than thirty seconds by Sharon, calling, 'Me turn, me turn.'
(A. P. Castle)

Gandalf gives counsel . . . 'Other evils there are that may come; for Sauron is himself but a servant or emissary. Yet it is not our part to muster all the tides of the world, but to do what is in us for the succour of those years wherein we are set, uprooting the evil in the fields that we know, so that those who live after may have clean earth to till. What weather they shall have is not ours to rule.' *(J. R. R. Tolkien)*

In one of the terrible concentration camps of the Second World War there was a Polish priest, called Father Kolbe. He had been put there because he had published comments about the Nazi Regime. One of the prisoners escaped from the camp and the camp commandant, to punish the prisoners, ordered ten of them to be starved to death. Among the prisoners was a young man who had a wife and children. When the prisoners' numbers were called out, Father Kolbe stepped forward and insisted on taking the young man's place. In the death cell, Father Kolbe helped the others prepare for death. He was the last to die, and because he had taken too long, they injected poison into his arm. After his death, if you had gone into his cell, you would have seen a picture of Jesus on the cross scratched on the wall with his nails. *(Anon)*

When Father Damien sailed as a missionary for the Hawaiian Islands in 1864 he probably knew little and thought nothing of the ever-growing colony of lepers by then segregated in part of the Island of Molokai. A day came when he happened to attend the dedication of a chapel recently erected on the Island of Mani. The Bishop, Monseigneur Maigret, was there, and in his address lamented that, owing to the scarcity of missioners, he was unable to send them a fixed pastor. Some young priests from the Picpus Congregation had just arrived for mission work, and before them Father Damien instantly spoke.

'Monseigneur,' said he, 'here are your new missioners. One of them could take my district; and if you will be kind enough to allow it, I will go to Molokai and labour for the poor lepers, whose wretched state of bodily and spiritual misfortune has often made my heart bleed within me.'

Thus simply was made, by an obscure priest on a faraway island, an offer of which the heroism, when the world came to know of it, made cowards shudder and brave men wish they had been braver. It was accepted and that same day, without any farewell, Father Damien embarked with the bishop on a boat that was taking some 50 lepers to Molokai. *(Anon)*

Useful texts

Unselfishness, Examples of:
Abraham, *Gen. 13:8-9*
David, 1 *Chr. 21:17*
Paul, 1 *Cor. 9:12-22*
Christ, *Mark 6:30-34*

See also: A33 Love your neighbour
B41 Generosity
B47 Dying to self
C34 The value of little things

A6

LIGHT OF THE WORLD

'The Lord is my light and my help.' *Psalm 27*

QUOTATIONS

The Spirit in a person is the candle of the Lord,
lighted by God, and lighting people to God.
(Benjamin Whichcote)

That Light whose smile kindles the Universe.
That Beauty in which all things work and more . . .
(Percy Bysshe Shelley)

No ray of light can shine
If severed from its source;
Without my inner light
I lose my course. *(Angelus Silesius)*

It is better to be saved by a lighthouse than by a lifeboat.
(Ernest Kunsch)

A Christian, like a candle, must keep cool and burn at the same
time. *(M. Rosell)*

I said to the man who stood at the gate of the Year, 'Give me a
light that I may tread safely into the unknown.' And he replied,
'Go out into the darkness and put your hand into the hand of
God. That shall be to you better than light and safer than a
known way.' *(Minnie Louise Haskins)*

PROVERBS

Don't curse the darkness – light a candle. *(Chinese proverb)*

There is more light than can be seen through a window.
(Russian proverb)

HUMOUR

The class had been told about the prodigious rate at which light travels. 'Isn't it wonderful,' the teacher said, 'to think of light coming to us from the sun at the speed of all those miles a second?' 'Not really,' said one boy, 'it's downhill all the way!'

Members of several religious Orders were together in a room one evening when suddenly the light went out, leaving them all in darkness. The Benedictine simply went on saying his Office, which he knew by heart anyway. The Franciscan knelt down and began to pray for light. The Dominican suggested to his companions that they should inquire into the nature of light, and consider the sequence of causes that might have led to its failure. But the Jesuit had left the room. He had gone to mend the fuse. (*Douglas Woodruff*)

STATEMENT

The Second Vatican Council's document on 'The Church' opens with the words: 'Christ is the light of all nations. Hence this sacred Synod, which has been gathered in the Holy Spirit, eagerly desires to shed on all men that radiance of His which brightens the countenance of the Church. This it will do by proclaiming the Gospel to every creature.'

WORD PICTURES

The Light of the World is the title of a famous picture by Holman Hunt painted in 1854. It portrays Christ, thorn-crowned, and carrying a lantern, knocking at a closed door.

When the artist showed the completed picture to some friends, one pointed out what seemed to be an omission. 'You have put no handle on the door,' he said to Holman Hunt. The artist replied, 'We must open to the Light – the handle is on the inside.'

When the scientific oil lamp was invented in 1783 by a Swiss chemist, Ami Argand, many people felt man's genius had gone far enough. The new lamp produced a light equal to nine candles and burned whale oil. An encyclopaedia of the time advised the use of a small screen between the eyes and the lamplight. At parties, ladies sometimes opened their parasols against the 'uncomplimentary' glare of the lamps.

Two legends enhance the lustre of the Koh-i-Noor diamond; that is that it must never be worn by a man, and its owner will rule the world.

The diamond's name means 'Mountain of Light'. It flashed among the possessions of the Mogul Emperor Mohammed when he fell to Nadir, the Shah of Persia who in turn died in a palace revolt of 1747. One hundred years later, it was the brightest jewel in the male-dominated Sikh empire that was conquered by the British Empire. Since then it has been worn by three English queens, but never by an English king.

There is a famous cave, some sixty miles from Auckland in New Zealand. It is known as the cave of the glow-worms. You reach it in a boat pulled by a wire for silence. As you glide down the stream, you suddenly come across a soft light gleaming in the distance; then you enter a magic world of fairyland. From the top of the cave, thousands of threads hang down from the glowing insects. So great is the light that it is possible to read a book there. But if there is the slightest noise, the bright light dies out, just as if a switch had been turned off.

The story goes that a little girl was with her family in a party being shown around one of our great cathedrals. As the guide was explaining an historic tomb nearby, the girl was staring at a great stained glass window through which the summer sun was streaming, bathing the cathedral floor in colour. As the group was about to move on she asked the guide in a shrill clear voice, 'Who are those people in the pretty window?'

'Those are the saints,' the man replied.

That night as she was undressing for bed she told her mother, 'I know who the saints are.'

'Do you dear?' replied her mother. 'Who are they?'

'They're the people who let the light shine through.'
(*Anon*)

Somewhere behind the dark clouds, something stirred. One hundred and eighty brightly dressed children stared hopefully at the distant, dark horizon.

This was Tromso, Norway – 215 miles inside the Arctic Circle and for the past two months in permanent darkness. Now, at eight minutes to midday the sun was due back. Not for long mind you – four minutes only on the first day. But it was enough to bring out a fair proportion of the 50,000 inhabitants of this, the world's most northerly city.

The bells pealed out and hundreds of colourful balloons were sent flying high into the gloom. There was just one snag: cloud – a grey morass that blanketed the region and cast a certain, understandable, shadow over proceedings.

They had been looking forward to this moment since, last November 25, the wan winter sun had finally sunk behind Bensfordtind Peak and day had become night. For the children, Sun Day – a celebration declared by King Olav in 1873 – means a day off school . . . but only if it is visible. If not, the children join the rest of the town in a midday break with a cup of cocoa and a Berlinerbolle, a kind of strawberry doughnut.

Down in the town as she ate hers outside Pedersen's Bakery 20-year-old Sigrid Finne said: 'I'm so happy today. If you haven't lived through such a winter as ours you can't imagine what it's like.' *(Jane Kelly)*

USEFUL TEXTS

Light, Descriptive of:
God, *1 John 1:5*
Jesus Christ, *John 8:12*
Christians, *Matt. 5:14*
Christian life, *1 John 1:7; 2:9-10*

See also: A37 Christ the King
          B4 Mary – Handmaid of God
          B8 The Word
          B46 Christ the Sacrament of God

A7

POOR IN SPIRIT

'How happy are the poor in spirit;
theirs is the kingdom of heaven.'
Matthew 5:3

QUOTATIONS

The spirit of poverty is to live in the gladness of today.
(Rule of Taizé)

He is rich enough who is poor with Christ. *(St Jerome)*

No man should praise poverty but he who is poor. *(St Bernard)*

Being poor in spirit means, above all, being unrestrained by
what is called fashion, it means freedom. *(Carlo Carretto)*

'Poor in spirit' refers, not precisely to humility, but to an
attitude of dependence on God and detachment from earthly
supports. *(Ronald Knox)*

Poverty – the poverty of spirit of the Sermon on the Mount – is
a total detachment from the material world. It is to recognise
that everything comes from God – our bodies, our breath, our
very existence. *(Bede Griffiths)*

Mother Teresa of Calcutta relates a story about her sisters . . .
Just as we arrived the sister brought in a man covered with
maggots. He had been picked up from a drain. 'I have been
taking care of him. I have been touching Christ. I knew it was
him', she said. *(William Johnston)*

PROVERBS

He is not poor that hath little, but he that desireth much.
(English Proverb)

Whoso stoppeth his ear at the poor shall cry himself and not be
heard. *(Hebrew proverb)*

Not he who has little, but he who wishes for more, is poor.
(Latin proverb)

HUMOUR

I've worked myself up from nothing to a state of extreme poverty.
(Groucho Marx)

A Franciscan and a Dominican came to a ford at a stream and
the Dominican asked the Franciscan to carry him over, as the
Franciscan was barefooted and his habit mattered less. The
Franciscan lifted him up and carried him half-way, and then
asked what money the Dominican had on him. 'Only two
reales,' said the Dominican. But it was enough for the
Franciscan, who promptly dropped his charge into the water,
excusing himself by saying 'You know our rule: we are not
allowed to carry money.' *(Douglas Woodruff)*

A Jesuit and a Franciscan were lunching together on a Friday.
There were two pieces of fish on the dish, one large and the
other very small. The Jesuit helped himself to the large piece
and put the small one on the other's plate.

'Is that Jesuitry?' asked the Franciscan.

'What do you mean?' said the Jesuit.

Only this,' the Franciscan replied. 'I've been trained in Holy
Poverty. Had I served the fish, I should have put the large piece
on your plate, and the small piece on mine.'

'That's exactly what you've got, isn't it'? said the Jesuit.
'What are you complaining about?' *(Douglas Woodruff)*

STATEMENTS

More than anything else is this vice of property to be cut off
root and branch from the monastery. Let no one presume to

give or receive anything without the leave of the abbot, or to retain anything as his own. He should have nothing at all; neither a book, nor tablets, nor a pen – nothing at all. For it is not allowed to the monks to have bodies or wills in their own power. *(Rule of St Benedict)*

Christians who take any active part in modern socio-economic development and defend justice and charity should be convinced that they can make a great contribution to the prosperity of mankind and the peace of the world. Whether they do so as individuals or in association, let their example be a shining one. After acquiring whatever skills and experience are absolutely necessary, they should in faithfulness to Christ and His Gospel observe the right order of values in their earthly activities. Thus their whole lives, both individual and social, will be permeated with the spirit of the beatitudes, notably with the spirit of poverty. *(Second Vatican Council – 'The Church Today')*

Poverty voluntarily embraced in imitation of Christ provides a witness which is highly esteemed, especially today . . . By it, a man shares in the poverty of Christ, who became poor for our sake when before He had been rich, that we might be enriched by His poverty. *(Second Vatican Council – 'The Religious Life')*

WORD PICTURE
The earth is a moon satellite
   Apollo 2 cost more than Apollo 1;
   Apollo 1 cost plenty.

   Apollo 3 cost more than Apollo 2;
   Apollo 2 cost more than Apollo 1;
   Apollo 1 cost plenty.

   Apollo 4 cost more than Apollo 3;
   Apollo 3 cost more than Apollo 2;
   Apollo 2 cost more than Apollo 1;
   Apollo 1 cost plenty.

Apollo 8 cost a fortune but nobody minded
because the astronauts were Protestants
and from the moon they read the Bible
to the delight and edification of all Christians
and on their return Pope Paul gave them his blessing.

Apollo 9 cost more than all of them together
and that includes Apollo 1, which cost plenty.

The great-grandparents of the Acahualinca people
were less hungry than the grandparents.
The great-grandparents died of hunger.

The grandparents of the Acahualinca people
were less hungry than the parents.
The grandparents died of hunger.

The parents of the Acahualinca people
were less hungry than the people are today.
The parents died of hunger.

The people who live today in Acahualinca
are less hungry than their children.
The children of the Acahualinca people
are not born because of hunger,
and they hunger to be born
so they can die of hunger.

And that is what the Acahualinca people do,
they die of hunger.

Blessed are the poor
for they shall possess the moon.
(Leonel Rugama (Nicaragua))

In a final challenge which must surely have sealed his fate even
if it had not already been settled, Romero appealed to the men
of the army and the national guard.

Brothers (he pleaded), you are part of our own people. You
are killing your own brothers and sisters. No soldier is
obliged to obey an order that is contrary to the law of God.

Nobody has to fulfil an immoral law . . . In the name of
God, and in the name of this suffering people, whose cries
rise to heaven each day more despairingly, I beg you, I
plead with you, I order you in the name of God
cease the repression.
When he had finished, the applause, which had interrupted him
five times in the course of this homily, went on for a full half-
minute. But in the eyes of the authorities what he had just said
was treason . . .

Only the last act remained to be played and the curtain had
already risen on it. On Monday morning he went to confession;
he was to say the 6 p.m. evening Mass in the chapel of the
cancer hospital where he lived. 'I want to feel clean in the
presence of the Lord', he told his confessor.

The Mass was for the mother of a friend, and unwisely its time
and location had been announced in the press. 'Though I walk in
the valley of the shadow of death, yet will I fear no evil, for thou
art with me', he read aloud from the 23rd Psalm, and the Gospel
reading took up this theme of death and resurrection: 'The hour
has come for the Son of Man to be glorified . . . Unless the grain
of wheat falls to the ground and dies, it remains only a grain. But
if it dies, it bears much fruit . . .'

As he always did, the Archbishop based his homily on the
readings . . . When he had finished speaking a shot rang out.
Romero died instantly, shot through a main artery. And in the
uproar that was let loose, the assailant or assailants made their
escape – and have never been brought to justice.

The news spread like a bush fire and the Salvadoreans were
stricken. Thousands waited to see the body as it lay in the
basilica, and when on the Wednesday it was moved to the
cathedral, the crowds filed weeping past the glass-topped
coffin, touching it, pressing against it. With difficulty, and at
enormous risk to themselves, *campesinos* poured into. the city,
queuing in the blazing sun for their turn to take a last look at the
man they had known as Monseñor.

To the anguished question, 'Why did he have to die?' the
people replied as one: 'Because he loved the poor.' *(Mary Craig)*

The poor are the hungry and the thirsty.
The poor are those who go about in rags.
The poor are the homeless.
The poor are the sick.

The poor are the physically and mentally handicapped.
The poor are the old.
The poor are the imprisoned.
The poor are the sad and depressed.

The poor are those who suffer injustice.
The poor are the unemployed and those on low wages.
The poor are the rejects and unwanted.
The poor are the lonely and the unloved.

The poor, in one way or another, are we ourselves.
Before God we are all poor.
May we never see poverty as a curse from God.
Rather may we know that when we are poor
the Kingdom of heaven is ours.
(Flor McCarthy)

USEFUL TEXTS

Poor People:
    Protection of, *Isa. 14:30*
    Blessings on, *Luke 6:20*
    Among believers, *Rev. 2:9*
    Provision for, *Ps. 68:10*

See also: A11 God's loving Providence
          C21 Rise above materialism
          C25 Humility
          C29 Not through luxury'

A8

THE LIGHT OF EXAMPLE

'Your light must shine in the sight of men.'
Matthew 5:16

QUOTATIONS

Example is not the main thing in influencing others – it is the only thing. *(Albert Schweitzer)*

A candle loses nothing by lighting another candle. *(Anon)*

There is not enough darkness in all the world to put out the light of one small candle. *(Anon)*

There is just one way to bring up a child in the way he should go and that is to travel that way yourself. *(Abraham Lincoln)*

A holy life will produce the deepest impression. Lighthouses blow no horns; they only shine. *(D. L. Moody)*

As far as we can discern, the sole purpose of human existence is to kindle a light in the darkness of mere being. *(C. G. Jung)*

To reflect God in all that is, both here and now, my heart must be a mirror empty, bright and clear. *(Angelius Silesius)*

There are two ways of spreading light; to be a candle, or the mirror that reflects it. *(Edith Wharton)*

If you would convince a man that he does wrong, do right. Men will believe what they see. Let them see. *(Henry Thoreau)*

No man is so insignificant as to be sure his example can do no hurt. *(Lord Clarendon)*

Example is the school of mankind, and they will learn at no other. *(E. Burke)*

Jesus said, 'Within a man of light, there is light; and he lights the whole world.' *(Gospel according to Thomas)*

PROVERBS

Example is the greatest of all seducers. *(French proverb)*

Precept begins, example accomplishes. *(French proverb)*

They do more harm by their evil example than by their actual sin. *(Latin proverb)*

HUMOUR

In the nursery the children were shouting and making a din. Mother went in and asked what they were quarrelling about. 'We're not quarrelling,' said the eldest, 'we're just playing Mummy and Daddy'.

WORD PICTURES

If all the matches produced in France were laid end to end they would stretch eight times the distance between the earth and the moon. So the state-controlled match industry reports.

What power to dispel darkness one little match has, if used properly. And what power for destruction when used carelessly – as witness many forest and city fires. *(Anon)*

An American teacher was employed in Japan on the understanding that during school hours he should not utter a word on the subject of Christianity. The engagement was faithfully kept, and he lived before his students the Christian life, but never spoke of it to them. Not a word was said to influence the young men committed to his care. But so beautiful was his character, and so blameless his example, that forty of the students, unknown to him, met in a grove and signed a secret covenant to abandon idolatry. Twenty-five of them entered the Kyoto Christian Training School, and some of them are now preaching the Gospel which their teacher had unconsciously commended. *(Anon)*

The following story is from Ernest Gordon's account of life and death in a Japanese POW camp on the river Kwai.

One incident concerned an Aussie private who had been caught outside the fence while trying to obtain medicine from the Thais for his sick friends. He was summarily tried and sentenced to death.

On the morning set for his execution he marched cheerfully between his guards to the parade ground. The Japanese were out in full force to observe the scene. The Aussie was permitted to have his Commanding Officer and a chaplain in attendance as witnesses. The party came to a halt. The CO and the chaplain were waved to one side and the Aussie was left standing alone. Calmly, he surveyed his executioners. He knelt down and drew a small copy of the New Testament from a pocket of his ragged shorts. Unhurriedly, his lips moving but no sound coming from them, he read a passage to himself. . . He finished reading, returned his New Testament to his pocket, looked up, and saw the distressed face of his chaplain. He smiled, waved to him, and called out, 'Cheer up, Padre, it isn't as bad as all that. I'll be all right.'

He nodded to his executioner as a sign that he was ready. He knelt down, and bent his head forward to expose his neck. The Samurai sword flashed in the sunlight. The examples set by such men shone like beacons. *(Ernest Gordon – 'Miracle on the River Kwai')*

USEFUL TEXTS

Example:
I have given, *John 13:15*
Of Christ, *1 Peter 2:21*
Of Believers, *1 Tim. 4:12*

See also: A9 Relationships
A33 Love your neighbour
B24 Go tell everyone

A9

RELATIONSHIPS

'All you need is "Yes" if you mean yes, "No" if you mean no.'
Matthew 5:37

QUOTATIONS

Loving relationships are a family's best protection against the challenges of the world. *(Bernie Wietre)*

Have a heart that never hardens, and a temper that never tires, and a touch that never hurts. *(Charles Dickens)*

Happiness is not perfected until it is shared. *(Jane Porter)*

We take care of our health, we lay up our money, we make our roof tight and our clothing sufficient, but who provides wisely that he shall not be wanting in the best property of all – friends? *(R. W. Emerson)*

I think people ought to fulfil sacredly their desires. And this means fulfilling the deepest desire, which is a desire to live unhampered by things that are extraneous, a desire for pure relationships and living truth. *(D. H. Lawrence)*

If a man does not make new acquaintances as he advances through life, he will soon find himself alone; one should keep his friendships in constant repair *(Samuel Johnson)*

Those are our best friends in whose presence we are able to be our best selves. *(C. W. Kohler)*

Lead the life that will make you kindly and friendly to everyone about you, and you will be surprised what a happy life you will live. *(C. M. Schwab)*

Life is mostly froth and bubble,
Two things stand like stone:
Kindness in another's trouble,
Courage in your own. *(Gordon Lindsay)*

Christianity is not a religion, it is a relationship. *(Dr Thieme)*

Every man is his own ancestor, and every man is his own heir.
He devises his own future; and he inherits his own past.
(H. F. Hedge)

The first half of our lives is ruined by our parents and the
second half by our children! *(C. S. Darrow)*

PROVERBS

A faithful friend is an image of God. *(French proverb)*

Better a good enemy than a bad friend. *(Yiddish proverb)*

WORD PICTURES

A blind man and a lame man happened to come at the same
time to a piece of very bad road. The former begged the latter
to guide him through his difficulties. 'How can I do that,' said
the lame man, 'as I am scarcely able to drag myself along? But
if you were to carry me I can warn you about anything in the
way; my eyes will be your eyes and your feet will be mine.' 'With
all my heart,' replied the blind man. 'Let us serve one another.'
So taking his lame companion on his back, they travelled in this
way with safety and pleasure. *(Aesop)*

Kevin, a ten-year-old from the country, came to spend the
Easter holidays with his aunt, who lived in the London suburb
of Wimbledon. Curious to explore not only her large garden
but also an overgrown path at the back, he heard odd noises
coming from a shed in a neighbour's garden. When he asked his
aunt about the noise she told him that she thought her
unmarried lady neighbour kept chickens. Kevin had been
brought up on a chicken farm and he knew immediately that
what he had heard was not 'chicken-noise'.

He went back through a hole in the fence to investigate. The neighbouring garden was very overgrown but with a clear path running from the house to the old shed. The shed door was padlocked and the window was blacked out but there was a large sort of letter-box slit in the door. First checking that no one was watching, Kevin peeped through the 'letter-box'. It was covered on the inside by a piece of hanging material but a powerful stench caught Kevin's nose. Just as he was about to turn away the cover was lifted and a pair of wild staring eyes appeared at the slit. Kevin gave a startled scream and bolted out of the garden back to his aunt's. He ran straight into her. He was so upset that he blurted out just what he had seen. His aunt called the police.

The dignified maiden lady was very indignant at first when the police asked to inspect her garden shed. When they insisted, her resistance collapsed and she gave them a key. On opening the door a sight met the eyes of the two constables that they are never likely to forget. Cowering in a darkened corner from the bright light, and the strange intruders, was a naked figure of what seemed to be a strange animal. It was on all fours, and had long black hair. There was fear in the wild eyes and 'it' made strange little noises. The police officers, taken aback by the sight and the stench, closed the door again and radioed for assistance.

The nine-year-old boy was taken into very special care. He had been in the shed for seven years, since the age of two, when the woman, fearing the discovery of her secret illegitimate child, had incarcerated him in the shed. Besides the filth, long hair and nails, his back was bent in such a way that he would never be able to learn to walk upright. Terrified at the presence of other people, he could not communicate but merely express emotions by grunts. He had never known any caring relationships and there was no hope of a return to full human existence. *(Paul Frost)*

Hundreds of years ago, the Romans were fighting against the Macedonians, and found great difficulty in breaking through their lines; for the Macedonians placed in front of their army a large square of foot soldiers armed with large shields and long, heavy pikes. This square was called the Phalanx. When the order was given to advance, each soldier linked his shield with that of the next man and thrust his pike forward. As this terrible line came on against the Romans, nothing could be seen but a row of glistening white shields and fierce pikes, and so long as the men kept together it was almost impossible to break through.

The Romans found that they could not pierce that terrible wall, and for a time they had to retreat as the enemy came on. But as the Macedonians advanced they came on broken and uneven ground, and the Phalanx began to be broken. This and that man broke away his linked shield from that of his neighbour; they could no longer stand in long lines linked shield to shield. It was then that the wise general Aemilius saw his chance. He sent little companies of his Roman soldiers to break through these gaps and make the divisions still wider. By this means the Macedonian army was routed and the Romans were victorious. *(Anon)*

USEFUL TEXTS

Relationships:
Of believers with one another, *1 Cor. 12:12-14*
Agreement necessary in, *Amos 3:3*
A continuing relationship, *Prov. 17:17*

See also: A33 Love your neighbour
B6 The family
B30 Married love
B52 God is Love
C10 Love your enemies
C19 Friendship

A10

SEEKING PERFECTION

'You must be perfect, just as your heavenly Father is perfect.'
(Matthew 5:48)

QUOTATIONS

By perfection, I mean the humble, patient,
gentle love of God and our neighbour,
ruling our tempers, words and actions. *(John Wesley)*

God did not make people perfect. He made them pilgrims after
perfection. *(Henry Ward Beeeher)*

To obtain the gift of holiness is the work of a life.
(Cardinal Newman)

Holiness consists not in doing uncommon things, but in doing
all common things with an uncommon fervour.
(Cardinal Manning)

It takes a long time to bring excellence to maturity.
(Publius Syrus)

It is only imperfection that complains of what is imperfect.
The more perfect we are, the more gentle and quiet we
become towards the defects of others. *(Fenelon)*

The serene, silent beauty of a holy life is the most powerful
influence in the world, next to the might of God. *(Pascal)*

No man can advance three paces on the road to perfection
unless Jesus Christ walks beside him. *(R. H. Benson)*

That soul is perfect which is guided habitually by the instinct of
the Holy Spirit. *(Isaac Hecker)*

PROVERBS

The diamond cannot be polished without friction, nor the man perfected without trials. *(Chinese proverb)*

Fear less, hope more; Eat less, chew more;
Whine less, breathe more; Talk less, say more:
Hate less, love more; and all good things will be yours.
(Swedish proverb)

HUMOUR

'Charity, dear Miss Prism, charity! None of us are perfect. I myself am peculiarly susceptible to draughts.' *(Oscar Wilde)*

Wife (heatedly)   'You're lazy, worthless, bad tempered; you're a liar.'

Husband (reasonably) 'Well, dear, no man is perfect!'

Bachelors' wives and old maids' children are always perfect. *(Chamfort)*

STATEMENTS

All the faithful, whatever their condition or state, are called by the Lord each in his own way, to the perfect holiness whereby the Father Himself is perfect.
(Second Vatican Council – 'The Church')

The Church recalls to the mind of all that culture must be made to bear on the integral perfection of the human person, and on the good of the community and the whole of society. Therefore, the human spirit must be cultivated in such a way that there results a growth in its ability to wonder, to understand, to contemplate, to make personal judgements and to develop a religious, moral and social sense. *(Second Vatican Council – 'The Church Today')*

WORD PICTURES

Youth is not a time of life . . . it is a state of mind.
Nobody grows old by merely living a number of years;
people grow old only by deserting their ideals.
Years wrinkle the skin, but to give up enthusiasm wrinkles
the soul. Worry, doubt, self-distrust, fear and despair . . .
these are the long, long years that bow the head and turn
the growing spirit back to dust.
Whether 70 or 16, there is in every being's
heart the love of wonder, the sweet amazement at the stars
and the starlike things and thoughts, the undaunted
challenge of events, the unfailing childlike appetite
for what next, and the joy of the game of life.
You are as young as your faith, as old as your doubt;
as young as your self-confidence, as old as your fear;
as young as your hope, as old as your despair. *(Anon)*

The great sculptor, Michelangelo, was at work on one of his
statues when a friend called on him, and said, 'I can't see any
difference in the statue since I came here a week ago. Have you
not been doing any work all the week?' 'Yes,' said the sculptor,
'I have retouched this part, softened this feature, strengthened
this muscle, and put more life into that limb.' 'But those are
only trifles,' said the friend. 'True,' said Michelangelo, 'but
trifles make perfection, and perfection is no trifle.'

Do all the good you can,
In all the ways you can,
In all the places you can,
At all the times you can,
To all the people you can,
As long as ever you can.
(John Wesley)

There is a rhythm, an ebb and
flow, in the spiritual life. We have to
acquire the patience and wisdom of
the farmer who accepts the barrenness of

winter as being as
much a part of the natural order as
the glory of high summer. He knows
that hidden forces are at work when
the fields are in the grip of frost and
snow. God's nurture of the soul which is orientated towards him
is not suspended during the times of
seeming sterility. *(Thomas Green)*

Florence Nightingale, who bandaged the world's battle wounds, said:

'I solemnly pledge myself before God and in the presence of this assembly:

'To pass my life in purity and to practise my profession faithfully. I will abstain from whatever is deleterious and mischievous, and will not take or knowingly administer any harmful drug.

'I will do all in my power to elevate the standard of my profession, and will hold in confidence all personal matters committed to my keeping and all family affairs coming to my knowledge in the practice of my profession.

'With loyalty will I endeavour to aid the physician in his work, and devote myself to the welfare of those committed to my care.' *(Anon)*

USEFUL TEXTS

Perfection:
Growing towards, *Heb. 6:1*
Limit of, *Ps. 119:96*
Prayer for, *2 Cor. 13:9*
Requirements for, *Matt. 19:21*

See also: A20 The Kingdom of God
A22 Seeking God
B26 The whole man
C47 The indwelling spirit

A11

God's Loving Providence

'Surely life means more than food, and the body more
than clothing! Look at the birds in the sky.'
Matthew 6:26

Quotations

Providence is the care God takes of all existing things.
(John of Damascus)

For, if the providence of God does not preside over human
affairs, there is no point in busying oneself about religion.
(St Augustine of Hippo)

People must pursue things which are just in present, and leave
the future to the divine Providence. *(Francis Bacon)*

The beginning of anxiety is the end of faith, and the beginning
of true faith is the end of anxiety. *(George Mueller)*

The doctrine of providence deals with the
history of created being as such, in the sense
that in every respect and in its whole span
this proceeds under the fatherly care of God
the Creator. *(Karl Barth)*

In all created things discern the providence and wisdom of
God, and in all things give Him thanks. *(St Teresa of Avila)*

The acts of our Maker ought always to be reverenced without
examining, for they can never be unjust. *(Pope St Gregory I)*

PROVERBS

Providence assists not the idle. *(Latin proverb)*

God builds the nest of the blind bird. *(Turkish proverb)*

He who gives us teeth will give us bread. *(Yiddish proverb)*

HUMOUR

'We mustn't question the ways of Providence,' said the Rector. 'Providence,' said the old woman. 'Don't talk to me about Providence. I've had enough of Providence. First he took my husband, and then he took my 'taters, but there's one above as'll teach him to mind his manners, if he doesn't look out!'

The Rector was much too distressed to challenge this remarkable piece of theology. *(Dorothy Sayers – 'The Nine Tailors')*

The story is told of the devout Irishman who, when his house was caught in a great flood, climbed for safety to the roof. Along came a rescue launch and offered to take him off. 'No thanks,' he said, 'I believe God will save me.' The rescuers on the launch could not persuade him and went away. The water rose and covered the roof and the Irishman climbed onto the chimney. A helicopter arrived and lowered a crewman. 'No thanks,' Paddy said, 'I believe God will save me.' He drowned. On arrival in heaven he met God and asked, 'Why didn't you save me?' 'I don't know what went wrong,' God replied 'I sent a launch and a helicopter!' *(Anon)*

STATEMENT

The People of God believes that it is led by the Spirit of the Lord, who fills the earth. Motivated by this faith, it labours to decipher authentic signs of God's presence and purpose in the happenings, needs and desires in which this People has a part along with other men of our age. For faith throws a new light on everything, manifests God's design for man's total vocation and thus directs the mind to solutions which are fully human. *(Second Vatican Council – 'The Church Today')*

WORD PICTURES

Providence requires three things of us before it will help us – a stout heart, a strong arm and a stiff upper lip. *(Sam Slick)*

God's providence is not in baskets lowered from the sky, but through the hands and hearts of those who love him. The lad without food and without shoes made the proper answer to the cruel-minded woman who asked, 'But if God loved you, wouldn't he send you food and shoes?'

The boy replied, 'God told someone, but he forgot'. *(George Buttrick)*

My life is but a weaving, between my God and me,
I do not choose the colours, he worketh steadily,
Of times he weaveth sorrow, and I in foolish pride,
Forget he sees the upper side, and I the underside.
Not till the loom is silent, and shuttle cease to fly,
Will God unroll the canvas and explain the reason why.
The dark threads are as needful in the skillful Weaver's hand
As the threads of gold and silver in the pattern he has
planned. *(Anon)*

The treasurer's voice droned on as he went through the accounts of the Papal States. Suddenly, Pope Pius V stood up, opened a window and stared out. After a few moments he relaxed, and turned back to his senior Vatican officials with eyes shining.

'Leave all this for now,' he said, waving towards the ledgers and financial statements, strewn about the table. 'We must go and give thanks to God. Victory has gone to the Christian fleet.'

The businesslike treasurer made a note of the strange incident in the minutes. It happened, he wrote, just before 5 p.m. on October 7, 1571.

Exactly a fortnight later, on October 21, a messenger galloped into Rome from Venice with news of an historic naval victory.

A Christian fleet, under Don John of Austria, had trounced the Turkish fleet at Lepanto. According to the official report, it had become clear that victory was theirs just before 5 p.m. on October 7. *(Anon)*

USEFUL TEXTS

Providence:

For Believers, *Matt. 6:33; Matt 10:28-31*

For salvation, *Luke 2:10-11; 2 Pet. 3:9*

For the earth, *Matt. 5:45*

See also: A7 Poor in Spirit

A19 Patience

B21 Trust in God

C39 Doing God's will

A12

HOLY SCRIPTURE

'Everyone who listens to these words of mine and acts on them will be like a sensible man who built his house on rocks.'
Matthew 7:24

QUOTATIONS

I read my Bible to know what people ought to do and my newspaper to know what they are doing. *(John H. Newman)*

Lay hold on the Bible until the Bible lays hold on you. *(William Houghton)*

People do not reject the Bible because it contradicts itself but because it contradicts them. *(E. Paul Hovey)*

What you bring away from the Bible depends to some extent on what you carry to it. *(Oliver Wendell Holmes)*

To be ignorant of the Scripture is not to know Christ. *(St Jerome)*

The Bible is a stream wherein the elephant may swim and the lamb may wade. *(Pope St Gregory I)*

The book of books, the storehouse and magazine of life and comfort, the holy scriptures. *(George Herbert)*

These writings bring back to you the living image of that most holy mind, the very Christ himself speaking, healing, dying, rising, in fact so entirely present, that you would see less of him if you beheld him with your eyes. *(Erasmus)*

Most people are bothered by those passages in Scripture which they cannot understand; but as for me, I always noticed that the passages in Scripture which trouble me most are those that I do understand. *(Mark Twain)*

In the twentieth century our highest praise is to call the Bible 'the World's Best-Seller'. And it has come to be more and more difficult to say whether we think it is a best-seller because it is great, or vice versa. *(D. Boorstin)*

Just as at the sea those who are carried away from the direction of the harbour bring themselves back on course by a clear sign, on seeing a tall beacon light or some mountain peak coming into view, so Scripture may guide those adrift on the sea of life back into the harbour of the divine will. *(St Gregory of Nyssa)*

HUMOUR

A Sunday School class had just been hearing about the parable of the prodigal son. 'Now,' said the Sunday School teacher, 'who was not glad to know of the prodigal's return?' 'Please, sir,' replied one boy, 'the fatted calf!' *(Anon)*

A lady was posting a gift of a Bible to a relative. The post office clerk examined the heavy parcel and inquired if it contained anything breakable. 'Nothing,' the lady told him, 'but the Ten Commandments.' *(Anon)*

In talking about the story of Jacob's dream, a Sunday School teacher asked the class, 'Why did the angels use the ladder when they had wings?'
One bright pupil quickly replied, 'Because they were moulting.'

After the teacher had told her class they could draw a picture of the Bible story she had told them, she went around to see what the children had done. She noticed that little Jenny hadn't drawn a Bible picture at all, so the teacher asked the child to tell the class about her picture.
'This is a car. The man in the front seat is God. The people in the back seat are Adam and Eve. God is driving them out of the Garden of Eden.'

There is a story of a Scottish minister who was reproved for only preaching from and thinking about the Old Testament, and was asked why he did not make more place in his ministry for the New. He replied, 'Aye, I know the New is there, and it is all very well in its way, but, as with other authors, the sequel is not quite up to the original work.' *(Douglas Woodruff)*

STATEMENTS

Let priests therefore . . . after they have themselves by diligent study perused the sacred pages and made them their own by prayer and meditation assiduously distribute the heavenly treasures of the divine word by sermons, homilies and exhortations; let them confirm the Christian doctrine by sentences from the Sacred Books . . . let them set forth all this with such eloquence, lucidity and clearness that the faithful may not only be moved and inflamed to reform their lives, but may also conceive in their hearts the greatest veneration for the Sacred Scripture. *(Pius XII – 'Divino Afflante Spiritu')*

Hence there exists a close connection and communication between sacred tradition and sacred Scripture. For both of them, flowing from the same divine wellspring, in a certain way merge into a unity and tend toward the same end. For sacred Scripture is the word of God inasmuch as it is consigned to writing under the inspiration of the divine Spirit. *(Second Vatican Council – 'Revelation')*

Those who search out the intention of the sacred writer must, among other things, have regard for 'literary forms'. For truth is proposed and expressed in a variety of ways, depending on wherther a text is a history of one kind or another, or whether its form is that of prophecy, poetry, or some other type of speech. The interpreter must investigate what meaning the sacred writer intended to express and actually expressed in particular circumstances as he used contemporary literary forms in acordance with the situation of his own time and culture. *(Second Vatican Council – 'Revelation')*

WORD PICTURES

Item, that you shall provide on this side the feast of Easter next coming, one book of the whole Bible of the largest volume, in English, and the same set up in some convenient place within the said church that you have cure of, whereas your parishioners may most commodiously resort to the same, and read it . . . Item, that you shall discourage no man privily or apertly from the reading or hearing of the said Bible, but shall expressly provoke, stir, and exhort every person to read the same, as that which is the very lively word of God, that every Christian man is bound to embrace, believe, and follow, if he look to be saved. *(Drawn up by Cromwell, submitted to Cranmer 1538, and sent out by him)*

Two poverty-stricken, illiterate men, one blind and the other at death's door, came to a mission hospital in India. On leaving the hospital some time later, the blind man asked for a copy of the 'Jesus Book.' 'Oh, what use is it to you? You cannot read.' 'No,' replied the blind man, 'but we will take it to those who can do so.' They returned to their village, the happy possessors of a Gospel. They were weavers by trade. Whenever men came to purchase cloth in that village they were met with the remark, 'Before we do any business with you, you must read us a few pages out of our Book.' When the tax-collectors came round, they, too, were told, 'We can do no business with you till you have read to us out of our Book.' When the doctor from the hospital visited that village two years afterward he found the heathen temple permanently closed and a church built and the whole village won for Christ. *(Life of Faith)*

A young man heard with disgust that his wealthy old uncle had left him a Bible in his will. The will read thus: 'To my nephew I leave a copy of God's priceless Word which I trust he will use daily and find within its pages real treasure.'

The beneficiary threw the Bible into an old trunk in the attic, disgusted and disappointed with his share in his uncle's bequests. Years later, at a time of depression, he turned to the good Book for comfort. Between its pages he found many thousands of pounds.

The seven wonders of the Word
1. The wonder of its formation – the way in which it grew is one of the mysteries of time.
2. The wonder of its unification – a library of 66 books, yet one book.
3. The wonder of its age – most ancient of all books.
4. The wonder of its sale – best seller of any book.
5. The wonder of its interest – only book in the world read by all classes.
6. The wonder of its language – written largely by uneducated men, yet the best from a literary standpoint.
7. The wonder of its preservation – the most hated of all books, yet it continues to exist. 'The word of our God shall stand for ever.' *(Anon)*

An American Soldier was taught a valuable lesson by a South Sea Islander during the Second World War.

The friendly host, trying to assure the visitor that they had many things in common, brought a copy of the Bible out of his hut and said: 'This is my most prized possession.'

With obvious disdain the soldier replied, 'We've outgrown that sort of thing, you know.'

The islander, who belonged to a tribe which had formerly practised cannibalism, was unimpressed by this lack of courtesy as well as faith. He calmly remarked, 'It's a good thing we haven't outgrown it here. If we had, you would have been a meal as soon as we saw you.' *(Anon)*

A 15-year-old Bedouin boy named Muhammed adh-Dhib was searching for a stray goat in a desert region close to the Dead Sea, when he saw the opening of a small cave in a rocky cliff. He lazily threw a few stones through the hole and heard something break.

Thinking it might be hidden treasure, Muhammed ran back to camp and brought a friend, Ahmed Muhammed, to the cave. They squeezed through the opening into the cave and found among pieces of broken pottery, a number of clay cylinders, two feet high.

Hoping for gold or precious stones, the boys wrenched off the lids, but instead of the treasure they expected, they found only dark musty-swelling lumps of material. They were 11 scrolls made of thin strips of sheepskin sewn together, and coated in gummy, decomposed leather. The scrolls, between 3 feet and 24 feet long, were marked in an ancient form of Hebrew script. The boys were disappointed, but their families managed to sell the fragments to a dealer in Jerusalem for a few pounds. That was in 1947. *(Anon)*

USEFUL TEXTS

Holy Scripture:
Given by God, *2 Tim 3:16*
Inspired by the Holy Spirit, *Acts 1:16; 2 Pet. 1:21*
Called Sword of the Spirit, *Eph. 6:17*
For instruction, *Rom. 15:4*
Bears witness to Christ, *John 5:39-40*

See also: B2 The Good News
B9 Revelation
B24 Go tell everyone
C6 The Old Testament Law

A13

The Church is for Sinners

'Indeed I did not come to call the virtuous, but sinners.'
Matthew 9:13

Quotations

The Church is the only institution in the world that has lower entrance requirements than those for getting on a bus.
(William Laroe)

The Church exists for the sake of those outside it.
(William Temple)

There are many sheep without, many wolves within.
(St Augustine of Hippo)

The Church and the sacraments exist to rescue character and bring out the best in it. Christ did this during his lifetime and has been doing it ever since. *(Hubert Van Zeller)*

The great criticism of the Church today is that no one wants to persecute it: because there is nothing very much to persecute it about. *(George McLeod)*

The Church is the one thing that saves a man from the degrading servitude of being a child of his own time.
(G. K. Chesterton)

Don't stay away from Church because there are so many hypocrites. There's always room for one more. *(A. R. Adams)*

The Church is not made up of people who are better than the rest, but of people who want to become better than they are.
(Anon)

Of course the fear that one's infidelity is being punished is just a stupid temptation. Our Lord came to save *sinners*, and we must not frustrate him by saying, '*Because* I have been a sinner, therefore I'm shut out from his mercy'. The devil would love us to say that but then he is the father of lies. *(Bishop Butler)*

HUMOUR

The retiring usher was instructing his youthful successor in the details of his office. 'And remember, my boy, that we have nothing but good, kind Christians in this Church – until you try to put someone else in their pew!'

There is one ingenious way of indulging in mild slander in the form of audible ejaculatory prayer, and I know a church in London where there is an Irish woman with a considerable gift for praying aloud in such a way as to make her personal opinions exceedingly clear.

One day, when the priest was a little late for Mass, she exclaimed as he came up the aisle, 'Oh, thanks be to the Mother of God, there's going to be the Holy Mass.' And at other times she has apostrophised before the statues of Our Lady and St Joseph, making it very plain that the saints are not deceived about the real character of other parties praying in the church; and I have often wondered what the exact legal position would be, for, if any conversation is privileged, it is surely prayer. *(Douglas Woodruff)*

STATEMENTS

Although by the power of the Holy Spirit the Church has remained the faithful spouse of her Lord and has never ceased to be the sign of salvation on earth, still she is very well aware that among her members, both clerical and lay, some have been unfaithful to the Spirit of God during the course of many centuries. In the present age, too, it does not escape the Church how great a distance lies between the message she offers and the human failings of those to whom the Gospel is entrusted. *(Second Vatican Council – 'The Church Today')*

While Christ, 'holy, innocent, undefiled,' knew nothing of sin, but came to expiate only the sins of the people, the Church, embracing sinners in her bosom, is at the same time holy and always in need of being purified, and incessantly pursues the path of penance and renewal.
(Second Vatican Council – 'The Church')

WORD PICTURES

Only one member has left the Church because of the behaviour of young people. It happened one hot summer evening. Bernice walked down the aisle and sat down with a bump in a pew. She kicked off her stiletto heels, hitched her skirt over her knees and placed her aching feet on the pew in front. She turned to the middle-aged man sitting next to her and said, 'Cor, ain't it bloody 'ot?' He left immediately and he has not been back since. In fact, it was bloody hot, and Bernice was just trying to be friendly in the only way she knew. Moreover, her greeting was in sharp distinction from the lack of welcome she received from him in the House of the Lord. Other adults have been driven close to despair at times by unexpected 'out of place' happenings, but it is to their credit that they still remain to tell the tale. *(Ernest Marvin – 'Odds Against')*

In any terms the picture of the Church as the flock of God is a lovely picture, but it is even lovelier when it is set against its Palestinian background. The pasture land of Judaea is no more than a narrow ridge like the backbone of the country. There were no walled fields, and the pasture land either plunged in cliffs down to the Dead Sea or fell away in infertile valleys through the Shephelah to the Mediterranean coast. The wandering sheep would certainly perish, and even on the pasture land itself grass was sparse and wells and springs were few and far between.

The result of this was that in Palestine a flock was never to be seen without its shepherd. Day and night the shepherd was on constant guard; without his constant and unsleeping care the sheep would certainly starve or wander to disaster.

The picture of the Church as the flock of God underlines the twin facts of God's unceasing care for his Church, and of the Church's complete dependence upon God. In the picture of the flock we see at one and the same time the love of God and the need of man. *(William Barclay)*

This was posted on a Bronx, New York, Church notice board: 'Do come in – Trespassers will be forgiven.' *(Anon)*

Notice put up at the church door by an Italian congregation: 'Home for Abandoned Old Men.' *(Anon)*

Among the regulations for the tenants of a new block of flats near Marble Arch, occurs the injunction 'No religious services or immorality permitted in these flats.' *(Anon)*

USEFUL TEXTS

Church:
The pillar of truth, *1 Tim. 3:15*
Gifts of, *1 Cor. 12:27-30*
Loved by Christ, *Eph. 5:25*

See also: B17 The Church – Bride of Christ
C12 The Church for all men
C27 The Father who receives us back

A14

THE SUCCESSORS OF THE APOSTLES

'He summoned his twelve disciples, and gave them authority over unclean spirits, with power to cast them out and to cure all kinds of diseases and sickness.' *Matthew 10:1*

QUOTATIONS

Whoever is sent by the Master to run his house, we ought to receive him as we would receive the Master himself. It is obvious, therefore, that we ought to regard the bishop as we would the Lord himself. *(St Ignatius of Antioch)*

Be obedient to your bishop and welcome him as the parent of your soul. *(St Jerome)*

Let him understand that he is no bishop, who loves to rule and not be useful to his flock. *(St Augustine)*

A bishop who is himself holy will most certainly have a following of holy priests, whose holiness will in turn redound to the religious perfection of the whole diocese. *(Pope John XXIII)*

'*For* you, I am Bishop', said St Augustine to his people, 'but *with* you, I am a Christian. The first is an office accepted, the second a grace received; one a danger, the other safety. If then, I am gladder by far to be redeemed *with you* than I am to be placed *over you*, I shall, as the Lord commanded, be more completely your servant.' *(St Augustine)*

It is very significant that in every recorded instance, the Apostles were busy at their daily work when the Master called them.
    Peter and Andrew were fishing;
    James and John were mending their nets;
    Matthew was sitting at the receipt of custom.
    God never visits an idle or unserviceable life. *(David Smith)*

Wherever the bishop appears, there let the people be; as wherever Jesus Christ is, there is the Catholic Church.
(St Ignatius of Antioch)

HUMOUR

Now hear an illusion: a mitre, you know,
Is divided above, but united below.
If this you consider, our emblem is right,
The bishops divide, but the clergy unite. *(Jonathan Swift)*

The bishop's last directions
Tell my Priests, when I am gone,
O'er me to shed no tears,
For I shall be no deader then
Than they have been for years.
(Anon)

STATEMENTS

As lawful successors of the apostles and as members of the episcopal college, bishops should always realise that they are linked one to the other, and should show concern for all the churches. *(Second Vatican Council – 'Bishops')*

In discharging their apostolic office, which concerns the salvation of souls, bishops of themselves enjoy full and perfect freedom, and independence from civil authority.
(Second Vatican Council – 'Bishops')

In exercising his office of father and pastor, a bishop should stand in the midst of his people as one who serves.
(Second Vatican Council – 'Bishops')

The pastoral office or the habitual and daily care of their sheep, is entrusted to them completely. Nor are they to be regarded as vicars of the Roman Pontiff, for they exercise an authority which is proper to them, and are quite correctly called 'prelates', or heads of the people whom they govern.
(Second Vatican Council – 'The Church')

WORD PICTURES

When Christ had finished his work on earth, it is said, and had returned to heaven, the angel Gabriel met him.

'Lord,' said Gabriel, 'is it permitted to ask what plans you have made for carrying on your work on earth?'

'I have chosen twelve men, and some women,' said Christ. 'They will pass my message on till it reaches the whole world.'

'But,' said the angel, 'supposing these few people fail you – what other plans have you made?'

Christ smiled. 'I have no other plan,' he said. 'I am counting on them.' *(Anon)*

The Apostles' symbols

The badges or symbols of the fourteen Apostles (i.e. the original twelve with Matthias and Paul) are as follows:

Andrew, an X-shaped cross, because he was crucified on one.

Bartholomew, a knife, because he was flayed with a knife.

James the Great, a scallop shell, a pilgrim's staff or a gourd bottle, because he is the patron saint of pilgrims.

James the Less, a fuller's pole, because he is said to have been killed by a blow on the head with a pole, dealt him by Simeon the Fuller.

John, a cup with a winged serpent flying out of it, in allusion to the tradition about Aristodemos, priest of Diana, who challenged John to drink a cup of poison. John made the sign of a cross on the cup, Satan like a dragon flew from it, and John then drank the cup which was quite innocuous.

Judas Iscariot, a bag, because he acted as a treasurer for Jesus and the Apostles.

Jude, a club, because he was martyred with a club.

Matthew, a hatchet or halberd, because he was slain at Nadabar with a halberd.

Matthias, a battleaxe, because it is believed he was first stoned, and then beheaded with a battleaxe.

Paul, a sword, because his head was cut off with a sword.

Peter, a bunch of keys, because Christ gave him 'the keys of the kingdom of heaven.'

Philip, a long staff surmounted with a cross, because he suffered death by being suspended by the neck from a tall pillar.

Simon, a saw, because according to tradition, he was sawn to death.

Thomas, a lance, because he was pierced to death through the body, at Meliapore. *(Anon)*

Stanislaus was born in the first half of the eleventh century in the town of Szczepanow. Because of his deep piety and his cultural preparation he was named a canon in the Cathedral of Bishop Lambert Zula. On the death of Bishop Lambert, Pope Alexander II, at the request of the clergy and the lay people as well as of King Boleslaus II himself, raised Stanislaus to the See of Krakow.

History tells how the relationship between Bishop Stanislaw and King Boleslaus II, serene at first, later deteriorated because of the injustices and cruelty visited by the king upon his subjects. The Bishop of Krakow, an authentic 'good shepherd' *(cf John 10:10-14)*, defended his flock. The king replied with violence. Bishop Stanislaus was killed while celebrating Mass.

On the venerated skull of the martyr, now preciously preserved in an artistic reliquary, one can still see the signs of the heavy mortal blows.

From that time on, Saint Stanislaus became the Patron of Poland. He became especially the benefactor and protector of poor people; he became, above all, an example to bishops as to how to communicate and defend the sacred deposit of faith with undaunted strength and unbending spirit. For centuries he has been considered an illustrious witness to genuine freedom and to the fruitful synthesis which is brought about in a believer between loyalty to an earthly fatherland and fidelity to the Church. *(Pope John Paul II)*

for useful texts see over

USEFUL TEXTS

Bishops:
Qualifications, *1 Tim. 3:1-7; Titus 1:6-9*
Responsibilities, *1 Thess. 5:14; Heb. 13:17*
Duties, *Acts 20:17; 28-30*

See also: A24 Papacy
A45 The Priesthood
B13 Authority

A15
SIN

'Sin entered the world through one man,
and through sin death.' *Romans 5:12*

QUOTATIONS

Really to sin, you have to be serious about it. *(Henrik Ibsen)*

Sin is essentially a departure from God. *(Martin Luther)*

To sin is nothing else than not to render to God his due.
(St Anselm)

Sin is the irrational in human consciousness. It is the failure of
free will to act reasonably. *(Charles Davis)*

So true is it that every sin is voluntary, that, unless it be
voluntary, it is not sin at all. *(St Augustine of Hippo)*

God loves us in our sin, and *through* our sin, and goes on loving
us, looking for a response. *(Donald Coggan)*

Pride is the ground in which all the other sins grow, and the
parent from which all the other sins come. *(William Barclay)*

For the religious man to do wrong is to defy his King; for the
Christian, it is to wound his Friend. *(William Temple)*

Sin is not a monster to be mused on, but an impotence to be got
rid of. *(Matthew Arnold)*

Keep yourself from opportunity and God will keep you from
sins. *(Jacob Cats)*

The greatest fault is to be conscious of none. *(Thomas Carlyle)*

For evil to triumph, it is only necessary for good men to do nothing. *(Edmund Burke)*

We are too Christian really to enjoy sinning, and too fond of sinning really to enjoy Christianity. Most of us know perfectly well what we ought to do; our trouble is that we do not want to do it. *(Peter Marshall)*

PROVERBS

Sin can be well-guarded, but cannot be free from anxiety. *(Latin proverb)*

You can get to the ends of the earth by lying, but you'll never get back. *(Russian proverb)*

Who is not ashamed of his sins, sins double. *(German proverb)*

HUMOUR

Testing a Sunday School class, the minister asked, 'What are sins of omission, my child?'

Little Cicely replied, 'They're the sins we ought to commit and don't.'

Mrs Brown was shocked to learn that her son had told a lie. Taking the youngster aside for a heart-to-heart talk, she graphically explained the consequences of falsehood:

'A tall black man with red fiery eyes and two sharp horns grabs little boys who tell lies and carries them off at night. He takes them to Mars where they have to work in a dark canyon for 50 years! Now,' she concluded, satisfied, 'you won't tell a lie again, will you, dear?'

'No, Mum,' replied her son, gravely. 'You tell better ones.' *(F. G. Kernan)*

One minister told his congregation that there are 700 different sins. He has already received 46 requests for the list. *(Anon)*

STATEMENTS

By himself and by his own power, no one is freed from sin or raised above himself, or completely rid of his sickness or his solitude or his servitude. On the contrary, all stand in need of Christ, their Model, their Mentor, their Liberator, their Saviour, their Source of Life. *(Second Vatican Council – 'Missions')*

Man is obliged to regard his body as good and honourable since God has created it, and will raise it up on the last day. Nevertheless, wounded by sin, man experiences rebellious stirrings in his body. But the very dignity of man postulates that man glorify God in his body and forbid it to serve the evil inclinations of his heart.
(Second Vatican Council – 'The Church Today')

WORD PICTURES

When Leonardo da Vinci was painting his masterpiece *The Last Supper*, he looked for a model for his Christ. At last, he located a chorister in one of the churches of Rome who was lovely in life and features, a young man named Pietro Bandinelli.

Years passed, and the painting was still unfinished. All the disciples had been portrayed save one – Judas Iscariot. Now he started to look for a man whose face was hardened and distorted by sin – and at last he found a beggar on the streets of Rome with a face so villainous that he shuddered when he looked at him. He hired the man to sit for him as he painted the face of Judas on his canvas. When he was about to dismiss the man, he said, 'I have not yet found out your name.' 'I am Pietro Bandinelli,' he replied, 'I also sat for you as your model of Christ.'

The sinful life of years so disfigured the once fair face of the young man that it now looked as though it were the most villainous face in all Rome! *(Indian Christian)*

Sin does not serve well as gardener of the soul. It landscapes the contour of the soul until all that is beautiful has been made ugly; until all that is high is made low; until all that is promising is

wasted. Then life is like the desert – parched and barren. It is drained of purpose. It is bleached of happiness. Sin, then, is not wise, but wasteful. It is not a gate, but only a grave.
(C. Neil Strait)

Persons called 'Sin-eaters' were hired at funerals in the Middle Ages to eat beside the corpse and so take upon themselves the sins of the deceased, that the soul might be delivered from Purgatory. In Carmarthenshire, the sin-eater used to rest a plate of salt on the breast of the deceased and place a piece of bread on the salt. After saying an incantation over the bread it was consumed by the sin-eater and it was thought that with it he ate the sins of the dead. *(Anon)*

In the ruins of Pompeii there was found a petrified woman who, instead of trying to flee from the city, had spent her time in gathering up her jewels. In one of the houses was found the skeleton of a man who, for the sake of 60 coins, a small plate and a saucepan of silver, had remained in his house till the street was half-filled with volcanic matter, then was trying to escape from the window. *(Anon)*

Sin has four characteristics:
self-sufficiency instead of faith,
self-will instead of submission,
self-seeking instead of benevolence,
self-righteousness instead of humility.
(E. Paul Hovey)

The Master was always teaching that guilt is an evil emotion to be avoided like the very devil – *all* guilt.
    'But are we not to hate our sins?' a disciple said, one day.
    'When you are guilty, it is not your sins you hate but yourself.' *(Anthony de Mello)*

As soon as we have disobeyed the voice of God, and sinned, another element enters into the situation, through sin we *come short* of the glory of God *(Romans 3:23)*. What does that mean?

When we go back to the old story of creation we find that God made man in his own image, and his own likeness *(Genesis 1:26)*. That is to say God made man to bear his own image, and therefore to reflect his own glory. Sin therefore is what keeps a man from being what he was meant to be and what he was created to be.

Here we come at the basic meaning of *hamartia*. *Hamartia* was not originally an ethical word at all. It was, in fact, a word from shooting; and it meant *a missing of the target*. Sin is the failure to hit the target; sin is the failure to be what we were meant to be; sin is falling below one's own possibilities. The moment a man begins to disobey he begins to lose the image of God, and therefore falls short of what he was meant to be. Here is the very foundation in practice of the universality of sin. To fail to do one's best as workman, to fail to be as good a father, mother, son, daughter as one might have been, to fail to use and to develop the gifts of hand and eye and mind and brain that God has given us, in any way to fall short of the best that we could be is a sin. Disobedience to God means failure in life; and failure to hit the target is sin. *(William Barclay)*

USEFUL TEXTS

Sin:
Consequences of, *Exod. 20:5; Prov. 14:11; Rom. 5:12*
Forgiveness of, *Exod. 24:7; Matt. 26:28*
God's displeasure in, *Gen. 6:6, Deut. 25:16; Ps. 5:4*

See also: A13 The Church is for sinners
           A38 Original Sin
           C37 Temptation

A16

THE SAINTS

'Anyone who welcomes a holy man because he is a holy man
will have a holy man's reward.'
Matthew 10:41

QUOTATIONS

To most, even good people, God is a belief. To the saints He is
an embrace. *(Francis Thompson)*

The saint is saint, not because he is 'good' but because he is
transparent for something that is more than he himself is. *(Paul
Tillich)*

Grace is indeed required to turn a man into a saint; and he who
doubts this does not know what either a man or a saint is.
(Blaise Pascal)

Can one be a saint without God? This is the only problem I
know of today. *(Albert Camus)*

It was because the saints were absorbed in God that they were
truly capable of seeing and appreciating created things, and it
was because they loved him alone that they alone loved
everybody. *(Thomas Merton)*

Nature requires the saint since he alone knows the miracle of
transfiguration; growth and development, the very highest and
most sustained incarnation, never weary him. *(Friedrick
Wilhelm Nietzsche)*

The only difference between a saint and a sinner is that every
saint has a past, and every sinner has a future. *(Oscar Wilde)*

The power of the soul for good is in proportion to the strength of its passions. Sanctity is not the negation of passion but its order. Hence great saints have often been great sinners. *(Coventry Patmore)*

What saint has ever won his crown without first contending for it? *(St Jerome)*

No devotion to the saints is more acceptable and more proper than if you strive to express their virtues. *(Erasmus)*

The way of this world is to praise dead saints and persecute living ones. *(Anon)*

PROVERBS

Saint cannot, if God will not. *(French proverb)*

The saint who works no miracles has few pilgrims. *(English proverb)*

HUMOUR

Every saint has a bee in his halo. *(E. V. Lucas)*

Saints are all right in heaven but they're hell on earth. *(Cardinal Cushing)*

Martyrdom, sir, is what these people like: it is the only way in which a man can become famous without ability. *(Bernard Shaw)*

There may have been disillusionments in the lives of the mediaeval saints, but they would scarcely have been better pleased if they could have foreseen that their names would be associated nowadays chiefly with racehorses and the cheaper clarets. *(Saki – H. H. Munro)*

There used to be an Italian who went about Liverpool selling plaster statues of the saints. One day he was barged into by a

sailor who knocked St Anthony out of his collection and broke off the arm with the Infant Jesus on it. The Italian was in the greatest distress. 'I can never sell him now,' he exclaimed. 'Sell him? Of course you can sell him,' said the sailor. 'Stick a patch on one of his eyes and sell him as Lord Nelson.'
(Douglas Woodruff)

STATEMENTS

In the lives of those who shared in our humanity and yet were transformed into especially successful images of Christ, God vividly manifests to men His presence and His face. He speaks to us in them, and gives us a sign of His kingdom, to which we are powerfully drawn, surrounded as we are by so many witnesses and having such an argument for the truth of the gospel. *(Second Vatican Council – 'The Church')*

WORD PICTURES

The festival of Hallowe'en originated in a pagan celebration, even though its name derives from the Christian festival of All Hallows or All Saints.

It was introduced in the seventh century to commemorate all those saints and martyrs who had no special day to themselves, and was held on May 13. But in the eighth century, All Hallows day was moved to November 1, to counteract the pagan celebrations held on that date.

October 31, the eve of November 1, was the last night of the year in the ancient Celtic calendar, and was celebrated as the end of summer and its fruitfulness. It was a festival which the Celts of Northern Europe marked with bonfires to help the sun through the winter.

Only since the late eighteenth and early nineteenth centuries has Hallowe'en developed as a jolly time for children, with costumes, lanterns and games. Before then it was regarded as a night of fear, and wise men, respectful of hobgoblins and wandering demons, stayed indoors. *(Anon)*

The cult of Saints' relics began with the cult of the martyrs, as the faithful soaked small cloths-brandea-in their blood, or put them in contact with the coffin. The cult of relics spread rapidly when elevation and translation of the holy person's body began to be practised, and bones became easily available. Every altar of the growing Church was supposed to have a relic under it, and kings and princes collected them, housing them in reliquaries that became objects of art. The demand for relics exceeded supply, and some saints, particularly venerated in several places, have a head in each place.

Gregory the Great refused a Byzantine empress' request for a piece of Saint Paul, but later on, there was no such hesitation about dismembering a body on the 'share-the-wealth' principle. Churchmen cut up the saints as farmers cut up seed potatoes, confident that the vital principle was in each fragment. Besides the relics of the saints, there were other relics with slips of ancient parchment attached to them saying that they were the bones of archangels. These brought a very high price and were thought to be particularly effective.

The number of saints increased rapidly; there were over 25,000 of them by the tenth century. Most of them were only local; getting a saint nationally recognised required the approval of a sovereign, international recognition that of the pope. The cults of really popular saints spread nearly as fast as the cults of motion-picture stars do today – the earliest representation we have of Saint Thomas Becket is in a Sicilian Cathedral.
(Ambrosini – 'The Secret Archives of the Vatican')

A saint is not pure spirit. He may not be mistaken for an angel: even death cannot make him one. For holiness belongs primarily to this world. It bears witness that the life we live on earth, a bodily life with all its weakness and pettiness, is yet capable of receiving the rays of supernatural light and of taking on a new and transcendent meaning. This teaches us not merely to endure life, but to desire and even to love it . . . The saint may mortify his passions, but they remain a condition and even an element of his holiness. For holiness is itself a passion . . .
(Louis Lavelle)

Yet the tale of heroic suffering for conscience's sake is told in our own day, and we have recently listened to the most inspiring account of modern martyrdom from the lips of Mrs Richard Wurmbrand, wife of the famous Romanian Pastor Richard Wurmbrand. She spent at least four years in prison under terrible conditions. She reminded me very much of another heroine of mine, Dorothy Day: there was the same serenity, the same poverty both of body and spirit, the same spiritual radiance. She is a woman in her early sixties, I think. Once a Jewess, intellectual and wealthy and thoroughly materialistic in outlook, she married the Jewish Richard and together they planned to have a pleasurable existence – until God erupted into their lives, challenged them, and conquered.

Mrs W. had been imprisoned with 1,000 women, some of them society women who only possessed the evening dress they were wearing at the time of their sudden arrest. She had stories only to be equalled in the annals of the early Christians, and listening to her I was transported to the past, to the times of St Cyprian and my own Felicitas and I began to realise something of the intense veneration felt for heroic confessors of the faith, for my instinct was to kneel and kiss Mrs Wurmbrand's feet.

She told of the nuns in her filthy overcrowded barrack-room who, in the face of all threats, calmly went on singing psalms and praising God. Their captors finally decided to make an exhibition of them. Summoning the whole camp as witnesses, they ordered them on to the frozen lake in bare feet and scant clothing. They should have died of exposure and frostbite. Instead, their song grew louder and sweeter. So the dogs – great specially trained brutes of terrifying ferocity – were set on them to tear them to pieces. The camp set up a wail and begged for pity – in vain. The dogs hurtled themselves on to the ice, ran in circles round the nuns, and then sat down quietly without a growl or menace. In angry frustration, the warders ordered everyone back to their cells, sent for a doctor, and asked for examination of the prisoners after their exposure. Not a single sign of injury. The nuns sang on.

The tale of their trial and victory very much resembles that of the Forty Martyrs of Sebaste which the higher critics would dismiss as myth – here it is a history in our own day. This, I felt, is where true ecumenism is to be found: no barriers whatever of confessional faiths. Only tribulations, anguish, persecutions, hunger, dangers, the sword, in fact the entire list given by St Paul in Romans – and over all, the joy of any man's inability to separate his own from Christ. *(Felicitas Corrigan)*

USEFUL TEXTS

Saint:
Called by God, *Rom. 1:7; 1 Cor. 1:2*
Any member of God's family, *Eph. 2:19*
Immorality not fitting, *Eph. 5:3*
God will not forsake, *Ps. 37:28*

See also: A10 Seeking perfection
B26 The whole man
B51 One with Christ
C8 God's messengers

A17

GENTLENESS

'Learn from me, for I am gentle and humble in heart.'
Matthew 11:30

QUOTATIONS

The gentle mind by gentle deeds is known. *(Edmund Spenser)*

Gentleness is invincible. *(Marcus Aurelius)*

Nothing appeases an enraged elephant so much as the sight of a little lamb. *(St Francis de Sales)*

It takes more oil than vinegar to make a good salad
(Jean Pierre Camus)

When you encounter difficulties and contradictions, do not try to break them, but bend them with gentleness and time.
(St Francis de Sales)

He who can preserve gentleness amid pains, and peace amid worry and multitude of affairs, is almost perfect.
(St Francis de Sales)

Nothing is so strong as gentleness, nothing so gentle as real strength. *(St Francis de Sales)*

Hail the small sweet courtesies of life, for smooth do they make the road of it. *(Laurence Sterne)*

This is the final test of a gentleman: his respect for those who can be of no possible service to him. *(William Lyon Phelps)*

Good manners and soft words have brought many a difficult thing to pass. *(Aesop)*

Well bred thinking means kindly and sensitive thoughts. *(Francois de la Rochefoucauld)*

A gentleman is a man who can disagree without being disagreeable. *(Anon)*

Meekness was the method that Jesus used with the apostles. He put up with their ignorance and roughness and even their infidelity. He treated sinners with a kindness and affection that caused some to be shocked, others to be scandalised, and still others to gain hope in God's mercy. Thus, he bade us to be gentle and humble of heart.*(St John Bosco)*

PROVERBS

The smile that you send out returns to you. *(Indian proverb)*

Kind words don't wear out the tongue. *(Danish proverb)*

A gentle hand may lead the elephant with a hair. *(Persian proverb)*

WORD PICTURES

Saint Anselm was riding one day with a group of young men, when one of them sighted a hare and the rest gave chase with their dogs. The hare took refuge under the feet of Anselm's horse. Anselm immediately reined in his steed, and forbade them to hunt the creature. When the men crowded round, noisy with the triumph of the capture, Anselm burst into tears.

'You laugh,' he said, 'but for this unhappy creature there is nothing to laugh at or be glad for, for its mortal foes are about it, and it flies to us for life, in its own way beseeching shelter.'

Then he rode on, and with a loud voice forbade that the dogs should touch the hare, while the creature, glad and at liberty, darted off to the fields and woods. *(Colin Goodman)*

The Wind and the Sun once had a quarrel. The Wind boasted that he was much stronger than the Sun. He said, 'I'll show you I'm stronger; see that old man over there with a big coat on? I bet I can make him take his coat off much quicker than you can.' 'All right,' said the Sun, 'we'll see.' So the Sun went behind a cloud, but left a little hole so that he could peep through and see what the Wind did. The Wind blew and blew as hard as he could, causing a terrible storm, but the harder he blew the tighter the old man wrapped his coat about him. In the end the poor old Wind had to become calm and give in.

Then it was the Sun's turn. He came out from behind the cloud and smiled with sunshine at the old man. After a while, the old man began to mop his brow, then he pulled his coat off. So the Sun beat the Wind. *(Anon)*

I always remember one incident that was told to me. A group of young priests wanted to make a pilgrimage to the Holy Land and greatly longed to have speech with the great Scripture scholar, Père Lagrange. They travelled by a French boat where they had the privilege of an altar for saying Mass. After going on the boat, a rather poorly-dressed gentle friar from the steerage came along, and asked them politely if he might say Mass the next morning. Rather unwillingly they agreed, telling him that he might say Mass after they had said theirs. Morning after morning he came humbly to say his Mass and then went back to the steerage.

When the young priests arrived at St Etienne to call on the great master it was the grubby little friar from the steerage that they found to be Lagrange. *(Vincent McNabb)*

A great bar of iron lay in a workshop. 'I can break that easily,' said the axe, and showered blow upon blow on its surface, but it was harder than he thought, and he made very little impression.

'You're trying the wrong way,' said the saw. 'Let me manage it.' So he set to work backwards and forwards across the iron. But it was very strong, and remained very much the same as before.

'I know how to break it,' said the hammer. 'Get out of my way, I'll do it.' Down it came with such a swing that its head fell off with the blow, but the iron was unmoved.

A quiet little flame was burning from a jet in the workshop. 'May I try ?' it said in a small voice. The louder voices heaped scorn upon it; but the flame rose gently and curled itself around the iron bar, with no noise or force, and gradually the iron melted and fell into two. *(Anon)*

USEFUL TEXTS

Gentleness:
A characteristic God likes, *1 Pet. 3:4*
Of Christ, *2 Cor. 10:1*
Deal with others in, *1 Cor. 4:21*

See also: A19 Patience
             B41 Generosity
             C18 Compassion
             C46 Loving kindness

A18

BALANCE IN NATURE

'It was not for any fault on the part of creation that it was
made unable to attain its purpose, it was made so by God.'
Romans 8:20

QUOTATIONS

All things are artificial, for nature is the art of God.
(Thomas Browne)

Nature is the living, visible garment of God. *(Goethe)*

Nature gives us life like a mother, but loves us like a step-
mother. *(Giacomo Leopardi)*

Nature is not inanimate; its daily toil is intelligent; its works are
duties. *(Cardinal Newman)*

Nature has some perfections, to show that she is the image of
God; and some defects, to show that she is only His image.
(Pascal)

Looked at in the wrong way, nature can be a substitute for God.
This is because relative beauty can be jealous of absolute beauty.
(Hubert Van Zeller)

Every flower of the field, every fibre of a plant, every particle of
an insect, carries with it the impress of its Maker, and can – if
duly considered – read us lectures of ethics or divinity. *(Thomas
Pope Blount)*

There is a sufficiency in the world for man's need but not for
man's greed. *(Mahatma Gandhi)*

The stuff of the universe, woven in a single piece according to one and the same system, but never repeating itself from one point to another, represents a single figure. Structurally it forms a Whole. *(Pierre Teilhard de Chardin)*

Here is the unity of blades of grass and bits of wood and stone, together with everything else . . . All that nature tries to do is to plunge into that unity, into the Father-nature, so that it may all be one, the one Son. *(Meister Eckhart)*

He showed me a little thing, the quantity of a hazel-nut, in the palm of my hand; and it was round as a ball. I looked thereupon with eye of my understanding, and thought: *What may this be?* And it was answered generally thus: *It is all that is made. (Julian of Norwich)*

PROVERBS

Nature does not proceed by leaps. *(Latin proverb)*

Nature is the art of God. *(Latin proverb)*

What is natural is graceful. *(Greek proverb)*

WORD PICTURES

St Malo would not move his cloak because a wren had nested in it. The other day a professional in a golf championship let go his chance of winning because he would not play his ball out of a thrush's nest. *(Helen Waddell)*

Francis of Assisi found a flowering meadow, there he preached: and he called upon it to praise the Lord, even as if it had been a rational being. In the same manner did he treat the sown fields and the vineyards, the stones and the forests, all the fair meads, the running streams, the green gardens, the earth, the fire, the air and the wind. And he counselled them all with upright purity of heart to love God; and in a strangely hidden way he penetrated into the heart of each creature with his sharp-sightedness; as though he were penetrating into the glorious freedom of the Son of God. *(Thomas of Celano)*

A child's view
I like the country because it is so peaceful. Out there the quiet just goes sliding along.

God sews up the buds of flowers very tight and after a while He lets the sun and rain open the stitches. When waves come in on the beach they look like big, open mouths ready to gobble up things. Sometimes they look like white, lacy arms hugging the whole world. *(Anon)*

Waste: man's single greatest product.
Each household discards about 3 lb of glass a week – five bottles.
Each household discards about 12 cans a week.
Each household discards about 13 lb of paper a week.
Each household discards about 1½ lbs of plastic a week.
Each household discards about 5½ lbs of food a week.

In AD 1309, an Aztec Indian inhabitant of what is now Mexico City was found guilty of burning charcoal in the city and polluting the air. He was ordered to be hanged for the offence.

Today, Mexico City has a carbon-monoxide level greater than metropolitan New York, a sulphur-dioxide level greater than that of London, and ten times the industrial contaminants of the industrialised Rhine River valley. *(John McLaughlin)*

On the morning of 14 October Fr Lito Satur was murdered near the town of Valencia in the province of Bukidnon in the southern Philippines. Three masked men shot him as he was returning to the parish house on his motorcycle after offering Mass at an outstation. Most local people feel they know why he was killed. He had been very active in local efforts to protect what remains of the tropical forest on the hills of Bukidnon.

In recent years the Department of Energy and Natural Resources in the Philippines, alarmed at its inability to stop the cutting, has authorised citizens to arrest illegal loggers on its behalf and seize the illegal timber. It is thought that Fr Satur ran foul of logging barons who paid to have him murdered.

One hopes that Fr Satur's death is not in vain and that it inspires others to commit themselves to protecting and healing the environment.

Fr Satur is not the first priest to be murdered for endeavouring to protect the environment in Mindanao. In 1988 Fr Mario Estorba SVD, who was active in an anti-logging campaign in the nearby province of Agusan del Sur, was also gunned down. Many fear that, given the ongoing war in the Philippines between the loggers and miners who are plundering the environment and Christians who are fighting to protect what is left, Fr Satur will not be the last religious leader to die in defence of God's creation. *(Sean McDonagh)*

Glance at the sun. See the moon and the stars.
Gaze at the beauty of earth's greenings.
Now, think.
What delight God gives to humankind
with all these things . . .
All nature is at the disposal of humankind.
We are to work with it. For
without we cannot survive.
(Hildegarde of Bingen)

When a person dies we bury the body in the land and it turns into earth. So we can't leave our land; it would be like leaving our dead, our bodies. Because the earth is our mother. The liver of the earth is coal; the lung is uranium. Earthquakes and tornados are her breath. Now she is in pain. When the government takes her organs she dies. The government only wants money, it doesn't think of her children. *(Navajo woman)*

We are faced with the need to make real present sacrifices in order to serve a future in which we may not even be alive. Not one person in 10,000 is capable of such self-denial . . . our own immediate welfare is bound up with the entire life of the Earth and its future. *(J. G. Bennett)*

We all moan and groan about loss of the quality of life through the destruction of our ecology, and yet each one of us, in our own little comfortable ways, contributes daily to that destruction. It's time now to awaken in each of us the respect and attention our beloved mother deserves. *(Ed Asner)*

USEFUL TEXTS

Earth:
Created by God, *Gen. 1:1*
To be inhabited, *Isa. 45:13*
As God's footstool, *Isa. 66:1*

See also:　B32 The Wonders of God
　　　　　B39 Creation
　　　　　B42 Signs of the times
　　　　　C34 The value of little things

A19

PATIENCE

'Do you want us to go and weed it out?' But he said, 'No, because when you weed out the darnel, you might pull up the wheat with it. Let them both grow till the harvest'.
Matthew 13:28

QUOTATIONS

Patience is needed with everyone, but first of all with ourselves. *(St Francis de Sales)*

Patience comes from two Greek words, meaning *stay under*, not always bobbing up. *(Robert A. Cook)*

Patience is the companion of wisdom. *(St Augustine of Hippo)*

A lot of the road to heaven has to be taken at thirty miles an hour. *(Evelyn Underhill)*

Be long-suffering and prudent, and you will obtain the mastery over wickedness and accomplish all justice.
(Shepherd of Hermas)

Patience is the root and guardian of all the virtues.
(Pope St Gregory I)

All men commend patience, although few be willing to practise it. *(Thomas à Kempis)*

We must wait for God, long, meekly, in the wind and wet, in the thunder and lightning, in the cold and the dark. Wait, and he will come. He never comes to those who do not wait.
(Frederick W. Faber)

'Take your needle, my child, and work at your pattern; it will come out a rose by and by.' Life is like that; one stitch at a time taken patiently, and the pattern will come out all right like embroidery. *(Oliver Wendell Holmes)*

PROVERBS

Patience is power; with time and patience the mulberry leaf becomes silk. *(Chinese proverb)*

One moment of patience may ward off great disaster, one moment of impatience may ruin a whole life. *(Chinese proverb)*

Patience is a bitter plant but it bears sweet fruit. *(German proverb)*

HUMOUR

Patience is something you admire in the driver behind you, but not in the one ahead. *(Bill McGlashen)*

The lovely thing about patience is that it annoys the person who is annoying you. *(Dublin Opinion)*

Angler   'You've been watching me for three hours. Why don't you try fishing yourself?'

Onlooker   'I ain't got the patience.'

That's the advantage of having lived 65 years. You don't feel the need to be impatient any longer. *(Thornton Wilder)*

WORD PICTURES

An aged man, whom Abraham hospitably invited to his tent, refused to join him in prayer to the one spiritual God. Learning that he was a fire-worshipper, Abraham drove him from his door. That night God appeared to Abraham in a vision and said 'I have borne with that ignorant man for 70 years; could you not have patiently suffered him one night?' *(The Talmud)*

Once some robbers came into the monastery and said, to one of the elders: 'We have come to take away everything that is in your cell.' And he said: 'My sons, take all you want.' So they

took everything they could find in the cell and started off. But they left behind a little bag that was hidden in the cell. The elder picked it up and followed after them crying out: 'My sons, take this, you forgot it in the cell!' Amazed at the patience of the elder, they brought everything back into his cell and did penance, saying: 'This one really is a man of God!'
(Tales of the Desert Fathers)

Found scratched on a wall at the Tower of London by prisoners: 'It is not adversity that kills, but the impatience with which we bear with adversity.'

When Stanley went out in 1871 and found Livingstone, he spent months in his company, but Livingstone never spoke to Stanley about spiritual things. Throughout those months, Stanley watched the old man. Livingstone's habits were beyond his comprehension, and so was his patience. He could not understand Livingstone's sympathy for the Africans. For the sake of Christ and His Gospel, the missionary doctor was patient, untiring, eager, spending himself and being spent for his Master. Stanley wrote, 'When I saw that unwearied patience, that unflagging zeal, those enlightened sons of Africa, I became a Christian at his side, though he never spoke to me about it.'
(Anon)

A little Scottish schoolgirl was asked, 'What is patience?' Her reply: 'Wait a wee while, and dinna weary.' *(Bob Edwards)*

USEFUL TEXTS

Patience:
Waiting for the Lord, *Ps. 130:5*
Need for, *Heb. 10:36*
Holy Spirit gives, *Gal. 5:22*
Produced by suffering, *Rom. 5:3*

See also: A11 God's loving Providence
B21 Trust in God
C39 Doing God's will

A20

THE KINGDOM OF GOD

'A disciple of the kingdom of heaven is like a householder
who brings out from his storeroom things both new and old.'
Matthew 13:52

QUOTATIONS

In the Gospel, Jesus is autobasileia, the kingdom himself.
(Origen of Alexandria)

To accept his kingdom and to enter in brings blessedness,
because the best conceivable thing is that we should be in
obedience to the Will of God. *(C. H. Dodd)*

To want all that God wants, always to want it, for all occasions
and without reservations, this is the kingdom of God which is
all within. *(Francois Fenelon)*

The kingdom of God is a kingdom of love; and love is never a
stagnant pool. *(Henry W. Du Bose)*

Is the kingdom of God a big family? Yes, in a sense it is. But in
another sense it is a prodigious biological operation – that of the
Redeeming Incarnation. *(Pierre Teilhard De Chardin)*

If you want to work for the kingdom of God, and to bring it,
and to enter into it, there is just one condition to be first
accepted. You must enter it as children, or not at all.
(John Ruskin)

The Kingdom of God will not come in a day; it will not be left
with the morning milk. *(S. Parkes Cadman)*

Many who are not yet 'in the Kingdom of God' in its earthly
manifestation, will enjoy its ultimate fulfilment in a world
beyond this. *(C. H. Dodd)*

STATEMENTS

In Christ's word, in His works, and in His presence this kingdom reveals itself to men.
(Second Vatican Council – 'The Church')

Before all things, however, the kingdom is clearly visible in the very person of Christ, Son of God and Son of Man, who came 'to serve and to give his life as a ransom for many' *(Mark 10:45)*.
(Second Vatican Council – 'The Church')

For the Lord wishes to spread His kingdom by means of the laity also, a kingdom of truth and life, a kingdom of holiness and grace, a kingdom of justice, love and peace. In this kingdom, creation itself will be delivered out of its slavery to corruption and into the freedom of the glory of the sons of God.
(Second Vatican Council – 'The Church')

WORD PICTURES

The kingdom is something within you which has the power of growth like a seed; something that you are searching for, and of whose values you become more confident and excited as the search proceeds and you discover truer, lovelier things which are constantly being surpassed; something for which you have to give everything you have, no less yet no more, including the earlier finds with which you were once so completely delighted.
(George Appleton)

Christ looked at the people.
He saw them assailed by fear:
He saw the locked door;
He saw the knife in the hand;
He saw the buried coin;
He saw the unworn coat,
   consumed by moth;
He saw the stagnant water
   drawn and kept in the pitcher,
   the musty bread in the bin –
   the defended,
   the unshared,
   the ungiven.

He told them then
  of the love
  that casts out fear,
  of the love that is four walls
  and a roof over the head:
  of the knife in the sheath,
  of the coin in the open hand,
  of the coin given
  warm with the giver's life,
  of the water poured in the cup,
  of the table spread –
  the undefended,
  the shared,
  the given –
  the Kingdom of Heaven.
(Caryll Houselander)

A Russian youth who had become a conscientious objector to war through the reading of Tolstoy and the New Testament was brought before a magistrate. With the strength of conviction he told the judge of the life which loves its enemies, which does good to those who despitefully use it, which overcomes evil with good, and which refuses war.

'Yes,' said the judge, 'I understand. But you must be realistic. These laws you are talking about are the laws of the kingdom of God; and it has not come yet.'

The young man straightened, and said, 'Sir, I recognise that it has not come for you, nor yet for Russia or the world. But the kingdom of God has come for me! I cannot go on hating and killing as though it had not come.' *(Neil H. Swanson)*

Though we achieve social justice, liberty, peace itself, though we give our bodies to be burned for these admirable causes, if we lack this – the transformation of the natural order by the Eternal Charity – we are nothing. For the kingdom is the Holy not the moral; the Beautiful not the correct; the perfect not the adequate; Charity not law. *(Evelyn Underhill)*

USEFUL TEXTS

The Kingdom:
Of God, *1 Chr. 29:11; Ps. 22:28*
Of Christ, *Matt. 16:28; 2 Pet. 1:11*
Of the World, *Rev. 11:15*

See also: A31 Heaven
B17 The Church – Bride of Christ
B51 One with Christ
C39 Doing God's will

A21
FEEDING THE HUNGRY

'Give them something to eat yourselves.'
Matthew 14:16

QUOTATIONS

Ticker tape ain't spaghetti. *(F. La Guardia)*

To a man with an empty stomach, food is God.
(Mohandas Gandhi)

It is not enough to free man from hunger imposed on him by an insufficiency of food. Man must be freed of all the forces that oppress him, of the natural, economic and political order. *(World Food Congress)*

If you give a man a fish, he will eat once.
If you teach a man to fish, he will eat for the rest of his life.
If you are thinking a year ahead, sow seed.
If you are thinking ten years ahead, plant a tree.
If you are thinking one hundred years ahead,
   educate the people.
By sowing seed, you will harvest once.
By planting a tree, you will harvest tenfold.
By educating the people, you will harvest one hundredfold.
(Kuantzu)

If you're put on bread and water, it's a punishment. The image conjures up visions of imprisonment and bare survival. In Africa these words mean exactly the opposite; bread and water means freedom – escape from the prison of starvation and death. *(Tear Fund)*

I suggest that we are thieves in a way. If I take anything that I do not need for my own immediate use, and keep it, I thieve it from somebody else . . . In India, we have got three millions of people having to be satisfied with one meal a day, and that meal consisting of unleavened bread (chapati) containing no fat in it, and a pinch of salt. You and I have no right to anything that we really have until these three millions are clothed and fed better. You and I, who ought to know better, must adjust our wants, and even undergo voluntary starvation in order that they may be nursed, fed and clothed. *(Mohandas Gandhi)*

PROVERBS

Hungry bellies have no ears. *(English Proverb)*

A man who wants bread is ready for anything. *(French proverb)*

When you're hungry, sing; when you're hurt, laugh. *(Jewish proverb)*

The full belly does not believe in hunger. *(Italian proverb)*

HUMOUR

The absent-minded professor called his biology class to order shortly after the lunch hour.

'Our special work this afternoon,' he said, 'will be cutting up and inspecting the inner workings of a frog. I have a dead frog here in my pocket to be used as a specimen.'

He reached into his pocket and pulled out a paper bag, shook its contents on the table and out rolled a nice looking ham sandwich. The professor looked at it, perplexed, scratched his head and muttered, 'That's funny, I distinctly remember eating my lunch.' *(Anon)*

A little Japanese boy called at the house of a retired gentleman and offered some picture postcards for sale at 10p each.

'What are you going to do with the money?' he asked him.

'I am raising one million pounds for the earthquake relief,' the boy answered, gravely, and he was so tiny and the sum he named was so large that the gentleman had to laugh.

'One million pounds?' he cried. 'Do you expect to raise it all by yourself?'

'No, sir,' he replied gravely. 'There's another little boy helping me.' *(Anon)*

STATEMENTS

Conscience, a new conscience for our times, is calling each of us to self-review. Am I really doing all I can to help the poor and hungry? Am I prepared to pay more taxes in order that the government can do more for development? Am I prepared to pay more in the shops for goods imported from abroad so that the people who produce these goods are paid a decent wage? Am I prepared to leave my country to help the younger nations? . . . It is still true, today, to say that charity begins at home. But home, today, is all the world. *(Pope Paul VI – 'Progressio Populorum')*

Since there are so many people in this world afflicted with hunger, this sacred Council urges all, both individuals and governments, to remember the saying of the Fathers: 'Feed the man dying of hunger, because if you have not fed him, you have killed him.' *(Second Vatican Council – 'The Church Today')*

The distribution of goods should be directed toward providing employment and sufficient income for the people of today and of the future. *(Second Vatican Council – 'The Church Today')*

WORD PICTURES

Christians alone straddle the whole spectrum of rich nations and therefore Christians can be a lobby of tremendous importance. When we come before our heavenly Father and he says, 'Did you feed them, did you give them to drink, did you clothe them, did you shelter them?' and we say, 'Sorry, Lord, but we did give them 0.3 per cent of our gross national product,' I don't think it will be enough. *(Barbara Ward)*

Your poverty is greater than ours . . . the spiritual poverty of the West is much greater than the physical poverty of the East. In the West, there are millions of people who suffer loneliness and emptiness, who feel unloved and unwanted. They are not the hungry in the physical sense; what is missing is a relationship with God and each other. *(Mother Teresa)*

Mother Teresa has shared her experience of one parent's response to this dilemma. 'Some time ago a gentleman came to our house and said 'There is a Hindu family with eight children that have not eaten for some time. Kindly go and see them.' I took rice with me and I went, and when I arrived I could see the children's faces shining with hunger. I gave the rice to their mother. She divided it into two and she went out. When she came back I asked her: 'Where did you go and what did you do?' And the only answer she gave me was, 'They are hungry also.'
'Who are *they?*' I asked.
She said: 'A Muslim family next door.'
'I was struck very much; not so much by what she did as by the fact she knew they were hungry; that she saw their hunger, she felt their hunger and therefore she had the courage to share with them. This is the greatness of poor people. Love, to be true, has to hurt. *(Dr Ittyerah)*

USEFUL TEXTS
Food:
Provided by God, *Gen. 1:29-30*
For strength, *Ps. 104:15*
To abstain from, *Gen. 2:16-17*
Christ provided, *Matt. 14:19-20*

See also: A33 Love your neighbour
B15 Jesus' friend of outcasts
C21 Rise above materialism
C29 Not through luxury

A22
SEEKING GOD

'After the fire there came the sound of a gentle breeze.'
I Kings 19:12

QUOTATIONS

The knowledge of God is naturally implanted in all.
(St Thomas Aquinas)

My only task is to be what I am, a man seeking God in silence and solitude with respect for the demands and realities of his own vocation, and fully aware that others too are seeking the truth in their own way. *(Thomas Merton)*

It is in silence that God is known, and through mysteries that He declares Himself. *(R. H. Benson)*

It was the man in the street who understood our Lord, and the doctor of the law who was perplexed and offended.
(R. H. Benson)

For the mind to attain to God in some degree is great beatitude.
(St Augustine of Hippo)

We know God better through grace than through unaided reason. *(St Thomas Aquinas)*

We cannot form an adequate concept of man unless we include God. He is mysterious, transcendent and ineffable, the eternal principle of the universe. But he watches over us, knows and observes us, penetrates and preserves us unceasingly. He is our Father. *(Pope Paul VI)*

Each conception of spiritual beauty is a glimpse of God.
(Moses Mendelssohn)

To have found God is not an end in itself but a beginning. *(Franz Rosenzweig)*

PROVERBS
Search yourself and you will find God. *(Kurdish proverb)*

Whosoever walks towards God one cubit, God runs towards him twain. *(Jewish proverb)*

STATEMENTS
From ancient times down to the present, there has existed among diverse peoples a certain perception of that hidden power which hovers over the course of things and over the events of human life; at times, indeed, recognition can be found of a Supreme Divinity and of a Supreme Father too. *(Second Vatican Council – 'Non-Christians')*

Since it has been entrusted to the Church to reveal the mystery of God, who is the ultimate goal of man, she opens up to man at the same time the meaning of his own existence, that is, the innermost truth about himself. *(Second Vatican Council – 'The Church Today')*

This sacred Synod affirms, 'God, the beginning and end of all things, can be known with certainty from created reality by the light of human reason.' *(Second Vatican Council – 'Revelation')*

WORD PICTURES
Carl Jung was counselling a man who had been receiving therapy for six months and was getting no better. Finally Dr Jung said: 'Friend, I cannot do any more for you. What you need is God.'

'How do I find God, Dr Jung?' the man asked.

'I do not know,' said Jung, 'but I suspect if you find a group of people that believe in Him passionately and just spend time with them you will find God.' *(Methodist Recorder)*

It was among, the Parthians the custom that none were to give their children any food in the morning before they saw the sweat on their faces . . . You shall find this to be God's usual course: not to give His children the taste of His delights till they begin to sweat in seeking after them. *(Richard Baxter)*

God, as the Christian knows him, is the *seeking* God. The great liberal Jewish scholar C. G. Montefiore held strongly that this is the one absolutely new thing which Jesus came to say. The idea of a God who will *invite* the sinner back is not new; the idea of a God who will *welcome* back the penitent sinner is not new; but the idea of a God who will go and seek for the sinner, and who wants men to do the same, is something completely new. Montefiore would find the very centre and soul and essence of the Christian Gospel in *Luke 15:1-10,* in the story of the shepherd searching for the lost sheep and the woman searching for the lost coin. He writes: 'Jesus sought to bring back into glad communion with God those whom sin, whether *moral* or *ceremonial,* had driven away. For him sinners (at least certain types of sinners) were the subject not of condemnation or disdain, but of pity. He did not avoid sinners, he sought them out. *(William Barclay)*

USEFUL TEXTS

Characteristics of God:
Omnipresence, *Ps. 139:7-12*
Omniscience, *Amos 9:2-3*
Omnipotence, *Jer. 32:17, 27*

Manifestations of God:
Voice of, *Deut. 5:22-26*
Glory of, *Exod. 40:34-35*
In Jesus, *John 14:9*

See also: A10 Seeking perfection
              B28 The Father who draws us to Himself
              C16 Come follow me
              C38 Discerning God's Will

A23
MERCY

'My salvation will come and my integrity be manifest.'
Isaiah 56:1

QUOTATIONS

Our faults are like a grain of sand beside the great mountain of the mercies of God. *(St John Vianney)*

Trust the past to the mercy of God,
The present to his love,
The future to his providence. *(St Augustine of Hippo)*

A God all mercy is a God unjust. *(Edward Young)*

For mercy is a greater thing than right. *(Chaucer)*

Mercy, also, is a good thing, for it makes men perfect, in that it imitates the perfect Father. Nothing graces the Christian soul so much as mercy. *(St Ambrose)*

Reason to rule, but mercy to forgive: The first is law, the last prerogative. *(Dryden)*

As freely as the firmament embraces the world, so mercy must encircle friend and foe. *(Schiller)*

Among the attributes of God, although they are all equal, mercy shines with even more brilliancy than justice. *(Cervantes)*

Teach me to feel another's woe, to hide the fault I see; that mercy I to others show, that mercy show to me.
(Alexander Pope)

The mercy of God (may be found) between the bridge and the stream. *(St Augustine of Hippo)*

There's a wideness in God's mercy
Like the wideness of the sea,
There's a kindness in his justice,
Which is more than liberty.
(Frederick W. Faber)

The sinner of today is the saint of tomorrow. Wherefore, unmindful of the sins and shortcomings of our neighbour, let us look to our own imperfections, surely forgetting what God has forgotten: sins truly repented, which God has forgotten, 'tis no business of ours to remember. *(Meister Eckhart)*

PROVERBS

If God were not willing to forgive sin, heaven would be empty. *(German proverb)*

Mercy is better than vengeance. *(Greek proverb)*

Mercy often gives death instead of life. *(Latin proverb)*

WORD PICTURES

A boy was sent by his teacher to the principal of the school for doing something wrong. After hearing the facts the principal took out a blank book and wrote down the boy's name, observing as he did so: 'You have not been sent to me before. Now, I don't know you: you may be a good boy, for all I know. Good boys sometimes make mistakes. Now I'll just make a note in pencil that you were sent to me today, and I will also note why you were sent. But you see I am making this memorandum in pencil, and I am not bearing on very hard. And if you are not sent to me again this year, I shall erase this from my book and no one will ever know anything about it.' It was a lesson in mercy the boy never forgot. *(F. H. Drinkwater)*

USEFUL TEXTS

Mercy:
Characteristic of God, *Lam. 3:22-23*
God showed in salvation, *Titus 3:4-5*
To characterise believers, *Matt. 5:7; Luke 6:36*

See also: A17 Gentleness
C14 Forgiveness
C18 Compassion
C46 Loving kindness

A24

PAPACY

'You are Peter and on this rock I will build my Church.'
Matthew 16:18

QUOTATIONS

When in the time of this Clement (Pope St Clement I), no little dissension arose among the Christians at Corinth, the Church in Rome sent a most powerful letter to the Corinthians urging them to peace and renewing their faith and in the tradition which they had recently received from the apostles.
(Eusebius of Caesarea)

Reckon up the priests from the days that Peter sat, and in their ancestral ranks, note who succeeded whom; for that is the rock over which the gates of hell shall never prevail.
(St Augustine of Hippo)

We think, too, that you should consult our holy brother, Bishop of the Church at Rome, for we presume that what you determine will in no way displease him. *(St Ambrose)*

The rejection of the primacy of St Peter has driven men on to a slippery course, where all the steps are downwards.
(Lord Acton)

The action and the theory of the modern papacy are the outcome of an agelong growth, and we must seek in the pages of history less for a proof of the papal claims than for the evidence that they have shared in, and been central to, the general development of that society which is our only historical link with the origins of Christianity. *(Dom. Butler)*

PROVERBS

We cannot all be Pope of Rome. *(German proverb)*

The corpse of the Pope takes up no more room than the sacristan's. *(Spanish proverb)*

HUMOUR

Pope Elopes, was the headline attributed to a Miss Dorothy Parker, who won the most sensational conceivable newspaper headline with it in an Algonquin Round-Table contest.

The tale is told of a newly-appointed minister of the Kirk who was calling on his new parishioners. At one cottage where he had been warmly received, he apologised at the end, saying, 'You have been most courteous, but I should not have come, for I see you are not part of my congregation, but are Roman Catholics.' The old cottager protested with some warmth that this was not so; neither he nor his wife were Roman Catholics, nor ever would be. 'Then why,' said the minister, 'do you have that brightly coloured picture of Pope Leo XIII on your wall?' The old man looked at it, then he exclaimed, 'Wait till I catch that Izzy Cohen in Glasgow. He sold it to me, telling me it was Robert Burns in his Mason's regalia.' *(Douglas Woodruff)*

STATEMENT

In order that the episcopate itself might be one and undivided, He placed Peter over the other apostles, and instituted in him a permanent and visible source and foundation of unity of faith and fellowship. And all this teaching about the institution, the perpetuity, the force and reason for the sacred primacy of the Roman Pontiff and of his infallible teaching authority, this sacred Synod again proposes to be firmly believed by all the faithful. *(Second Vatican Council – 'The Church')*

WORD PICTURES

Before a crowded concert in the Paris Conservatoire, the composer Gounod arrived in the audience, and found all seats occupied. A young priest rose and said, 'Please take my seat, you are older than I.' But Gounod replied: 'No, my friend, you are the Church. I recall a remark of Pope Gregory XVI. Some visitor said to him once 'Holy Father, I'm an older man than you.' The Pope said 'Older than me? I have lived over eighteen hundred years.'

'Your reverence is eighteen hundred years old: you must keep the seat.' *(Mgr Luigi Vigna)*

The last non-Italian Pope, Adrian of Utrecht, had been the tutor of the young Emperor Charles V and enjoyed his confidence. He was ruling Spain for him when the messengers arrived at Vitoria with the disconcerting news that he had been elected Pope, and he set out on a very slow journey, not without dangers, to Rome, to his short and unhappy pontificate. *(Douglas Woodruff)*

When Hildebrand became Pope St Gregory VII, with the new fashion, or fairly new one, of the Pope taking a new name, he chose to be Gregory VII because of his great respect for Gregory VI, a little known Pope, but a man with a most remarkable history.

Quite often, in bad patches of the extraordinary history of the See of Rome, ambitious cardinals or rulers have tried bribery. But Gregory bought the Papacy outright from his immediate predecessor, because that predecessor was a quite unfit young man, and Gregory, who was an elderly priest at Grottaferrata, bought the Papacy not from ambition, but to get it back into good hands.

He was apparently allowed to do so, and we can be sure that Hildebrand, a leading figure in the great reform that began with St Leo IX, would not have honoured Gregory VI as he did if the story had not been creditable to him. No-one has yet succeeded in purchasing the See of Westminster. *(Douglas Woodruff)*

In 1509, the Emperor Maximilian I wrote to his 'Very dear and beloved daughter, Margaret,' who ruled the Netherlands, to say that he could see no sensible reason why he should marry again; and went on to tell her his plans. 'Tomorrow we are sending the

Bishop of Gurk to Rome to the Pope, for him to treat with him that he appoint Us his coadjutor, so that We may be assured of the Papacy after his death, later to become priest, and eventually saint, so that you will be obliged to pray to Me once I find myself in heavenly glory.' And he signed himself – 'Your good father Maximilian, future Pope.'

USEFUL TEXTS

Peter:
Called by Christ, *Matt. 4:18-20*
Walked on water, *Matt. 14:22-23*
Confessed Jesus as Christ, *Matt. 16:13-18*
Denied knowing Jesus, *Matt. 26:69-75*
Witnessed empty tomb, *John 20:1-9, etc*

See also: A14 The successors of the Apostles
B13 Authority
B17 The Church – Bride of Christ
C44 Feed my sheep

A25

COURAGE

'Jesus began to make it clear to his disciples that he was destined to suffer grievously at the hands of the elders.'
Matthew 16:21

QUOTATIONS

Courage is grace under pressure. *(Ernest Hemingway)*

He who loses wealth loses much; he who loses a friend loses more; but he that loses his courage loses all. *(Cervantes)*

Courage does not consist in calculation, but in fighting against chances. *(John Henry Newman)*

It needs courage to throw oneself forward; but it needs not less to hold oneself back. *(Désiré Joseph Mercier)*

Courage is doing what you're afraid to do. There can be no courage unless you're scared. *(Eddie Rickenbacker)*

Courage is almost a contradiction in terms. It means a strong desire to live taking the form of a readiness to die.
(G. K. Chesterton)

The principal act of courage is to endure and withstand dangers doggedly rather than to attack them. *(St Thomas Aquinas)*

Courage is not merely *one* of the virtues but the form of every virtue at the testing point, which means at the point of highest reality. *(C. S. Lewis)*

We learn courageous action by going forward whenever fear urges us back. A little boy was asked how he learned to skate. 'Oh, by getting up every time I fell down,' he answered.
(David Seabury)

Mere physical courage – the absence of fear – simply is not worth calling bravery. It's the bravery of the tiger, not the moral bravery of the man. *(R. H. Benson)*

PROVERBS

True courage grapples with misfortune. *(Latin proverb)*

Two-thirds of help is to give courage. *(Irish proverb)*

Great things are done more through courage than through wisdom. *(German proverb)*

You can't answer for your courage if you have never been in danger. *(French proverb)*

WORD PICTURES

The Victoria Cross is the premier British award for conspicuous bravery in the presence of the enemy. Instituted by Queen Victoria in 1856, the ribbon is claret coloured, but was formerly blue for the Royal Navy and red for the Army. It consists of a bronze Maltese Cross with the royal crown surmounted by a lion under which is a scroll bearing the words *For Valour*. One of the first awards was to a boy-midshipman who when a bomb from a Russian battery fell on the deck of his warship, went and picked it up with its fuse burning, carried it to the side and dropped it into the sea.

After over a hundred years, the Victoria Cross had been awarded to 1,344 brave men altogether. *(Anon)*

One of the most famous stories of unselfishness and courage is the epic of Captain L. E. Oates, of the Inniskilling Dragoons, who marched with Scott to the South Pole. It was an ill-fated expedition. One disaster after another overtook the little party of men struggling over hundreds of miles of snow and ice in temperatures as low as minus 46, without machines or dogs to help them. Captain Oates was badly afflicted by frostbite; he could hardly hobble along, let alone pull his share of the weight of sledge and stores. March 17 (1912) was his birthday and, in the evening, he quietly left his tent and walked out into the blizzard knowing that without him to hamper them, his companions had a better chance of survival. His sacrifice was unavailing but is none the less memorable for that. Today in the Antarctic wastes, now crossed and recrossed by scientists with all their latest modern equipment, there is still a cairn and a cross and a plaque which begins, 'Hereabouts died a very gallant gentleman . . .' (R. C. Macrobie)

The word 'courage' takes on added meaning if you keep in mind that it is derived from the Latin term *cor* meaning 'heart'.

The dictionary defines it as a 'quality which enables one to pursue a course deemed right, through which one may incur contempt, disapproval, or opprobrium.'

Some 300 years ago, La Rochefoucauld went a step further when he said: 'Perfect courage is to do unwitnessed what we should be capable of doing before all men.' (*Anon*)

One Friday morning in February 1975, an underground train, with 300 people on it, crashed against a stone wall at Moorgate station killing 41 people. Among the passengers was a 19-year-old girl, named Margaret, who had just become a policewoman. When the train hit the wall, she found herself sitting on the floor with one of her legs under her body and a man on top of her. Neither could move without hurting the other. It was completely dark. The man on top said to her, 'You are being very brave.' 'I have to be,' she said, 'I am a policewoman.' For many hours, firemen tried to pull them out. Then they found that Margaret's left leg was trapped under a huge steel girder. The firemen marvelled that she could still laugh and joke. They could do nothing more to get her out. Then a surgeon came and told her that she was going to be put to sleep so that she could be got out. 'That's fine,' she said, 'who's going to take me?' Five minutes later, the surgeon took Margaret's left foot off above the ankle. Within two days she was sitting up in hospital, chatting cheerfully to visitors. She received more than 2,000 gifts and cards from all over the world. (*M. Nassan*)

USEFUL TEXTS

Courage:
Call to, *Deut. 31:7; Ps. 27:14*
Paul testified to having, *2 Cor. 5:6-8*

See also: B35 The Grace of God
C13 Coping with grief
C41 Starting afresh

A26

SACRAMENT OF PENANCE

'Whatever you bind on earth
shall be considered bound in heaven;
whatever you loose on earth
shall be considered loosed in heaven.'
Matthew 18:18

QUOTATIONS

It is better for a person to confess their sins than to harden their heart. *(Pope St Clement I)*

How could a man live at all if he did not grant absolution every night to himself and all his fellows! *(Goethe)*

You shall confess your offences in church, and shall not come forward to your prayer with a bad conscience. *(Didache)*

Even when one confesses his sins, he ought to do so with praise of God; nor is a confession of sins a pious one unless it be made without despair, and with a prayer for God's mercy.
(St Augustine of Hippo)

Within the Church, sins are forgiven in three ways; by baptism, by prayer and by the greater humility of penance.
(St Augustine of Hippo)

Through the office of priests, those should be reconciled to Holy Church by doing penance, who have departed from its society by sinning. *(St Bede the Venerable)*

Be a lion in the pulpit, but a lamb in the confessional.
(St Alphonsus of Liguori)

The life of Christ was massively a ministry of reconciliation.
(J. D. Crichton)

PROVERBS

Open confession is good for the soul. *(Scottish proverb)*

In every pardon there is love. *(Welsh proverb)*

HUMOUR

A priest hearing children's confessions was puzzled to find child after child adding, after the recital of more familiar and intelligible sins, that of 'throwing peanuts in the river'. He wondered whether they were repenting of wasting food or of river pollution, and then decided to press for a little more explanation when the last and smallest child came in. But the smallest penitent failed to confess this. 'Yes,' said the priest, 'is that all – isn't there something you've forgotten? What about throwing peanuts in the river?' 'But, Father,' said a bewildered voice, 'I am Peanuts'. *(Douglas Woodruff)*

Fr Vincent McNabb was once speaking in Hyde Park on the Sacrament of Penance. A heckler was positive that Catholics pay for absolution. 'You're really quite sure about that?' asked Fr Vincent. The heckler said he was quite certain. 'Then I've been done!' said the priest. 'I've been hearing confessions for 50 years, and nobody ever paid me.' *(F. H. Drinkwater)*

After a vigorous brotherly and sisterly disagreement, our three children retired only to be aroused at 2 o'clock by a terrific thunderstorm. Hearing an unusual noise upstairs, I called to find, out what was going on. A little voice answered, 'We are in the cupboard forgiving each other.' *(Robert Tuttle)*

STATEMENT

In the spirit of Christ the Shepherd, priests should train them to submit their sins with a contrite heart to the Church in the sacrament of Penance. Thus mindful of the Lord's words: 'Repent, for the kingdom of God is at hand' *(Matt. 4:17)*, the , people will be drawn ever closer to Him each day.
(Second Vatican Council – 'Priests')

WORD PICTURE

A Moslem soldier had beaten a Christian prisoner until he was only half-conscious, and while he kicked him he demanded, 'What can your Christ do for you now?' The Christian quietly replied, 'He can give me strength to forgive you. *(R. Earl Allen)*

There is an Oriental story of a Sultan who failed to waken one morning at the hour of prayer. The devil waked him up and told him to get up and pray. 'Who are you?' asked the Sultan. 'Never mind. My act is good, is it not?' replied the devil. 'No matter who does the good action, so long as it is good.' 'Yes, but I think you are Satan and you must have some bad motive,' the Sultan persisted. 'You are the tempter; that's your business, and I wish to know why you want me to get up and pray.' 'Well,' said the devil, 'if you had slept and forgotten your prayers, you would have been sorry for it afterwards, and penitent; but if you go on as now, and do not neglect a single prayer for ten years, you will be so satisfied with yourself that it will be worse for you than if you had missed one and repented of it. God loves your fault mixed with penitence more than your virtue seasoned with pride.'

USEFUL TEXTS

Reconciliation:
To God, *Rom. 5:10-11*
To brother, *Matt. 5:23-24, Matt. 18:15-17*

See also: A27 As we forgive those
B16 Christ heals and forgives
C14 Forgiveness
C40 Reconciliation

A27

AS WE FORGIVE THOSE

'Not seven, I tell you, but seventy-seven times.'
Matthew 18:22

QUOTATIONS

Only one petition in the Lord's Prayer has any condition attached to it; it is the petition for forgiveness. *(William Temple)*

To err is human, to forgive divine. *(Alexander Pope)*

We pardon to the extent that we love.
(Francois De La Rochefoucauld)

'I can forgive, but I cannot forget' is only another way of saying 'I cannot forgive.' *(Henry Ward Beecher)*

Humanity is never so beautiful as when praying for forgiveness or else forgiving another. *(Jean Paul Richter)*

He that cannot forgive others breaks the bridge over which he must pass himself: for every man has need to be forgiven. *(Thomas Fuller)*

Every person should have a special cemetery plot in which to bury the faults of friends and loved ones. *(Anon)*

May God forgive him! I want him in heaven. *(Maria Goretti, 11, fatally stabbed while resisting the advances of a 19-year-old youth)*

PROVERBS

The noblest vengeance is to forgive. *(English proverb)*

He who forgives ends the quarrel. *(African proverb)*

To forgive is beautiful. *(Greek proverb)*

Forgiving the unrepentant is like drawing pictures on water. *(Japanese proverb)*

WORD PICTURES

A minister tells the story of a clergyman who was given a flowery introduction before a speech. When he stood up to present his address, he said, 'May the Lord forgive this man for his excesses, and me for enjoying them so much.' *(Alice Murray)*

O Lord, remember not only the men and women of goodwill, but also those of ill-will. But do not remember all the suffering they have inflicted on us, remember the fruits we have bought, thanks to this suffering – our comradeship, our loyalty, our humility, our courage, our generosity, the greatness of heart which has grown out of all this, and when they come to the judgement, let all the fruits that we have borne be their forgiveness. *(Found on a piece of paper by the body of a dead child at Ravensbruck concentration camp)*

Brother Rufino was extremely gentle, and no one doubted his sincerity. Prayer came more naturally to him than preaching. Indeed, to speak in public terrified him. When he was asked to preach he became confused, then completely speechless. This handicap, however, could not be permitted when he had vowed to preach the Gospel of Christ.

Normally kind and tolerant, and ever prepared to counsel and befriend a brother, Francis could be harsh when a friar broke the Rule. He regarded it as an insult to Christ. Thus, hoping to overcome Rufino's weakness, he ordered him to go and preach in Assisi. Desperately Rufino pleaded to be excused and grew so obstinate that Francis fiercely rebuked him. As a penance, Francis again commanded Rufino to go, this time without his habit and wearing only his breeches.

It is easy to imagine Rufino's painful ordeal. People thought that this man, who had once walked Assisi as a prince, was now crazy as he entered the city half-naked. With urchins laughing and jeering at his heels, he passed through the streets, and when he started to preach on honesty, the words came so falteringly that the people laughed.

After Rufino had left the Porziuncola, Francis, regretting his treatment of him, turned his wrath upon himself. 'Please God,' he cried, 'thou shalt have experience of what thou hast made another endure.' With that, he threw off his habit and, dressed like Rufino, went to Assisi. Brother Leo, tactfully picking up both habits, followed some distance behind.

Rufino was still preaching when Francis reached the city. When the badly delivered sermon ended, Francis stood beside Rufino and spoke so marvellously on the poverty and nakedness of Christ that the congregation turned from laughter to tears. Leo then handed the habits to the friars, and the people crowded around them and kissed the hems of their robes. *(Douglas Liversidge)*

A small boy, repeating the Lord's Prayer one evening prayed: 'And forgive us our debts as we forgive those who are dead against us.' *(Anon)*

USEFUL TEXTS

Forgiveness:
Of enemies, *Luke 6:27*
Among believers, *Eph. 4;32*
Of sin, by God, *Ps. 130:4*
Of sin, by Christ, *Acts 10:43*

See also: A26 Sacrament of Penance
B16 Christ heals and forgives
C14 Forgiveness
C40 Reconciliation

A28
WORK

'Call the workers and pay them their wages,
starting with the last arrivals and ending with the first.'
Matthew 20:8

QUOTATIONS

No one has a right to sit down and feel hopeless. There's too much work to do. *(Dorothy Day)*

I like work, it fascinates me. I can sit and look at it for hours. *(Jerome K. Jerome)*

Work is the greatest thing in the world, so we should always save some of it for tomorrow. *(Don Herold)*

Light is the task where many share the toil. *(Homer)*

Some are bent with toil, and some get crooked trying to avoid it. *(Anon)*

God gives every bird its food, but he does not throw it into the nest. *(J. G. Holland)*

He who labours as he prays lifts his heart to God with his hands. *(St Bernard)*

The best worship, however, is stout working. *(Thomas Carlyle)*

Nothing is really work unless you would rather be doing something else. *(James M. Barrie)*

Iron rusts from disuse, stagnant water loses its purity and in cold weather becomes frozen; even so does inaction sap the vigours of the mind. *(Leonardo Da Vinci)*

My grandfather once told me that there are two kinds of people: those who do the work and those who take the credit. He told me to try to be in the first group; there was much less competition there. *(Indira Gandhi)*

PROVERBS
Work is worship. *(French proverb)*

Never was good work done without much trouble.
(Chinese proverb)

Work is no disgrace: the disgrace is idleness. *(Greek proverb)*

He who begins too much accomplishes little.
(German proverb)

A man grows most tired while standing still. *(Chinese proverb)*

HUMOUR
No man goes before his time – unless the boss leaves early.
(Groucho Marx)

'Been to the zoo recently?' asked the manager.
'No, sir,' answered the new delivery boy.
'Well, you should,' said the manager. 'You'd enjoy it and get a big kick out of watching the turtles zip by.'

Employer   'Sorry, I have no job for you. I couldn't find enough work to keep you busy.'
Applicant   'But you have no idea how little work it takes to keep me busy.'

'How many people work in the Vatican City, Holy Father?'
'About half.' *(Story told of Pope John XXIII)*

A man who needed a job saw an ad in the local paper for a position open at the zoo. He accepted the job and was to dress up as a monkey and perform in one of the cages. All went well for several days and then, as he was going from limb to limb, he fell.

'Help, help,' he cried.

'Shut up,' said the lion in the next cage, 'or we'll both lose our jobs.'

STATEMENTS

Everyone who works has the right to just and favourable remuneration insuring for himself and his family an existence worthy of human dignity . . . *(United Nations Universal Declaration of Human Rights, Article 23)*

According to natural reason and Christian philosophy, working for gain is creditable, not shameful, to a man, since it enables him to earn an honourable livelihood; but to misuse men as though they were things in the pursuit of gain, or to value them solely for their physical powers – that is truly shameful and inhuman. *(Pope Leo XIII : Rerum Novarum 1891)*

It is ordinarily by his labour that a man supports himself and his family, is joined to his fellow men and serves them, and is enabled to exercise genuine charity and be a partner in the work of bringing God's creation to perfection. Indeed, we hold that by offering his labour to God a man becomes associated with the redemptive work itself of Jesus Christ, who conferred an eminent dignity on labour when at Nazareth He worked with His own hands. *(Second Vatican Council – 'The Church Today')*

WORD PICTURES

A man who works with his hands is a labourer; a man who works with his hands and his brain is a craftsman; a man who works with his hands and his brain and his heart is an artist. *(Louis Nizer)*

Work is love made visible.
And if you cannot work with love, but only with distaste, it is
  better that you should leave your work and sit at the gate of
  the temple and take alms of those who work for joy.

For if you bake bread with indifference, you bake a bitter bread
that feeds but half man's hunger.
And if you grudge the crushing of the grapes, your grudge
distils a poison in the wine.
And if you sing though as angels, and love not the singing, you
muffle man's ears to the voices of the day and the voices of
the night. *(Kahlil Gibran)*

If I use my faculties and my resources to their full potential,
limited and faulty though these may be, I feel that I can expect
that the Providence of God will make good whatever I cannot
do myself, provided, of course, that what I am doing is in
conformity with his will. Yet I emphasise the absolute necessity
of working as if everything depended upon yourself, for I hold
no brief for the view that if only you have sufficient faith you
can sit back and God will provide. *(Leonard Cheshire)*

John Wesley travelled 250,000 miles on horseback, averaging 20
miles a day for 40 years; preached 40,000 sermons; produced
400 books; knew 10 languages. At 83, he was annoyed that he
could not write more than 15 hours a day without hurting his
eyes, and at 86, he was ashamed he could not preach more than
twice a day. He complained in his diary that there was an
increasing tendency to lie in bed until 5.30 in the morning!
(The Arkansas Baptist)

Somebody said that it couldn't be done,
But he with a chuckle replied,
That maybe it couldn't, but he would be one
Who wouldn't say so till he'd tried.
So he buckled right in with a bit of a grin
On his face. If he worried, he hid it;
And he started to sing as he tackled the thing
That couldn't be done – and he did it! *(Anon)*

Recent studies have shown that the key to success is not so
much talent or natural gifts but rather one's drive and
enthusiasm. A researcher studied the top performers among

tennis players, neurosurgeons, pianists, and other fields of endeavour and found that 'these superstars, who were rarely the best in their school classes and often appeared not to be physically or mentally qualified, succeeded because they cultivated proficiency. Practice and motivation determined their success . . . There are three key factors that help us cultivate proficiency: enthusiasm, optimism and creativity.' *(Jo Berry)*

It is not only prayer that gives glory to God but work,
    smiting on an anvil, sowing a beam,
    white-washing a wall, driving horses,
    reaping, scouring, everything gives God glory.
It being in his grace, you do it as your duty.
To go to Communion worthily gives God great glory,
    but simply to take food in thankfulness
    and temperance gives God glory too.
To lift up the hands in prayer gives God glory.
    But a man with a dung-fork in his hand
    or a woman with a slop-pail,
They give God glory too.
All things give God glory if you mean they should.
So then, my brethren, this is the way to live.
(Gerard Manley Hopkins, S. J.)

St Benedict elevated work from a servile occupation to be avoided or limited as far as possible, often called the Curse of Adam, into something positively good.

It was my friend's thesis that St Benedict's Rule never reached Russia where work continued to be looked down upon, just as further east, the Chinese delighted to grow their finger nails to enormous lengths as the visible proof they had no need to work. So while serfdom disappeared in Christian Europe, the opposite happened in Russia, and it became worse at the end of the Middle Ages. The western monks practised what they preached, especially the reformed Benedictines, Cistercians and Carthusians. The official marking for quality steel in France is still the Carthusian emblem, the ball and the cross.
(Douglas Woodruff)

Useful texts

Physical Work:
Forbidden on the Sabbath, *Exod. 23:12*
Be diligent in, *Eccles. 9:10; Col. 3:23; 1 Thess. 4:11*
Illustrated by parables, *Matt. 21:28; Matt. 25:21*
With God's help, *Rom. 8:26; 1 Cor. 3:6-9*

See also: A1 The value of time
A18 Balance in Nature
A36 Using talents
A39 The glory of God

A29
TRUE OBEDIENCE

'He became as men are; and being as all men are, he was humbler yet, even to accepting death, death on a cross.'
Philippians 2:7

QUOTATIONS

Thirty years of Our Lord's life are hidden in these words of the Gospel: 'He was subject unto them.' *(Jacques B. Bossuet)*

Every great person has first learned how to obey, whom to obey, and when to obey. *(William A. Ward)*

Don't listen to friends when the Friend inside you says, 'Do this!' *(Mohandas Gandhi)*

Every revelation of God is a demand, and the way to knowledge of God is by obedience. *(William Temple)*

Obedience is the fruit of faith; patience the bloom on the fruit. *(Christina Rosetti)*

The devil does not fear austerity but holy obedience. *(St Francis de Sales)*

The first degree of humility is obedience without delay. *(St Benedict)*

No man securely commands but he who has learned to obey. *(Thomas à Kempis)*

Blessed are the obedient, for God will never suffer them to go astray. *(St Francis de Sales)*

When God puts inspirations into a heart, the first he gives is obedience. *(St Francis de Sales)*

Obedience responds to obedience. When someone obeys God, God obeys his request. *(Mios of Belos)*

How will you find good? It is not a thing of choices; it is a river that flows from the foot of the invisible throne, and flows by the path of obedience. *(George Eliot)*

PROVERBS

Obedience is the mother of success, the wife of safety. *(Greek proverb)*

No one can rule except one who can be ruled. *(Latin proverb)*

HUMOUR

Teacher	'This is the fifth time this week that I have had to punish you. What have you to say, Charlie?'
Charlie	'I'm glad it's Friday!'

A teacher left her class one day and on returning found all the children sitting in profound silence with their arms folded. She was not only surprised at such silence, but bewildered and asked for an explanation. A little girl arose and said:

'Miss, you told us one day if you ever left the class room and came back and found all of us sitting perfectly silent, you would drop dead.'

Three year old Bobby insisted in standing up in his highchair although mother had admonished him to remain seated, then emphasised her admonishment twice reseating him. After the third time, little Bobby remained seated but looked at his mother searchingly and said, 'Mummy, I'm still standing up inside.'

STATEMENTS

With ready Christian obedience, laymen, as well as all disciples of Christ, should accept whatever their sacred pastors, as representatives of Christ, decree in their role as teachers and rulers in the Church. *(Second Vatican Council – 'The Church Today')*

It also follows that political authority, whether in the community as such or in institutions representing the state, must always be exercised within the limits of morality and on behalf of the dynamically conceived common good, according to a juridical order enjoying legal status. When such is the case citizens are conscience-bound to obey.
(Second Vatican Council – 'The Church Today')

WORD PICTURE

Centuries ago, in one of the Egyptian monasteries, a man came and asked to be admitted. The abbot told him that the chief rule was obedience, and the man promised to be patient on all occasions, even under excessive provocation. It chanced that the abbot was holding a dried-up willow wand in his hand; he forthwith fixed the dead stick into the earth and told the newcomer that he was to water it until, against all the rules of nature, it should once again become green. Obediently the new monk walked two miles every day to the River Nile to bring back a vessel of water on his shoulders and water the dry stick. A year passed by, and he was still faithful to his task, though very weary. Another year, and still he toiled on. Well into the third year he was still trudging to the river and back, still watering the stick, when suddenly one day it burst into life.

This story is related in the *Dialogues of Sulpicius Severus*, on the authority of an acquaintance named Postumianus who had travelled in the East. 'I myself', said the latter, 'have beheld the green bush – the former dead stick – which flourishes to this day in the atrium of the monastery. Its waving green foliage is a living witness to the mighty virtues of obedience and faith.'
(F. H. Drinkwater)

Already in 1940, the order had gone out—incurables and the insane were no longer to be a burden on the Reich. Three high officials descended upon the Bethel institution (a huge hospital for epileptics and the mentally ill). 'Herr Pastor,' they said, 'the Fuehrer has decided that all these people must be gassed.' Von Bodelschwingh looked at them calmly. 'You can put me into a concentration camp, if you want; that is your affair. But as long as I am free, you do not touch one of my patients. I cannot change to fit the times or the wishes of the Fuehrer. I stand under orders from our Lord Jesus Christ.' *(John Foster)*

USEFUL TEXTS

Obedience:
To God, *1 Sam. 15:22*
To Christ, *2 Cor. 10:5*
To the covenant, *Exod. 24:7*
To the Gospel, *2 Thess. 1:8, 1 Pet. 4:17*

See also: A14 The successors of the Apostles
A32 Civic duty
B13 Authority
B31 The commandments of life
C25 Humility

A30

THE JEWISH PEOPLE

'The vineyard of the Lord of hosts is the House of Israel
and the men of Judah that chosen plant!' *Isaiah 5:7*

QUOTATIONS
Spiritually we are all Semites. *(Pope Pius XI)*

The race of the Hebrews is not new but is honoured among all
men for its antiquity and is itself well known to all.
(Eusebius of Caesarea)

In Israel, in order to be a realist you must believe in miracles.
(David Ben-Gurion)

The Jew's home has rarely been his 'castle'; throughout the ages
it has been something far higher—his sanctuary.
(Joseph H. Hertz)

If my theory of relativity is proven successful, Germany will
claim me as a German and France will declare that I am a
citizen of the world. Should my theory prove untrue, France
will say that I am a German and Germany will declare that I am
a Jew. *(Albert Einstein)*

The pursuit of knowledge for its own sake, an almost fanatical
love of justice, and a desire for personal independence – these
are features of the Jewish tradition which make me thank my
stars that I belong to it. *(Albert Einstein)*

The Hebrews have done more to civilise men than any other
nation. If I were an atheist, and believed in blind eternal fate, I
should still believe that fate had ordained the Jews to be the
most essential instrument for civilising the nations.
(John Adams)

The English always imagine God as the perfect Englishman; but when God became man he was a Jew. *(Paul Frost)*

PROVERBS

Jews are just like everyone else – only more so. *(Jewish proverb)*

No misfortune avoids a Jew. *(Yiddish proverb)*

No Jew is a fool, no hare is lazy. *(Spanish proverb)*

Even Moses couldn't get along with the Jews. *(Yiddish proverb)*

STATEMENTS

The Church cannot forget that she received the revelation of the Old Testament through the people with whom God in his inexpressible mercy deigned to establish the Ancient Covenant. Nor can she forget that she draws sustenance from the root of that good olive tree onto which have been grafted the wild olive branches of the Gentiles.
(Second Vatican Council – 'Non-Christians')

Since the spiritual patrimony common to Christians and Jews is thus so great, this sacred Synod wishes to foster and recommend that mutual understanding and respect which is the fruit above all of biblical and theological studies, and of brotherly dialogues. *(Second Vatican Council – 'Non-Christians')*

WORD PICTURES

Because he was a man
As well as he was God
He loved his own goat-nibbled hills,
His crumbling Jewish sod.
He bowed to Roman rule
And dared none to rebel
But Oh the windflowers out of Nain
We know he loved them well!

He must have loved its tongue,
His Aramaic brogue,
As much as any Norman loves
The accents of La Hogue.
Discountried and diskinged
And watched from pole to pole,
A Jew at heart remains a Jew –
His nation is his soul.
Had he upon that day
Of headlong cloaks and boughs
Surrendered all mankind to race
And lifted David's brows,
They would not on his cross
Have writ as mocking news
That he the man from Nazareth
Was monarch of the Jews.
As heifers' to their young
Christ's bowels yearned to his sod.
He was the very Jew of Jews
And yet since he was God –
Oh you with frontiered hearts,
Conceive it if you can –
It was not life alone he gave,
But country up for man.
(Eileen Duggan)

Hath not a Jew eyes? Hath not a Jew hands, organs, dimensions, senses, affections, passions, fed with the same food, hurt with the same weapons, subject to the same diseases, healed by the same means, warmed and cooled by the same winter and summer, as the Christian is? If you prick us, do we not bleed? If you tickle us, do we not laugh? If you poison us, do we not die? And if you wrong us, shall we not revenge?
(From the Merchant of Venice by William Shakespeare)

There are three impudent creatures: among beasts, the dog; among birds, the cock; among people, Israel. But Rabbi Ammi added 'Do not consider this as blame; it is praise, for to be a Jew means to be ready to be martyred.'
(Midrash: Exodus Rabbah)

Not long ago I was reading the Sermon on the Mount with a rabbi. At nearly every verse he showed me very similar passages in the Hebrew Bible and Talmud. When he reached the words 'Resist not evil', he did not say 'this too is in the Talmud', but asked, with a smile, 'Do the Christians obey this command?' I had nothing to say in reply, especially as at that particular time, Christians, far from turning the other cheek, were smiting the Jews on both cheeks.
(Leo Tolstoy)

USEFUL TEXTS

Israel:
Name given to descendants of, *Gen. 43:32*
New name of Jacob, *Gen. 32:28*
What God required of, *Deut. 10:12-22*
Final conversion of, *Rom. 11:26-27*

See also: A12 Holy Scripture
B36 The Family of God
C8 God's messengers

A31

HEAVEN

'The Lord of hosts will remove the mourning veil covering all
peoples, and the shroud enwrapping all nations,
he will destroy Death for ever.' *Isaiah 25:7*

QUOTATIONS

The world has forgotten, in its concern with Left and Right, that
there is an Above and Below. *(Glen Drake)*

Heaven means to be one with God. *(Confucius)*

The main object of religion is not to get a man into heaven; but
to get heaven into him. *(Thomas Hardy)*

Earth hath no sorrow that heaven cannot heal. *(Thomas Moore)*

When I reflect upon the number of disagreeable people who I
know have gone to a better world, I am moved to lead a
different life. *(Mark Twain)*

Heaven is not to be looked upon only as the reward, but as the
natural effect, of a religious life. *(Joseph Addison)*

God may not give us an easy journey to the Promised Land, but
He will give us a safe one. *(Bonar)*

I'm not going to heaven because I've preached to great crowds
of people. I'm going to heaven because Christ died on that
cross. None of us are going to heaven because we're good. And
we're not going to heaven because we've worked. We're not
going to heaven because we pray and accept Christ. We're going
to heaven because of what He did on the Cross. All I have to do
is receive Him. And it's so easy to receive Christ that millions
stumble over its sheer simplicity. *(Billy Graham)*

I say to my people who are dying: 'Soon after you're dead – we're not sure how long, but not long – you'll be united with the most ecstatic love you've ever known. As one of the best things in your life was human love, this will be love, but much more satisfying, and it will last FOR EVER.' *(Cardinal Basil Hume)*

If you insist on having your own way, you will get it. Hell is the enjoyment of your own way forever. If you really want God's way with you, you will get it in heaven, and the pains of purgatory will not deter you, they will be welcomed as means to that end. *(Dante Alighieri)*

PROVERBS

Men go laughing to heaven. *(Dutch proverb)*

Heaven is mine if God says amen. *(Spanish proverb)*

HUMOUR

The Irish have a story of an Irishman who appeared before St Peter, expecting admission, and when his ledger showed pages and pages of heavy debit entries, said that the books had been badly kept, for he knew he had once given twopence to a beggar. St Peter, after much flipping over of pages, found it was so indeed; but was twopence sufficient to outweigh all else? Then the Irishman said he had a friend called Patrick. If they would have the common politeness to call him, he would make it alright. St Patrick was summoned, looked at the ledger, and he and St Peter exchanged doubtful glances. 'What are we to do with this countryman of yours?' asked St Peter. 'You see how it is.' 'Yes,' said St. Patrick, 'I see how it is. Give him back his twopence.' *(Douglas Woodruff)*

A teacher once said to a class of small boys, 'Hands up those who want to go to heaven.' All the boys put up their hands, except one. 'Don't you want to go to heaven, Georgie?' she asked, 'Nah, not if that lot's going.' The teacher did not ask Georgie where he would like to go.

There was a great plague in the world which killed off all the mice. When they went to heaven, they were amazed how beautiful and plentiful it was.

After a few days, God was doing his rounds and came across the mice. 'How are you doing?' he asked, 'Have you got everything you need?'

The mice replied what a wonderful place this heaven was and thank you, yes, they had everything they needed.

'There is one thing we could use some help with,' spoke up one small mouse.

'What's that?' asked God.

'Well,' the mouse replied, 'this is such a vast place and with our tiny legs, we find it difficult to get around and see everything. I don't suppose you could fix us up with some sort of transport? Nothing elaborate, in fact, a skateboard will do nicely.'

God smiled and immediately set Joseph the carpenter about the task of producing a skateboard.

Some time later there was another great plague and this time all the cats died. They in turn went to heaven and again in turn met God whilst he was doing his rounds.

'What do you think of heaven?' asked God.

'What a wonderful place!' answered the cats. 'It's absolutely delightful and so well organised. Especially the meals on wheels!' *(Anon)*

'How is your wife?' the man asked a friend he hadn't seen for years.

'She's in heaven,' replied the friend.

'Oh, I'm sorry.' Then he realised that was not the thing to say, so he added, 'I mean, I'm glad.' And that was even worse. He finally came out with, 'Well, I'm surprised.'

(Christian Herald)

STATEMENT

The Church, to which we are all called in Christ Jesus, and in which we acquire sanctity through the grace of God, will attain her full perfection only in the glory of heaven. Then will come the time of the restoration of all things. Then the human race as well as the entire world, which is intimately related to man and achieves its purpose through him, will be perfectly re-established in Christ. *(Second Vatican Council – 'The Church')*

WORD PICTURES

The Curé of Ars used to say in the pulpit, 'My dear parishioners, we must all do our very best to get to heaven. There we shall see God. How happy we shall be! We ought to go there all in a procession, with the parish priest in front. We must all of us get to heaven. If some of you get lost on the way, it will spoil everything!'

To over-fussy pilgrims who wanted to take too much time talking to him, he would say, 'We can talk in heaven.' *(Anon)*

Here lies a woman who was always tired,
She lived in a house where help was not hired.
Her last words on earth were: 'Dear friends, I am going
Where washing ain't done, nor sweeping, nor sewing
But everything there is exact to my wishes;
For where they don't eat, there's no washing of dishes.
I'll be where loud anthems will always be ringing,
But having no voice, I'll be clear of the singing.
Don't mourn for me now, don't mourn for me never –
I'm going to do nothing for ever and ever.' *(Anon)*

USEFUL TEXTS

Heaven,
Characteristics of:
No death, *Luke 20:36*
No pain, *Rev. 21:4*
No corruption, *1 Cor. 15:42, 50*
Joy, *Luke 15:7*
Peace, *Luke 16:25*
Glory, *Rom. 8; 17-18*

See also: A20 The Kingdom of God
B3 Joy in Christ
B51 One with Christ
C48 One in us

A32

CIVIC DUTY

'Give back to Caesar what belongs to Caesar –
and to God what belongs to God.' *Matthew 22:21*

QUOTATIONS

Whatever makes people good Christians makes them good citizens. *(Webster)*

Nothing is politically right which is morally wrong.
(Daniel O'Connell)

Morality is the very soul of good citizenship.
(Archbishop Ireland)

Liberty has never come from the government . . . The history of liberty is the history of the limitations of governmental power, not the increase of it. *(Woodrow Wilson)*

When a politician says, 'We're all in the same boat,' he usually means he wants to play captain while the rest of us do the rowing. *(Anon)*

No better citizen is there, whether in time of peace or war, than the Christian who is mindful of his duty; but such a one should be ready to suffer all things, even death itself, rather than abandon the cause of God or of the Church. *(Pope Leo XIII)*

A state without the means of some change is without the means of its conservation. *(Edmund Burke)*

A lesson that our country learned early and well, and which some countries unfortunately never learned or learned too late, is that each citizen had better take an active interest in running his country or he may suddenly find the country running him. *(Art Linkletter)*

We are justified, from the point of view of exegesis, in regarding the democratic conception of the State as an expansion of the thought of the New Testament. *(Karl Barth)*

We need politicians who dare to make practical decisions, sometimes right, sometimes wrong. We need churchmen who dare to insist that life is larger than politics, and God grander than governments. *(John Harriott)*

HUMOUR
Hymn and prayer for civil servants

O Thou who seest all things below,
Grant that Thy servants may go slow,
That they may study to comply
With regulations till they die.

Teach us, O Lord, to reverence
Committees more than common sense;
To train our minds to make no plan
And pass the baby when we can.

So when the tempter seeks to give
Us feelings of initiative,
Or when alone we go too far,
Chastise us with a circular.

Mid war and tumult, fire and storms,
Give strength, O Lord, to deal out forms.
Thus may Thy servants ever be
A flock of perfect sheep for Thee.
(Published anonymously in The Daily Telegraph)

STATEMENTS
Citizens should develop a generous and loyal devotion to their country, but without any narrowing of mind. In other words, they must always look simultaneously to the welfare of the whole human family, which is tied together by the manifold bonds linking races, peoples, and nations.
(Second Vatican Council – 'The Church Today')

Let all Christians appreciate their special and personal vocation in the political community. This vocation requires that they give conspicuous example of devotion to the sense of duty and of service to the advancement of the common good.
(Second Vatican Council – 'The Church Today')

It is highly important, especially in pluralistic societies, that a proper view exist of the relation between the political community and the Church. Thus the faithful will be able to make a clear distinction between what a Christian conscience leads them to do in their own name as citizens, whether as individuals or in association, and what they do in the name of the Church and in union with her shepherds.
(Second Vatican Council – 'The Church Today')

WORD PICTURES

The Church is a place where the politician, like the citizen, must be able to step out of the wind, to find again the whole vision, the whole truth, and forgiveness for falling short of either. He can expect sympathy, but not too much, for his predicaments, tenderness for his frailties. What he should not expect is wholehearted endorsement of his policies or a seal of approval for his party. *(John Harriott)*

Few people are aware that the word 'govern' comes from the Latin term 'guberno' meaning 'to steer a ship.'

This thought was graphically illustrated by one man who said that a 'dictatorship is like a high-powered ocean liner. It can go straight ahead at a fast clip. The danger is that it may hit an iceberg.'

'Democracy,' he added, 'is like a log raft. You can't guide the thing very well; you wallow all over the place; your feet are always wet.'

'But you can never sink a log raft,' he concluded, 'and if you keep trying you eventually get there. That's what we've got to do, keep trying.'

The inefficiencies of self-government are often exasperating. But it is within the power of citizens, thank God, to right most wrongs.

Many years ago when a total eclipse of the sun became visible in Connecticut, USA, candles were lighted in many houses. Birds fell silent and disappeared, and domestic fowls retired to roost. The people were impressed by the idea that the day of judgement was at hand. This opinion was entertained by the Legislature, at that time sitting at Hartford. The House of Representatives adjourned; the Council proposed to follow the example. Colonel Davenport objected. 'The Day of Judgement,' he said, 'is either approaching, or it is not. If it is not, there is no cause for an adjournment; if it is, I choose to be found doing my duty. I move, therefore, that candles be brought.' *(Anon)*

USEFUL TEXTS

Citizenship:
Obligations, *Rom. 13:1-7; I Pet. 13-17*
Punishment for neglect, *Ezra 7:26*
Jesus discussed, *Matt. 17:24-27; 22:17-21*

See also: A29 True obedience
B14 Freedom to serve
B33 Faith and good works
B34 Human rights

A33

LOVE YOUR NEIGHBOUR

'The second commandment resembles it: You must love your neighbour as yourself.' *Matthew 22:39*

QUOTATIONS

Love your neighbour, yet pull not down your hedge.
(George Herbert)

No man can be a friend of Jesus Christ who is not a friend to his neighbour. *(R. H. Benson)*

To love our neighbour in charity is to love God in man.
(St Francis de Sales)

Nothing in life is happier than to love faithfully – and to be loved in return. *(Adam of Perseigne)*

The Bible tells us to love our neighbours, and also to love our enemies; probably because they are generally the same people.
(G. K. Chesterton)

He alone loves the Creator perfectly who manifests a pure love for his neighbour. *(St Bede the Venerable)*

We make our friends; we make our enemies; but God makes our next door neighbour. *(G. K Chesterton)*

All is well with him who is beloved of his neighbours.
(George Herbert)

Man becomes a holy thing, a neighbour, only if we realise that he is the property of God and that Jesus Christ died for him.
(Helmut Thielecke)

The love of our neighbour is the only door out of the dungeon of self. *(George MacDonald)*

Though we do not have our Lord with us in bodily presence, we have our neighbour, who, for the ends of love and loving service, is as good as our Lord himself. *(St Teresa of Avila)*

Next to the Blessed Sacrament itself, your neighbour is the holiest object presented to your senses. If he is your Christian neighbour, he is holy in almost the same way, for in him also Christ *vere latitat* – the glorifier and the glorified, Glory Himself, is truly hidden. *(C. S. Lewis)*

I sought my soul, the soul I could not see.
I sought my God and God eluded me.
I sought my brother and found all three.
(Anon)

PROVERBS

Mix with your neighbours, and you learn what's doing in your own house. *(Yiddish proverb)*

God grant us no neighbour with two eyes. *(Arab proverb)*

No one is rich enough to do without a neighbour.
(Danish proverb)

Love thy neighbour, even when he plays the trombone.
(Jewish proverb)

HUMOUR

If you have an unpleasant neighbour, the odds are that he does too. *(Frank A. Clark)*

A mother was telling her six-year-old about the Golden Rule. 'Always remember,' she said, 'that we are here to help others.'
    The youngster mulled this over for a minute and then asked, 'Well, what are the others here for?' *(Christian Herald)*

Have you heard the story of the little girl who was sucking a lolly on the top of a bus and rubbing it now and again against the fur coat of the lady in front of her? Her mother said 'Don't do that, darling, you'll get hairs all over your lolly!' *(Anon)*

STATEMENTS

This Council lays stress on reverence for man; everyone must consider his every neighbour without exception as another self, taking into account first of all his life and the means necessary to living it with dignity.
(Second Vatican Council – 'The Church Today')

In our times a special obligation binds us to make ourselves the neighbour of absolutely every person, and of actively helping him when he comes across our path, whether he be an old person abandoned by all, a foreign labourer unjustly looked down upon, a refugee, a child born of an unlawful union and wrongly suffering for a sin he did not commit, or a hungry person who disturbs our conscience.
(Second Vatican Council – 'The Church Today')

WORD PICTURES

A visionary miracle influenced the conversion of a fourth-century Hungarian cavalry officer who later became the Bishop of Tours. St Martin, as he is generally remembered, was leading his troops, when he came upon a poorly clad beggar suffering from the frigid temperatures. Moved by the man's suffering, Martin took off his own elegant cape and put it on the beggar, and he was about to go on his way when he was stopped by an amazing sight: the beggar was Jesus Christ, searching among men for evidence of the charity He had said was the greatest virtue. Soon after that incident Martin resigned his position in the military and became a monk. He founded a monastic community and became known for his healing miracles and good deeds to the poor. So popular was he that he was later chosen to be bishop, an office that he very reluctantly accepted.
(Glenn D. Kittler)

A little boy was heartbroken to find his pet turtle lying on its back, lifeless and still, beside the pond.

His father did his best to console him: 'Don't cry, son. We'll arrange a lovely funeral for Mr Turtle. We'll make him a little coffin all lined in silk and get the undertaker to make a headstone for his grave, with Mr Turtle's name carved on it. Then we'll have fresh flowers placed on the grave each day and make a little picket fence to go all around it.'

The little boy dried his eyes and became enthusiastic about the project. When all was ready, the cortege was formed – father, mother, maid, and child, the chief mourner – and began to move solemnly toward the pond to bring in the body. But the body had vanished.

Suddenly they spied Mr Turtle emerging from the depths of the pond and swimming around merrily. The little boy stared at his friend in bitter disappointment, then said, 'Let's kill him.'

It isn't really you I care about, but the thrill I get from loving you. *(Bill Bausch)*

I chose Christianity because I felt that in it I had found the best way of serving my neighbour. I was elected by Christ to be a priest forever, motivated by the desire to devote myself full-time to loving my fellow man.

As a sociologist, I wished this love to become effective through science and technology. Upon analysing Colombian society, I realised the need for a revolution that would give food to the hungry, drink to the thirsty, clothing to the naked and bring about the well-being of the majorities in our country.

I feel that the revolutionary struggle is a Christian and priestly struggle. Only through this, given the concrete circumstances of our country, can we fulfil the love that men should have for their neighbours. *(Camilo Torres)*

The Rabbi Hillel was a renowned scribe in Jerusalem about the time of Christ's birth; he seems to have died about AD 10, aged 80. He was called 'the Great' or 'the Elder', and his interpretations of the Law were less severe than others. He is said to have been the grandfather of Gamaliel *(Acts 22:3)* who taught St Paul. Our Lord must have heard often of Hillel, and could possibly have spoken with him during the three days before the Finding in the Temple.

Here is one of the tales Our Lord might have heard. A certain gentile came to Shammai (Shammai was the leader of the more strict school of interpretation) and said that he would like to become a proselyte, but could not stay long in Jerusalem. 'Can you teach me the whole Torah while I am standing on one foot?' Shammai sent him away angrily. So the gentile went to Hillel with the same question. Hillel admitted him as a convert, and said, 'Whatever is hateful to thee, do not do to thy fellow-man. This is the whole Torah: all the rest is commentary. Now go and study.' *(F. H. Drinkwater)*

USEFUL TEXTS

Love your neighbour:
Love towards, *Rom. 13:9-10; Matt. 22:39*
Speak the truth to; *Eph. 4:25*
Urged to be good, *Luke 10:29-37*

See also: A9 Relationships
B52 God is Love
C10 Love your enemies
C19 Friendship

A34

HYPOCRISY AND AMBITION

'Do not be guided by what the Pharisees do; since they do not practise what they preach.' *Matthew 23:3*

QUOTATIONS

A Pharisee is a man who prays publicly and preys privately. *(Don Marquis)*

Thou shalt hate all hypocrisy, and everything that is not pleasing to the Lord. *(Didache)*

I will have nought to do with a man who can blow hot and cold with the same breath. *(Aesop)*

Where there is no religion, hypocrisy becomes good taste. *(George Bernard Shaw)*

May the man be damned and never grow fat
Who wears two faces under one hat. *(H. G. Bohn)*

There's not much practical Christianity in the man who lives on better terms with angels and seraphs than with his children, and neighbours. *(Henry Ward Beecher)*

Most people would succeed in small things if they were not troubled by great ambitions. *(Longfellow)*

Most of the trouble in the world is caused by people wanting to be important. *(T. S. Eliot)*

Hew not too high lest the chip fall in thine eye. *(John Heywood)*

Ambition is the mind's immodesty. *(Sir William Davenant)*

Well is it known that ambition can creep as well as soar. *(Edmund Burke)*

You cannot be anything if you want to be everything. *(Solomon Schechter)*

PROVERBS

Many go out for wool and come back shorn. *(Spanish proverb)*

Every eel hopes to become a whale. *(German proverb)*

Every ambitious man is a captive and every covetous one a pauper. *(Arab proverb)*

WORD PICTURES

Get place and wealth; if possible, with grace;
If not, by any means get wealth and place. *(Alexander Pope)*

Cineas, when dissuading Pyrrhus from undertaking a war against the Romans, said, 'Sir, when you have conquered them, what will you do next?'

'Sicily is near at hand and easy to master,' replied Pyrrhus.

'And what when you have conquered Sicily?'

'Then we will pass on to Africa and take Carthage.'

'When these are conquered, what will be your next attempt?' asked Cineas.

'Then,' said Pyrrhus, 'we will fall upon Greece and Macedon and recover what we have lost there.'

'Well, when all are subdued, what fruit do you expect from all your victories?'

'Then,' said Pyrrhus, 'we will sit down and enjoy ourselves.'

Sir!' said Cineas, 'may we not do it now? Have you not already a kingdom of your own? He that cannot enjoy himself with a kingdom cannot with a whole world.' *(Anon)*

Cardinal Wolsey, dying, charged Cromwell:
'I charge thee, Cromwell, fling away ambition. By that sin, fell the angels: how can man, then, the image of his Maker, hope to gain by't?' *(Shakespeare in Henry VIII)*

The original Jack Horner, the story goes, was steward to Richard Whiting, the last of the abbots of Glastonbury. In the 1530s, the time of the Dissolution of the Monasteries, it is said that the abbot, hoping to placate Henry VIII, sent His Majesty an enormous Christmas pie containing the deeds of 12 manors. Horner was entrusted to take the pie to the King. On the way he managed to open the pie and extract the deeds of the Manor of Mells in Somerset – presumably the 'plum' referred to in the rhyme.

An architect, who had worked for a large company for many years, was called in one day by the board of directors and given plans for a fine house to be built in the best quarter of the town. The chairman instructed him to spare no expense, using the finest materials and best builders. As the house began to go up, the architect began to think, 'Why use such costly materials?' So he began to use poor materials and to hire poor quality workmen, and he put the difference in the cost into his own pocket. When the house was finished, it looked very fine on the outside, but it certainly would not last long. Shortly after it was finished, the board of directors held another meeting to which the architect was called. The chairman made a speech, thanking the architect for his long service to the company, as a reward for which they were making him a present of the house! *(Anon)*

Useful texts

Hypocrisy:
Description of;
  Blindness, *Matt. 23:17-26*
  Unclean hearts, *Luke 11:39*
  Seeks self-acclaim, *Matt. 6:2-5*
Ascribed to Pharisees, *Matt. 23:13-15; Luke 12:1*

See also: A2 Integrity
      A15 Sin
      B26 The whole man
      B44 The dignity of the individual

A35

PREPARING FOR DEATH

'Stay awake, because you do not know either the day
or the hour.' *Matthew 25:13*

QUOTATIONS

Death is the supreme festival on the road to freedom.
(Dietrich Bonhoeffer)

Do not seek death. Death will find you, But seek the road which
makes death a fulfilment. *(Dag Hammarskjöld)*

What is death at most? It is a journey for a season: a sleep longer
than usual. If thou fearest death, thou shouldest also fear sleep.
(St John Chrysostom)

Blessed be God for our sister, the death of the body.
(St Francis)

Of this at least I am certain, that no one has ever died who was
not destined to die some time. *(St Augustine of Hippo)*

Some people decide to be saved at the eleventh hour, and die at
ten-thirty. *(Anon)*

Take heed, dear friend, in passing by,
As you are now, so once was I;
As I am now, you soon will be,
Prepare for death and follow me.
(On a tombstone)

By God's body, master More, *Indignatio principis mors est.*
Is that all, my lord? quoth he. Then in good faith is there no
more difference between your grace and me, but that I shall die
today and you tomorrow. *(St Thomas More at his trial)*

See me safe up: for my coming down, I can shift for myself.
(St Thomas More, as he ascended the scaffold)

There is a moment in every man's life when he has to make
ready for a departure, and at last the moment comes for him to
leave his earthly home, and to give an account of his labour.
May every one of us then be able to say: I have looked those
who did not share my ideals straight in the eyes and treated
them with brotherly affection, in order not to impede the
carrying out of God's great purpose, in his good time – a
purpose which must bring about the fulfilment of the divine
teaching and command of Jesus, 'that we may all be one.'
(Pope John XXIII)

Once you accept your own death, all of a sudden you're free to
live. You no longer care about your reputation, you no longer
care except so far as your life can be used for others.
(Saul Alinsky)

Christ leads me through no darker rooms
Than he went through before;
He that unto God's kingdom comes,
Must enter by this door.

My knowledge of that life is small,
The eye of faith is dim
But 'tis enough that Christ knows all,
And I shall be with him.
(Richard Baxter)

Death is only a level-crossing from one life to another;
From life in its beginnings to life in full achievement;
From this incomplete life to that transformed one.
For the true Christian, death has the character of any other
    natural event –
no longer agonising or tragic, because decisive.
(Raoul Plus)

PROVERBS

To die well is the chief part of virtue. *(Greek proverb)*

Six feet of earth make all men equal. *(Italian proverb)*

A good death does honour to a whole life. *(Italian proverb)*

HUMOUR

Two small boys saw their grandmother walking up and down reading her prayer book. One boy said to the other, 'What's Grandma doing?' The other boy replied, 'She's swotting for her finals!'

WORD PICTURES

Francis of Assisi, hoeing his garden, was asked what he would do if he were suddenly to learn that he was to die at sunset that day. He said, 'I would finish hoeing my garden.' *(Anon)*

In years gone by, the Court Jester was an important member of the king's household. By means of quips, he kept the king in good humour, and entertained the members of the royal household.

Some writer tells us that what he believes to be the best retort any Court Jester gave. It was the retort given to his Sovereign, a dyspeptic dictator who had the ancient 'power of life or death' over all his subjects, and it was supposed to be legally impossible for the king to change any sentence he set on a subject. Becoming irritated by his Court Jester, in a sudden rage of wrath, the king sentenced his Court Jester to death. Then realising too late his rash decree, the king said to the Court Jester: 'In consideration of your faithful services, I will permit you to select the manner in which you prefer to die.' The Court Jester instantly answered: 'I select to die of old age.' *(Anon)*

A sick man asked Sengai to write something for the continued prosperity of his family, to be treasured from generation to generation. Sengai wrote: 'Father dies, son dies, grandson dies'. The sick, rich man was indignant. 'Is that what you write for the happiness of my family?' Sengai replied, 'If your son would die before you, that would be very sad. If your grandson would die before you and your son, you would be broken-hearted. If your family dies in the order I have written down, isn't that prosperity and happiness?' *(Sengai)*

If I should never see the moon again
Rising red gold across the harvest field,
Or feel the stinging of soft April rain,
As the brown earth her hidden treasures yield.

If I should never taste the salt sea spray
As the ship beats her course against the breeze,
Or smell the dog-rose and the new mown hay,
Or moss and primrose beneath the tree.

If I should never hear the thrushes wake
Long before the sunrise in the glimmering dawn
Or watch the huge Atlantic rollers break
Against the rugged cliffs in baffling scorn.

If I have said goodbye to stream and wood,
To the wide ocean and the green clad hill,
I know that He who made this world so good
Has somewhere made a heaven better still.

This I bear witness with my latest breath
Knowing the love of God,
I fear not death.
(Lines found in the Bible of Major Malcolm Boyle, killed in action after the landing on D-day, June 1944)

USEFUL TEXTS

Mortality:
Death, common experience, *Heb. 9:27*
End of earthly life, *Eccles. 9:10*
Consequence of sin, *Rom. 5:12*

See also: A42 Life after death
                  B21 Trust in God
                  B22 Death
                  B23 Pastoral care of the sick
                  B47 Dying to self

A36
USING TALENTS

'To one he gave five talents, to another two, to a third one;
each in proportion to his ability.' *Matthew 25:15*

QUOTATIONS

The buried talent is the sunken rock on which most lives strike
and founder. *(Frederick W. Faber)*

No one respects a talent that is concealed. *(Erasmus)*

Talents are distributed unevenly, it is true: to one ten, and to
another five; but each has one pound, all alike. *(R. H. Benson)*

Alas for those who never sing, but die with all their music in
them. *(Oliver Wendeu Holmes)*

Encourage individiduals to use their talents in their own ways
and they will often turn a squirrel cage of frustration into a
ladder of success. *(Crawford H. Greenewalt)*

As tools become rusty, so does the mind. A garden uncared for
soon becomes smothered in weeds; a talent neglected withers
and dies. *(Ethel Page)*

The real tragedy of life is not in being limited to one talent, but
in the failure to use the one talent. *(Edgar W. Work)*

There is a great deal of unmapped country within us.
(George Eliot)

Doing easily what others find difficult is talent; doing what is
impossible is genius. *(Amiel)*

If people knew how hard I have to work to gain my mastery, it
would not seem wonderful at all. *(Michelangelo)*

Iron rusts from disuse; stagnant water loses its purity, and in
cold weather becomes frozen; even so does inaction sap the
vigours of the mind. *(Leonardo Da Vinci)*

Talent is the capacity of doing anything that depends on application and industry; it is voluntary power, while genius is involuntary. *(Hazlitt)*

Nature has concealed at the bottom of our minds talents and abilities of which we are not aware. *(La Rochefoucauld)*

PROVERBS

Nobody don't never get nothing for nothing nowhere, no time, nohow. *(American proverb)*

Often the greatest talents lie unseen. *(Latin proverb)*

HUMOUR

Author 'Well, sir, the upshot of it was that it took me ten years to discover that I had absolutely no talent for writing literature.'

Friend 'You gave up?'

Author 'Oh, no; by that time I was too famous.'

Teacher 'When George Washington was your age, he was head of his class.'

Pupil 'Yes, sir. And when he was your age, he was President of the United States!'

STATEMENT

Since Christians have different gifts *(cf Rom. 12:6)* each one must collaborate in the work of the gospel according to his own opportunity, ability, charismatic gifts, and call to service *(cf 1 Cor. 3:10).*

Hence all alike, those who sow and those who reap *(cf Jn. 4:37),* those who plant and those who irrigate, must be united *(cf 1 Cor. 3:8).*

Thus, 'in a free and orderly fashion co-operating toward a common goal,' they can spend their forces harmoniously for the upbuilding of the Church. *(Second Vatican Council – 'Missions')*

WORD PICTURES

What you are
  is God's gift to you,
What you become
  is your gift to God.
(Anon)

One day, Michelangelo saw a block of marble which the owner said was of no value. 'It's valuable to me,' said Michelangelo. 'There is an angel imprisoned in it and I must set it free.' *(Anon)*

An impoverished French farm lad was rated a genius by the recruiting officers who were inducting him into the army.

He amazed specialists in his aptitude test by scoring the highest of the 40,000 previously examined. One expert compared his mental capacity with that of Leonardo da Vinci and other great minds of the past.

The 20-year-old farmer never got more than rudimentary education because, as the ninth child of eleven children, he was needed to help at home.

Instead of inducting him immediately, the army sent him to a special school, where he completed six years of education in five months. *(Anon)*

USEFUL TEXTS

Gifts:
Given to each, *1 Cor. 12:4-11*
Comes from Father, *James 1:17*
Good stewards of, *I Pet. 4:10*
Of Holy Spirit, *Luke 11:13*

See also: A1   The value of time
              A28 Work
              A39 The Glory of God

A37

Christ the King

'For he must be king until he has put all his enemies under his feet and the last of the enemies to be destroyed is death.'
1 Corinthians 15:25

Quotations

Eighty-six years I have served Him, and He has done me no wrong. How can I blaspheme my King who has saved me?
(St Polycarp's answer when told to revile Christ)

The true Christ, the divine and heavenly *Logos*, the only High Priest of the world, the only King of all creation, the only Archprophet of prophets of the Father. *(Eusebius of Caesarea)*

Christian Joy is the flag which is flown from the castle of the heart when the King is in residence there. *(P. Rainy)*

Wherever God rules over the human heart as King, there is the Kingdom of God established. *(Paul W. Harrison)*

Statement

Christ obeyed even at the cost of death, and was therefore raised up by the Father *(cf Phil. 2:8-9)*. Thus He entered into the glory of His kingdom. To Him all things are made subject until He subjects Himself and all created things to the Father that God may be all in all. *(cf 1 Cor. 15:27-28)*.
(Second Vatican Council – 'The Church')

Word pictures

Some years ago, an American soldier on a bus in Sweden told the man sitting next to him, 'America is the most democratic country in the world. Ordinary citizens may go to the White House to see the President and discuss things with him.'

The man said, 'That's nothing. In Sweden, the King and the people travel on the same bus.'

When the man got off the bus, the American was told by other passengers that he had been sitting next to King Gustav Adolf VI. *(Anon)*

Dame Julian of Norwich tells us that Our Good Lord showed Himself to her in different ways, as on earth. One was His sweet Incarnation, when He was born of His Mother. Another was His blessed Passion, when He showed Himself dying on the Cross. Another time, she saw Him as if in a point, that is, His presence as Creator in everything, upholding it. Another time, He showed Himself as if leading a pilgrimage, with Himself going in front of us all, making the pilgrimage to heaven. At other times, He showed her Himself reigning as a king. But the way He showed Himself to her most often was as King reigning in man's soul. 'There He has fixed His resting place, and His royal city: and out of this worshipful throne He shall never rise, nor move His dwelling-place from it for ever.'
(F. H. Drinkwater)

USEFUL TEXTS

Christ the King:
Kingdom of, *2 Pet. 1:11, Matt. 16:28*
Born to be, *Matt. 2:2*
'Are you?' *Matt. 27:11; Luke 23:3*
Title over cross, *Luke 23:38*
King of kings, *Rev. 17:14; Rev. 19:16*

See also: A4 Emmanuel – Mary's child
A44 Meeting Christ in the sacraments
B4 Mary – Handmaid of God
B8 The Word

A38

ORGINAL SIN

'Sin entered the world through one man,
and through sin death.' *(Romans 5:12)*

QUOTATIONS

The whole clay of humanity is a condemned clay.
(St Augustine of Hippo)

Adam was but human – this explains it all. He did not want the
apple for the apple's sake; he wanted it only because it was
forbidden. The mistake was in not forbidding the serpent –
then he would have eaten the serpent. *(Mark Twain)*

The kingdom of death dominated mankind to such an extent as
to drive all, by due penalty, headlong into the second death, of
which there is no end, except that the undue grace of God has
delivered some. *(St Augustine of Hippo)*

Augustine's theory of the transmission of original sin by way of
the sexual urge which is the typical form of 'concupiscence', the
lusting of flesh against spirit, has had a most disastrous influence
upon much of traditional Christian ethics. *(J. Burnaby)*

If only there were evil people somewhere insidiously
committing evil deeds and it was necessary only to separate
them from the rest of us and destroy them. But the line dividing
good and evil cuts through the heart of every human being and
who is willing to destroy a piece of his own heart? . . . Socrates
taught us *know thyself. (Alexander Solzhenitsyn)*

The Lord will never ask how successful we were in overcoming
a particular sin or imperfection. He will ask: 'Did you humbly
and patiently bear this mystery of iniquity in your life? How did
you deal with it? Did it teach you not to trust in your own ability

but in my love? Did it enable you to understand and be compassionate with the mystery of iniquity in the lives of others? Did it above all give you the most typical characteristic of the truly religious person – that he never judges or condemns the sin of others? The Christian knows from his own life that the demon of evil can be stronger than man . . . he knows that it is the patience, charity and humility learned which counts. Success or failure are accidental. The joy of the Christian is never based on his personal religious success, but on the knowledge that his Redeemer lives. *(Adrian van Kamm)*

PROVERB
All the evil in the world was brought into it by an apple. *(Mala mali malo mala contulit omnia mundo.)* *(Medieval proverb)*

STATEMENTS
Affected by original sin, men have frequently fallen into multiple errors concerning the true God, the nature of man, and the principles of the moral law. The result has been the corruption of morals and human institutions and not rarely, contempt for the human person himself.
(Second Vatican Council – 'Laity')

If any one does confess that the first man Adam, when he had transgressed the command of God in Paradise, straightway lost that holiness and righteousness in which he had been established, and through the offence of this disobedience incurred the wrath and indignation of God, and therefore incurred death, which God had before threatened to him, and with death, captivity under the power of him who therefore had the power of death, namely the devil, and that the whole of Adam, through offence of that disobedience, was changed for the worse in respect of body and soul; let him be anathema. *(Council of Trent – Session 5)*

WORD PICTURES
It is from the Talmud and not from Genesis that we get our traditional idea of Adam and Eve with a fig leaf apiece, as

though foliage had been rationed from the start: and from the Talmud, too, comes the story that Eve made all the animals eat some fruit too, so that they should all be involved in the same catastrophic consequences, and only the Phoenix had the sense to refuse and fly . . . *(Douglas Woodruff)*

There is an Indian fable of a swan, that, pitying a poor pig in its muddy environment, began to describe the beautiful country further up the river, with green banks and rising slopes, and invited the pig to join the happy company of white swans that lived there. The pig was willing enough to go, but asked the question, 'Is there any mire up in that fine country?' 'Oh no!' replied the swan, 'it is clean and free from mud and mire.' 'Then,' said the pig, 'I'm sorry I cannot accompany you. I must stay here in the mire.' *(Anon)*

Eden is on no map, and Adam's fall fits no historical calendar. Moses is not nearer the Fall than we are, because he lived 3,000 years before our time. The Fall refers not to some datable aboriginal calamity in the historic past but to a fact of human experience which is always present – namely, that we, who have been created for fellowship with God, repudiate it continually; and that the whole of mankind does this along with us. Every man is his own 'Adam,' and all men are solidarily 'Adam'. Thus Paradise before the Fall is . . . our 'memory' of a divinely intended quality of life, given to us along with our consciousness of guilt. *(J. S. Whale)*

USEFUL TEXTS

Sin:
God displeased with, *Gen. 6:6; Deut. 25:16*
Upright do not condone, *Gen. 39:9; Deut. 7:26*
Consequences of, *Exod. 20:5; Rom. 5:12*
Forgiveness of, *Exod. 34:7; Matt. 26:28*

See also: A15 Sin
B10 Baptism
C26 The human condition
C37 Temptation

A39

THE GLORY OF GOD

'He was transfigured; his face shone like the sun and his clothes became as white as the light.' *Matthew 17:2*

QUOTATIONS

Grace is but glory begun, and glory is but grace perfected. *(Jonathan Edwards)*

Provided that God be glorified, we must not care by whom. *(St Francis de Sales)*

God's majesty speaks to us by the works of his almighty Hands. *(R. H. Benson)*

If you say that God is good, great, blessed, wise or any such thing, the starting point is this: God is. *(St Bernard)*

Short is the glory that is given and taken by men; and sorrow followeth ever the glory of this world. *(Thomas à Kempis)*

God is proved not only by the zeal of those who seek Him, but by the blindness of those who seek Him not. *(Pascal)*

To God alone be glory. *Soli Deo gloria.*
(Latin phrase (Medieval))

May none of God's wonderful works
keep silence, night or morning.
Bright stars, high mountains, the depths of the seas,
sources of rushing rivers:
may all these break into song as we sing
to Father, Son and Holy Spirit.
May all the angels in the heavens reply:
Amen! Amen! Amen!

Power, praise, honour, eternal glory
to God, the only Giver of grace.
Amen! Amen! Amen!
(An Egyptian doxology, third century)

WORD PICTURES

On the margin of many of his masterpieces, Johann Sebastian Bach jotted down the words: 'To God Alone the Glory.'

And indeed, the prodigious quantity and sublime quality of his music, literally woven of religious contemplation and exaltation, reflect his lofty intention.

Although Bach was one of the greatest German organists of the eighteenth century, few besides his family and pupils knew of his genius in musical composition. At his death in 1750, after a lifetime of total dedication, poverty, and struggle, many of his priceless works were lost.

Music lovers today owe the 'rediscovery' of Bach to Felix Mendelssohn. As a young boy, he was enraptured by Bach's manuscript of the St Matthew Passion. At the age of 20, he gave a private performance of it. As a result, Bach's genius was widely acclaimed. *(Anon)*

I AM   is the unqualified fullness of being
is the supreme indication of presence
is the one statement that cannot be uttered
   without being completely true
is the one completely and immediately
   personal statement
is the presupposed in every intelligible utterance
is true equally of God and man
is true in every time and place
is the name of God.
(T. S. Gregory)

There is a legend that Jerome, who lived for many years in a cave near Bethlehem, was visited by the Christ Child and talked with him. One day Jerome asked: 'What may I give to Thee, O Christ Child?' But the Holy Child replied: 'I need nought but that thou should'st sing, "Glory to God in the highest, and on earth peace, goodwill." ' But Jerome persisted: 'I would give thee gifts – money.' 'Nay,' repeated the Child. 'I need no money, give it to my poor, for my sake. Thus shalt thou be giving to me.' *(Anon)*

USEFUL TEXTS

Glory of God:
Exod. 24:15-17, 40:34; Luke 2:9; Acts 7:55
Reflected In Christ, *John 1:14*
Reflected in man, *1 Cor. 11:7*

See also: A20 The Kingdom of God
            B40 One God
            C31 Thanksgiving
            C39 Doing God's will

A40

THE EQUALITY OF WOMEN

'His disciples returned, and were surprised to find him speaking to a woman.' *John 4:27*

QUOTATIONS

Women's styles may change, but their designs remain the same. *(Oscar Wilde)*

Mother is the name for God in the lips and hearts of little children. *(William Makepeace Thackeray)*

I think it must somewhere be written, that the virtues of the mothers shall be visited on their children as well as the sins of the fathers. *(Charles Dickens)*

Woman's basic fear is that she will lose love. *(Sigmund Freud)*

Spiritually a woman is better off if she cannot be taken for granted. *(Germaine Greer)*

It was to a virgin woman that the birth of the Son of God was announced. It was to a fallen woman that His resurrection was announced. *(Fulton J. Sheen)*

There is in every true woman's heart a spark of heavenly fire, which lies dormant in the broad daylight of prosperity, but which kindles up and beams and blazes in the dark hour of adversity. *(Washington Irving)*

Being a woman is a terribly difficult trade, since it consists principally of dealing with men. *(Joseph Conrad)*

PROVERBS

An ounce of mother is worth a pound of clergy.
(Spanish proverb)

When three women join together the stars come out in broad daylight. *(Talugu proverb)*

HUMOUR

I hate women because they always know where things are. *(James Thurber)*

Actually, the original meaning of 'lady' was 'bread kneader' and if the dictionary adds 'See dough' it refers, we add sternly, to bread only. *(Cleveland Amory)*

My 13-year-old daughter and I were talking about women's liberation one day, and I said firmly, 'I don't want to be liberated.'

My daughter said, 'I don't want to be liberated either – at least not until I know how it feels to be captured.'
(Lynn Cannon)

STATEMENT

For in truth it must still be regretted that fundamental personal rights are not yet being universally honoured. Such is the case of a woman who is denied the right and freedom to choose a husband, to embrace a state of life, or to acquire an education or cultural benefits equal to those recognised for men. *(Second Vatican Council – 'The Church Today')*

WORD PICTURES

Woman was made from the rib of man.
She was not created from his head – to top him,
nor from his feet – to be stepped upon.

She was made from his side – to be equal to him;
from beneath his arm – to be protected by him:
near his heart – to be loved by him. *(Anon)*

No one can read through the Gospels without realising what a deep appreciation Jesus had for women. They were the last at the cross and the first at the tomb, and for good reason. Dorothy Sayers, in her book *Are Women Human?* comments on Jesus' attitude and the female response.

'They had never known a man like this Man – there never has been such another. A prophet and teacher who never nagged at them, never flattered or coaxed or patronised; who never made arch jokes about them, never treated them either as 'The women, God help us!' or 'The ladies, God bless them'; who rebuked without querulousness and praised without condescension; who took their questions and arguments seriously; who never mapped out their sphere for them, never urged them to be feminine or jeered at them for being female; who had no axe to grind and no uneasy male dignity to defend; who took them as he found them and was completely unselfconscious. There is no act, no sermon, no parable in the whole Gospel that borrows its pungency from female perversity; nobody could possibly guess from the words and deeds of Jesus that there was anything 'funny' about woman's nature.' *(Dorothy Sayers)*

The difficulty of housework and male aversion to it are illustrated in *The Marvellous Land of Oz*:
'As they passed the rows of houses they saw through the open doors that men were sweeping and dusting and washing dishes, while the women sat around in groups, gossiping and laughing.

"What has happened?" the Scarecrow asked a sad-looking man with a bushy beard, who wore an apron and was wheeling a baby-carriage along the sidewalk.

"Why, we've had a revolution, your Majesty – as you ought to know very well," replied the man, "and since you went away the women have been running things to suit themselves. I'm glad you have decided to come back and restore order, for doing housework and minding children is wearing out the strength of every man in the Emerald City."

"Hm!" said the Scarecrow, thoughtfully. "If it is such hard work as you say, how did the women manage it so easily?"

"I really do not know," replied the man, with a deep sigh. "Perhaps the women are made of cast-iron." '*(L. Frank Baum)*

In the beginning, said a Persian poet – Allah took a rose, a lily, a dove, a serpent, a little honey, a Dead Sea apple, and a handful of clay. When he looked at the amalgam – it was a woman. *(William Sharp)*

As a young woman, Florence Nightingale longed to be involved in Christian ministry, but all she encountered was roadblocks. 'I would have given her (the church) my head, my hand, my heart. She would not have them. She did not know what to do with them. She told me to go back and do crochet in my mother's drawing-room. "You may go to Sunday school if you like," she said, but she gave me no training even for that. She gave me neither work to do for her, nor education for it.' *(Marlys Taege)*

Useful Texts
Woman:
Creation of, *Gen. 1:27; 2:21-23*
Devout, *1 Sam. 1:15; Luke 1:25*
Heirs with Christ, *Gal. 3:26-29*

See also: B34 Human rights
B44 The dignity of the individual
C33 Equality

A41

SPIRITUAL BLINDNESS

'I only know that I was blind and now I can see.'
(John 9:26)

QUOTATIONS

There are too many people we just leave asleep.
(Antoine Saint Exipéry)

The very limit of human blindness is to glory in being blind.
(St Augustine of Hippo)

The devil is ready to put out men's eyes that are content
willing to wax blind. *(St Thomas More)*

In the country of the blind, the one-eyed man is king.
(Erasmus)

Blind men should judge no colours. *(John Heywood)*

A blind man will not thank you for a looking-glass. *(Anon)*

PROVERBS

The eyes are blind when the mind is elsewhere. *(Latin proverb)*

When the blind man carries the banner, woe to those who
follow. *(French proverb)*

WORD PICTURES

A world of darkness and silence was the lot of Helen Keller who
lived from 1880 to 1968. Blinded and made deaf by a fever
when she was only 19 months old, she overcame her handicaps
to become one of America's most famous authors and lecturers.
When she was six-years-old, her teacher began to spell words
into Helen's palm while the child felt the objects with the other

hand. There was no progress. There came a breakthrough when the teacher spelled the word 'water' while holding Helen's other hand under a pump. Her sense of touch rapidly became her window to the world. *(Anon)*

A three-year-old girl in Glasgow was the eyes of her blind mother and father.

Wearing a leather harness, the child was a familiar sight as she led her parents along streets, across intersections and in and out of shops.

'I trust her judgement completely,' said her totally blind father. 'She is a blessing to us,' agreed her nearly blind mother.

I noticed a man walking towards me down the village street. He was barefoot and dressed in a long robe. He came slowly along, feeling his way by tapping with his stick. He was blind. We sat down by the roadside to talk. He was the village postman, messenger and general errand man. He had heard that a stranger had arrived in the village, so he came along to greet me. He had two parcels with him. Out of one came a typewriter and there on the roadside he tapped out on a piece of rough paper a message, in the Braille language, of welcome to me and a greeting to friends in England.

Then he unwrapped his second parcel. Out came a large book about the size of a family Bible. Made of thick brown paper, the pages were studded with Braille characters. He ran his fingers along the lines until he found the passage from *St John 14*: 'Let not your heart be troubled; believe in God, believe also in me.' We sat there by the side of the dusty road in silence. Then he packed away his treasures, shook hands, and away he padded down the road . . . I was moved by the man's inner serenity. He had turned blindness into sight and dark into light. *(Cecil Northcott: Christianity in Africa)*

In the African country of Ghana, a river was going to be used to make electricity and supply water for the people and their crops. But at the head of the river there was a place called 'the Valley of the Blind.' The people who lived there had trouble with their eyes. The trouble was caused by a fly which lived in the shrubs along the river. When this little fly bit someone it put into that person's blood a little creature called a parasite and this made the person blind. Before the huge work on the river could be properly started, it was necessary to find ways of getting rid of this little fly. *(M. Nassan)*

USEFUL TEXTS

Spiritual blindness:
Prov. 4:19; Matt. 6:23
Condition of;
Jewish leaders, *Matt. 15:14; 23:19, 24, 26*
Israel, *2 Cor. 3:14-16*
Unbelievers, *2 Cor. 4:3-4*

See also: A22 Seeking God
B49 Coping with doubt
C26 The human condition

A42

LIFE AFTER DEATH

'I am the resurrection. If anyone believes in me,
even though he dies he will live, and whoever lives and
believes in me will never die!' *John 11:25*

QUOTATIONS

The shortest life is the best if it leads us to the eternal.
(St Francis de Sales)

Eternal life does not begin with death; it begins with faith.
(Samuel Shoemaker)

To be immortal is to share in Divinity. *(Clement of Alexandria)*

Without love immortality would be frightful and horrible.
(Theodor Haecker)

I know as much about the afterlife as you do – nothing. I must
wait and see. *(William Inge)*

After the royal throne comes death; after the dunghill comes the
Kingdom of Heaven. *(St John Chrysostom)*

After the resurrection of the body shall have taken place, being
set free from the condition of time, we shall enjoy eternal life,
with love ineffable and steadfastness without corruption.
(St Augustine of Hippo)

Nobody is excluded from the kingdom of heaven except
through human fault. *(St Thomas Aquinas)*

If you were to destroy the belief in immortality in mankind, not
only love but every living force on which the continuation of all
life in the world depended, would dry up at once. Moreover,
there would be nothing immoral then, everything would be
permitted *(Fyodor Dostoyevsky)*

If individuals live only 70 years, then a state, or a nation, or a civilisation, which may last for a thousand years, is more important than an individual. But if Christianity is true, then the individual is not only more important but incomparably more important, for he is everlasting and the life of a state or a civilisation, compared with his, is only a moment. *(C. S. Lewis)*

PROVERBS

Those who live in the Lord never see each other for the last time. *(German proverb)*

When one is dead, it is for a long time. *(French proverb)*

HUMOUR

There was a meeting of the board of directors going on in Hell. Satan was concerned over the fact that business was not increasing. He wanted to reach as many people as possible and draw them into Hell.

One demon jumped up and said: 'I'll go back to earth and convince the people that there is no Heaven.'

'That won't do,' said Satan. 'We've tried it before and it doesn't work.'

'I'll convince them that there is no Hell,' offered a second demon.

'No – that doesn't work either,' said Satan.

A wise old veteran in the back of the room rose and said, 'If you let me go back to earth, I can fill this place. I'll just convince them that there is no hurry.' *(Anon)*

WORD PICTURES

A man who was entirely careless of spiritual things died and went to hell. And he was much missed on earth by his old friends. His business agent went down to the gates of hell to see if there was any chance of bringing him back. But, though he pleaded for the gates to be opened, the iron bars never yielded.

His priest went also and argued: 'He was not really a bad fellow, let him out, please!'

The gates remained stubbornly shut against all their voices.

Finally his mother came, she did not beg for his release.

Quietly, and with a strange catch in her voice, she said to Satan, 'Let me in.' Immediately the great doors swung open upon their hinges. For love goes down through the gates of hell and there redeems the damned. *(G. K. Chesterton)*

Princess Tou Wan died about 104 BC, but it was thought she would live for ever, because she was buried in a jade suit. Her husband, who had died nine years earlier, was given a similar suit. The pair were laid to rest in vast tombs hollowed out of a rocky hillside. In China, in 1969, their tombs were discovered and they created a sensation because of the staggering wealth of the 2,800 funeral offerings. Most spectacular of all were the jade suits, each made up of more than 2,000 tiny plates of thin jade, sewn together with gold thread. Nobles of the period believed gold and jade would stand the ravages of time, and so confer immortality. *(A. P. Castle)*

Over the triple doorway of the Cathedral of Milan, there are three inscriptions spanning the splendid arches.

Over one doorway is carved a beautiful wreath of roses, and underneath is the legend 'All that pleases is but for a moment.'

Over another is sculptured a cross, and these are the words beneath: 'All that troubles is but for a moment.'

But underneath the great central entrance in the main aisle is the inscription 'That only is important which is eternal.' *(Anon)*

USEFUL TEXTS

Life after death:
Of the righteous, *Matt. 25:46*
Gift of God, *Rom. 6:23*
Promise of, *1 John 2:25*
Through Jesus, *John 3:15*

See also: A31 Heaven
            B22 Death
            C35 Hope

A43
BELIEVING COMMUNITY

'These remained faithful to the teaching of the apostles, to the brotherhood, to the breaking of bread and to the prayers.'
Acts 2:42

QUOTATIONS

A community is only a community when the majority of its members are making the transition from 'the community for myself' to 'myself for the community'. *(Jean Vanier)*

The church after all is not a club of saints; it is a hospital for sinners. *(George Craig Stewart)*

The church is never a place, but always a people; never a fold, but always a flock; never a sacred building, but always a believing assembly. The church is you who pray, not where you pray. A structure of brick or marble can no more be a church than your clothes of serge or satin can be you. There is in this world, nothing sacred but man, no sanctuary of God but the soul. *(Anon)*

A church exists for the double purpose of gathering in and sending out. *(Anon)*

PROVERB

There is little piety in big churches. *(Italian proverb)*

HUMOUR

Lots of folks spend more on dog food than on the church – maybe because the dog pays them more attention. *(Frank Clark)*

One Sunday morning, a man entered the church and sat down the front with his hat on. Noting the man, one of the ushers spoke to him, asking him if he knew he had forgotten to remove his hat.

'Yes,' the man replied, 'I realise I have my hat on. I've been coming to this church for two months and this is the only way I could get anyone to speak to me.'

Father told his little son that he couldn't go to church because he was suffering from a severe case of voluntary inertia.
'I bet you aren't,' the little boy answered, 'I bet you're just lazy.'

The Devil's Beatitudes
Blessed are those who are too tired,
    busy or disorganised to meet with
    fellow Christians on Sundays each week.
    They are my best workers.

Blessed are those who enjoy noticing
    the mannerisms of clergy and choir.
    Their hearts are not in it.

Blessed are those Christians who wait
    to be asked and expect to be thanked.
    I can use them.

Blessed are the touchy.
    With a bit of luck they may even stop
    going to Church.
    They are my missionaries.

Blessed are those who claim to love God
    at the same time as hating other people.
    They are mine forever.

Blessed are the troublemakers.
    They shall be called my children.

Blessed are those who have not time to pray.
    They are easy prey for me.

Blessed are your when you read this and
    think it is about other people and
    not about yourself.
    I've got you. *(John Stowell)*

STATEMENT

Thus the Church, at once a visible assembly and a spiritual community, goes forward together with humanity and experiences the same earthly lot which the world does. She serves as a leaven and as a kind of soul for human society as it is to be renewed in Christ and transformed into God's family. *(Second Vatican Council – 'The Church Today')*

WORD PICTURES

Humanity is one in Christ, men are branches of one vine, members of one body. The life of each man enlarges itself infinitely into the life of others, the communion of saints, and each man in the church lives the life of all men in the church; each man is humanity. He belongs not only to that part of humanity which, living on earth at the moment, stands before God in prayer and labour, for the present generation is only a page in the book of life. In God and in his church, there is no difference between living and dead, and all are one in the love of the Father. Even the generations yet to be born are part of this one divine humanity. *(Sergius Bulgakov)*

There was once a family who brought their youngest child, a girl, to be baptised. When the time came for the baptism, the family went forward, including a very happy three-year-old brother. When the baptism was over, the minister carried the baby into the middle of the congregation, expressing what a delight it was to welcome this child into the larger family, the Church. The three-year-old brother had followed the minister, and standing beside the minister, the little boy noticed a grandpa-aged man sitting and smiling with a very happy smile. In a voice that all could hear, the little boy said, 'Would you like to touch our baby?'

'I would,' said the elderly man.

So the minister gently held out the baby for the man to touch. The man seemed so pleased that the little boy said, 'Maybe someone else would like to touch her.'

The minister walked down the aisle, and hands reached out to touch the baby. 'Now,' said the minister, 'those of you who have touched this child should pass that loving touch to others around you, until all have been touched.' And so it happened. People were so thrilled with that service that they asked if the same thing might not be done at each baptism. *(John Ambrose)*

USEFUL TEXTS

Church:
Loved by Christ, *Eph. 5:25*
Pillar of truth, *1 Tim 3:15*
Head of, *Eph. 1:22*
Building of, *Matt. 16:18; Eph. 2:20-21*

See also: B17 The Church – Bride of Christ
B36 The Family of God
C12 The Church for all men

A44

MEETING CHRIST IN THE SACRAMENTS

'He took the bread and said the blessing; then he broke it
and handed it to them. And their eyes were opened
and they recognised him.' *Luke 24:30-31*

QUOTATIONS

A sacrament is a material object sanctified and consecrated by
the Word of God. *(Peter Lombard)*

With these sacraments (i.e. baptism and the eucharist) Christ
feeds His Church; by them, the soul's very being is
strengthened. *(St Ambrose)*

The Spiritual Presence cannot be received without a
sacramental element, however hidden the latter might be.
(Paul Tillich)

Christ cannot live his life today in this world without our
mouth, our eyes, without our going and coming, without our
heart. When we love, it is Christ loving through us.
(Leon Joseph Suenens)

The liturgy is . . . not only a school of literary taste and a mine
of marvellous subjects, but it is infinitely more; it is a great
sacramental built around the six sacraments which surround the
greatest sacrament who is Christ Himself dwelling among us
even unto the consummation of the world. *(Thomas Merton)*

STATEMENT

To accomplish so great a work, Christ is always present in His
Church, especially in her liturgical celebrations. He is present in
the sacrifice of the Mass, not only in the person of His minister,
'the same one now offering, through the ministry of priests, who
formerly offered himself on the cross,' but especially under the

Eucharist species. By His power, He is present in the sacraments, so that when a man baptises it is really Christ Himself who baptises. *(Second Vatican Council – 'Liturgy')*

WORD PICTURES

Thou shalt know him
When he comes
Not by any din of drums
Nor the vantage of his airs
Nor by anything he wears
Neither by his crown
Nor his gown
For his presence known shall be
By the holy harmony
That his coming makes in me.
(Anon c. 1500)

Look backward – see Christ dying for you.
Look upward – see Christ pleading for you.
Look inward – see Christ living in you.
Look forward – see Christ coming for you.
(Anon)

At one of the settlements on a Red Indian reservation, where the priest was able to visit the Catholics only rarely, a Government agent came one day in his prairie-cart. He had things to give away, waistcoats and shirts and tobacco.

To one old man, who was a Catholic, the agent said jokingly, 'Your priest doesn't look after you, he doesn't seem to have brought you any presents, does he?'

The old man pointed to his bare chest, 'Can you see into my soul?'

'No, I can't,' said the agent.

'Well, if you could you would see the beautiful white garment that God gave me when the Blackrobe baptised me. And every time he comes he washes it clean for me in the blood of Jesus Christ. And when he gives me Communion, He puts Jesus Himself into my heart. Your tobacco soon goes off in smoke, and your shirts soon wear out, but the presents that the Blackrobe brings will stay with me and take me to heaven. *(Anon)*

See also: A37 Christ the King
B4 Mary – Handmaid of God
B46 Christ the Sacrament of God
B51 One with Christ
C45 The Divinity of Christ

THE PRIESTHOOD

'The Lord is my Shepherd there is nothing I shall want.'
(Psalm 23)

QUOTATIONS

The clergy can be the greatest barrier to spiritual growth in the world. *(Cardinal Suenans)*

The work of the ministry is an exalted work and leads to the kingdom of heaven. *(St Basil)*

The priesthood requires a great soul; for the priest has many harassing troubles of his own, and has need of innumerable eyes on all sides. *(St John Chrysostom)*

The priesthood is the spiritual power conferred on the ministers of the Church by Christ for the purpose of dispensing the sacraments to the faithful. *(John of Paris)*

The end of man is the glory of God. The end of a Christian is the greater glory of God. The end of a priest is the greatest glory of God. *(Cardinal Manning)*

Beware of spending too much time doing the work of the Lord without spending enough time with the Lord of the work!
(Pope John Paul II to priests)

Our Lord's plan for each priest is personal partnership: 'We: Jesus and I'. This is how He would have each priest live and act – in the first person plural. Our Lord wants to share every moment of our life, especially every moment of our ministry. *(M. Eugene Boylan)*

I always like to associate with a lot of priests because it makes me understand anti-clerical things so well. *(Hilaire Belloc)*

STATEMENT

The divinely established ecclesiastical ministry is exercised on different levels by those who from antiquity have been called bishops, priests and deacons. Although priests do not possess the highest degree of the priesthood, and although they are dependent on the bishops in the exercise of their power, they are nevertheless united with the bishops in sacerdotal dignity. By the power of the sacrament of orders, and in the image of Christ the eternal High Priest *(Heb. 5:1-10; 7:24; 9:11-28)*, they are consecrated to preach the gospel, shepherd the faithful and celebrate divine worship as true priests of the New Testament. *(Second Vatican Council – 'The Church')*

WORD PICTURES

Graham Greene's *The Power and the Glory* was greatly influenced by the courageous underground work and death of Father Miguel Pro. During the Mexican religious persecution under President Calles, 35-year-old Miguel Pro, a Jesuit priest, secretly ministered to hundreds of Mexicans every day. A master of disguise, he escaped the police again and again. Finally he was arrested with his two brothers. No evidence was produced against them; there was not even a mock trial. When he faced the firing squad, Father Pro threw open his arms in the form of a cross and as the soldiers took aim cried, 'Long live Christ the King'. *(A. P. Castle)*

The priesthood is a passionate commitment, a fiery-eyed vision, and an insatiable thirst for holiness and practical justice. The priest is called to be challenger, enabler, life-giver, poet of life, music maker, dreamer of dreams. He must be a man of personal faith, conformed to Christ, a man who loves the scriptures, draws sustenance from the sacramental life of the Church, and truly knows the community with and for whom he offers sacrifice. A priest is a man with a clear sense of his own self, and one who strives to develop all his natural talents to the limit for the good of the Church. He is a man of unreasonable hopes and expectations, who takes seriously, for himself and others, the injunction to be perfect as the heavenly Father is.
(Cardinal Joseph Bernardin)

If the priest preaches more than ten minutes, he is
   too long-winded,
If his sermon is short, he is too easy-going.
If the parish funds are low, he's a bad businessman,
If he mentions money, he's too grasping.
If he visits his parishioners, he's never home,
If he doesn't, he's snobbish.
If he runs bazaars and ballots, he's bleeding the people,
If he doesn't, the parish is lacking social life.
If he takes time in the confessional, he's too slow,
If he doesn't, he has no time for people.
If he starts Mass on the minute, his watch is fast,
If he's a bit late, he's holding up the congregation.
If he decorates the church, he's spending too much,
If he doesn't, he's letting it run down.
If he's young, he's inexperienced,
If he's old, he should retire.

If he dies, there will never be his equal again!
(Anon)

USEFUL TEXTS

Priest:
Jesus as;
   appointed by God, *Heb 5:5*
   appointed for ever, *Heb. 5:6*
   intercessor, *Rom. 8:34*
   able to sympathise, *Heb. 4:14*
Priesthood of
Aaron, *Exod. 28:1, Heb. 5:1-5*
Melchizedek, *Gen 14:18*
Christ, *Heb. 4:14, Heb 5:5-10*

See also: A14 The successors of the Apostles
          A46 Priesthood of the laity
          B13 Authority

A46

PRIESTHOOD OF THE LAITY

'You are a chosen race, a royal priesthood, a consecrated
nation, a people set apart, to sing the praises of God.'
1 Peter 2:9

QUOTATIONS

Laypersons do not *belong to* the Church,
nor do they *have a role* in the Church.
Rather, through baptism, they *are* the Church.
(Leonard Doohan)

Confirmation is the sacrament of the common priesthood of the
laity. *(Gerald Vann)*

What is the people itself but priestly? To whom it was said, 'You
are a chosen race, a royal priesthood, a consecrated nation'
(1 Peter 2:9), as the apostle Peter says. Everyone is anointed to
the priesthood, is anointed to the kingdom also; but it is a
spiritual kingdom and a spiritual priesthood. *(St Ambrose)*

By the waters of baptism, as by common right, Christians are
made members of the mystical Body of Christ the Priest, and by
the 'character' which is imprinted on their souls, they are
appointed to give worship to God; thus they participate,
according to their condition, in the priesthood of Christ.
(Pope Pius XII)

STATEMENTS

The earth's goods must be divided fairly and this right of every
man to a just share comes first. Even the right to private
property, and the right to free enterprise, must yield to justice.

Those who have money, cannot just spend as they please, or
speculate, regardless of the way that others are affected.

The laity must act, using their initiative, not waiting for
instructions. The laity must take the Christian Spirit into the

minds and hearts of men, into morality and laws, into the structures of society. The laity must breathe the Spirit of the Gospel into the changes and reforms that have to come.
(Pope Paul VI – 'This is Progress')

The Lord Jesus, 'whom the Father has made holy and sent into the world' *(John 10:36),* has made his whole mystical body share in the anointing by the Spirit with which he himself has been anointed. For in him all the faithful are made a holy and royal priesthood. They offer spiritual sacrifices to God through Jesus Christ, and they proclaim the perfections of him who has called them out of darkness into his marvellous light. Hence, there is no member who does not have a part in the mission of the whole Body. Rather, each one ought to hallow Jesus in his heart and bear witness to Jesus in the spirit of prophecy.
(Second Vatican Council – 'Priests')

It is through the sacraments and the exercise of the virtues that the sacred nature and organic structure of the priestly community is brought into operation. Incorporated into the Church through baptism, the faithful are consecrated by the baptismal character to the exercise of the cult of the Christian religion. *(Second Vatican Council – 'The Church')*

Are not we laymen priests also? It is written: 'He hath also made us a kingdom and priests to God and his Father.' The difference between the Order and the people is due to the authority of the church and the consecration of their rank by the reservation of a special bench for the order. *(Tertullian, writing as a Montanist)*

USEFUL TEXTS
Priesthood of Believers:
   1 Pet. 2:5; Rev. 1:6

See also: B10 Baptism
          B44 The dignity of the individual
          C49 Receive the Holy Spirit

A47

THE SPIRIT OF TRUTH

'The Father will give you another Advocate to be with you for
ever, that Spirit of truth whom the world can never receive.'
John 14:16-17·

QUOTATIONS

Let us begin by committing ourselves to the truth, to see it like
it is and to tell it like it is, to find the truth, to speak the truth
and live with the truth. That's what we'll do. *(Richard Nixon)*

When truth is discovered by someone else, it loses something of
its attractiveness. *(Alexander Solzhenitsyn)*

All truth, wherever it is found, belongs to us as Christians.
(St Justin Martyr)

Nothing conquers except truth: the victory of truth is charity.
(St Augustine of Hippo)

Every truth without exception – and whoever may utter it – is
from the Holy Ghost. *(St Thomas Aquinas)*

We arrive at the truth, not by the reason only, but also by the
heart. *(Pascal)*

No truth can really exist external to Christianity.
(Cardinal Newman)

Let us rejoice in the Truth, wherever we find its lamp burning.
(Albert Schweitzer)

PROVERBS

Individuals may perish; but truth is eternal. *(French proverb)*

Time discovers truth. *(Latin proverb)*

Tell the truth and run. *(Jugoslav proverb)*

The name of God is Truth. *(Hindu proverb)*

STATEMENT

Truth, however, is to be sought after in a manner proper to the dignity of the human person and his social nature. The inquiry is to be free, carried on with the aid of teaching or instruction, communication and dialogue. In the course of these, men explain to one another the truth they have discovered, or think they have discovered, in order thus to assist one another in the quest for truth. Moreover, as the truth is discovered, it is by a personal assent that men are to adhere to it.
(Second Vatican Council – 'Religious Freedom')

WORD PICTURES

Become an expert in the art of discovering the good in every person. No one is entirely bad.

Become an expert in the art of finding the truthful core in views of every kind. The human mind abhors total error.
(Dom Helder Camara)

Without the Holy Spirit:
God is far away,
Christ stays in the past,
the Gospel is a dead letter,
the Church is simply an organisation,
authority is a matter of domination,
mission a matter of propaganda,
the liturgy no more than an evocation,
Christian living a slave morality.

But in the Holy Spirit:
the risen Christ is there,
the Gospel is the power of life,
the Church shows forth the life of the Trinity,
authority is a liberating service,
mission is a Pentecost,
the liturgy is both memorial and anticipation,
human action is deified.
(Patriarch Athenagoras)

There is only one God
His name is 'True', for he is true,
And all truth comes from him.

He made everything: he knows no fear:
He knows no hate.

He was not born. and will not die:
He is life itself: he is great,
And gives generously to all.

His name is 'True':
He was there when everything began:
He watched while the universe was born.
His name is 'True'.

He has lived in the years gone by:
He is living now, and will live for ever.
(D. G. Butler: The words of the 'Mool Mantra',
sacred to Sikhs from the Guru Granth)

But there are seven sisters ever serving Truth,
Porters of the Posterns, one called Abstinence,
Humility, Charity, Chastity be the chief maidens there;
Patience and Peace help many a one;
Lady Almsgiving lets in full many.
(William Longland, 'Piers Plowman')

Truth does not consist in minute accuracy of detail, but in conveying a right impression; and there are vague ways of speaking that are truer than strict facts would be. When the Psalmist said, 'Rivers of water run down mine eyes, because men keep not thy law', he did not state the fact, but he stated a truth deeper than fact, and truer. *(Henry Alford)*

USEFUL TEXTS

Truth:
Attribute of God, *Isa. 65:16*
Spirit of, *John 15:26*
Christ is, *John 14:6*
Word of God is, *John 17:17*

See also: B53 Consecrated in Truth
C47 The indwelling Spirit
C49 Receive the Holy Spirit

A48

WORSHIP

'All these joined in continuous prayer, together with several
women, including Mary the mother of Jesus,
and with his brothers.' *Acts 1:14*

QUOTATIONS

All who follow in the steps of Christ live both for other people
and for God. They do not separate prayer and action.
(Bro. Roger of Taizé)

We are working with God to determine the future! Certain
things will happen in history if we pray rightly. We are to change
the world by prayer. *(Richard Foster)*

The most pressing duty of Christians is to live the liturgical life,
and increase and cherish its supernatural spirit. *(Pope Pius XII)*

Christian worship can never let us be indifferent to the needs of
others, to the cries of the hungry, of the naked and of the
homeless, of the sick and the prisoner, of the oppressed and
disadvantaged. *(Archbishop Tutu)*

The worship of God is not a rule of safety – it is an adventure of
the spirit, a flight after the unattainable. *(A. N. Whitehead)*

SOMEHOW, about 40 per cent of churchgoers seem to have
picked up the idea that 'singing in church is for singers'. The
truth is that 'singing is for believers'. The relevant question is
not, 'Do you have a voice?' but 'Do you have a song?'
(Donald Hustad)

It is a law of man's nature, written into his very essence, and just
as much a part of him as the desire to build houses and cultivate
the land and marry and have children and read books and sing
songs, that he should want to stand together with other men in
order to acknowledge their common dependence on God, their
Father and Creator. *(Thomas Merton)*

PROVERBS

Prayers travel faster when said in unison. *(Latin proverb)*

They that worship God merely from fear, would worship the devil too, if he appear. *(Anon)*

HUMOUR

The shopkeeper had just handed me a demonstration pair of binoculars. I was getting the distant wall nicely into focus when a passer-by, seeing my Roman collar, quietly advised, 'Just tell them to move to the front of the church, Father.' *(John Stewart)*

WORD PICTURES

God is the supreme artist. He loves to have things beautiful. Look at the sunset and flowers and the snow-capped mountains and the stars. They are beautiful because they come from God. God loves to have things beautiful in Church, too. And the same goes for church courtesies. To show our reverence for the Cross on which he died for us, and for the Sacrament in which he comes to our hearts, is just to be polite to God. This is not required, but it is the part of Christian good breeding. It has the importance that courtesy has the world over. *(John S. Baldwin)*

The centuries which followed the fall of the Empire in the West, in spite of the impoverishment of their material culture, were from the liturgical point of view a great creative age, and it is remarkable that this is no less true of the semi-barbarian West than of the stable and comparatively prosperous Byzantine world. All these ages possessed of poetry, music and art found expression in the liturgy—an expression no later age has been able to surpass. *(C. Dawson)*

I have a treasured missal of the Sarum or old English rite, printed at Ingoldstadt in 1555. When it was planned, Edward VI was still on the throne, and when I peruse it I regret more than ever that there was no Englishman in Rome in 1570 when St Pius V, while tidying up the immemorial Roman rite, exempted from the discipline of that rite any other which could show 200 years of continuity.

The Sarum rite shows how confusing a misnomer it is to call the Roman rite 'tridentine' when it is incomparably older than Trent. The canon of the Mass in the Sarum rite is identical all the way from *Te igitur* until the communion. One of the small differences was that in the *Te igutur* prayer, after mentioning the Pope and the local bishop, the King was also prayed for, as he was not prayed for at Rome where the Pope was also the King. Let us repair the omission of 1570 and apply now for Sarum to be licensed. *(Douglas Woodruff)*

How natural it is to have a cup of tea or coffee when we meet friends! There is nothing more unifying than sitting round a fire, warming one's hands on a mug of chocolate and sharing experiences! The psalmist says 'his cup is overflowing' when he is happy. Jesus asked his disciples if they could drink the cup of suffering he was to drink. Why not use this universal symbol in our family prayer?

It is a good idea to have a special cup that may be called our 'blessing cup'. There are so many lovely pottery cups and goblets these days. It can be kept in the home in a prominent place and then when we want to pray together it can be placed on the table with a candle and flowers and our Bible. We begin our prayer with a few well chosen verses from the Bible. Then we pray especially according to our needs and what we are celebrating. Finally the cup is filled carefully with Ribena or orange squash or hot chocolate – we have chosen beforehand - and it is a privilege to be the one to fill the blessing–cup. The cup is passed from one to the other, sharing in peace and love the nourishment, the refreshment, the enjoyment: the sense of belonging.

Our celebration ends with the family holding hands and saying together the Lord's Prayer, followed by a well-known hymn or song.

Every family strives to strengthen its bonds by mutually sharing hopes and fears, joys and sorrows. The blessing cup is a family tradition you can begin in your home to help you towards this goal. *(Sr Jean Daniel RLR)*

The word 'Worship' is an Anglo-Saxon word and means 'worthship' or 'worthiness'. The word commonly translated 'worship' in the New Testament – though there are several other Greek words – is 'Proskuneo', to kiss the hand toward. This is thought to be derived from the slave's manner of salutation and homage when he entered the presence of his master, the act being a mark of reverence and respect, and also implying affection. Hence, in ascriptions of worship, we have the expression 'Thou art worthy'. *(Anon)*

When the guru sat down to worship each evening the ashram cat would get in the way and distract the worshippers. So he ordered that the cat be tied up during evening worship.

Long after the guru died the cat continued to be tied up during evening worship. And when the cat eventually died, another cat was brought to the ashram so that it could be duly tied up during evening worship.

Centuries later learned treatises were written by the guru's disciples on the essential role of a cat in all properly conducted worship. *(Anon)*

USEFUL TEXTS

Worship:
Of God, *Exod. 20:3; Deut. 5:7; Matt. 4:10*
Of Christ, *John 9:38; Heb. 1:6; Rev. 5:8-9*
Attitude in, *Lev. 10:3; Ps. 5:7; John 4:24*

See also: B25 Quiet – time for prayer
            B29 The Eucharist
            C32 Prayer

B1

Waiting on the Lord

'Stay awake, because you do not know when the master of the house is coming.' *Mark 13:35*

Quotations

When you do not know what to do – wait. *(Anon)*

True waiting means waiting without anxiety.
(St Francis de Sales)

They also serve who only stand and wait. *(John Milton)*

There are three distinct comings of the Lord of which I know, his coming to men, his coming into men, and his coming against men. *(St Bernard)*

To him that waits all things reveal themselves, provided that he has the courage not to deny, in the darkness, what he has seen in the light. *(Coventry Patmore)*

We do not obtain the most precious gifts by going in search of them but by waiting for them. Man cannot discover them by his own powers, and if he sets out to seek for them he will find in their place counterfeits of which he will be unable to discern the falsity. *(Simone Weil)*

Proverbs

Everything comes to those who wait. *(French proverb)*

The future belongs to him who knows how to wait.
(Russian proverb)

It's good to hope, it's the waiting that spoils it.
(Yiddish proverb)

WORD PICTURES

Three hundred years ago, a man condemned to the Tower of London carved these words on the stone wall of the prison:
'It is not adversity that kills,
but the impatience with which we bear adversity.'

The Emperor Hadrian once said to Rabbi Joshua, 'I want to see your God.' The rabbi replied, 'That is impossible.' The emperor said, 'You must show him to me.' The rabbi made the emperor go outside with him. It was summer. He said to the emperor, 'Look at the sun,' 'I cannot,' answered the emperor. Then the rabbi replied, 'If you cannot even look at the sun, which is but one of the servants of the Holy One, blessed be he, how shall you look at the Holy One himself?' *(The Talmud)*

At a moment in history there was a great meeting between 'Time' and, 'Love' and the result was a weak helpless baby. When God came into our world that's how he came. On the first Christmas night the Son of God, 'Love' itself, became one of us.

In the Church's season of 'the coming', we find not one meeting of 'Love' and 'Time' prepared for and celebrated, but three. The liturgy of Advent speaks of the three 'comings' of Jesus. This can be a little confusing, unless clearly spelt out and thought about:

(1.) The coming of 'Love' as a baby – the first coming of Jesus as a member of a family.

(2.) The coming of 'Love' as the Word of God – the second coming of Jesus at the age of 30 as a preacher.

(3.) The coming of 'Love' as the judge – the final coming of Christ at the end of time as our judge.

In the four weeks of Advent these three 'comings' of Jesus are recalled. *(A. P. Castle)*

USEFUL TEXTS

Waiting:
On the Lord, *Ps. 27:14; Isa. 40:31*
For the promise of God, *Acts 1:4*
For guidance and teaching, *Ps. 25:5*
For the Coming of Christ, *1 Cor. 1:7; 1 Thess. 1:10*

See also: A1 Value of time
A22 Seeking God
A35 Preparing for death
B21 Trust in God
C1 Liberation from fear
C36 The Day of the Lord

B2
THE GOOD NEWS

'Go up on a high mountain, joyful messenger to Zion.
Shout with a loud voice, joyful messenger to Jerusalem.'
Isaiah 40:9

QUOTATIONS

The Gospel was not good advice but good news.
(William Ralph Inge)

How petty are the books of the philosophers with all their
pomp, compared with the gospels! *(Jean Jacques Rousseau)*

Our reading of the Gospel story can be and should be an act of
personal communion with the living Lord. *(William Temple)*

God writes the gospel not in the Bible alone, but on trees, and
flowers, and clouds, and stars. *(Martin Luther)*

The Gospel is neither a discussion nor a debate. It is an
announcement. *(Paul S. Rees)*

It is no use walking anywhere to preach unless we preach as we
walk. *(St Francis of Assisi)*

We had no use for the policy of the Gospels: if someone slaps
you, just turn the other cheek. We had shown that anyone who
slapped us on our cheek would get his head kicked off.
(Nikita Khrushchev)

Go to the people
Learn from them
Love them
Start with what they know
Build with what they have
But of the best leaders
When the job is done
When the task is accomplished

The people will say
'We have done it ourselves'
(Lao Tzu)

HUMOUR

The sexton had been laying the new carpet on the pulpit platform and had left a number of tacks scattered on the floor. 'See here, James,' said the parson, 'what do you suppose would happen if I stepped on one of those tacks right in the middle of my sermon?'

'Well, sir,' replied the sexton, 'I reckon there'd be one point you wouldn't linger on!' *(Anon)*

Old Mrs Mac was hard of hearing but would never admit it, so she always sat close to the pulpit.

'You'll have to come up to date, Father, and get micro-phones,' she told the P. P. 'The agnostics in this church are very poor.'

STATEMENTS

In his gracious goodness, God has seen to it that what he had revealed for the salvation of all nations would abide perpetually in its full integrity and be handed on to all generations. Therefore, Christ the Lord, in whom the full revelation of the supreme God is brought to completion *(cf. 2 Cor. 1:20; 3:16; 4:6.)*, commissioned the apostles to preach to all men that Gospel which is the source of all saving truth and moral teaching, and thus to impart to them divine gifts. This Gospel had been promised in former times through the prophets and Christ Himself fulfilled it and promulgated it with his own lips.
(Second Vatican Council – 'Revelation')

Holy Mother Church has firmly and with absolute constancy held, and continues to hold, that the four Gospels just named, whose historical character the Church unhesitatingly asserts, faithfully hand on what Jesus Christ, while living among men, really did and taught for their eternal salvation until the day he was taken up into heaven *(see Acts 1:1-2)*.
(Second Vatican Council – 'Revelation')

WORD PICTURES

Everyone has inside himself
a piece of good news.
The good news is that you really don't know
how great you can be,
how much you can love,
what you can accomplish, and
what your potential is.
How can you top good news like that?
(Anon)

You are writing a Gospel,
A chapter each day,
By the deeds that you do,
And the words that you say.

Men read what you write,
If it's false or it's true.
Now what is the Gospel
According to you?
(Anon)

In the home
    it is kindness;
In society
    it is courtesy;
In business
    it is honesty;
In work
    it is fairness;
Towards the weak
    it is help;
Towards the unfortunate
    it is sympathy;
Towards the wicked
    it is resistance;
Towards the strong
    it is trust;

Towards the penitent
   it is forgiveness;
Towards the successful
   it is congratulations;
And towards God
   it is reverence and obedience.
(Anon)

Ruskin says that many people read the Scriptures as the hedgehog gets grapes. The old monks said that this animal rolled over among the grapes and carried what happened to stick to its spines or quills. So the 'hedgehoggy' readers roll themselves over on a portion of the Scriptures and get only what happens to stick. But you can get only the skins of Bible verses that way. If we want the juice, we must press them in clusters.
(Anon)

Author Lloyd Douglas used to tell how he loved to visit an old violin teacher who had a homely wisdom that refreshed him. One morning, Douglas walked in and said 'Well, what's the good news today?'
   Putting down his violin, the teacher stepped over to a tuning fork suspended from a cord and struck it. '*There* is the good news for today,' he said. 'That, my friend, is the musical note A. It was A all day yesterday, will be A next week and for a thousand years.' *(Purnell Bailey)*

USEFUL TEXTS

Good News:
Of Christ, *2 Cor. 2:12*
Preached by Paul, *Acts 14:15*
Of God, *Rom. 1:1*
As Refreshment, *Prov. 15:30*

See also: B9 Revelation
          B12 On a mission
          B24 Go tell everyone
          C2 Joy of salvation

JOY IN CHRIST

'Be happy at all times.'
1 Thessalonians 5:16

QUOTATIONS

God is infinite fun. *(Mary O'Hara)*

We are all strings in the concert of his joy. *(Jakob Boehme)*

The sweet mark of a Christian is not faith, or even love, but joy. *(Samuel M. Shoemaker)*

Joy is prayer – Joy is strength – Joy is love – Joy is a net of love by which you can catch souls. *(Mother Teresa)*

The thought of God, and nothing short of it, is the happiness of man. *(Cardinal Newman)*

Happiness is a mystery like religion, and should never be rationalised. *(G. K Chesterton)*

Happiness is a butterfly, which, when pursued is always beyond our grasp, but which, if you will sit down quietly, may alight upon you. *(Nathaniel Hawthorne)*

This is the secret of joy. We shall no longer strive for our own way; but commit ourselves, easily and simply, to God's way, acquiesce in his will and in so doing find our peace. *(Evelyn Underhill)*

PROVERBS

Those who wish to sing always find a song. *(Swedish proverb)*

Great joys weep, great sorrows laugh. *(French proverb)*

One joy dispels a hundred cares. *(Oriental proverb)*

HUMOUR

There is a story of an Irishman who died suddenly and went up for divine judgement, feeling extremely uneasy. He didn't think he had done much good on earth! There was a queue ahead of him, so he settled down to look and listen.

After consulting his big book, Christ said to the first man in the queue: 'I see here that I was hungry and you gave me to eat. Good man! Go on into Heaven.' To the second he said: 'I was thirsty and you gave me to drink,' and to the third: 'I was in prison and you visited me.' And so it went on.

As each man ahead of him was sent to Heaven the Irishman examined his conscience and felt he had a great deal to fear. He'd never given anyone food or drink, he hadn't visited prisoners or the sick.

Then his turn came. Trembling he watched Christ examining the book. Then Christ looked up and said: 'Well there's not much written here, but you did do something: I was sad and discouraged and depressed; you came and told me funny stories, made me laugh and cheered me up. Get along to Heaven!'

That story makes the point that no form of charity should be neglected or undervalued. (*Anon*)

Out of the gloom a voice said unto me,
'Smile and be happy: things could be worse.'
So I smiled and was happy and, behold,
things did get worse. (*Anon*)

'There was a little Indian girl at school today,' announced my son proudly. 'Does she speak English?' I asked. 'No,' came the reply, 'But it doesn't matter because she laughs in English.' (*Anon*)

WORD PICTURES

An Athenian one day found Aesop amusing himself by talking to a group of boys and began to laugh and jeer at him for it. Aesop took a bow unstrung and laid it upon the ground. Then, calling the Athenian, 'Now, philosopher,' said he, 'expound the riddle if you can, and tell me what the unstrung bow implies.' The man, after racking his brain a considerable time to no purpose, at last gave it up. 'Why,' said Aesop, smiling, if you keep a bow always bent, it will presently lose its elasticity; but if you let it go slack, it will be fitter for use when you want it. *(Aesop)*

It has long been my belief that one of the things which have enabled man to survive is the ability to laugh. No matter how difficult the situation may be, man somehow has always been able to find humour in his situation. If I were given the opportunity to present a gift to the next generation, it would be the ability for each individual to learn to laugh at himself. I have not always had this ability, but have envied those who do, and I think it is one of God's greatest blessings. *(Charles Schulz)*

Can we not say to the young apprentice who has just learnt the use of a high precision lathe, and is thrilled at his new ability to use so apparently heavy and bulky a machine to prepare a piece of metal to a given shape with an accuracy of one ten-thousandth of an inch, that God is equally thrilled, and that this sheer joy in the situation is not wholly different from that of the angels who behold God's glory and rejoice? *(C. A. Coulson)*

Health enough to make work a pleasure.
Wealth enough to support your needs.
Strength to battle with difficulties and overcome them.
Grace enough to confess your sins and forsake them.
Patience enough to toil until some good is accomplished.
Charity enough to see some good in your neighbour.
Love enough to move you to be useful and helpful to others.
Faith enough to make real the things of God.
Hope enough to remove all anxious fears concerning the
     future.
(Johann Wolfgang von Goethe)
There was a mediaeval king who regularly used the advice of a wise man. This sage was summoned to the king's presence. The

monarch asked him how to get rid of his anxiety and depression of spirits, how he might be really happy, for he was sick in body and mind. The sage replied, 'There is but one cure for the king. Your Majesty must sleep one night in the shirt of a happy man.'

Messengers were dispatched throughout the realm to search for a man who was truly happy. But everyone who was approached had some cause for misery, something that robbed them of true and complete happiness. At last they found a man – a poor beggar – who sat smiling by the roadside and, when they asked him if he was really happy and had no sorrows, he confessed that he was a truly happy man.

Then they told him what they wanted. The king must sleep one night in the shirt of a happy man, and had given them a large sum of money to procure such a shirt. Would he sell them his shirt that the king might wear it? The beggar burst into uncontrollable laughter, and replied, 'I am sorry I cannot oblige the king. I haven't a shirt on my back.' *(Anon)*

It is a proven fact that some of the happiest people in this world have the least amount of material wealth. Their happiness comes rather from the joy they derive from giving themselves in service to others who are needy. This is true of Mother Teresa and those who work with her. In a tribute to her and her single missionary sisters, Malcolm Muggeridge writes:

Their life is tough and austere by worldly standards, certainly: yet I never met such delightful, happy women, or such an atmosphere of joy as they create. Mother Teresa, as she is fond of explaining, attaches the utmost importance to this joyousness. The poor, she says, deserve not just service and dedication, but also the joy that belongs to human love . . . The Missionaries of Charity . . . are multiplying at a fantastic rate. Their Calcutta house is bursting at the seams, and as each new house is opened, there are volunteers clamouring to go there. As the whole story of Christendom shows, if everything is asked for, everything – and more – will be accorded; if little, then nothing.

for useful texts see over

Joy:
In the Holy Spirit, *Rom. 14:17*
Of the Lord, *Neh. 8:10*
In trials, *Jas. 1:2*
When a sinner repents, *Luke 15:10*

See also: B51 One with Christ
            C2 Joy of salvation
            C47 The indwelling spirit

B4
MARY – HANDMAID OF GOD

'I am the handmaid of the Lord,' said Mary. 'Let what you have said be done to me.' *Luke 1:38*

QUOTATIONS

Mary's humble acceptance of the divine will is the starting point of the story of the redemption of the human race from sin. *(Alan Richardson)*

There is no more excellent way to obtain graces from God than to seek them through Mary, because her Divine Son cannot refuse her anything. *(St Philip Neri)*

Mary can teach us kindness. 'They have no wine,' she told Jesus at Cana. Let us, like her, be aware of the needs of the poor, be they spiritual or material and let us, like her, give generously of the love and grace we are granted. *(Mother Teresa)*

WORD PICTURES

The Virgin Mary's 'yes' finds its fulfilment in an attitude of offering: in faith, simple trust in God, Mary did not hold on to her Son for herself; she gave him to the world. We too wish to find our fulfilment in trusting and, in the spirit of praise, by giving all that God gives to us.

But how can we place our trust in God when a question rises incessantly from the hearts of many: if God existed, he would not permit wars, injustice, illness and the oppression of even one human being on this earth. If God existed, he would keep us from doing evil.

In a leper hospital in Calcutta, where I was sharing the life of the poorest for a time, I saw a leper raise his arms and what remained of his hands and sing these words: 'God has not inflicted a punishment on me; I praise him because my illness has turned into a visit from God'.

On either side of him, to be sure, other lepers were moaning with pain and with despair. But this one had realised that suffering is not sent by God; it is not a consequence of wrong-doing. God is not the author of evil, nor a tormentor of the human conscience. *(Bro. Roger of Taizé)*

Mary is the closest one to priests. No one could have been a better priest than Our Lady. She really can, without difficulty, say 'This is my Body', because it was really her body that she gave to Jesus.

And yet Mary remained only the handmaid of the Lord, so that you and I can always turn to her as our Mother. She is one of our own so that we can always be one with her.

That of course is why Mary was left behind after the Ascension: to strengthen the priesthood of the apostles, to be a mother to them, until the Church, the young Church, was formed. *(Mother Teresa)*

What Mary wants throughout the ages of the Church is not that we should venerate her as an individual but that we should recognise the depth of God's love in the work of his incarnation and redemption. Since she lived in the house of the beloved disciple, it would be astonishing if the gospel of the love of the triune God made manifest in Christ had not been inspired also by her presence and what she had to say. Certainly it is characteristic that the first apparition of Our Lady about which we learn from trustworthy sources is the vision of Origen's pupil Gregory the Wonder-worker, recounted by Gregory of Nyssa, which he had when preparing to be ordained as a bishop.

While one night he was pondering on the words of faith, a form appeared to him, an old man in the attitude and dress of a priest, who told him he would show him the divine wisdom in order to remove his uncertainty. Then he gestured sideways with his hand and showed him another form of more than human dignity and almost unbearable splendour. This said to John the Evangelist that he should expound the mystery of faith to the young man, whereupon John said he would gladly comply with the wishes of the mother of the Lord, and explained the mystery of the trinity to Gregory in clear words. Gregory wrote what was said down at once and later preached on this to his people. *(H. U. von Balthasar)*

USEFUL TEXTS

Mary:
Mother of Jesus, *Matt. 1:1-16*
Present at first miracle, *John 2:1-10*
Present at crucifixion, *John 19:25-26*
Cared for by the disciple, *John 19:27*

See also: A4 Emmanuel – Mary's child
A40 The equality of women
B7 Mary, Mother of God

B5

A Saviour is Born for Us

'Today in the town of David a Saviour has been born to you;
he is Christ the Lord.' *Luke 2:11*

Quotations

For he was made Man that we might be made God.
(St Athanasius)

By His divine nature, Christ is simple,
By His human nature, He is complex. *(St Thomas Aquinas)*

The incarnation is not an event; but an institution. What Jesus
once took up He never laid down. *(Vincent McNabb)*

He is what God means by man.
He is what man means by God. *(J. S. Whale)*

The Word of God, Jesus Christ, on account of His great love for
mankind, became what we are in order to make us what He is
Himself. *(St Irenaeus)*

I do hope your Christmas has had a little touch of Eternity in
among the rush and pitter patter and all. It always seems such
a mixing of this world and the next – but that after all is the
idea! *(Evelyn Underhill)*

We pray for visions but seldom watch a sunset. We marvel at the
gift of tongues but are bored listening to babies. We desire
proofs for the existence of God even as life in all its marvels
continues all around us.

We tend to look for God everywhere, except in the place
where incarnation took place – our flesh. *(Ronald Rolheiser)*

That there was no room in the inn was symbolic of what was
to happen to Jesus. The only place where there was room for
him was on the Cross. *(William Barclay)*

HUMOUR

Dialogue from a church nativity play, written, directed and acted by a class of nine-year-olds, opens with the scene at the inn. Joseph and Mary ask for a room overlooking Bethlehem:

Innkeeper   Can't you see the 'No Vacancy' sign?

Joseph   Yes, but can't you see that my wife is expecting a baby any minute?

Innkeeper   Well, that's not my fault.

Joseph   Well it's not mine either! *(Anon)*

A Nativity play was to be performed in the church hall and a country vicar went to town to get a streamer for display. Unfortunately, he forgot the measurements so he wired his wife for details. The telegraph clerk at the other end nearly had a fit when the reply message was received. It read: 'Unto us a Child is Born – seven feet six by one foot three.' *(Anon)*

STATEMENT

Since human nature as He assumed it was not annulled, by that very fact it has been raised up to a divine dignity in our respect too. For by His incarnation the Son of God has united Himself in some fashion with every man. He worked with human hands, He thought with a human mind, acted by human choice, and loved with a human heart. Born of the Virgin Mary, He has truly been made one of us, like us in all things except sin. *(Second Vatican Council – 'The Church Today')*

WORD PICTURES

The first Christmas card was believed to have been sent by W. C. T. Dobson, R.A., in 1844. Sir Henry Cole and J. C. Horsley produced the first commercial Christmas card in 1846, although it was condemned by temperance enthusiasts because members of the family group in the centrepiece were cheerfully drinking wine. After Tucks, the art printers, took to printing them in the 1870s, they really came into vogue. *(Anon)*

Fr Robert was invited to preach the Novena for Christmas in a Parish of Sao Paulo (Brazil). In every sermon he promised that for Christmas they would have a great 'living crib'. People were anxious to see it.

The 25th December was approaching, but nothing new could be seen. The usual crib was prepared in the usual way and place, by the usual ladies. Two days before Christmas he again announced the great event. After the sermon he called three students and told them: 'In these two days before Christmas you are exempt from coming to the church. You will go to the poorest areas of the Parish and look for the poorest families. Write down the names of the parents, the number of children and their ages, and their exact address. You will bring the results of this census on Christmas Eve.'

The students came back with about a hundred addresses. Fr Robert had them written on separate papers, folded and placed in a tray. A few minutes before Midnight Mass, he placed the tray on a small table beside the altar. When the celebration of the Mass started, he went towards the altar carrying two posters. He brought one to the usual crib and left it there, with the writing 'Dead Crib'. Then he laid the other beside the tray and people could read on it, 'Living Crib'.

There was a dead silence. People were wondering what was the meaning of that gesture and waiting for an explanation. Fr Robert talked briefly: 'Social injustice, unemployment, lack of housing, lack of love and respect for the human person and his rights, ignorance and poverty, have forced Christ to change his address. Today, Christmas day, he is waiting for your visit at his new address that you will find in this tray.'

After Mass the church remained empty, and so did the tray. The baker that day sold more bread, the butcher more meat, the shops more rice and beans, and the milk disappeared. Clothes, shoes, exercise books, pens, toys, found new owners.
(M. Cristofolini)

Light looked down and beheld Darkness:
'Thither will I go,' said Light.
Peace looked down and beheld War:

'Thither will I go,' said Peace.
Love looked down and beheld Hatred:
'Thither will I go,' said Love.
So came Light and shone.
So came Peace and gave rest.
So came Love and brought life.
And the Word was made flesh and dwelt among us.
(Laurence Housman)

Christmas celebrates the domestic God, the God born into ordinary life.

Several years ago, at a prayer seminar I was attending, a lady was giving a talk on Zen. She was describing how she spent more than two hours a day in meditation and how she would, through this practice, have very deep and lucid connections with the transcendent.

During the question period, I asked her how she would compare the feelings of God that she experienced during meditation with the feelings she had when she ate dinner with her family.

'No comparison', she replied. 'Eating dinner with my family can be a good experience, holy even in its own way. But the experience of God in meditation dwarfs everything else.'

I do not want to question the importance of meditation, nor indeed the value of Lourdes, Fatima and Padre Pio, but I am Christian enough to be pagan enough to demand some qualifications here. We should pray meditatively, and perhaps we can benefit from Fatima, Lourdes and Padre Pio. But, in the end, we must realise that God is domestic more than monastic.

1 John 4:7-16 says: 'God is love and whoever abides in love abides by God and God abides in him/her'. Love is a thing that happens in ordinary life, in kitchens, at tables, in the flesh. God abides in us when we abide there. The Christ-child is also to be found in church, in the sacraments and in private meditations (for these, too, are ordinary).

All of these are ordinary and the incarnation crawls into them and helps us to abide in God. *(Ronald Rolheiser)*

Deliveries with a difference
In February a British Airways jumbo jet landed at Heathrow with one more passenger than when it had taken off from Delhi – a new born girl. Mrs Rajapir Randhawa, seven months pregnant, went into labour two hours after take-off and, helped by three doctors, gave birth to a 6 lb baby at 30,000 ft in Soviet airspace.

Last November mum-to-be Sharon Young couldn't wait any longer for a taxi – so she had to give birth to her son on a grass verge. Sharon from Manchester, said that it was all over very quickly. 'I was in labour 24 hours with my first two children, but Robert arrived in two minutes after I walked a quarter of a mile to the phone box.'

And last October 31-year-old Karen Kelly gave birth to her son on an M25 slip road. Ambulancemen delivered the baby after Karen from Farnham, began to get twinges while driving with a friend. *(Womans Own)*

USEFUL TEXTS
Saviour:
    Applied to Christ, *2 Tim. 1:10*
    Incarnation, *Matt. 1:18-21; John 1:1-18*

See also: A4 Emmanuel – Mary's Child
             B3 Joy in Christ
             C2 Joy of salvation
             C7 The humanity of Christ

B6
THE FAMILY

'The Lord honours the father in his children, and upholds the rights of a mother over her sons.' *Ecclesiasticus 3:2*

QUOTATIONS

Home is where the heart is. *(Pliny the Elder)*

Without a family, man, alone in the world, trembles with the cold. *(André Maurois)*

He is the happiest, be he king or peasant, who finds peace in his home. *(Goethe)*

Few are born to do the great work of the world, but the work that all can do is to make a small home circle brighter and better. *(George Eliot)*

What a father says to his children is not heard by the world, but it will be heard by posterity. *(Jean Paul Eixhter)*

The union of the family lies in love; and love is the only reconciliation of authority and liberty. *(R. H. Benson)*

Where does the family start? It starts with a young man falling in love with a girl – no superior alternative has yet been found. *(Sir Winston Churchill)*

The family, grounded on marriage freely contracted, monogamous and indissoluble, is and must be considered the first and essential cell of human society. *(Pope John XXIII)*

The family is more sacred than the state, and men are begotten not for the earth and for time, but for heaven and eternity. *(Pope Pius XI)*

People say to us, 'There is this problem of the family. How are we to preserve it? It seems to be dissolving before our eyes.' That has been true perhaps always and everywhere. Everywhere good things have seemed to be going. Yet everywhere they are merely struggling to their new birth. *(Bede Jarrett)*

PROVERBS

None but a mule denies his family. *(Moroccan proverb)*

Pity the home where everyone is the head. *(Jewish proverb)*

There are no praises and no blessings for those who are ashamed of their families. *(Jewish proverb)*

Nobody's family can hang out the sign 'Nothing the matter here.' *(Chinese proverb)*

HUMOUR

The one thing children wear out faster than shoes is parents. *(John Plomp)*

Children are very adept at comprehending modern statistics. When they say, 'Everyone else is allowed to,' it is usually based on a survey of one. *(Paul Sweeney)*

A woman got on a bus with seven children. The conductor asked 'Are these all yours, lady, or is it a picnic?'
'They're all mine,' came the reply, 'and it's no picnic.' *(Anon)*

Dad volunteered to baby-sit one night so Mum could have an evening out. At bedtime he sent the youngsters upstairs to bed and settled down to look at the newspapers. One child kept creeping down the stairs, but Dad kept sending him back. At 9 p.m. the doorbell rang, it was the next-door neighbour, Mrs Smith, asking whether her son was there. The father brusquely replied, 'No!' Just then a little head appeared over the banister and a voice shouted, 'I'm here, Mum, but he won't let me go home!' *(Anon)*

STATEMENTS

The family has received from God its mission to be the first and vital cell of society. It will fulfil this mission if it shows itself to be the domestic sanctuary of the Church through the mutual affection of its members and the common prayer they offer to God, if the whole family is caught up in the liturgical worship of the Church and if it provides active hospitality and promotes justice and other good works for the service of all the brethren in need. *(Second Vatican Council – 'The Laity')*

Thus the Christian family, which springs from marriage as a reflection of the loving covenant uniting Christ with the Church, and as a participation in that covenant, will manifest to all men the Saviour's living presence in the world and the genuine nature of the Church.
(Second Vatican Council – 'The Church Today')

WORD PICTURES

Most people have forgotten nowadays what a home can mean, though some of us have come to realise it as never before. It is a kingdom of its own in the midst of the world, a haven of refuge amid the turmoil of our age, nay more, a sanctuary. It is not founded on the shifting sands of private and public life, but has its peace in God. For it is God who gave it its special meaning and dignity, its nature and privilege, its destiny and worth. It is an ordinance God has established in the world, the place where peace, quietness, joy, love, purity, continence, respect, obedience, tradition, and, to crown them all, happiness may dwell, whatever else may pass away in the world.
(Dietrich Bonhoeffer)

What makes a Christian home
It is a place of love, consideration and understanding.
It is a place where they pray for the homeless.
It is not a place where Father and Mother are always
    away at Church meetings.

It is a place of family fun and enjoyment.
It is a place where children are welcome.

It is a place of welcome and hospitality.
It is not just a home for the family.

It is a place where the stranger can feel at home.
It is a place where God is given thanks for all things.
It is a place where the family can bring their friends.
It is a place where parents pray for their family.

It is a place where children can learn to pray.
It is not just a clean respectable house.
IT IS A HOME.
A place where Jesus himself would feel at ease,
A place where Jesus lives
And callers who come with doubts, fears and sorrows
    will meet him. They will find faith, hope and love,
    company and understanding.
(The Methodist Diary)

Any wise parent knows that real parenthood does not mean doing things for the child; it means enabling the child to do things for himself. One of the great stories of history concerns Edward the First and his son the Black Prince. In battle the prince was sorely pressed. There were courtiers who came to the king to tell him that his son was up against it. 'Is he wounded or unhorsed?' asked the king. When they said 'No', the king replied: 'Then I will send him no help. Let him win his spurs.'

To take the matter on a much more everyday level, it is much easier for a parent, when his child asks help with a school exercise, to do the exercise and then to allow the child to copy out the answer. But by that way the child will make no progress at all. By far the wiser way is to teach and to encourage the child to do it for himself. *(William Barclay)*

In many ways, children suffer more from divorce than their parents do. This is due in part to the fact that most children of divorce have no past experience of being without both parents. The parents can recall their independent lives prior to marriage and know that a life without a spouse is not an experience that is entirely unknown to them.

Debbie Barr writes:

'A child, however, has no such assurance. He can recall no time in his life when he lived without father or mother. In fact, just trying to imagine life apart from a parent may be nearly impossible for him to do. One of his greatest natural fears has always been that of being abandoned and left to fend for himself. When separation and divorce breathe life into that fear, an unprecedented crisis can occur. For some, life will never really be the same again.'

USEFUL TEXTS

The Family,
Responsibilities within:
  Husbands, *Col. 3:19*
  Wives, *Col. 3:18; Prov. 31:11-15*
  Children, *Col. 3:20*
  Fathers, *Col. 3:21*
  Mothers, *Prov. 31:15; 27-28*

See also: A9 Relationships
          B30 Married love
          C5 The institution of marriage

B7

MARY, MOTHER OF GOD

'The shepherds found Mary and Joseph,
and the baby lying in the manger.' *Luke 2:16*

QUOTATIONS

The dignity of virginity began with the Mother of the Lord.
(St Augustine of Hippo)

Though she was the Mother of the Lord, yet she desired to learn
the precepts of the Lord, and she who brought forth God, yet
desired to know God. *(St Ambrose)*

They all were looking for a king
To slay their foes and lift them high;
Thou cam'st, a little baby thing
That made a woman cry.
(George MacDonald)

Upon these two titles, Mary Mother of God, and Mary the
Mother of mankind, the whole practice of the Catholic's
devotion to the Blessed Virgin Mary is built.
(Archbishop Goodier)

I fully grant that devotion towards the blessed Virgin has
increased among Catholics with the progress of centuries; I do
not allow that the doctrine concerning her has undergone a
growth, for I believe that it has been in substance one and the
same from the beginning. *(Cardinal Newman)*

The blessed Virgin, by becoming the Mother of God, received
a kind of infinite dignity because God is infinite; this dignity
therefore is such a reality that a better is not possible, just as
nothing can be better than God. *(St Thomas Aquinas)*

God loved the world so much that he gave his Son Jesus, entrusting him to the Virgin Mary. To prove his Father's love for the world, Jesus became so small, so helpless, that he had to have a mother to look after him.

And at the foot of the cross, too, Mary became our mother. Just before he died, Jesus gave his mother to Saint John and Saint John to his mother. And so, all of us became her children. *(Mother Teresa)*

PROVERB

God could not be everywhere, so He made mothers.
(Jewish proverb)

STATEMENTS

If anyone does not confess that Emmanuel is true God, and that therefore the holy Virgin is Mother of God *(Dei genetricem Theotokon)*, since she bore, after the flesh, the incarnate Word of God, let him be anathema. *(Council of Alexandria)*

At the message of the angel, the Virgin Mary received the Word of God in her heart and in her body, and gave Life to the world. Hence she is acknowledged and honoured as being truly the Mother of God and Mother of the Redeemer. Redeemed in an especially sublime manner by reason of the merits of Her Son, and united to Him by a close and indissoluble tie, she is endowed with the supreme office and dignity of being the Mother of the Son of God.
(Second Vatican Council – 'The Church')

WORD PICTURES

When I arrived in Taizé in 1940, I was welcomed from the very first days by some of the old women of the village with hearts of gold. One of them, Marie Auboeuf, was for me like a mother according to the Gospel.

In those days I was alone. The community did not exist yet. I was preparing its creation and I was offering shelter to people who had to be hidden to avoid the worst. It was wartime in Europe. Marie Auboeuf was poor; she had raised ten children.

Where in her heart did she find the simple intuition that allowed her to understand the vocation I was trying to live out?

That elderly woman told me that one night, many years before I arrived, while she was praying the rosary, the Virgin Mary appeared to her in a vision. The next morning, when she got up, she was cured of a paralysis of the hip that was making it harder and harder for her to walk and to take care of her children.

That appearance of the Virgin took place in Taizé long before I myself had even heard of the name of that village, and yet it still continues to have an effect. *(Bro. Roger of Taizé)*

In Michelangelo's masterpiece of sculpture, the Pietà, the Mother seems far too young to be the Mother of the dead Son. Someone said this to Michelangelo, and he replied, 'You don't know anything. Chaste women retain their fresh looks longer than those who are not chaste. The Madonna was without sin, without even the least unchaste desire, and so she was always young'. *(F. H. Drinkwater)*

The great importunity of Sir Walter Raleigh, court favourite during part of the reign of good Queen Bess, wearied Queen Elizabeth. One day, when he came to ask a fresh favour from her, she turned and said, 'Raleigh, when will you cease to be a beggar?' Immediately came Raleigh's reply, 'When your Majesty ceases to be a benefactress and to grant me favours.' *(Anon)*

See also: A4 Emmanuel – Mary's Child
A40 The equality of women
B4 Mary, handmaid of God
C7 The humanity of Christ
C45 The Divinity of Christ

B8

THE WORD

'In the beginning was the Word, the Word was with God,
and the Word was God. He was with God in the beginning.'
John 1:1

QUOTATIONS

Jesus Christ is the centre of all, and the goal to which all tends.
(Blaise Pascal)

If you have the Word without the Spirit, you dry up. If you have
the Spirit without the Word, you blow up. But if you have both
together you grow up. *(David Smith)*

The divine and creative Word was not uttered once for all, but
it receives perpetual utterance in the radiation of light, in the
movements of the stars, in the development of life, in the reason
and conscience of man. *(William Temple)*

The Word, in a manner indescribable and inconceivable, united
personally to himself flesh animated with a reasonable soul, and
thus became man and was called the Son of man.
(St Bernard of Clairvaux)

The Word of God is not a sounding but a piercing Word, not
pronounceable by the tongue but efficacious in the mind, not
sensible to the ear but fascinating to the affection. His face is
not an object possessing beauty of form but rather it is the
source of all beauty and all form. It is not visible to the bodily
eyes, but rejoices the eyes of the heart. And it is pleasing not
because of the harmony of its colour but by reason of the ardour
of the love it excites. *(St Bernard of Clairvaux)*

For it has been clearly demonstrated that the Word which exists
from the beginning with God, by whom all things were made,

who was also present with the race of men at all times, this Word has in these last times, according to the time appointed by the Father, been united to his own workmanship and has been made passible man. *(St Irenaeus)*

STATEMENT

For God's Word, by whom all things were made, was himself made flesh so that as perfect man he might save all men and sum up all things in himself. The Lord is the goal of human history, the focal point of the longings of history and of civilisation, the centre of the human race, the joy of every heart, and the answer to all its yearnings.
(Second Vatican Council – 'The Church Today')

WORD PICTURES

The five most expressive words are alone, death, faith, love, no. *(Wilfred Frost)*

Cold words freeze people, and hot words scorch them, and bitter words make them bitter, and wrathful words make them wrathful. Kind words also produce their image on men's souls; and a beautiful image it is. They smooth, and quiet, and comfort the hearer. *(Blaise Pascal)*

The Word was made flesh and dwelt amongst us. God, dwelling amongst us. God, dwelling in inaccessible light, steps into the arena of the visible world, and lives visibly among his own creatures. His power and presence, his operations within the world, his 'personality', are no longer just a matter for speculation and guesswork; the door is open, the lights are burning, the fire is glowing in the hearth.

The Word was made flesh, the Word was made visible. And just as God made himself visible in Christ, tangible, clutchable, so his power and presence are made visible and tangible in our own times. In the Church which is the visible community that Christ brought into being two thousand years ago, in its central activity, the Mass, in the bread of life which he gives us to eat, in the living word of the Scriptures, in the signs that we call sacraments, and in each other – temples of the Holy Spirit. Through these we may not know all there is to be known about God; but we know enough. *(John Harriott)*

And so the Word had breath, and wrought
With human hands the creed of creeds
In loveliness of perfect deeds,
More strong than all poetic thought.
(Tennyson: 'In Memoriam')

USEFUL TEXTS

The Word
   John 1:1
   John 1:14

See also: A4 Emmanuel – Mary's Child
          A37 Christ the King
          B4 Mary – Handmaid of God
          C45 The Divinity of Christ

B9

REVELATION

'It was by a revelation that I was given the knowledge
of the mystery.' *Ephesians 3:3*

QUOTATIONS

As prayer is the voice of humanity to God, so revelation is the
voice of God to humanity. *(Cardinal Newman)*

Human salvation demands the divine disclosure of truths
surpassing reason. *(St Thomas Aquinas)*

Truths above reason can be believed on authority alone; where
that is lacking, we have to take hints from the workings of
nature. *(St Thomas Aquinas)*

Every revelation of truth felt with interior savour and spiritual
joy is a secret whispering of God in the ear of a pure soul
(Waker Hilton)

He who shall introduce into public affairs the principles of
primitive Christianity will revolutionise the world.
(Benjamin Franklin)

The Lord Jesus Christ loves to reveal Himself to those who dare
to take the bleak side of the hill with Him. *(Anon)*

A revelation is religious doctrine viewed on its illuminated side;
a mystery is the self-same doctrine viewed on the side
unilluminated. *(Cardinal Newman)*

A Christian cannot live by philosophy. Only the light of
Christian revelation gives the end as well as the means of life. It
is the same for you as for me and the man in the street. If one
has more learning, another has more grace, it is all one.
(Abbot Chapman)

We do not believe that God has added, or ever will add, anything to His revelation in His Son. But we can now see many things in that revelation which could not be seen by those who first received it. Each generation of Christians, and each people to which the Christian Gospel is preached, makes its own contribution to the understanding of the riches of Jesus Christ. *(C. B. Moss)*

God hides nothing. His very work from the beginning is revelation – a casting aside of veil after veil, a showing unto men of truth after truth. On and on from fact divine he advances, until at length in his son Jesus he unveils his very face. *(George MacDonald)*

STATEMENT

Then, after speaking in many places and varied ways through the prophets, God 'last of all in these days has spoken to us by his son' *(Heb. 1:1-2)*. For he sent his Son, the eternal Word, who enlightens all men, so that he might dwell among men and tell them the innermost realities about God *(cf. John 1:1-12)*. Jesus Christ, therefore, the Word made flesh, sent as 'a man to men' speaks the words of God *(John 3:34)*, and completes the work of salvation which his Father gave him to do *(cf. John 5:36, 17:4)*. To see Jesus is to see his Father *(John 14:9)*. For this reason, Jesus perfected revelation by fulfilling it through his whole work of making himself present and manifesting himself: through his words and deeds, his signs and wonders, but especially through his death and glorious resurrection from the dead and final sending of the Spirit of Truth.
(Second Vatican Council – 'Revelation')

WORD PICTURES

Jesus said: 'You test the face of the sky and of the earth: but him who is before your face you have not known, and you do not know how to test this moment.'
(The Gospel according to Thomas)

In Cracow, a rabbi dreamt three times that an angel told him to go to Livovna. 'In front of the palace there, near the bridge,' the angel said, 'you will learn where a treasure is hidden.' The rabbi went to Livovna. When he arrived at the palace, he found a sentinel near the bridge, so he told him the dream. The sentinel replied; 'I, too, have had a dream, The angel told me to go to a rabbi's house in Cracow, where a treasure is buried in front of the fireplace.' Hearing this, the rabbi returned home and dug in front of the fireplace. There he found the treasure. All revelation will show that God is to be found nowhere else but within. *(Paul Frost)*

We must be saved together or we will not be saved at all. That would seem to be the deepest truth about the atonement, a profoundly mysterious truth, not wholly congenial to our mutual self-centredness, but lying as it were somewhere near the base of the whole structure of divine revelation. The Bible is a book about Man and not about individual men, except insofar as they show us Man in his infinite need and Man as the object of God's infinite grace. *(Max Warren)*

USEFUL TEXTS
Revelation:
Through Jesus, *John 15:15*
By the Spirit, *1 Cor. 2:10; Eph. 3:1-6*
Through the prophets, *Deut. 18:18*

See also: A12 Holy Scripture
             B2 The Good News
             B24 Go tell everyone
             C8 God's messengers
             C38 Discerning God's will

B10

BAPTISM

'He will baptise you with the Holy Spirit.'
Mark 1:8

QUOTATIONS

The day when a person is baptised is more important than the day when a person is ordained priest and bishop.
(Raymond E. Brown)

Our adoptive sonship is in its supernatural reality a reflection of the sonship of the Word. God has not communicated to us the whole of his nature but a participation of it.
(R. Garrigou-Lagrange)

Baptise as follows: After first explaining all these points, baptise in the name of the Father and of the Son and of the Holy Spirit, in running water. But if you have no running water, baptise in other water; and if you cannot in cold, then in warm. But if you have neither, pour water on the head three times in the name of the Father and of the Son and of the Holy Spirit.
(Teaching of the Twelve Apostles)

Christians are made, not born. *(St Jerome)*

Happy is our sacrament of water, in that by washing away the sins of our early blindness, we are set free and admitted into eternal life . . . But we, little fishes, after the example of our ICHTHYS *(Jesous Christos Theou Uios Soter: Jesus Christ Son of God Saviour)* are born in water, nor have we safety in any other way than by permanently abiding in water.
(Tertullian) (The Greek word for fish is ichthys)

You have been baptised, but think not that you are straightway a Christian . . . The flesh is touched with salt: what then if the mind remains unsalted? The body is anointed, yet the mind remains unanointed. But if you are buried with Christ within, and already practise walking with Him in newness of life, I acknowledge you as a Christian. *(Erasmus)*

HUMOUR

When a negro was asked whether he believed in baptism, he replied, 'Sure I believe in it, boss, I've seen it done.' *(Anon)*

A Presbyterian and a Baptist minister were discussing baptism. After a beautiful dissertation on the subject by the Baptist minister, the Presbyterian minister asked if the Baptist considered a person baptised if he were immersed in water up to his chin. 'No,' said the Baptist.

'Is he considered baptised if he is immersed up to his nose?' asked the Presbyterian.

Again the Baptist's answer was, 'No.'

'Well, if you immerse him up to his eyebrows, do you consider him baptised?' queried the Presbyterian.

'You don't seem to understand,' said the Baptist. 'He must be immersed completely in water – until his head is covered.'

'That's what I've been trying to tell you all along,' said the Presbyterian, 'it's only a little water on the top of the head that counts.' *(Anon)*

STATEMENT

By the sacrament of baptism, whenever it is properly conferred in the way the Lord determined, and received with the appropriate dispositions of soul, a man becomes truly incorporated into the crucified and glorified Christ and is reborn to a sharing of the divine life, as the apostle says: 'For you were buried together with Him in Baptism, and in Him also rose again through faith in the working of God who raised Him from the dead.' *(Col. 2:12; cf. Rom. 6:4)*

Baptism, therefore, constitutes a sacramental bond of unity linking all who have been reborn by means of it. But baptism, of itself, is only a beginning, a point of departure, for it is wholly directed toward the acquiring of fullness of life in Christ.

Baptism is thus oriented toward a complete profession of faith, a complete incorporation into the system of salvation such as Christ Himself willed it to be, and finally, toward a complete participation in Eucharistic communion.
(Second Vatican Council – 'Ecumenism')

WORD PICTURES

Earth retains all the water ever created – an estimated 326 million cubic miles of it. Water responds to a variety of powerful forces – the heat of the sun, the pull of earth's gravity and the tidal forces of the sun and moon. The result is a natural cycle in which water has been used, purified and re-used for 3,000 million years. *(Anon)*

About 1877 a class of Zulu boys were being prepared for baptism.

Among those who dropped in casually was a middle-aged man, Maqumusela, one of the King's soldiers, who, coming regularly, and staying long, at last asked for baptism with the rest.

But the King's word was that if any of his soldiers became Christians he would have him killed. This was put before Maqumusela, who, having gone away and thought and prayed, returned, and asked still to be baptised by the missionaries .

The King came to hear about it, and just before the baptism sent soldiers to put Maqumusela to death. He asked first for time to pray, and after prayers for himself, the missionaries, the King, the soldiers and Zululand, said to the soldiers who were sitting around, waiting, that he was ready. They were, however, so impressed that they could not perform their duty, but beckoned to another man near, who dispatched the first Zulu martyr. *(Anon)*

When the Roman youth reached manhood, he put on the Toga Virilis, the robe of manhood. The day was one of special ceremonial, a great day for him.

When the Hindu youths of certain castes reached manhood, they put on the Yagnopavitam or sacred cord. The day is one of special ceremonial, a great day for the youth who is invested with the sacred cord.

So the believer at his baptism acknowledges that he has 'put on Christ' – a new robe of righteousness to display to the world, a new cord of holiness that links him with the holiness of his God, a 'Holy Father'. *(Anon)*

A holy man returned to his native village after making the long and arduous pilgrimage to the Ganges. He walked bearing aloft the brass bowl in which he had brought home some of the sacred water. A poor beggar man watching him, knelt and begged a drop of the water that all Hindus consider washes away sins. At first the holy man ignored him, but when he persisted, turned and cursed him. Then said the beggar, 'He has washed his body in the Ganges but his heart is not washed' – and his faith in his ancient religion was broken. *(Anon)*

St Louis of France used to sign his documents not, 'Louis IX, King' but 'Louis of Poissy.' Someone asked him why, and he answered: 'Poissy is the place where I was baptised. I think more of the place where I was baptised than of Rheims Cathedral where I was crowned. It is a greater thing to be a child of God than to be the ruler of a Kingdom: this last I shall lose at death, but the other will be my passport to an everlasting glory.' *(F. H. Drinkwater)*

St Ambrose, in a disquisition on baptism, makes a big point that the newly baptised is about to be received in the very best society. With baptism, one becomes a member of the communion of saints, one of the richest Catholic doctrines, but one which I feel is being increasingly neglected today. This is not at all the mind of the Church, and word 'holidays' serve as a constant reminder how important the Church always thought it to keep in remembrance, for encouragement and edification, the lives of heroic sanctity, and impressive as the company was of which St Ambrose was thinking in the 4th century, it is vastly more numerous now, with striking additions every generation. *(Douglas Woodruff)*

USEFUL TEXTS

Baptism:
Jesus' baptism, *Matt. 3:11; 13-17*
By John the Baptist, *Matt. 3:5-12*
Commanded by Christ, *Matt. 28:19-20*
In the Early Church, *Acts 8:12; 36-38, 9:17-18*

See also: A38 Original Sin
B36 The Family of God
C26 The human condition
C47 The indwelling spirit
C49 Receive the Holy Spirit

B11

VOCATION

'Speak, Lord, your servant is listening.'
1 Samuel 3:10

QUOTATIONS

Only God knows what is one's real work. *(Anton Chekhov)*

When I have learned to do the Father's will, I shall have fully realised my vocation. *Carlo Carretto)*

The vocation of every man and woman is to serve other people. *(Leo Tolstoy)*

The test of a vocation is the love of the drudgery it involves. *(Logan Pearsall Smith)*

Blessed is he who has found his work; let him ask no other blessedness. *(Thomas Carlyle)*

We must not forget that our vocation is so to practise virtue that men are won to it; it is possible to be morally upright repulsively. *(William Temple)*

Do not despise your situation. In it you must act, suffer and conquer. From every point on earth, we are equally near to heaven and the infinite. *(Henri F. Amiel)*

A good vocation is simply a firm and constant will in which the called person has to serve God in the way and in the places to which Almighty God has called him. *(St. Francis de Sales)*

If a person shows a firm and persevering determination to serve God in the manner and place to which His divine majesty calls her, she gives the best proof she can that she has a true vocation. *(St Francis de Sales)*

HUMOUR

This story comes from Rome, but I expect the rest of the world has its variants. Two American Catholic young men encountered a little nun seated alone just outside a bar. Conversation began, and ended thus:

'Well Sister, we're just going along to the bar for a drink. Can we bring you out anything? A coca-cola or something?'

'Well, that's very kind of you. What are you going to drink? I don't care much for coca-cola.'

'We're having a dry Martini.'

'Well, so will I. But bring it to me in a cup and saucer, not a glass.'

Boys to waiter: 'Three large dry Martinis. Put one in a tea-cup, please.'

Waiter: 'Gee, is that little nun STILL sittin' there?'
(Douglas Woodruff)

This is the season when American nuns peregrinate and arrive at the London Hotels. Of two of them I am told this tale, that, sitting in the restaurant-car opposite two young men, the youths thought they would try to shock them. Said one, 'I am going home for my parents' wedding, they think it's about time.' Said the other, 'Mine thought of getting married but they've turned it down for the expense.' Said one of the nuns, 'Would one of you two bastards mind passing the mustard?'
(Douglas Woodruff)

STATEMENT

Yet a man must so respond to God's call that, without consulting flesh and blood (*cf Gal. 1:16*), he can devote himself wholly to the work of the Gospel. This response, however, can be made only when the Holy Spirit gives his inspiration and strength. For he who is sent enters upon the life and mission of him who 'emptied himself, taking the nature of a slave' (*Phil. 2:7*). Therefore, he must be ready to stand by his vocation for a lifetime, and to renounce himself and all those whom he thus far considered as his own, and instead to become 'all things to all men' (*1 Cor. 9:22*). (*Second Vatican Council – 'Missions'*)

WORD PICTURES

When Christ calls a man, he bids him come and die. It may be a death like that of the first disciples who had to leave home and work to follow him, or it may be a death like Luther's, who had to leave the monastery and go out into the world. But it is the same death every time—death in Jesus Christ, the death of the old man at his call. That is why the rich young man was so loath to follow Jesus, for the cost of following was the death of his will. In fact every command of Jesus is a call to die, with all our affections and lusts. But we do not want to die, and therefore Jesus Christ and his call are necessarily our death and our life. *(Dietrich Bonhoeffer, 'The Cost of Discipleship')*

Seven young nuns of the Franciscan Missionaries of Mary, none older than 36, martyred in China in 1900, were beatified by Pius XII in 1946.

This order first sent its Sisters to China in 1886, and in 1899, Mother M. Hermine, aged 33, was sent with a party to start a new orphanage at Taiyuanfu in Shansi province. They quickly won the love of the children and the respect of the townsfolk. But the 'Boxer' society against foreigners was already working havoc in the neighbouring province, and by June 1900, the population of Shansi also were being stirred up to 'destroy the devils from the West and slay all Christians'. The storm came near to Taiyuanfu. Bishop Grassi advised the nuns to flee while there was time, but Mother Hermine said she and her Sisters must remain with the orphans. She begged the Bishop 'not to deprive them of the palm of martyrdom which God in his mercy was reaching down to them from heaven'.

On 28th June, they started out with their orphans to reach a safer place, but at the gates of the town they were turned back. There was nothing to do but wait for the arrival of the Boxer troops. Two Bishops and three other Franciscans waited also. The Sisters remained quiet and calm. Soldiers came and took away the orphans by force. Then on 9th July, the Boxers, led by the Governor Yu-Hsien, broke into the building. Bishop Grassi at once pronounced the final absolution. Yu-Hsien gave orders for the Catholics to be bound, and bundled them roughly out

into the yard, where, without even the pretence of a trial, the butchery began. First of all, the nuns had to witness the brutal murder of the Bishops and friars, then came their own turn. With the words of the *Te Deum* on their lips, the sisters knelt and raised their veils, baring their necks to receive the blow from the sword which cut off their heads. One after another, these holy women gladly laid down their lives for Christ.
(M. R. Walsh)

I asked God for strength that I might achieve;
I was made weak that I might learn humbly to obey.

I asked for help that I might do greater things;
I was given infirmity that I might do better things.

I asked for riches that I might be happy;
I was given poverty that I might be wise.

I asked for all things that I might enjoy life;
I was given life that I might enjoy all things.

I was given nothing that I asked for;
But everything that I had hoped for.

Despite myself, my prayers were answered;
I am among all men most richly blessed.
(Anon)

USEFUL TEXTS

Vocation:
 Worthy of, *Eph. 4:1*
 From God, *Rom. 8:30; 11:29*
 Obedience to one's, *1 Cor. 7:17-24*

See also: A10 Seeking perfection
    A22 Seeking God
    C16 Come follow me
    C38 Discerning God's will

B12

ON A MISSION

'The time has come,' Jesus said, 'and the kingdom of God is close at hand. Repent, and believe the Good News.'
Mark 1:15

QUOTATIONS

Mission is the Church in love with the whole world.
(Charles Slattery)

The Spirit of Christ is the spirit of missions, and the nearer we get to him the more intensely missionary we must become.
(Henry Martyn)

The Church exists by mission, as fire exists by burning.
(Emil Brunner)

The world has many religions; it has but one Gospel.
(George Owen)

The fact of the missions reveals the Church's faith in herself as the Catholic unity of mankind. *(J. C. Murray)*

The reason some folks don't believe in mission is the brand of religion they have isn't worth propagating. *(Anon)*

If God calls you to be missionary, don't stoop to be a king.
(Jordan Grooms)

Your love has a broken wing if it cannot fly across the sea.
(Maltble D. Babcock)

If people ask 'Why did he not appear by means of other parts of creation, and use some nobler instrument, as the sun or moon or stars or fire or air, instead of man merely?', let them know that the Lord came not to make a display, but to teach and heal those who were suffering. *(Athanasius of Alexandria)*

HUMOUR

A young Canadian mission worker said that he was always looking for guidance from the Lord and he had come to South America because when he was considering his vocation he had suddenly seen a chocolate bar with a Brazil nut. 'What would you have done if it had been a Mars bar?' asked his sceptical friend. *(Anon)*

STATEMENTS

The members of the Church are impelled to carry on such missionary activity by reason of the love with which they love God and by which they desire to share with all men in the spiritual goods of both this life and the life to come.
(Second Vatican Council – 'Missions')

Missionary activity is nothing else and nothing less than a manifestation or epiphany of God's will and the fulfilment of that will in the world and in world history. *(Second Vatican Council – 'Missions')*

WORD PICTURES

One cannot be Christian in name alone. It is not enough to say that one possesses the faith in one's own individual conscience. The faith is both a communal and outgoing thing. Consequently, it carries with it the obligation of involving oneself with it and of spreading it. You yourselves must be apostles of the faith, and grow in love for the Church. You must foster within yourselves a deep missionary spirit, showing interest and zeal not only for the missionary countries but also for all those people you meet in the contacts of daily life.
(Pope Paul VI)

Fr Nussbaum was martyred in Tibet in 1941. He was a tough little blue-eyed Alsatian, 50-years-old, with a blond beard; always gentle and good humoured, he lived in Tibetan-fashion at a post in Chinese Tibet. After years of efforts, he got some Swiss priests from the St Bernard Pass to start a mountain hospice at the Latsa Pass (1935). Leaving his mission to the Swiss, Fr Nussbaum moved on into Tibet proper (a forbidden land) to start a mission again at Yerkalo. (Over the years many priests had tried to set up a mission there but all had died martyrs' deaths.)

Fr Nussbaum duly established himself in the village of Yerkalo, with one of the Swiss priests, and in three years, they had baptised 350 Tibetans. They then earned the enmity of the chief Lama of the nearby monastery of Karmda. He sent messages to the Dalai Lama demanding expulsion of all Western priests, but got no reply. Meanwhile the Second World War broke out, and the Lama of Karmda took counsel with a local bandit-leader.

In September 1941, Fr Nussbaum went to Mission headquarters at Tse-chung for a retreat. Returning to Yerkalo, with his bearer and three Tibetan girl-catechists whom he had recruited, he was warned of an ambush and camped in the village of Napu, where no house would give them shelter.

During the night, bandits attacked, but were bought off with some money and blankets and all the caravan's tea. Next day, they moved on to the mission-house at Pame. There another night attack took place and the priest and his party were all bound while they watched the looting of the mission. Then they were dragged along a rocky path (Fr Nussbaum with bare and bleeding feet) and at the edge of a ravine the priest was shot in the back. The other prisoners were then allowed to go. A group of Christians from Pame came and recovered the body.
(Henri Daniel-Rops)

Azariah was tall and very dark, quick in movement and speech, with the knack of stirring up enthusiasm by his swift passionate words. A phrase that was constantly on his lips was 'Every Christian a witness'. It was absolutely necessary, he said, that every convert should at once bear witness. He drove this home at Madras in his own vivid way. 'It was,' he said, 'by the witness of the common man that the Gospel spread in the early church,

from slave to slave, from soldier to soldier, from artisan to artisan: and as I have gone around among the churches, I have had the baptised members place their hands on their heads and repeat after me, "I am a baptised Christian. Woe is me if I preach not the Gospel".'
(A. M. Chirgwin – 'These I have Known')

USEFUL TEXTS

Mission:
Of Christ;
    to do God's will, *John 6:38*
    to save the lost, *Luke 19:10*
    to reveal God, *Heb. 1:1-3*
    to fulfil the law, *Matt. 5:17*
Of all Christians;
    to make disciples, *Matt. 28; 16-20*

See also: B2 The Good News
           B24 Go tell everyone
           C12 The Church for all men
           C16 Come follow me

B13

AUTHORITY

'Here is a teaching that is new,' they said, 'and with authority behind it.' *(Mark 1:27)*

QUOTATIONS
He who is firmly seated in authority soon learns to think security and not progress. *(J. R. Lowell)*

If you accept the authority of Jesus in your life, then you accept the authority of his words. *(Colin Urquhart)*

The man who cannot control himself becomes absurd when he wants to rule over others. *(Isaac Arama)*

It is right to submit to higher authority whenever a command of God would not be violated. *(St Basil)*

The highest duty is to respect authority, and obediently to submit to just law. *(Pope Leo XIII)*

Authority without wisdom is like a heavy axe without an edge, fitter to bruise than polish. *(Anne Bradstreet)*

There are three theories of power and therefore of authority, to wit: the robber theory that all power is for mastery; the hireling theory that all power is for wealth; the good shepherd theory that all power is for service. *(Vincent McNabb)*

No authority has power to impose error, and if it resists the truth, the truth must be upheld until it is admitted. *(Lord Acton)*

Authority is not a short way to the truth; it is the only way to many truths; and for men on earth, it is the only way to divine truths. *(Vincent McNabb)*

Next to power without honour, the most dangerous thing in the world is power without humour. *(Eric Sevareid)*

STATEMENTS

Now, if the political community is not to be torn to pieces as each man follows his own viewpoint, authority is needed. This authority must dispose the energies of the whole citizenry toward the common good, not mechanically or despotically, but primarily as a moral force which depends on freedom and the conscientious discharge of the burdens of any office which has been undertaken.
(Second Vatican Council – 'The Church Today')

Therefore, this Vatican Synod urges everyone, especially those who are charged with the task of educating others, to do their utmost to form men who will respect the moral order and be obedient to lawful authority. Let them form men who will be lovers of true freedom – men, in other words, who will come to decisions on their own judgement and in the light of truth, govern their activities with a sense of responsibility, and strive after what is true and right, willing always to join with others in co-operative effort.
(Second Vatican Council – 'Religious Freedom')

WORD PICTURES

One of the most solemn facts in all history – one of the most significant for anybody who cares to ponder over it – is the fact that Jesus Christ was not merely murdered by hooligans in a country road; he was condemned by everything that was most respectable in that day, everything that pretended to be most righteous – the religious leaders of the time, the authority of the Roman Government, and even the democracy itself which shouted to save Barabbas rather than Christ.
(Herbert Butterfield, 'History and Human Relations')

The Church does not exist in a social vacuum. If attitudes towards authority have changed, the Church must take account of them. If tensions exist between parents and children, teachers and pupils, management and workers, politicians and electorate, they will also exist between Church leaders and people. It would require impossible psychological acrobatics for people to practise uncritical obedience in one area of life which they practise in no other, or to judge Church authorities by a different set of standards from those by which they judge others, even if they initially feel a greater willingness to indulge apparent failings among bishops and priests.

If people are suspicious of all authorities they will not exempt the Church authorities. If they demand honesty, justice, truthfulness, openness of secular authorities, they will demand them still more of Church authorities. And if the Church claims, as it rightly does, that its origins, message and principle of life are divine, this claim which goes beyond human understanding will be judged against those actual human operations which are well within human understanding. Such divine inspiration does not mean Church leaders can arrive at truth and justice at a bound. They too must pursue truth and administer justice by the same arduous processes as other men. *(John Harriott)*

A Government surveyor one day brought his theodolite along to a farm, called on the farmer and asked permission to set it up in a field nearby to take readings. Seeing the farmer's unwillingness to let him enter the field, he produced his papers and explained that he had Government authority for entering the field and could, on the same authority, go anywhere in the country to take necessary readings. Reluctantly the farmer opened the barred gate and allowed him to enter and set up his survey table, but went to the other end of the field and let in the fiercest of his bulls. The surveyor was greatly alarmed at seeing the bull approach, and the farmer from the other side of the gate shouted to him, 'Show him your credentials: show him your authority.' The surveyor had the authority to enter but had not the power to resist the bull. *(Anon)*

USEFUL TEXTS

Authority:
  Jesus taught with, *Matt. 7:29*
  To forgive sin, *Matt. 9:6*
  To cast out evil spirits, *Mark 3:15*
  None except from God, *Rom. 13:1*
  Submit to, *Titus 3:1*

See also: A14 The successors of the Apostles
       A24 Papacy
       A29 True obedience
       A32 Civic duty
       B14 Freedom to serve

B14
FREEDOM TO SERVE

'I made myself all things to all men in order to save some at any cost' *1 Corinthians 9:22*

QUOTATIONS

The moment we understand that we are no more than instruments of God is a beautiful one.
(Archbishop Oscar Romero)

Freedom is that faculty which enlarges the usefulness of all other faculties. *(Immanuel Kant)*

Freedom is not worth having if it does not include the freedom to make mistakes. *(Gandhi)*

There are two freedoms – the false, where a man is free to do what he likes; the true, where a man is free to do what he ought. *(Charles Kingsley)*

If you wish to be a leader you will be frustrated, for very few people wish to be led. If you aim to be a servant you will never be frustrated. *(Frank F. Warren)*

Freedom's just another word for nothing left to lose. *(Kris Kristofferson)*

I cannot and will not give any undertaking at a time when I, and you, the people, are not free. Your freedom and mine cannot be separated. *(Nelson Mandela)*

No freedom is so great as that of the children of God who are fast bound by the perfect law of love and liberty. *(R. H. Benson)*

A Christian man is the most free lord of all, and subject to none; a Christian man is the most dutiful servant of all, and subject to everyone. *(Martin Luther)*

He who does not enjoy solitude will not love freedom. *(Arthur Schopenhauer)*

True liberty is liberty to do what we ought to do. It is not liberty to do as we like. *(Field-Marshal Lord Montgomery)*

God forces no one, for love cannot compel, and God's service, therefore, is a thing of perfect freedom. *(Hans Denk)*

PROVERBS

Better to be a free bird than a captive king. *(Danish proverb)*

No bad man is free. *(Greek proverb)*

No man is free who is not master of himself. *(Greek proverb)*

HUMOUR

It is by the goodness of God that in our country we have those three unspeakably precious things: freedom of speech, freedom of conscience and the prudence never to practise either of them. *(Mark Twain)*

We are not free; it was not intended we should be. A book of rules is placed in our cradle and we never get rid of it until we reach our graves. Then we are free and only then. *(E. W. Howe)*

STATEMENT

For its part, authentic freedom is an exceptional sign of the divine image within man. For God has willed that man be left 'in the hand of his own counsel' so that he can seek his Creator spontaneously, and come freely to utter and blissful perfection through loyalty to him. Hence man's dignity demands that he act according to a knowing and free choice. Such a choice is personally motivated and prompted from within. It does not result from blind internal impulse nor from mere external pressure. *(Second Vatican Council – 'The Church Today')*

WORD PICTURES

In 1961 a lawyer, Peter Benenson, was disturbed at the case of two overseas students jailed for seven years for drinking a toast to freedom in a cafe. He wrote an article in a newspaper to publicise the plight of people detained for peacefully expressing their beliefs. Within a week, 1,000 people offered support. This was the birth of Amnesty International. In 1977 Amnesty won the Nobel Peace Prize.

Our Urgent Action campaigns are one of our most successful ways of fighting injustice. When we hear of a prisoner needing aid, we set out to get the facts. We rely on meticulous research. When the facts are verified, our supporters write to authorities overseas to plead the prisoner's case. Last year we ran appeals for 2,000 detainees in 80 countries.

How effective are they? In two out of five cases, the victim's condition improves . . . torture stops . . . the prisoner sees a doctor or lawyer or is taken from solitary confinement. *(M. Staunton)*

The largest category of slaves today are children grossly exploited at work, and those living on the streets. Most of the latter are found in Latin America where Brazil alone has 36 million. Some of these are the *aviaozinhos*, or 'little aeroplanes' who run between the drug dealers and their customers.

But the saddest children are probably those who are sold into exploitation. Children like 11-year-old Binlah whose story was told in January in the *Sunday People Magazine*, after the Anti-Slavery Society had put reporters on the track. Binlah, like most of the 2 million or perhaps even 5 million child slaves exploited in Thailand, comes from the desperately poor north-east, from Korat, a village, 300 miles from Bangkok. Her father had parted with her for £85 offered by a recruiting agent from the capital. Binlah was willing to go to the promised restaurant job, and £85 is not only a year's wage, it is the difference between eating plain rice and rice with a little fish in it.

As is usually the case, Binlah did not go to her promised job. She was sold on by a staff agency to an ice-cream factory. There, for five months, until her screams alerted neighbours which led to her release, she was brutally beaten and semi-starved, her one meal a day consisting of rice and a steamed egg. She had to eat and sleep where she worked among the ice-making machines. Because she was given no gloves to protect her from the ice, her fingers were badly swollen and blistered .

Binlah received nothing out of her (roughly) £2 a week wages. And she still had to pay back the money – advanced to her father together with interest, of course. She told her rescuers:

'I started work at 5 am and finished around midnight every day. The man used to hit me all the time to make me work faster I was so tired. I cried a lot because I wanted to go home.'

Binlah is one of the lucky ones. Many children in Thailand are worn out at 16 and have only the slums built around Bangkok's rubbish mountains to live in. There they fall prey to drugs, alcoholism and very cheap prostitution. Their life is brutal and short. *(Anti-Slavery Association)*

Believe me, if you have been shut up for a year and a half, it can get too much for you some days. In spite of all justice and thankfulness, you can't crush your feelings. Cycling, dancing, whistling, looking out into the world, feeling young, to know that I'm free – that's what I long for; still, I mustn't show it, because I sometimes think if all eight of us began to pity ourselves, or went about with discontented faces, where would it lead us? *(Anne Frank)*

Incredible as it is, 2370 years after Socrates drank hemlock, 1970 years after the crucifixion of Christ, 435 years after Thomas More was beheaded and 370 years after Giordano Bruno was burnt at the stake, thousands of men and women waste away their days in prison for their opinions. But opinions should be free, and if he is behind bars it is not he but those who keep him there that are dishonoured.
(Salvador de Madariaga)

There is room in the world for loving;
there is no room for hate.
There is room in the world for sharing;
there is no room for greed.

There is room for justice;
no room for privilege.
There is room for compassion;
no room for pride.

The world is ample enough for the needs of all;
too small for the greed of a few.
Let us learn that we depend on each other;
that the eye cannot say to the hand
'I need you not'.

Let us be delicate with persons.
Let us touch the earth lightly with hands like petals.
Let us speak softly and carry no stick.
Let us open the clenched fist and extend the open palm.
Let us mourn till others are comforted,
    weep till others laugh.

Let us be sleepless till all can sleep untroubled.
Let us be meek till all stand up in pride.
Let us be frugal till all are filled.
Let us give till all have received.
Let us make no claims till all have had their due.
Let us be slaves till all are free.
Let us lay down our lives
    till others have life abundantly.
Let us be restless for others, serene within ourselves.
Let us be as gods.
(John Harriott)

USEFUL TEXTS

Ministry:
> Example of Christ, *Mark 10:45*
> As servanthood, *Matt. 20:22-27*
> Of God's messengers, *1 Cor. 3:5*
> Of angels, *Ps. 103:20*

See also: B34 Human rights
     B45 Free will
     C1 Liberation from fear

B15

JESUS, FRIEND OF OUTCASTS

A leper came to Jesus and pleaded on his knees;
'If you want to' he said, 'you can cure me.' *Mark 1:40*

QUOTATIONS

God says to man 'With thy very wounds I will heal thee'
(The Talmud)

The poor are our brothers and sisters . . . people in the world
who need love who need care who have to be wanted.
(Mother Teresa)

If Jesus Christ is not true God, how could he *help* us?
If he is not true man, how could he help *us*?
(Dietrich Bonhoeffer)

If Jesus had been indicted in a modern court, he would have
been examined by two doctors, found to be obsessed by a
delusion, declared to be incapable of pleading, and sent to an
asylum . . . *(George Bernard Shaw)*

PROVERBS

A poor man is hungry after eating. *(Portuguese proverb)*

Not he who has little, but he who wishes for more, is poor.
(Latin proverb)

Many can bear adversity, but few contempt. *(English proverb)*

STATEMENT

The greatest commandment in the law is to love God with one's
whole heart and one's neighbour as oneself *(cf Matt. 22:37-40)*
Christ made this commandment of love of neighbour his own
and enriched it with a new meaning. For he wanted to identify

himself with his brethren as the object of this love when he said, 'As long as you did it for one of these, the least of my brethren, you did it for me' *(Matt. 25:40)*.
(Second Vatican Council – 'The Laity')

WORD PICTURES

Chad Varah was an Anglican priest. In 1953, he buried a girl of 18 who had killed herself. The coroner, at her inquest, suggested that she might not have done this desperate act if someone had been around who would have listened to her troubles. Chad Varah decided to use his London church and a telephone to listen to people who were in despair. He put a small advertisement in the local paper, and during the first week he had 27 calls.

Soon he was listening and advising people 12 hours each day. There were so many people waiting in his outer office to see him that he asked some of his congregation to come and provide cups of tea for them. Then he found that often people who had come into the outer office in great distress had become different people by the time they reached him, and some did not even wait to see him because one of the helpers had befriended them. So he decided to train a group of his congregation so that they could be more helpful in the way they befriended the clients.

That is how the Samaritans were formed. *(Patricia Curley)*

When I first went to teach in South East London, I learnt that within the boundaries of the parish where I lived, a short walk from the parish church, was a huge GLC (as it was then) Reception Centre for down and outs. It had a capacity of 800 beds; and provided little else, the men having to be out and about during the day. Its proximity to the church guaranteed a regular stream of visitors to the kitchen door!

The parish repository, with the usual assortment of statues and rosary beads, was situated in the run-down hall next to the church. The following story appeared in the parish magazine at the time and was written by Fr Paul Frost, the young assistant priest in the parish:

'One morning I was quite alone sweeping the hall floor when I noticed in the display case (an old glass-panelled bookcase) some small wooden crosses, measuring about 5in x 3in lying on the bottom shelf, "Now that's something I've never done," I thought to myself, "I've never carried a crucifix in my pocket." It suddenly felt so important that I put the broom down and went across the house for the cupboard key and some money. I felt impelled to get one *now*. When my chore in the hall was completed I placed the crucifix in my inside coat pocket and thought no more about it.

About three hours later, just after lunch, a call came through from the Reception Centre asking if a priest could come immediately as one of the gentlemen of the road, known to them as Paddy, was very seriously ill. Equipped with the Holy Oils I went as quickly as I could to the Centre. I had never been inside before and I was struck by the stark, white-washed, simplicity of the place. There was no one much about, except for the warden (or supervisor), who took me through a large hall into a side room where there were four beds.

Lying on the first one, just inside the door on the right-hand side, was the sad figure of Paddy. He lay on his back, covered by a single blanket, his face was ashen and his eyes were closed.

"He's not long with us," remarked the warden, adding, as he turned to leave, "the ambulance is on its way." There was no bed-side locker, no chair to sit on and no sign of any possessions. I knelt on the floor, close to his head, and bending close to his ear asked if he could hear me. There was no response, so I took hold of the rough-skinned hand that lay along the top of the blanket and said, "If you can hear me squeeze my hand." I was pleased and relieved when there was a very definite tightening and loosening of the hand in reply.

"It's the priest, Paddy", I said, "Would you like me to anoint you with the holy oils? Squeeze my hands if you want to". There was another squeeze. After the anointing and the prayers spoken into his ear, the warden appeared in the doorway with the words, "the ambulance is here". I desperately wanted to do something more, then I remembered the crucifix in my pocket. I held it to Paddy's lips and told him what it was. The hand tightened and loosed. I told him I was giving it to him as a little present to take to hospital with him. The hand squeezed and seemed momentarily longer than before.

I pressed the crucifix to his lips again and told him it would be in his left hand, the one that I had been holding. He understood. The ambulance men were hovering behind me. I laid his left hand, holding the crucifix across his chest. As they lifted him off the bed I was suddenly struck by the utter desolation of the scene. Paddy had nothing and no one. It was Calvary all over again. He was going naked out of the world with nothing but the crucifix in his hand.

As I walked meditatively back to the presbytery I felt quite upset and immediately rang a neighbouring parish to speak to the curate who was the hospital chaplain. Fortunately I just caught him as he was leaving to visit the hospital. He said he would look out for Paddy. Later that evening he rang back to tell me that Paddy had died in the ambulance on the way to the hospital.' *(Contact Magazine)*

It had been such a thought-provoking experience for the priest concerned. He told me it made him realise how wonderfully God works. He had never carried a crucifix before and as far as I know he has never felt the need to since. Paddy had left the world grasping his only possession, he had nothing but Jesus, and him crucified. And what more was necessary? To have only Jesus was to have everything. The Kingship of Christ asks us to be stripped of the world and to have nothing that is more important to us than Jesus. The great St Bernard of Clairvaux's favourite saying was 'To prefer nothing to the love of Jesus' *(Luke 14:26), (A. P. Castle)*.

They borrowed a bed to lay His head
    When Christ the Lord came down;
They borrowed an ass in the mountain pass
    For Him to ride to town;
But the crown He wore and the cross He bore
    Were His own –
    The cross was His own *(Anon)*

Useful texts

Jesus and outcasts:
  Friend of, *Luke 7:34*
  Welcomes, *Luke 15:1-2*
  Came to invite, *Luke 5:32*
  Saviour, *Acts 2:36-38*

See also: A21 Feeding the hungry
           A33 Love your neighbour
           B38 The Suffering Servant
           C3 Sharing possessions

B16

CHRIST HEALS AND FORGIVES

Jesus said to the paralytic, 'my child, your sins are forgiven.'
Mark 2:5

QUOTATIONS

Nothing in this lost world bears the impress of the Son of God so surely as forgiveness. *(Alice Cary)*

I can forget my earlier sins and failings: they rest in the bosom of God's mercy. What is important is that I should put my present life in order. *(Cardinal Augustin Bea, S. J.)*

Forgiveness is the answer to the child's dream of a miracle by which what is broken is made whole again, what is soiled is again made clean. *(Dag Hammarskjöld)*

When, through my tears, I began to tell him (Jesus) something of the years during which I betrayed him, he lovingly placed his hand over my mouth in order to silence me. His concern was that I should muster enough courage to pick myself up again to try to carry on walking, in spite of my weakness, and to believe in his love in spite of my fears. *(Carlo Carretto)*

To be persons, in the Christian sense, means that we must bear one another's burdens. We must be prepared to suffer pain for one another and to carry each other in love through times of darkness and dread. We must take on what we can of each other's violence and woundedness without allowing ourselves the relief of retaliation. Only if we are prepared to do this do we enter the privilege of the Gospel, which is to heal each other and find our healing in and through each other. *(Angela Tilby)*

PROVERBS

He who has health has hope; and he who has hope has everything. *(Arab proverb)*

The offender never forgives. *(Russian proverb)*

STATEMENT

God, who 'wishes all men to be saved and come to the knowledge of the truth' *(1 Tim. 2:4)*, 'in many and various ways . . . spoke of old to our fathers by the prophets' *(Heb. 1:1)*. When the fullness of time had come he sent his Son, the Word made flesh, anointed by the Holy Spirit, to preach the gospel to the poor, to heal the contrite of heart *(cf. Isa. 61:1; Luke 4:18)*, to be a 'bodily and spiritual medicine', the Mediator between God and man *(cf 1 Tim. 2:5)*. *(Second Vatican Council – 'Liturgy')*

WORD PICTURES

A Christian doctor in Scotland was very lenient with his poor patients, and when he found that it was difficult for them to pay his fees he wrote in red ink across the record of their indebtedness the one word – 'Forgiven'. This was of such frequent occurrence that his case book had few pages where the red letters did not appear. After his death, his executors thought the doctor's estate would be greatly benefited if some of the 'Forgiven' debts could be collected. After unsuccessful applications to the poor patients, the executors took legal proceedings to recover the amounts. But when the judge examined the case book and saw the word 'Forgiven' cancelling the entry, he said, 'There is no tribunal in the land that could enforce payment of these accounts marked "Forgiven,"' and he dismissed the case. *(Indian Christian)*

During October 1806, John Newton entered his pulpit to preach for the last time. The occasion was a special service to raise money for the sufferers from the battle of Trafalgar. A friend of the First Lord of the Admiralty, and an old sailor himself, he was exerting his last strength on behalf of the victims of war. But as he addressed the crowded congregation, his mind wandered away. Perhaps it was to the day when he had been taken by the Press Gang, or to the time he had himself seen action as a midshipman, or to the disgrace and agony of the flogging for desertion, or even to his voyages as a slave captain. Wherever his mind went, he clean forgot what he was doing and somebody had to go into the pulpit to remind him.

He lived for another year, and a few weeks before the end, said to a friend, 'My memory is nearly gone; but I remember two things, that I am a great sinner and that Christ is a great Saviour'. He died on 21st December 1807, and his epitaph written by his own hand is 'John Newton (Clerk), Once an infidel and libertine, A servant of slaves in Africa: Was by the rich mercy of our Lord and Saviour Jesus Christ, Preserved, restored, pardoned, And appointed to preach the faith he had long laboured to destroy.' *(Anon)*

USEFUL TEXTS

Forgiveness of sin:
Forgiveness, *Exod. 34:7; Matt. 26:28*
Consequences of, *Exod. 20:5; Prov. 14:11; Rom. 5:12*
Confession of sin, *Neh. 1:6; James 5:16; 1 John 1:9*

See also: A15 Sin
A26 Sacrament of Penance
A27 As we forgive those
C14 Forgiveness
C27 The Father who receives us back
C40 Reconciliation

B17

THE CHURCH – BRIDE OF CHRIST

'I will betroth you to myself for ever, betroth you with
integrity and justice, with tenderness and love.'
Hosea 2:21

QUOTATIONS

The Church is in Christ as Eve was in Adam. *(Richard Hooker)*

Beware when you take on the Church of God.
Others have tried and have bitten the dust.
(Archbishop Desmond Tutu)

What matters in the Church is not religion but the form of
Christ, and its taking form amidst a band of men.
(Dietrich Bonhoeffer)

The Church of Christ is not an institution; it is a new life with
Christ and in Christ, guided by the Holy Spirit.
(Sergius Belgakov)

This Church, imitating His (i.e. Christ's) Mother, daily gives
birth to His members, and likewise remains a virgin.
(St Augustine of Hippo)

I have laboured with all my might that holy Church, the bride
of God, our mistress and our mother, should recover her
honour and remain chaste, and free and Catholic.
(Pope St Gregory VII)

The *name* itself shows how much the Church would be
committed, is committed, to the cause of its Lord . . . Its source
was the Byzantine popular form *Kyrike* and thus means
'belonging to the Lord' or, in a wider sense, 'house of the Lord.'
(Hans Küng)

The Church, like blessed Mary ever Virgin, both espoused and immaculate, conceives us as a virgin by the Spirit, bears us as a virgin without pain, and both espoused as it were to one, but made fruitful by another, through the single parts which compose the one Catholic Church is joined visibly to the pontiff set over it, but is increased through the visible power of the Holy Spirit. *(St Bede the Venerable)*

How I would like to engrave this great idea on each one's heart: Christianity is not a collection of truths to be believed, of laws to be obeyed, of prohibitions. That makes it very distasteful. Christianity is a person, one who loved us so much, one who calls for our love. Christianity is Christ. *(Archbishop Oscar Romero)*

HUMOUR

A child on the way home from school decided to call in the church to have a look around. When he arrived home he told his grandmother he had been to God's house

'Oh,' said grandma, did you see God?'

'No' replied the little boy, 'but I did see his wife scrubbing the floor.' *(Anon)*

STATEMENT

Having become the model of a man loving his wife as his own body, Christ loves the Church as His Bride *(cf Eph. 5:25-28)*. For her part, the Church is subject to her Head *(cf Eph. 5:22-23)*. 'For in him dwells all the fullness of the Godhead bodily' *(Col. 2:9)*. He fills the Church, which is His Body and His fullness, with His divine gifts *(cf Eph. 1:22-23)* so that she may grow and reach the fullness of God *(cf Eph. 3:19)*.
(Second Vatican Council – 'The Church')

WORD PICTURES

'I cannot get used to being called a Person of God,' said the layman, 'when I was brought up to think of myself as a sheep; and I quite understand why I was a sheep for my pastors to count, because counting sheep is the best way to enable our pastors to go to sleep.' *(Douglas Woodruff)*

When I found myself singing – a courtesy term in my case – with my fellow parishioners the rousing hymn that assures us that 'The Church's one foundation is Jesus Christ Our Lord', the memory came back to me of the very different circumstances in which I had first learnt it among the Evangelicals of the Church of England. I recalled how lustily my Protestant uncles and aunts sang it, as one in the eye for the Pope, for it was written against the Roman claim 'Thou art Peter and upon this Rock I will build my Church'. The one foundation, says the hymn, is elsewhere. Still, this is not said in so many words, and there is nothing in the words which Catholics cannot sing with full conviction.

Anglicans, for their part, have never hesitated about 'Lead, Kindly Light' either, though they do not like the scene to which the 'Kindly Light' eventually led the author of the Hymn which was, when he wrote it, the very much distant scene he did not ask to see, and would have shuddered at, had he glimpsed it. *(Douglas Woodruff)*

USEFUL TEXTS

Church:
 Loved by Christ, *Eph. 1:22*
 Persecuted by Paul, *Gal 1:13*
 Gifts of, *I Cor. 12:27-30*
 Bride, *2 Cor. 11:2; Eph. 5:31-32*

See also: A13 The Church is for sinners
 B36 The Family of God
 C12 The Church for all men

B18

SUNDAY

'The Sabbath was made for man, not man for the Sabbath; so the Son of Man is master even of the Sabbath.' *Mark 2:27*

QUOTATIONS

Everything has its weekday side and its Sunday side.
(G. C. Lichtenberg)

The Sabbath is the golden clasp that binds together the volume of the week. *(Macaulay)*

Going to church doesn't make you a Christian any more than going to a garage makes you an automobile. *(Billy Sunday)*

Better a man ne'er be born.
Than he trims his nails on a Sunday morn.
(Warwickshire: Traditional)

God ended all the world's array,
And rested on the seventh day:
His holy voice proclaimed it blest,
And named it for the sabbath rest.
(St Bede the Venerable)

The Lord's Day is so called, because on that day, the joy of our Lord's resurrection is celebrated. This day the Jews did not observe, but it was declared by the Christians in honour of the Lord's resurrection, and the celebration began from that time. *(St Isidore)*

A world without a Sabbath would be like a man without a smile, like a summer without flowers and like a homestead without a garden. It is the joyous day of the whole week.
(Henry Ward Beecher)

Sunday, indeed, is the day on which we hold our common assembly because it is the first day on which God, transforming the darkness and matter, created the world; and our Saviour, Jesus Christ, arose from the dead on the same day. For they crucified Him on the day before, that of Saturn, and on the day after, Sunday, He appeared to His apostles and disciples, and taught them the things which we have passed on to you also for consideration. *(St Justin Martyr)*

HUMOUR

A small boy, on his way to church for the first time, was being briefed by his elder sister. 'They won't allow you to talk,' she warned him. 'Who won't?' asked the boy. 'The Hushers.'
(Sign, London)

A child – one of the many who get taken to church these days much too young, partly with the idea of accustoming them to church as a normal part of life, but often because there is nobody to leave them with – was bored and restless, kept looking at the sanctuary lamp, and finally whispered: 'When the red light changes to green, can we go?' *(Douglas Woodruff)*

During the Second World War, for basic training, the men were divided according to their religious denominations and expected to attend service at the Anglican, Roman Catholic or Jewish places of worship, as the case might be. One of the men in an attempt to evade attendance proclaimed himself an atheist.

'Don't you believe in God?' asked the officer.

'No,' said he.

'Nor in keeping the Sabbath Day holy?'

'No, one day is as good as another to me.'

'Then', said the officer, 'you are just the man we have been looking for. You will stay and clean out the latrines!' *(Anon)*

STATEMENT

By an apostolic tradition which took its origin from the very day of Christ's resurrection, the Church celebrates the paschal

mystery every eighth day; with good reason, this, then, bears the name of the Lord's day or the day of the Lord. For on this day Christ's faithful should come together into one place so that, by hearing the word of God and taking part in the Eucharist, they may call to mind the passion, the resurrection and the glorification of the Lord Jesus, and may thank God who 'has begotten us again, through the resurrection of Jesus Christ from the dead, unto a living hope' *(1 Pet. 1:3)*. Hence the Lord's day is the original feast day, and it should be proposed to the piety of the faithful and taught to them in such a way that it may become in fact a day of joy and of freedom from work. Other celebrations, unless they be truly of overriding importance, must not have precedence over this day, which is the foundation and nucleus of the whole liturgical year.
(Second Vatican Council – 'The Liturgy')

WORD PICTURES

Even in the slave-camps of Russia under Stalin, Sunday was not always forgotten.

Slavomir Rawicz, in *The Long Walk*, describes his experiences in forced-labour Camp 303, in northern Siberia, from which he escaped with a few others, reaching India after many months of terrible endurance across the Gobi desert and the Himalayas.

At Camp 303, soup and bread were the regular diet, but 'There was an occasional treat on Sunday when we were given dried fish . . . We worked hard for six days and had an easy day on the seventh.'

'Sunday was the day when the Commandant addressed the prisoners.' *(F. H. Drinkwater)*

Various forms of legalism have always been a significant part of Protestantism, though the specifics have differed from generation to generation. The Puritans and their descendants were particularly concerned about Sabbath keeping, and according to Colleen McDannell, 'By the nineteenth century the New England Calvinist Sabbath had reached almost mythical proportions and stood for all forms of unreasonable, harsh religious devotion. The Puritan, who hung his cat on Monday for killing a mouse on Sunday, became a symbol for New England rigidity and old fashioned attitudes. Even writers within the Reformed tradition commented that previous generations had been too extreme in their demands for a sacred Sabbath. And yet, the Sabbath continued to be a day devoted to God, devoid of work, amusements, and secular activities. Few Protestant writers would challenge the Sabbath's religious nature.' *(Colleen McDannell)*

Thirty-nine work activities are prohibited on the Jewish Sabbath. There is a popular misconception that these restrictions give rise to an onerous, rule-ridden, joyless day. On the contrary, the experience of observant Jews is that these well-defined guidelines make possible, every seven days, the physical and spiritual renewal which modern men and women need.

Just visualise the feeling of liberation from the telephone, traffic jams, dislocation and responsibility; imagine having the leisure to be within a few minutes of your home, available to your family, local friends and neighbours, able to absorb the details of the neighbourhood that you choose to live within, without the pressure to fix it, change it, resolve it, transform it; picture the periodic opportunity of carrying on a conversation with an acquaintance or a friend, finishing a story with your child, or just staring into space without feeling that you are guilty of not using your time constructively. People pay a lot of money to go on structured weekends for this very purpose.

The universe is larger than my ego and its demanding needs. I am part of a community of creatures and substances whose significance goes far beyond my own existence. I feel awe and humility when I stand still in such a spectacular theatre of reality. My attention is directed to the preservation of this environment of which I am a part.

On the Sabbath we experience time in a new way. This requires us to change social and psychological habits. Taking a bath, making a change of clothes, setting the table decoratively, responding to the schedule of the sunset rather than the timepiece – these are aids to the difficult task of changing

spiritual gear. 'Six days shall you labour and do all your work'
(Exod. 20:8). The sages of the tradition humorously (or perhaps
not so humorously) ask: is it possible for a human being to do
all his/her work in six days? To which they answer: Rest on the
Sabbath *as if* all your work were done. This capacity to shift
one's mental and spiritual state from doing to being is the crux
of the Sabbath programme. The Sabbath is a time for love and
love-making. The Song of Songs is its hymn. *(Rabbi Tzvi Marx)*

One Sunday, our young minister announced that he would
dispense with the formality of standing at the door to shake
hands with the faithful at the end of the service.

Instead, he now goes out and shakes hands with the parents
waiting to pick up their children from Sunday-school. *(C. W. F.)*

It is a theory cherished by those who love to find the continuity
in history, that the Puritans were really the down-trodden
Saxons and poor Danes taking a very belated revenge on the
haughty Norman-French nobility. One line of argument is the
attitude to Sunday, which was treated very seriously in Saxon
England, with colossal penalties for working or making servants
work-penalties that might include being reduced to bondage.

Then came the Normans, bringing what later came to be
called 'the Continental Sunday', choosing it as the most
auspicious day of the week for every kind of public event, the
lucky day, and the day for jollification. This, it is thought, was
always secretly disapproved of, though there was for a long time
no gainsaying the feudal lords, who did as they pleased.

Sunday was so gay that there were some French missionaries
who came to England in 1200 AD to preach against the
excessively Continental English Sunday. But they got a bad
reception in southern England, and their leader, Eustatius, went
back to France for more ammunition. He returned in the
following year with a letter from the Almighty, which had come
via Jerusalem, having been found on St Simeon's altar in the
church of the Holy Sepulchre. When the letter arrived, those in
the church had prostrated themselves and nobody liked to
touch it, till the Patriarch had the boldness to do so, and read

out a terrible denunciation from the Lord for those who did not keep the Lord's Day holy, as ordered in the Ten Commandments. There followed a threat that from the Heavens there would rain down on them stones and wood and scalding water, to be followed by a new set of ravenous and loathsome beasts, with the heads of lions and the tails of camels.

Eustatius, on his second visit to England, left the south alone, and had a better reception in York, where it was agreed to stop Sunday marketing. Stories soon circulated round Yorkshire of the misfortunes that had promptly overtaken millers and others who had worked on the Sabbath. These injunctions applied any time after three o'clock on Saturday afternoon, when the observance of the Sabbath should begin.

But this was only a foretaste of Wycliffe's time, when the Lollards started in earnest to enforce the English Sunday, and there was plenty of legislation to stop tradesmen and shopkeepers. Well before the seventeenth century, Sunday had been tightened up, by Henry VIII among others. Queen Mary tried to go back to an earlier and laxer tradition, in a way that no doubt had its contrary effect on the growing Puritans of Elizabeth's reign. Although the Commonwealth Puritans lost their cause, they left their mark on the eighteenth-century Sabbath, and after the French Revolution it tightened up again. *(Douglas Woodruff)*

USEFUL TEXTS

Sunday:
First of week, *John 20:1*
Breaking bread on, *Acts 20:7*

See also: A48 Worship
B29 The Eucharist

B19

CONSCIENCE

'Let anyone blaspheme against the Holy Spirit and he will never have forgiveness.' *Mark 3:29*

QUOTATIONS

Conscience is God's presence in man. *(Emmanuel Swedenborg)*

A good conscience is a continual Christmas. *(Benjamin Franklin)*

No more conscience than a fox in a poultry farm. *(George Bernard Shaw)*

Conscience warns us as a friend before it punishes us as a judge. *(King Stanislas I)*

Conscience is the royalty and prerogative of every private man. *(Dryden)*

Conscience is nearer to me than any other means of knowledge. *(Cardinal Newman)*

Conscience and reputation are two things. Conscience is due to yourself, reputation to your neighbour. *(St Augustine of Hippo)*

Conscience is the voice of the soul, as the passions are the voice of the body. No wonder they often contradict each other. *(Jean Jacques Rousseau)*

The best preacher is the heart; the best teacher is time; the best book is the world; the best friend is God. *(The Talmud)*

In matters of conscience, the law of the majority has no place. *(Mohandas Gandhi)*

Most of us follow our conscience as we follow a wheelbarrow. We push it in front of us in the direction we want to go. *(Billy Graham)*

The more faithfully you listen to the voice within you, the better you will hear what is sounding outside. *(Dag Hammarskjöld)*

PROVERBS

All too often a clear conscience is merely the result of a bad memory. *(Ancient proverb)*

There is no pillow so soft as a clear conscience. *(French proverb)*

A bad conscience is a snake in one's heart. *(Yiddish proverb)*

HUMOUR

Hewitt 'You don't seem to think much of him.'

Jewell 'If he had his conscience taken out, it would be a minor operation.' *(Anon)*

Small boy's definition of conscience: 'Something that makes you tell your mother before your sister does.' *(Anon)*

The teacher had given her English class a test. As she began to read off the correct answers, one of the boys changed an answer further down on the page. This troubled him as he thought the teacher might think he had changed the answer she had just given. He raised his hand and asked what he should do about changing answers after the teacher started reading the correct ones.

'Let you conscience be your guide,' the teacher told him.

The boy scratched his head and seemed so puzzled that the teacher asked him what was the matter.

'My conscience can't make up its mind,' the boy replied. *(Anon)*

STATEMENTS

Conscience is the most secret core and sanctuary of a man. There he is alone with God, whose voice echoes in his depths. In a wonderful manner conscience reveals that law which is fulfilled by love of God and neighbour.
(Second Vatican Council – 'The Church Today')

On his part, man perceives and acknowledges the imperatives of the divine law through the mediation of conscience. In all his activity, a man is bound to follow his conscience faithfully, in order that he may come to God, for whom he was created. It follows that he is not to be forced to act in a manner contrary to his conscience. Nor on the other hand, is he to be restrained from acting in accordance with his conscience, especially in matters religious.
(*Second Vatican Council – 'Religious Freedom'*)

WORD PICTURES

King David and King Solomon led merry, merry lives,
With many, many lady friends and many, many wives,
But when old age crept over them, with many, many qualms,
King Solomon wrote Proverbs and King David
    wrote the Psalms.
(*Dr James Ball Naylor*)

Cowardice asks, Is it safe?
Expediency asks, Is it politic?
Vanity asks, Is it popular?
But Conscience asks, Is it right?
(*W. Morley Punshon*)

'Oh, yes,' said the Indian, 'I know what my conscience is. It is a little three-cornered thing in here,' he laid his hand on his heart, 'that stands still when I am good; but when I am bad, it turns round, and the corners hurt very much. But if I keep on doing wrong, by-and-by the corners wear off and it doesn't hurt any more.' (*J. Ellis*)

A cat's conscience
A dog will often steal a bone,
But conscience lets him not alone,
And by his tail his guilt is known.

But cats consider theft a game,
And, howsoever you may blame,
Refuse the slightest sign of shame.

When food mysteriously goes,
The chances are that Pussy knows
More than she leads you to suppose.

And hence there is no need for you,
If Puss declines a meal or two,
To feel her pulse and make ado.
(*Anon*)

Two men once visited a holy man to ask his advice. 'We have done wrong actions,' they said 'and our consciences are troubled. Can you tell us what we must do so that we may be forgiven and feel clear of our guilt?'

'Tell me of your wrongdoings, my sons,' said the old man.

The first man said, 'I have committed a great and grievous sin.'

'What about you?' the holy man asked the second.

'Oh,' said he, 'I have done quite a number of wrong things, but they are all quite small, and not at all important.'

The holy man considered for a while. 'This is what you must do,' he said at last. 'Each of you must go and bring me a stone for each of his misdeeds.'

Off went the men: and presently the first came back staggering with an enormous boulder, so heavy that he could hardly lift it, and with a groan he let it fall at the feet of the holy man. Then along came the second, cheerfully carrying a bag of small pebbles. This he also laid at the feet of the saint.

'Now,' said the holy man, 'take all those stones and put them back where you found them.'

The first man shouldered his rock again, and staggered back to the place from which he had brought it. But the second man could only remember where a few of his pebbles had lain. After some time, he came back, and said that the task was too difficult.

'You must know, my son,' said the old man, 'that sins are like these stones. If a man has committed a great sin, it lies like a heavy stone on his conscience; but if he is truly sorry, he is forgiven and the load is taken away. But if a man is constantly doing small things that are wrong, he does not feel any very great load of guilt, and so he is not sorry, and remains a sinner. So, you see, my son, it is as important to avoid little sins as big ones.' *(Anon)*

USEFUL TEXTS

Conscience:
Maintaining a good, *Acts 24:16*
Bears witness to God, *Rom 2:15*
Maintains truth, *1 Tim. 3:9*

See also: A2 Integrity
A10 Seeking perfection
A34 Hypocrisy and ambition
B45 Free will
C47 The indwelling Spirit

B20

GROWTH TO MATURITY

'Of its own accord the land produces first the shoot,
then the ear, then the full grain in the ear.' *Mark 4:28*

QUOTATIONS

Mature people are made not out of good times but out of bad
times. *(H. J. Schachtel)*

God gets His best soldiers out of the highlands of affliction.
(Anon)

If God sends us on stony paths, He will provide us with strong
shoes. *(Alexander Maclaren)*

Men come to their meridian at various periods of their lives.
(Cardinal Newman)

Sometimes great difficulties are permitted only in order to
strengthen character. *(R. H. Benson)*

A woman deserves no credit for her beauty at 16 but beauty at
60 is her own soul's doing. *(Anon)*

God develops spiritual power in our lives through pressure of
hard places. *(Anon)*

Experience is not what happens to a man; it is what a man does
with what happens to him. *(A. Huxley)*

Your theology, fancy or plain, is what you are when the talking
stops and the action starts. *(Colin Morris)*

For it is the part of a truly great man not merely to be equal to
great things, but also to make little things great by his own
power. *(St Basil)*

The greater the difficulty, the more glory in surmounting it. Skilful pilots gain their reputation from storms and tempests. (*Epicurus*)

'Whenever I find myself in the cellar of affliction, I always look about for the wine.' (*Samuel Rutherford*)

At 16 I was stupid, confused, insecure and indecisive. At 25 I was wise, self-confident, prepossessing and assertive. At 45 I am stupid, confused, insecure and indecisive. Who would have supposed that maturity is only a short break in adolescence? (*Jules Feiffer*)

STATEMENTS

The law of Christian maturity demands that we lose ourselves in concern for others. One must not wait until all problems at home are solved before beginning to address oneself to those of the neighbour. In fact, an awareness of the immensity of the tasks and problems of progress which face humanity as a whole can stir individuals to work more seriously for progress in their own society. (*Pope Paul VI*)

Indeed, everyone should painstakingly ready himself personally for the apostolate, especially as an adult. For the advance of age brings with it better self-knowledge, thus enabling each person to evaluate more accurately the talents with which God has enriched his soul and to exercise more effectively those charismatic gifts which the Holy Spirit has bestowed on him for the good of his brothers. (*Second Vatican Council – 'The Laity'*)

WORD PICTURES?

A maturity check-up
1. A mature person does not take himself too seriously – his job, yes!
2. A mature person keeps himself alert in mind.
3. A mature person does not always 'view with alarm' every adverse situation that arises.

4. A mature person is too big to be little.

5. A mature person has faith in himself which becomes stronger as it is fortified by his faith in God.

6. A mature person never feels too great to do the little things and never too proud to do the humble things.

7. A mature person never accepts either success or failure in themselves as permanent.

8. A mature person never accepts any one of his moods as permanent.

9. A mature person is one who is able to control his impulses.

10. A mature person is not afraid to make mistakes.

(Leonard Wedel)

In psychological writings the definition of maturity has frequently been a rather negative one ... According to this view, the emotionally mature person is able to keep a lid on his feelings. He can suffer in silence; he can bide his time in spite of present discomfort. He is not subject to swings in mood, he is not volatile. When he does express emotion he does so with moderation, decently, and in good order. He is not carried away by his feelings ... Actually, in the writer's opinion, a person can live up to all of these prescriptions and still be an abjectly immature person, as well as a very cold fish *(Arthur T. Jersild)*

Benjamin Franklin's practical suggestions on how to get along with others are as timely today as they were when he wrote them nearly 200 years ago:
'The best thing to give your enemy is forgiveness:
   – to an opponent, tolerance;
   – to a friend, your ear;
   – to your child, good example;
   – to a father, reverence;
   – to your mother, conduct that will make her proud of you;
   – to yourself, respect;
   – to all men, charity.'

Brian Keenan in his book, *An Evil Cradling* knows the truth that 'pain is a holy angel which shows treasure to men which otherwise remains forever hidden'. But he knows too the cost of that vision. He weighed it up immediately after his release in August 1990:

'I feel like a cross between Humpty Dumpty and Rip Van Winkle – I have fallen off the wall and suddenly awake I find all the pieces of me, before me.

'There are more parts than I began with. All the King's horses, and all the King's men, cannot put Humpty together again.' *(Sheila Cassidy)*

'What is REAL?' asked the rabbit one day, when they were lying side by side near the nursery fender, before Nana came to tidy the room. 'Doesn't it mean having things that buzz inside you and a stick-out handle?'

'Real isn't how you are made,' said the skin horse. 'It's a thing that happens to you. When a child loves you for a long, long time, not just to play with, but REALLY loves you, then you become REAL.'

'Does it happen all at once, like being wound up,' he asked, 'or bit by bit?' 'It doesn't happen all at once,' said the skin horse. 'You become. It takes a long time. That's why it doesn't often happen to people who break easily, or have sharp edges, or who have to be carefully kept. Generally, by the time you are REAL, most of your hair has been loved off, and your eyes drop out and you get loose in the joints and very shabby.' *(Margery Williams – 'The Velveteen Rabbit')*

USEFUL TEXTS

Growth:
> In grace and knowledge of God, *2 Pet. 3:18*
> In Christlikeness, *Eph. 4; 13*
> In Christ, *Eph. 4; 15*

See also: A2 Integrity
> A7 Poor in Spirit
> A10 Seeking perfection
> B26 The whole man

B21

TRUST IN GOD

'Why are you so frightened?
How is it that you have no faith?'
Mark 4:40

QUOTATIONS
All shall be well and all shall be well and all manner of things shall be well. *(Dame Julian of Norwich)*

What is more elevating and transporting, than the generosity of heart which risks everything on God's word?
(Cardinal Newman)

Consider seriously how quickly people change, and how little trust is to be had in them; and cleave fast unto God, who changeth not. *(St Teresa of Avila)*

Cast yourself into the arms of God and be very sure that if he wants anything of you, he will fit you for the work and give you strength. *(St Philip Neri)*

Have courage for the great sorrows of life, and patience for the small ones. And when you have laboriously accomplished your daily task, go to sleep in peace. God is awake. *(Victor Hugo)*

When a train goes through a tunnel and it gets dark, you don't throw away your ticket and jump off. You sit still and trust the engineer. *(Corrie Ten Boom)*

Many men have just enough faith to trust God as far as they can see Him, and they always sing as far as they can see providence go right; but true faith can sing when its possessors cannot see. It can take hold of God when they cannot discern Him.
(Charles Haddon Spurgeon)

This trust Jesus showed is tied up with the intimate knowledge he had of his disciples. He knew their strengths and weaknesses; he knew just how reliable they were; and yet taking all this into consideration, he trusted them with his life and his work. And he treats us likewise. *(Michael Hollings)*

PROVERBS

One of them, a grave and sensible man . . . repeated a Spanish proverb, which though I cannot repeat in just the same words that he spoke it in, yet I remember I made it into an English proverb of my own thus:

'In trouble to be troubled
Is to have your trouble doubled.' *(Daniel Defoe)*

Trust in God, but mind your business. *(Russian proverb)*

From those I trust, God guard me;
from those I mistrust, I will guard myself.
(Italian proverb)

WORD PICTURES

As the marsh-hen secretly builds on the watery sod,
Behold I will build me a nest on the greatness of God:
I will fly in the greatness of God as the marsh-hen flies,
In the freedom that fills all the space 'twixt the marsh and
    the skies:
By so many roots as the marsh-grass sends in the sod,
I will heartily lay me a-hold on the greatness of God.
(Sydney Lanier)

'Worry' we are told, is from an Anglo-Saxon word which means 'harm' and is another form of the word 'wolf'. It is something harmful and bites and tears as a wolf which mangles a sheep. There are times, no doubt, when we must feel anxious because of harm suffered or anticipated by ourselves or others, and this may be beneficial because it rouses to necessary activity; but often worry has the opposite effect, it paralyses us and unfits us for duty, and also distracts our thoughts and obscures our vision. *(Anon)*

An old story tells of an angel who met a man carrying a heavy sack and enquired what was in it. 'My worries,' said the man. 'Let me see them,' asked the angel. When the sack was opened, it was empty. The man was astonished and said he had two great worries. One was of yesterday which he now saw was past; the other of tomorrow which had not yet arrived. The angel told him he needed no sack, and the man gladly threw it away. *(Anon)*

Compare two world-class athletes. At the 1988 Olympics in Korea, the two fastest runners in the world, Ben Johnson of Canada and Florence Griffith-Joyner (nicknamed Flo-Jo) both broke world records and won gold medals. However, Ben Johnson was discovered to have taken drugs; he had cheated and was sent home in disgrace. In contrast Flo-Jo ran with a relaxed smile on her face and immediately after the new world record, when interviewed, said, 'I thank God that he helped me to win.' The lesson to all young people must be clear; put not your trust in drugs but in God. *(Paul Frost)*

USEFUL TEXTS
Trust in God:
   For peace, *Isa. 26:3*
   For safety, *Prov. 29:25*
   Forever, *Isa. 26:4*
   Not in wealth, *Prov. 11:28; Luke 12:19-20*
   Not in man, *Ps. 118:89; Jer. 17:5*

See also: A11 God's loving Providence
         A19 Patience
         B52 God is love
         C39 Doing God's will

B22

DEATH

'Death was not God's doing, he takes no pleasure
in the extinction of the living.'
Wisdom 1:13

QUOTATIONS

Every parting gives a foretaste of death; every coming together
again a foretaste of the resurrection. *(Arthur Schopenhauer)*

Death is the side of life which is turned away from us.
(Rainer Maria Rilke)

I depart from life as from an inn, and not as from my home.
(Marcus Tullius Cicero)

It is a poor thing for anyone to fear that which is inevitable.
(Tertullian)

We understand death for the first time when he puts his hand
upon one whom we love. *(Mme de Stael)*

Death is but a sharp corner near the beginning of life's
procession down eternity. *(John Ayscough)*

When a man dies he clutches in his hands only that which he
has given away in his lifetime. *(Jean Jacques Rousseau)*

The foolish fear death as the greatest of evils, the wise desire it
as a rest after labours and the end of ills. *(St Ambrose)*

Men fear death as children fear to go in the dark; and as that
natural fear in children is increased with tales, so is the other.
(Francis Bacon)

Why is it that we rejoice at a birth and grieve at a funeral? It is because we are not the person involved. *(Mark Twain)*

I am able to follow my own death step by step.
Now I move softly towards the end.
(Pope John XXIII; Remark made two days before he died)

PROVERBS

Death is a debt we must all pay. *(Greek proverb)*

Death does not take the old but the ripe. *(Russian proverb)*

The angel of Death has many eyes. *(Yiddish proverb)*

HUMOUR

I am ready to meet my Maker. Whether my Maker is prepared for the ordeal of meeting me is another matter.
(Sir Winston Churchill)

The ageing but still active French comedian, Maurice Chevalier, was asked how he felt about old age. 'I prefer it', he said, 'to the alternative.' *(K. Edwards)*

Children sometimes have very adult questions about death, but they express them more simply. In *Children's Letters to God*, a young boy writes, 'Dear God, What is it like when a person dies? Nobody will tell me. I just want to know, I don't want to do it. Your friend, Mike.' *(Eric Marshall and Stuart Hample)*

At the last moment, a minister was asked to preach a funeral sermon for another minister who had suddenly become ill.
Realising he had forgotten to ask if the deceased had been a man or woman, he frantically tried to catch a mourner's eye. Finally succeeding, he pointed to the casket and whispered, 'Brother or sister?'
'Cousin' came the faint reply.
(Together)

It's not that I'm afraid to die. I just don't want to be there when it happens. *(Woody Allen)*

Epitaphs
For a Mr Box

Here lies one Box within another.
The one of wood was very good,
We cannot say so much for t'other.

For the Earl of Kildare

Who killed Kildare? Who dared Kildare to kill?
Death killed Kildare – who dare kill whom he will.

For Dr Chard

Here lies the corpse of Chard,
Who filled the half of this churchyard.

For Arabella

Here rests in silent clay
Miss Arabella Young,
Who on the 21st May,
Began to hold her tongue.

STATEMENTS

It is in the face of death that the riddle of human existence becomes more acute. Not only is man tormented by pain and by the advancing deterioration of his body, but even more so by a dread of perpetual extinction. He rightly follows the intuition of his heart when he abhors and repudiates the absolute ruin and total disappearance of his own person.
(Second Vatican Council – 'The Church Today')

Such is the mystery of man, and it is a great one, as seen by believers in the light of Christian revelation. Through Christ and in Christ, the riddles of sorrow and death grow meaningful. Apart from his Gospel, they overwhelm us. Christ has risen, destroying death by his death. He has lavished life upon us so that, as sons in the Son, we can cry out in the Spirit: Abba, Father! *(Second Vatican Council – 'The Church Today')*

WORD PICTURES

I have seen death too often to believe in death.
It is not ending – but a withdrawal.
As one who finished a long journey,
   Stills the motor,
   Turns off the lights,
   Steps from his car,
And walks up the path
To the home that awaits him.
(Blanding)

The Church is the only society on earth that never loses a member through death! As a Christian I believe, not just in life *after* death but in life *through* death. In the words of a Russian Christian, 'The moment of death will be in the inrush of timelessness.' *(David Watson)*

If I should die before the rest of you
Break not a flower nor inscribe a stone;
Nor, when I'm gone, speak in a Sunday voice,
But be the usual selves that I have known.

Weep if you must.
Parting is hell.
But life goes on.
So sing as well.
(Joyce Grenfell)

I dreamt death came the other night
and heaven's gate swung wide.
With kindly grace an angel came
and ushered me inside;
and there to my astonishment
stood folks I'd known on earth:
some I had judged quite unfit,
or of but little worth.
Indignant words rose to my lips
but never were set free,
for every face showed stunned surprise.
NO-ONE EXPECTED ME.
(Len Dean)

If I should never see the moon again
Rising red gold across the harvest field,
Or feel the stinging of soft April rain,
As the brown earth her hidden treasures yield.

If I should never taste the salt sea spray
As the ship beats her course against the breeze,
Or smell the dog-rose and the new mown hay,
Or moss and primroses beneath the tree.

If I should never hear the thrushes wake
Long before sunrise in the glimmering dawn,
Or watch the huge Atlantic rollers break
Against the rugged cliffs in baffling scorn.

If I have said goodbye to stream and wood,
To the wide ocean and the green clad hill,
I know that He who made this world so good
Has somewhere made a heaven better still.

This I bear witness with my latest breath
Knowing the love of God, I fear not death.

*(Lines found in the Bible of Major Malcolm Boyle,
killed in action after the landing on D-Day, June 1944)*

My body is to be buried in the place near the
chapel that I caused to be made in the south aisle
of St Magnus' Church.

For tithes forgotten: 3s 4d.

For masses to be said in the church for my soul,
my wife's soul and all Christian souls, every
month for one year after my death: £6.

Every Friday for a year after my death 3s 4d to
be given to prisoners in Newgate one Friday,
those in Ludgate the next Friday.

The very best canvas for shirts and smocks for
the poor people in Bedfordshire.

£100 towards the making of an altar table.

The will of Richard Berne, London, 1525)

God says:
Do not fear your death.
For when that moment arrives
I will draw my breath
and your soul will come to Me
like a needle
to a magnet.
(Anon)

Death is nothing at all,
I have only slipped away into the next room.
I am I and you are you;
Whatever we were to each other that we are still.

Call me by my old familiar name,
speak to me in the easy way which you always used.
Put no difference into your tone;
wear no forced air of solemnity or sorrow.
Laugh as we always laughed
at the little jokes we enjoyed together.
Play, smile, think of me, pray for me.
Let my name be ever the household word it always was.
Let it be spoken without effect,
without the ghost of a shadow on it.
Life means all that it ever meant.

It is the same as it ever was;
there is absolutely unbroken continuity.

What is this death but a negligible accident;
why should I be out of mind because I am out of sight?
I am but waiting for you, for an interval,
somewhere very near,
just around the corner.
All is well.
(Canon Henry Scott-Holland)

for useful texts see overleaf

USEFUL TEXTS

Death:
    Consequence of sin, *Gen. 3:3;Rom. 5:12*
    End of earthly life, *Eccles. 9:10*
    Lot of all, *Heb. 9:27*
    Second death, *Rev. 20:14*

See also: A35 Preparing for death
            A42 Life after death
            B47 Dying to self
            C36 The Day of the Lord

B23

PASTORAL CARE OF THE SICK

'My grace is enough for you; my power is at its best in weakness.' *2 Corinthians, 12:9*

QUOTATIONS

The best prayers have often more groans than words. *(John Bunyan)*

We are so fond of one another, because our ailments are the same. *(Jonathan Swift)*

I enjoy convalescence. It is the part that makes the illness worthwhile. *(George Bernard Shaw)*

Disease makes men more physical; it leaves them nothing but body. *(Thomas Mann)*

The sick on the other hand are to be admonished to realise that they are sons of God by the very fact that the scourge of discipline chastises them. For unless it were his plan to give them an inheritance after their chastisements, he would not trouble to school them in affliction. *(Pope St Gregory I)*

Now the custom of the Church is that the sick should be anointed by the priests with consecrated oil and through the accompanying prayer restored to health. If, therefore, the sick be in sins and shall have confessed these to the priests of the Church and shall have sincerely undertaken to relinquish and amend them, they shall be remitted to them. For sins cannot be remitted without the confession of amendment.
(Venerable Bede)

Cheer up, God is with you. You suffer, it is true. But he is near you, trust in him as you would your own father. If he has let you suffer, it is because he sees something in it which today you do not yet know. Your peace of mind is in your trust in God who can never let you down. *(Pope John Paul II)*

Before all things and above all things, care must be taken of the sick, so that they may be served in very deed as Christ himself . . . But let the sick on their part consider that they are being served for the honour of God, and not provoke their brethren who are serving them by their unreasonable demands. Yet they should be patiently borne with, because from such as these is gained a more abundant reward. *(St Benedict)*

PROVERBS

In time of sickness the soul collects itself anew. *(Latin proverb)*

Sickness shows us what we are. *(Latin proverb)*

Sickness is every man's master. *(Danish proverb)*

Every invalid is a physician. *(Irish proverb)*

HUMOUR

It is a cold, which God Almighty in justice did give me while I sat lewdly sporting with Mrs Lane the other day with the broken window in my neck. *(Samuel Pepys)*

WORD PICTURES

Hilary Pole was a young woman who was totally physically handicapped, while being extremely active, mentally and intellectually. She was only able to move her left big toe one-sixteenth of an inch.

To make it possible for Hilary to communicate with her family and the world around her, Reg Maling, a medical scientist, who had invented the Possum, developed in 1967, a special mechanism to make use of Hilary's minute movement.

The Possum is a machine which makes it possible to dial a telephone number, open a front door, switch on a light or fire without lifting a finger, by using special electronic equipment.

A sequence of lights on a display board is operated by blowing on a stem pipe, or in Hilary's case, tapping lightly with her big toe. The release of pressure activates the gadget. A code of sucks and blows enables disabled people to operate an electric typewriter at up to 40 words a minute.

Hilary made good use of her Possum, winning the MBE in 1973 for her work for the handicapped! She died on 18th June 1975, aged 37. (*A. P. Castle*)

Kathryn Kuhlman, the well-known healing evangelist who captured the hearts of her millions of followers for most of three decades from the 1940s to the 1970s, was a woman of deep emotion. Her healing ministry focused not on herself but on others as she compassionately bent over them, seeking to alleviate their pain. Her biographer, Jamie Buckingham, poignantly describes this love that was so evident in her ministry.

'I saw her, on dozens of occasions, take a child that was lame, maybe paralysed from birth, and hug that child to her breast with the love of a mother. I am convinced she would have, at any moment required of her, given her life in exchange for that child's healing.

She would hug bleary-eyed alcoholics and mix her tears with theirs. And the prostitutes who came to her meetings, with tears smearing their mascara, knew that if they could but touch her they would have touched the love of God. And those little old women, hobbling along on canes and crutches, some of whom couldn't even speak the English language but were drawn by the universal language of love.

No man could have ever loved like that. It took a woman, bereft of the love of a man, her womb barren, to love as she loved. Out of her emptiness – she gave. To be replenished by the only lover she was allowed to have – the Holy Spirit.'
(*Jamie Buckingham*)

A devout Anglican, Dorothy Kerin had been an invalid in bed for nearly five years and semi-conscious for two weeks. The doctor said the end had come. She then had a vision of Jesus, who smiled and said: 'No, Dorothy, you are not coming yet.' An angel told her to get up and walk and, to the amazement of all present, she did. She had not been able to walk for years, but when the doctor examined her next morning he found that the tubercular peritonitis and other illnesses had miraculously disappeared and the emaciated body had regained a normal, healthy shape and strength: surely one of the most remarkable physical healing miracles of all time – and well documented.

In a vision, Dorothy was then given the commission to 'heal the sick, comfort the sorrowing and give faith to the faithless'. A period of 17 years' preparation followed, during which she received the stigmata, and was encouraged, perhaps mistakenly, to take private vows of poverty, chastity and obedience.

Her public healing ministry started in 1929 in Ealing, and lead to the founding of the Burrswood Christian healing centre in Kent, where the practice of praying for healing is still combined with the medical services of a nursing home. She exercised her ministry under the spiritual direction, successively, of three Anglican bishops and in her later years undertook journeys to Sweden, Switzerland, France and the United States in furtherance of her mission. *(Benedict Heron)*

USEFUL TEXTS

Sickness:
>   Because of sin, *Lev. 26:14-16; 2 Chr. 21:12-15*
>   Result of excesses, *Hos. 7:5; Prov. 25:16*
>   Under God's control, *Deut. 32:39; 1 Cor. 11:30*
>   Pray for those in, *Acts 28:8; Jas. 5:14-15*

See also: A35 Preparing for death
>   B38 The Suffering Servant

B24

GO TELL EVERYONE

'Jesus summoned the Twelve and began to send them out in
pairs . . . to preach repentance.' *Mark 6:7, 13*

QUOTATIONS

The half-baked sermon causes spiritual indigestion.
(Austin O'Malley)

When you preach the Gospel, beware of preaching it as the
religion which explains everything. *(Albert Schweitzer)*

To love to preach is one thing – to love those to whom we
preach, quite another. *(Richard Cecil)*

I preached what I felt, what I smartingly did feel. *(John Bunyan)*

It is very important to live your faith by confessing it, and one
of the best ways to confess it is to preach it. *(Thomas Merton)*

Some people accuse us of too much emotionalism. I say we have
too little. That is why we are losing church people to other
interests. We need not only to capture their minds: we've got to
touch their hearts. We've got to make people feel their faith.
(Billy Graham)

The expertise of the pulpit can only be learned slowly and it
may well be, with a strange mixture of pain and joy.
(Donald Coggan)

Sermons remain one of the last forms of public discourse where
it is culturally forbidden to talk back. *(Harvey Cox)*

The test of a preacher is that his congregation goes away saying,
not 'What a lovely sermon!' but 'I will do something.'
(St Francis de Sales)

When I preach I regard neither doctors nor magistrates, of whom I have above 40 in my congregation; I have all my eyes on the servant maids and on the children. And if the learned men are not well pleased with what they hear, well, the door is open. *(Martin Luther)*

PROVERBS

Who teaches, often learns himself. *(Italian proverb)*

Those having torches will pass them on to others. *(Greek proverb)*

The teacher is like the candle, which lights others in consuming itself. *(Italian proverb)*

HUMOUR

A famous preacher once told his congregation, 'Every blade of grass is a sermon.'

A few days later, a parishioner saw him mowing his lawn. 'That's right, Father,' the man said, 'cut your sermons short.' *(Anon)*

A well-known preacher delivered a sermon before a congregation in which his wife was a worshipper. When the service was over, he went over to her and asked, 'How did I do?' She replied, 'You did fine, only you missed several opportunities to sit down.' *(Asbury Lenox)*

A preacher whose sermon had gone down very badly asked a friend afterwards, 'How would you have delivered that sermon?'

'Under an assumed name,' he replied. *(Anon)*

WORD PICTURES

Paganini, the great violinist, came out before his audience one day and made the discovery just as they ended their applause that there was something wrong with his violin. He looked at it for a second and then saw that it was not his famous and valuable one. He felt paralysed for a moment, then turned to his audience and told them there had been some mistake and he did not have his own violin. He stepped back behind the curtain thinking that it was still where he had left it, but discovered that someone had stolen his and left that old second-hand one in its place. He remained back of the curtain a moment, then came out before his audience and said,

'Ladies and gentlemen: I will show you that the music is not in the instrument but in the soul.' And he played as he had never played before; and out of that second-hand instrument, the music poured forth until the audience was enraptured with enthusiasm and the applause almost lifted the roof off the building, because the man had revealed to them that the music was not in the machine but in his own soul.

It is your mission . . . to walk out on the stage of this world and reveal to all earth and Heaven that the music is not in conditions, not in things, not in externals, but the music of life is in your own soul. *(Anon)*

Clinton Locy of West Richland, Washington put all long-winded preachers to shame in February, 1955, when he preached 48 hours and 18 minutes and set a world's record for the length of a sermon. He took texts from every book of the Bible, and eight listeners stayed for the completion. *(Anon)*

Somewhere, I read about an Eskimo hunter who asked the local missionary priest, 'If I did not know about God and sin, would I go to hell?' 'No,' said the priest, 'not if you did not know.' 'Then why,' asked the Eskimo earnestly, 'did you tell me?' *(Annie Dillard)*

The great eighteenth-century actor David Garrick was once asked by a church leader how he produced such wonderful effects on his listeners, when reciting fiction. 'Because', said Garrick, 'I recite fiction as if it were truth, and you preach truth as if it were fiction.' *(Richard Bewes)*

The decline of the Ministry of the Word in Protestant England can perhaps be traced in hour glasses. In the seventeenth century they lived up to their name, and it was really at the end of an hour that the preacher, if in good form, would turn them over and say 'another glass'. If he stopped before the sand, he was thought an idle, shirking dog.

But early in the last century, habits changed, and Queen Victoria restoring the Chapel Royal in 1867 had an hour-glass fitted which gave the preachers 18 minutes. Her son, Edward, improved on this royal hint, and made it known that to go beyond 10 minutes was to displease him.

Of Isaac Barrow, in Charles II's reign, it is related that 'he was three-and-a-half hours delivering a sermon on charity before the Lord Mayor and aldermen; and on one occasion when preaching in Westminster Abbey the servants of the Church caused the organ to be struck up against him and he was fairly blown out of the pulpit'. *(Douglas Woodruff)*

USEFUL TEXTS

Mission:

Of Christ;
    to do God's will, *John 6:38*
    to save the lost, *Luke 19:10*
    to reveal God, *Heb. 1:1-3*
    to give his life, *Mark 10:45*
    to fulfil the Law, *Matt. 5:17*

Of Christians;
    to make disciples, *Matt. 28:15-20*

See also: B2 The Good News
          B12 On a mission
          C8 God's messengers

B25

QUIET – TIME FOR PRAYER

'You must come away to some lonely place all by yourselves and rest for a while.' *Mark 6:31*

QUOTATIONS

Recollection is the only paradise from which we cannot be turned out. *(Jean Paul Richter)*

All the troubles of life come upon us because we refuse to sit quietly for a while each day in our rooms. *(Blaise Pascal)*

Make your prayer simple, as simple as you can. Reason little, love much, and you will pray well. *(Fr Willie Doyle, S. J.)*

I am convinced that nothing in Christianity is so rarely attained as a praying heart. *(Charles G. Finney)*

There is no true solitude except interior solitude.
(Thomas Merton)

Mere silence is not wisdom, for wisdom consists in knowing when and how to speak and when and where to keep silent.
(J. P. Camus)

The self-sufficient do not pray, the self-satisfied will not pray, the self-righteous cannot pray. No man is greater than his prayer life. *(Leonard Ravenhill)*

If we have not quiet in our minds, outward comfort will do no more for us than a golden slipper on a gouty foot. *(John Bunyan)*

To go up alone into the mountain and come back as an ambassador to the world, has ever been the method of humanity's best friends. *(Evelyn Underhill)*

Solitude, though it be silent as light, is like light, the mightiest of agencies; for solitude is essential to man. All men come into this world alone; all leave it alone. *(Thomas De Quincey)*

How can you expect God to speak in that gentle and inward voice which melts the soul, when you are making so much noise with your rapid reflections? Be silent, and God will speak again. *(Francois Fenelon)*

PROVERB
Quiet sow, quiet mow. *(English proverb)*

WORD PICTURES
Luigi Tarisio was found dead one morning with scarce a comfort in his home, but with 246 fiddles, which he had been collecting all his life, crammed into an attic, the best in the bottom drawer of an old rickety bureau. In very devotion to the violin, he had robbed the world of all that music all the time he treasured them; others before him had done the same, so that when the greatest Stradivarius was first played, it had 147 speechless years. *(W. Y. Fullerton)*

After I enter the chapel I place myself in the presence of God and I say to him. 'Lord, here I am; give me whatever you wish.' If he gives me something, then I am happy and I thank him. If he does not give me anything, then I thank him nonetheless, knowing, as I do, that I deserve nothing. Then I begin to tell him of all that concerns me, my joys, my thoughts, my distress, and finally, I listen to him. *(St Catherine Labouré)*

The greatest thing that we can do for any man is to pray for him. Alexander Whyte told a story of a servant girl who was a member of his congregation. When she came asking to become a member, he asked her what she could do for her church and for the work of Jesus Christ. It was in the old days when the work of a domestic servant lasted all day and half the night.

'I haven't much time to do things,' the girl said, 'but at night, when I go to bed, I take the morning newspaper with me.' 'Yes,' said Whyte, wondering what could possibly be coming next.

'And,' the girl went on, 'I read the birth notices, and I pray for the little babies who have just come into the world. I read the marriage notices, and I pray that God will give these people happiness. I read the death notices, and I pray that God will comfort those who are sad.'

No one in this world will ever know what blessing to unknown people came from an attic bedroom from one who prayed. If we love someone, then surely we cannot help praying for them. *(William Barclay)*

Come now, little man! Flee for a while from your tasks, hide yourself for a little space from the turmoil of your thoughts. Come, cast aside your burdensome cares, and put aside your laborious pursuits. For a little while, give your time to God, and rest in him for a little while. Enter into the chamber of your mind, shut out all things save God and whatever may aid you in seeking God; and having barred the door of your chamber, seek him. *(St Anselm of Canterbury)*

USEFUL TEXTS

Prayer:
    Of faith, *Jas. 5:15*
    Of the righteous, *Prov. 15:29*
    Hindrance to, *1 Pet. 3:7*
    Of Christ, *John 17*
    For forgiveness, *Ps. 51:1-9*

See also: A1 The value of time
          A10 Seeking perfection
          C32 Prayer
          C47 The indwelling Spirit

B26

THE WHOLE MAN

'Bear with one another charitably, in complete selflessness, gentleness and patience.' *Ephesians 4:2*

QUOTATIONS

The body is the socket of the soul. *(Anon)*

The soul, like the body, lives by what it feeds on. *(J. Gilbert Holland)*

You can easily judge the character of a man by how he treats those who can do nothing for him. *(James Miles)*

I wished for all things that I might enjoy life, and was granted life that I might enjoy all things. *(An anonymous soldier)*

Despise the flesh, for it passes away; be solicitous for your soul which will never die. *(St Basil)*

It is the glory of man to continue and remain in the service of God. *(St Irenaeus)*

The soul is the user, the body for use; hence the one is master, the other servant. *(St Ambrose)*

What a man is in the sight of God, so much he is and no more. *(St Francis of Assisi)*

The eyes of the soul should not be hindered by the eyes of the body. *(R. H. Benson)*

Never has there been so little discussion about the nature of men as now, when, for the first time, anyone can discuss. *(G. K Chesterton)*

Man is an exception, whatever else he is. If he is not the image of God, then he is a disease of the dust. If it is not true that a divine being fell, then we can only say that one of the animals went entirely off his head. *(G. K Chesterton)*

PROVERBS

What soap is for the body, tears are for the soul.
(Jewish proverb)

The diamond cannot be polished without friction, nor the man perfected without trials. *(Chinese proverb)*

STATEMENTS

According to the almost unanimous opinion of believers and unbelievers alike, all things on earth should be related to man as their centre and crown.
(Second Vatican Council – 'The Church Today')

Thus the ideal of 'the universal man' is disappearing more and more. Nevertheless, it remains each man's duty to preserve a view of the whole human person, a view in which the values of intellect, will, conscience, and fraternity are pre-eminent. These values are all rooted in God the Creator and have been wonderfully restored and elevated in Christ.
(Second Vatican Council – 'The Church Today')

WORD PICTURES

Mankind has taken up just a fraction of earth's time. It is almost impossible to imagine the vast expanse of time since the earth was born out of gas and cosmic dust 5,000 million years ago.

Imagine the planet's history condensed into a single century. On the time scale produced by this leap of imagination, the oldest-known rocks began to form at the dawn of year 15, and life in its most primitive form of bacteria and algae appeared in the year 26. Until the year 80 life evolved slowly as the continents drifted about, and it was not until eight years ago that the first amphibians struggled ashore.

Dinosaurs were dominant three years ago, but by the following year they had become extinct.

Three weeks ago, the first man emerged in Africa, using tools and walking upright. The last Ice Age ended two hours ago, the Industrial Revolution started two minutes ago . . . and four seconds ago man set foot on the moon. *(Anon)*

A man was walking down a dark alley, thinking his own thoughts, so he didn't notice the approach of a hold-up man until he felt a gun in his back and heard a low voice whispering: 'Your money or your life.'

'Take my life.' the victim replied promptly, 'I'm saving my money for my old age.'

Some of us not only save our money for our old age, but seem to save our lives for our old age as well. We are reluctant to give ourselves to living, to dedicate our time and our spirit to a full life of the spirit, a life that concerns itself with our neighbour, whether he is next door or half a world away. Yet the truth is that only through this wholehearted living do we really live at all. *(Anon)*

Once Hodja was invited to a very important formal banquet but he didn't dress up for the occasion but rather went in everyday clothing. Once there he was treated with disrespect and was looked upon with contempt. No one paid him any attention and the servants ignored him and didn't serve him dinner. After a short while he slipped out of the banquet unnoticed and went home. There he changed into his finest clothes, putting on his magnificent turban, a fine silk robe, very valuable jewellery and a large expensive fur coat over all. Then he returned to the banquet.

This time he was received with open arms. The host himself bade him to sit beside him at the highest seat and offered him a plate filled with the choicest delicacies. Much to their bewildered amazement, Hodja took off his coat held it to the plate and said:

'Eat, my master eat!'

'Hodja, what are you doing?' exclaimed his astonished host.

'It is the clothes that you are giving these delicacies to, not the man inside!' *(From Minyatur Yayinlari)*

There are three qualities you must have if you are going to succeed finally, however technically proficient you may be.

First, you must have integrity, which I would say in your own profession (of commerce) is particularly important.

Second, you must have courage, not necessarily physical courage, because not everyone has that, but moral courage, standing firm by what one believes to be right.

Third, you must have enthusiasm, the ability to get something out of life by putting something into it in an enthusiastic way. *(Lord Montgomery)*

See also: A2 Integrity
            A10 Seeking perfection
            B20 Growth to maturity

B27

BREAD FROM HEAVEN

'It is my Father who gives you the bread from heaven, the true bread; for the bread of God is that which comes down from heaven and gives life to the world.' *John 6:32-33*

QUOTATIONS

The history of man from the beginning has been the history of the struggle for daily bread. *(Jesue de Castro)*

Bread for myself is a material matter: bread for other people is a spiritual matter. *(Nikolai Berdyaev)*

Christ is food for me; Christ is drink for me; the Flesh of God is food for me, the Blood of God is drink for me. Christ is ministered to me daily. *(St Ambrose)*

As to the truth of the Flesh and Blood there is no room left for doubt. For both from the declaration of the Lord Himself and from our own faith, it is truly Flesh and truly Blood. And when These are eaten and drunk, it is brought to pass that we are both in Christ and Christ is in us. Is this not so? *(St Hilary of Poitiers)*

Therefore you hear that as often as sacrifice is offered, the Lord's death, the Lord's resurrection, the Lord's ascension and the remission of sins is signified, and will you not take the Bread of life daily? He who has a wound needs medicine. The wound is that we are under sin; the medicine is the heavenly and venerable Sacrament. *(St Ambrose)*

PROVERBS

When God gives us bread, men will supply the butter. *(Yiddish proverb)*

A mother's bread costs dear. *(Spanish proverb)*

Whose bread I eat, his song I sing. *(German proverb)*

STATEMENT

The Lord left behind a pledge of this hope and strength for life's journey in that sacrament of faith where natural elements refined by man are changed into His glorified Body and Blood, providing a meal of brotherly solidarity and a foretaste of the heavenly banquet.

(Second Vatican Council – 'The Church Today')

WORD PICTURES

It is told of Sadhu Sundar Singh that many years ago he was distributing gospels in the Central Provinces of India and he came to some non-Christians on a train and offered a man a copy of John's Gospel. The man took it, tore it into pieces in anger and threw the pieces out of the window.

That seemed the end, but it so happened in the providence of God, there was a man idly walking along the line that very day, and he picked up, as he walked along, a little bit of paper and looked at it, and the words on it in his own language were 'the Bread of Life'. He did not know what it meant; but he enquired among his friends and one of them said: 'I can tell you; it is out of the Christian book. You must not read it or you will be defiled.'

The man thought for a moment and then said: 'I want to read the book that contains that beautiful phrase': and he bought a copy of the New Testament. He was shown where the sentence occurred – our Lord's words 'I am the Bread of Life'; and as he studied the Gospel, the light flooded into his heart. Later he became a preacher of the gospel, in the Central Province of India. That little bit of paper, through God's Spirit, was indeed the bread of life to him. *(Anon)*

In 1956, news came through about one of Stalin's forced-labour camps in Siberia, by way of a Dr Joseph Scholmer who had been a prisoner there. He said that four bishops, 700 priests and 700 monks and nuns had been deported from Lithuania, as well as many lay Catholics. They worked in mines 600 feet below ground, and Mass was said often down there by some priest dressed in his usual overalls. The altar-wafers came by post from

Lithuania, allowed through as 'Lithuanian bread', and the wine was from the Crimea.

The miners had made a tiny silver chalice only one-and-a-quarter inches high. At Easter (said Dr Scholmer) over 400 of the Lithuanian miners received their Easter communion hidden in tins of cigarettes which were being distributed. Each host, wrapped in a small piece of linen, was hidden under a top layer of cigarettes, and broken up for four communicants.
(*F. H. Drinkwater*)

Be gentle
When you touch bread.
Let it not lie
Uncared for – unwanted.
So often bread
Is taken for granted.
There is much beauty in bread.
Beauty of sun and soil,
Beauty of patient toil,
Winds and rain have caressed it.
Christ often blessed it.
Be gentle
When you touch bread.
(*Anon*)

The story is told of a certain minister who was disturbed to see a shabby old man go into his church at noon every day and come out again after a few minutes. What could he be doing? He informed the caretaker and bade him question the old man. After all, the place contained valuable furnishings.

'I go to pray,' the old man said in reply to the caretaker's questioning.

'Come, come now,' said the other, 'you are never long enough in the church to pray.'

'Well, you see,' the shabby old man went on, 'I cannot pray a long prayer, but every day at 12 o'clock, I just comes and says, "Jesus, it's Jim" and waits a minute and then comes away. It's just a little prayer, but I guess He hears me.'

When Jim was injured some time later and taken to hospital, he had a wonderful influence in the ward. Grumbling patients became cheerful and often the ward would ring with laughter.

'Well, Jim,' said the sister to him one day, 'the men say you are responsible for this change in the ward. They say you are always happy.'

'Aye, sister, that I am. I can't help being happy. You see, it's my visitor. Every day he makes me happy.'

'Your visitor?' The sister was puzzled. She always noticed that Jim's chair was empty on visiting days, for he was a lonely old man, with no relations. 'Your visitor? But when does he come?'

'Every day,' Jim replied, the light in his eyes growing brighter. 'Yes, every day at 12 o'clock he comes and stands at the foot of my bed. I see him and he smiles and says, "Jim, it's Jesus" ' *(William Aitken)*

USEFUL TEXTS

Bread:
Unleaven for Passover, *Exod. 12:15; 17-20*
In the tabernacle, *Lev. 24:5-9; Heb. 9:2*
Miraculous provision of, *1 Kgs. 17:6; Matt. 14:19-21*
'Bread of life', *John 6:25-59*
Eucharist, *Luke 22:7-19; 1 Cor. 11:23-29*

See also: A21 Feeding the hungry
A44 Meeting Christ in the sacraments
B29 The Eucharist

B28

THE FATHER
WHO DRAWS US TO HIMSELF

'No one can come to me unless he is drawn
by the Father who sent me.' *John 6:44*

QUOTATIONS

The Father is our fount and origin, in whom our life and being
is begun. *(John of Ruysbroeck)*

Our Heavenly Father never takes anything from His children
unless He means to give them something better.
(George Mueller)

The child is not likely to find a father in God unless he finds
something of God in his father. *(Robert Ingersoll)*

The Mohammedans have 99 names for God, but among them
all they have not 'Our Father'. *(Anon)*

Whosoever walks toward God one cubit, God runs toward him
twain. *(Anon)*

God does not ask about our ability or our inability, but our
availability. *(The Arkansas Baptist)*

An old mystic says somewhere, 'God is an unutterable sigh in
the innermost depths of the soul.' With still greater justice, we
may reverse the proposition and say the soul is a never ending
sigh after God. *(Theodor Christlieb)*

When we pray to God, says Cyprian, with entire assurance, it is
himself who has given us the spirit of our prayer. Then it is the
Father listening to the words of his child; it is he who dwells in
the depths of our hearts, teaching us how to pray.
(François Fénelon)

PROVERBS

He who has no friend has God. *(Egyptian proverb)*

God never shuts one door but He opens another.
(Irish proverb)

With God, go over the sea – without him, not over the threshold.
(Russian proverb)

WORD PICTURES

When G. K. Chesterton was a child he had a cardboard toy theatre with cut-out characters. One of the characters was a man with a golden key; he never could remember what character that man with the golden key represented; but that character was always identified in his mind with his father, whom he saw as a man with a golden key who unlocked all sorts of doors leading to all sorts of wonderful things.
(William Barclay)

It was the widespread rebellion against the central government in 1964 which was to bring persecution and death to many Congo Christians. The actions of the Simbas, or Lions, were usually unpredictable . . . 'Why did you shelter a white woman?' asked the Simba military court of one pastor. 'Because she is my sister in Christ, the child of my own Heavenly Father,' was the reply. Although he was condemned by the court to be shot, the effect of his bearing on the Simba major was such that he set him free. *(T. A. Beetham 'Christianity and the New Africa')*

The daughter of Karl Marx once confessed to a friend that she had never been brought up in any religion and had never been religious. 'But,' she said, 'the other day I came across a beautiful little prayer which I very much wish could be true'. 'And what was the prayer?' She was asked. Slowly the daughter of Karl Marx began repeating in German, 'Our Father, which art in heaven . . .' *(Robert Latham – 'God for all Men')*

A nineteenth-century prototype of what would today be a number one record was a song called *Come Home, Father*. It was about a little girl who went to a saloon every night to plead with her father to come home:

Father, dear father come home with me now,
The clock in the steeple strikes one.
You said you were coming right home from the shop,
As soon as your day's work was done.

Every hour on the hour she returned. The clock struck two and little Willie was sick and calling for him. The clock struck three and little Willie was worse, coughing and crying. The clock struck four, five, six. The fire went out; the house got cold; mother was waiting. When the clock struck ten in the morning father finally went home. Too late. Willie was dead.

It was a tearjerker if ever there was one. In those days it was alcohol that intoxicated fathers. Today it is almost as likely to be work. (*Jessie Bernard*)

Have you ever realised that the words 'I', 'my' and 'me' do not occur once in the Lord's Prayer? Yet while saying 'Our Father', it is easy to mean only 'my Father'; to utter the words 'give us this day our daily bread' and still think only in terms of 'give me my daily bread'.

These lines of Charles Thompson may help you avoid the tendency to be self-centred while praying:

You cannot pray the Lord's Prayer,
And even once say 'I'.
You cannot pray the Lord's Prayer,
And even once say 'My'.
Nor can you pray the Lord's Prayer,
And not pray for another;
For when you ask for daily bread,
You must include your brother.
For others are included
In each and every plea:
From the beginning to the end of it,
It does not once say 'Me'.

USEFUL TEXTS

Fatherhood:
   Of God to all he created, *Deut. 32:6*
   Of God to all who believe in his Son, *Gal. 4:4-6*
   Of God to Jesus Christ, *Col. 1:3*

See also: B40 One God
              C20 Our Father in heaven
              C27 The Father who receives us back

B29

THE EUCHARIST

'For my flesh is real food and my blood is real drink.
He who eats my flesh and drinks my blood lives in me
and I live in him.' *John 6:55-56*

QUOTATIONS

If you have received worthily, you are what you have received.
(St Augustine of Hippo)

The Christian metaphysics is – that he eats God.
(Theodor Hoecker)

At the Sacrament of the Body and Blood of Christ, nothing shall
be offered but bread and wine mixed with water.
(Council of Hippo)

The worthiest thing, most of goodness, in all this world, it is the
Mass. *(Lay Folk's Mass Book, thirteenth Century)*

The effect of our communion in the Body and Blood of Christ
is that we are transformed into what we consume, and that he
in whom we have died and in whom we have risen from the
dead lives and is manifested in every movement of our body and
of our spirit. *(Pope Leo I)*

The sacrament (mystery) of sacraments. *(Pseudo-Dionysius)*

Here, Lord Jesus, art Thou both Shepherd and Green Pasture.
(St Thomas Aquinas)

The noblest sacrament, consequently, is that wherein His Body
is really present. The Eucharist crowns all the other sacraments.
(St Thomas Aquinas)

I am God's wheat; I am ground by the teeth of the wild beasts that I may end as the pure bread of Christ.
(*St Ignatius of Antioch*)

Great is this mystery, and great the dignity of priests, to whom that is given which is not granted to angels. For priests alone, rightly ordained in the Church, have power to celebrate and to consecrate the body of Christ. (*Thomas à Kempis*)

For all the other things which are said in the earlier parts of the service are said by the priest . . . when it comes to the consecration of the venerable sacrament, the priest no longer uses his own language, but he uses the language of Christ. Therefore, the word of Christ consecrates this sacrament.
(*St Ambrose*)

Be zealous, then, in the observance of one Eucharist. For there is one Flesh of our Lord, Jesus Christ, and one Chalice that brings union in His Blood. There is one altar, as there is one bishop with the priests and deacons, who are my fellow workers. And so, whatever you do, let it be done in the name of the Lord. (*St Ignatius of Antioch*)

HUMOUR

Up in the north-west of England, they told me the tale of two Irish labourers over here for work who, having inadvertently and carelessly strayed into a very advanced Anglo-Catholic church, were resolved to be particularly careful about Mass the following Sunday. They watched everything closely and suspiciously until the second collection came round, and then, with great relief, one whispered to the other, 'It's alright, Mick, we're all right this time.' (*Douglas Woodruff*)

This is an appropriate moment to tell the tale of the half-crown and the penny. As they came down adjoining chutes at the Royal Mint they agreed to try to keep in touch, and to recount their adventures when they met. After a good while, meet they did. The half-crown had quite a good time, being gratefully fondled as a tip of a generous order, and had crossed many counters for useful purposes, and the penny could not match the history. His story was largely of slot machines, bus rides, and buying newspapers in the street; but, he said triumphantly, he had one big thing to boast about, that he had never once missed Mass. *(Douglas Woodruff)*

STATEMENT

As often as the sacrifice of the cross in which 'Christ, our passover has been sacrificed' *(1 Cor. 5:7)* is celebrated on an altar, the work of our redemption is carried on. At the same time, in the sacrament of the Eucharistic bread, the unity of all believers who form one body in Christ *(cf 1 Cor. 10:17)* is both expressed and brought about. All men are called to this union with Christ, who is the light of the world, from whom we go forth, through whom we live, and toward whom our journey leads us. *(Second Vatican Council – 'The Church')*

WORD PICTURES

Stories continue to come out of China, from time to time, of the heroic efforts of the few remaining bishops and priests to keep the Faith alive and nourish the underground Church. One such story tells of a priest who lives and works as a coolie. By means of prearranged sign language, he gets messages around of where he is to be found – usually in the corner of a local market ostensibly selling soap. Customers who, like the early Christians, give a secret sign, are given a piece of soap, between the wrappings of which is hidden a small wafer of consecrated bread. The Chinese Christian takes his purchase home and usually, after a short family service, receives Communion. *(Anon)*

As Christ willed it and spake it
And thankfully blessed it and brake it,
And as the sacred words do make it
So I believe and take it.

My life to give therefor,
In earth to live no more.
*(Lines appearing in various Catholic sources, quoted by
Princess Elizabeth when pressed to declare her opinion of
the Holy Eucharist. She characteristically omitted the last two.
Sixteenth Century)*

See also: A44 Meeting Christ in the sacraments
B18 Sunday
B27 Bread from heaven

B30

MARRIED LOVE

'A man must leave his father and mother and be joined
to his wife, and the two will become one body.'
Genesis 2:24

QUOTATIONS

Let there be spaces in your togetherness. *(Kahlil Gibran)*

A successful marriage is an edifice that must be rebuilt every
day. *(André Maurois)*

Don't over-analyse your marriage; it's like yanking up a fragile
indoor plant every 20 minutes to see how its roots are growing.
(Anon)

Success in marriage is more than finding the right person: it is a
matter of being the right person. *(Rabbi B. R. Brickner)*

The sum which two married people owe to one another defies
calculation. It is an infinite debt, which can only be discharged
through all eternity. *(Goethe)*

The state of marriage is one that requires more virtue and
constancy than any other; it is a perpetual exercise of
mortification. *(St Francis de Sales)*

The best way to compliment your wife is frequently. *(Anon)*

It is necessary to be almost a genius to make a good husband.
(Balzac)

A good marriage is one which allows for change and growth in
the individuals and in the way they express their love.
(Pearl Buck)

A good marriage is that in which each appoints the other guardian of his solitude. *(Rainer Maria Rilke)*

To be happy with a man you must understand him a lot and love him a little. To be happy with a woman you must love her a lot and not try to understand her at all. *(Helen Rowland)*

PROVERBS

A man too good for the world is no good for his wife. *(Yiddish proverb)*

Do not choose your wife at a dance, but in the field among the harvesters. *(Czech Proverb)*

Everyone can keep house better than her mother until she trieth. *(English proverb)*

A good husband should be deaf and a good wife blind. *(French proverb)*

HUMOUR

By all means marry. If you get a good wife, you will become very happy; if you get a bad one, you will become a philosopher – and that is good for any man. *(Socrates)*

Adam and Eve had an ideal marriage. He didn't have to hear about all the men she could have married – and she didn't have to hear about the way his mother cooked. *(Bob Orben)*

A young bride complained to her friend: 'My husband and I are getting along together fairly well, but he simply can't bear children.'

'Oh, well,' the friend consoled her, 'you can't expect men to do everything'. *(General features)*

To keep your marriage brimming,
With love in the loving cup,
Whenever you're wrong, admit it,
Whenever you're right, shut up. *(Ogden Nash)*

Boy   'Do you know, Dad, that in some parts of Africa a man doesn't know his wife until he marries her?'

Dad   'Why single out Africa?' *(Anon)*

Husband 'Did you see that pretty girl smile at me?'

Wife   'That's nothing, the first time I saw you,
I laughed out loud.' *(Anon)*

To her sympathetic neighbour the unhappy wife confessed, 'My husband doesn't show any interest in what I do. All he cares about is whatever it is he does at that place – wherever it is – that he works!' *(Anon)*

A police car stopped a motorist on the highway and informed the driver that his wife fell out of the auto a mile back.
    'Good!' exclaimed the motorist. 'I thought I'd gone deaf'. *(Anon)*

When the late Mr and Mrs Henry Ford celebrated their golden wedding anniversary, a reporter asked them, 'To what do you attribute your 50 years of successful life?'
'The formula,' said Ford, 'is the same formula I have always used in making cars – just stick to one model.' *(Anon)*

Questioning the children before Confirmation, the Bishop asked one nervous little girl, 'What is matrimony?' She answered, 'a place where souls suffer for a time on account of their sins.'
    'No, no,' said the parish priest, 'that's purgatory.'
    'Let her alone,' said the Bishop. 'She may be right. What do you and I know about it?' *(F. H. Drinkwater)*

STATEMENTS

Authentic married love is caught up into divine love and is governed and enriched by Christ's redeeming power and the saving activity of the Church. Thus this love can lead the spouses to God with powerful effect and can aid and strengthen them in the sublime office of being a father or a mother. *(Second Vatican Council – 'The Church Today')*

Such love, merging the human with the divine, leads the spouses to a free and mutual gift of themselves, a gift proving itself by gentle affection and by deed. Such love pervades the whole of their lives. Indeed, by its generous activity it grows better and grows greater. Therefore, it far excels mere erotic inclination, which, selfishly pursued, soon enough fades wretchedly away.

This love is uniquely expressed and perfected through the marital act. The actions within marriage by which the couple are united intimately and chastely are noble and worthy ones. Expressed in a manner which is truly human, these actions signify and promote that mutual self-giving by which spouses enrich each other with a joyful and a thankful will.

Sealed by mutual faithfulness and hallowed above all by Christ's sacrament, this love remains steadfastly true in body and in mind, in bright days or dark. It will never be profaned by adultery or divorce. Firmly established by the Lord, the unity of marriage will radiate from the equal personal dignity of wife and husband, a dignity acknowledged by mutual and total love. *(Second Vatican Council – 'The Church Today')*

WORD PICTURES

Marriage is like a three-speed gearbox: affection, friendship, love. It is not advisable to crash your gears and go right through to love straight away. You need to ease your way through. The basis of love is respect, and that needs to be learnt from affection and friendship. *(Peter Ustinov)*

Before President Ford married Elizabeth Bloomer, in 1948, they drew up a private marriage contract together.

'We sat down before the wedding and, in a very businesslike way, defined our objectives,' says Mrs Ford.

'We decided the number of children we would have, and ardently agreed to the mutual promise that one would never try to "change" the other.'

'We decided, too, that a successful marriage is never really a 50-50 proposition and settled for a 75-25 arrangement. Sometimes the 75 would emanate from my side. Sometimes it would have to be Jerry's gesture. We have carefully worked out the art of generous compromise.' *(Marian Christy)*

In Imperial China, where wise justice was legendary, the law maintained a careful balance between the sexes. The first time a wife was unfaithful, it was her seducer who was punished, for he was presumed to have taken advantage of her innocence. At the second breach, it was the fickle spouse herself who was whipped. On the third occasion, her husband was imprisoned for having brought the venerable institution of marriage into disrepute. *(James de Coquet)*

The art of marriage
A good marriage must be created.
In the marriage, the little things are the big things . . .
It is never being too old to hold hands.
It is remembering to say 'I love you' at least once
    each day.
It is never going to sleep angry.
It is having a mutual sense of values and common
    objectives.
It is standing together and facing the world.
It is forming a circle of love that gathers in the
    whole family.
It is speaking words of appreciation and
    demonstrating gratitude in thoughtful ways.
It is having the capacity to forgive and forget.
It is giving each other an atmosphere in which each
    can grow.
It is a common search for the good and the
    beautiful.
It is not only marrying the right person,
It is being the right partner.
(Anon)

Useful Texts

Marriage:
  Permanent bond, *Matt. 19:5-6*
  Instituted by God, *Gen. 2:18-24*
  Honourable for all, *Heb. 13:4*
  Means of preventing immorality, *1 Cor. 7:2-4*

See also: A46 Priesthood of the laity
          B6 The Family
          C5 The institution of marriage

B31

THE COMMANDMENTS OF LIFE

'Accept and submit to the word which has been planted
in you and can save your souls.'
James 1:21

QUOTATIONS

Live by the commandments; do not die by them. *(Talmud)*

Wherever law ends, tyranny begins. *(John Locke)*

Love, and do what you will. *(St Augustine of Hippo)*

Man is an able creature, but he has made 32,647,389 laws and
hasn't yet improved on the Ten Commandments. *(Anon)*

What else are the laws of God written in our hearts but the very
presence of the Holy Ghost? *(St Augustine of Hippo)*

The precepts of the law are these: to live honourably, to injure
no other man, to render to every man his due.
(Institutes of Justinian)

God's precepts are light to the loving, heavy to the fearful.
(St Thomas Aquinas)

To say 'It is only a man-made law' is to miss the point. Only
when civil laws are at variance with the laws of God are they
strictly man-made. *(Hubert Van Zeller)*

Love of God is the root, love of our neighbour the fruit, of the
Tree of Life. Neither can exist without the other; but the one is
cause and the other effect, and the order of the Two Great
Commandments must not be inverted. *(William Temple)*

All laws are promulgated for this end: that every man may know his duty; and therefore the plainest and most obvious sense of the words is that which must be put on them. *(St Thomas More)*

HUMOUR
Overheard: 'If God believed in today's permissiveness, He would have given us the Ten Suggestions!' *(Anon)*

'The boys are in such a mood that if someone introduced the Ten Commandments, they'd cut them down to eight'. *(Senator Norris Cotton (Reference to economy-minded Senate))*

WORD PICTURES
Life must be based on positive and permanent values. The value of love will always be stronger than the value of hate; since any nation which employs hatred is eventually torn to pieces by hatred within itself. The value of truth and sincerity is always stronger than the value of lies and cynicism. No process has been invented which can permanently separate men from their own hearts and consciences or prevent them from seeing the results of their own false ideas. You cannot make men believe that a way of life is good when it spreads poverty, misery, disease and death. Men cannot be everlastingly loyal unless they are free. *(Franklin D. Roosevelt)*

In Oscoda, Michigan, Rev John Silen gives the Ten Commandments the Chippewa Indians had long ago. They are:
1. Never steal, except from an enemy.
2. Respect the aged and harken to them.
3. Be kind to the sick and deformed.
4. Obey your parents.
5. Be modest.
6. Be charitable.
7. Be of good courage, suffer in silence.
8. Avenge personal and family wrongs.
9. Be hospitable.
10. Pray to the Great Spirit.

Many people criticise some of these Chippewa commandments and at the same time look upon God's Ten Commandments as ghostly whispers of a dead age.

Six hundred and thirteen commandments were given to Moses: 365 negative, corresponding to the days of the year, and 248 positive, corresponding to the number of joints in the human body. *(Talmud)*

USEFUL TEXTS

The Commandments:
    Of God, *John 15:12*
    Of Christ, examples, *Matt. 5:16, 27-28, 31-32, 34*
    Of a father, *Prov. 6:20, 7:1*

See also: A29 True obedience
              C6 The Old Testament Law
              C39 Doing God's will.

B32

THE WONDERS OF GOD

'He has done all things well,' they said 'he makes the deaf hear and the dumb speak.' *Mark 7:37*

QUOTATIONS

Seeing, hearing, feeling are miracles, and each part and tag of me is a miracle. *(Walt Whitman)*

It is impossible on reasonable grounds to disbelieve miracles. *(Pascal)*

God raises the level of the impossible. *(Corrie Ten Boom)*

A miracle is a transgression of a law of nature by a particular volition of the Deity, or by the interposition of some invisible agent. *(David Hume)*

The miracles of Jesus were the ordinary works of his Father, wrought small and swift that we might take them in. *(George MacDonald)*

Jesus was himself the one convincing and permanent miracle. *(Ian MacLaren)*

Miracles are not contrary to nature, but only contrary to what we know about nature. *(St Augustine of Hippo)*

A miracle is no argument to one who is deliberately, and on principle, an atheist. *(Cardinal Newman)*

It would have approached nearer to the idea of miracle if Jonah had swallowed the whale. *(Thomas Paine)*

I should not be a Christian but for the miracles. *(St Augustine of Hippo)*

All miracles are simply feeble lights like beacons on our way to the port where shines the light, the total light of the resurrection. *(Jacques Ellul)*

For those who believe in God, no explanation is needed; for those who do not believe in God, no explanation is possible. *(John LaFarge)*

PROVERBS

Miracles are the swaddling-clothes of infant churches. *(English proverb)*

Little saints also perform miracles. *(Danish proverb)*

STATEMENT

If any one shall say that miracles are impossible, and therefore that all the accounts regarding them, even those contained in Holy Scripture, are to be dismissed as fabulous or mythical; or that miracles can never be known with certainty, and that the divine origin of Christianity is not rightly proved by them; let him be anathema. *(First Vatican Council – Session 3)*

WORD PICTURES

When Moses threw the wand into the Red Sea, the sea quite contrary to the expected miracle, did not divide itself to leave a dry passage for the Jews. Not until the first man had jumped into the sea did the promised miracle happen and the waves recede. *(Jewish legend)*

Shortly after the end of Eritrea's 30-year war with Ethiopia, Gioacchino Catanzaro, a Franciscan who lives and works in the capital, Asmara, sent this account of how he perceived the momentous changes in his country:

This time last year we were all living in a nightmare of almost intolerable tension. Missiles fell at random in the city, killing and injuring many innocent victims. Explosions and shots could be heard near and far. Battles killed thousands and wounded many more. There were assassinations. Jet bombers, like giant wasps, angrily cleft the air. Our hearts were constantly filled with fear and panic.

'Then on 10 May 1991, there appeared around the sun above Asmara, a brilliant circle. We all saw it. The people – the voice of God – immediately declared that the bright circle in the sky was a sign of the covenant between God and ourselves. On 11 May, President Menghistu fled Addis Ababa. On 24 May, the Ethiopian army fled, disappeared as if by magic from Asmara and the whole of Eritrea, without another shot being fired.

'This is a miracle! A great miracle, worked through the intercession of Our Lady, our Mother and our Queen. We join with her in thanking God who has cast down the mighty from their seats and raised the lowly, who has filled the hungry with good things and sent the rich away empty.'

If you say, but no one has seen miracles performed, then I answer that once upon a time everybody worshipped false gods and persecuted Christians, and then afterwards all were converted including the wise, noble, powerful, by a few poor and unlettered preachers. Either this was miraculous or not. If so, then the point is granted; if not, then I ask, what greater miracle could there have been than to convert so many without miracles? *(St Thomas Aquinas)*

Jack Traynor, of Liverpool, was hit in the head with a piece of shrapnel at the start of the First World War, but he recovered and was posted to Egypt, where as a result of the wound he began to have epileptic fits. In May 1915, at Gallipoli, he was cut down by three Turkish machine-gun bullets. Two passed through his chest and the third went through his right arm and lodged under his collar bone, severing the main nerves in his armpit and paralysing the limb. After four unsuccessful attempts to reunite the severed nerves, he was awarded a one hundred per cent pension in 1917.

A statement signed by three doctors who accompanied him to Lourdes in 1923 attested that he was then epileptic and incontinent, and without any voluntary movement in his legs.

His arm was still paralysed and there was a resultant atrophy of chest and shoulder muscles.

It was after Traynor's ninth and last visit to the baths that he suddenly felt he could walk, and the following day, during the Procession of the Blessed Sacrament, his right arm began to twitch. On the third day, the same three doctors confirmed that Traynor could walk, had recovered the use of his arm and that a hole in his skull, through which it had been possible to see his brain pulsating, had completely closed.

Traynor returned to Liverpool to take charge of the family coal business and, being an honest man, informed the Ministry of Pensions of his recovery. Since they had no administrative machinery to cope with miracles, he continued to receive his pension until he died, aged 64. *(Anon)*

Some of the Christians referred to in the documents we present are in prison for the crime of 'miraculous healings'. According to the Communist authorities, such things are impossible!

However, I myself was sick in prison with lung, spinal and intestinal tuberculosis and recurring jaundice. The 'medicines' I received were beatings, neglect and lack of food. Doctors in Oslo who later examined me and took X-rays could not believe at first that I had survived the Rumanian prison conditions, with four vertebrae infected with tuberculosis, lungs like sieves, and without food and drugs. The healing virtue of Christ had proved to be the same as in the times of the Gospel. Today He delivers many of the fighters of the Underground Church from their infirmities through the prayers of the faithful.

We read in the *Journal* of George Fox, the founder of the Quakers, that when he was released from the prison in Newcastle he could heal. So can many who have passed through Communist jails.

The Communists may mock such healings as fakes – again they put the dunce's caps on our heads! But I know that I was mortally sick and I know that I am now very much alive! Thousands can tell the same story. *(Richard Wurmbrand)*

USEFUL TEXTS

Miracles:
  Attributed to;
  God's power, *Acts 15:12*
  Christ's power, *John 2:11*
  Spirit's power, *Matt. 12:28*
  To reveal God's glory, *John 11:40*

See also: A18 Balance in nature
           B39 Creation

B33

FAITH AND GOOD WORKS

'Faith is like that, if good works do not go with it,
it is quite dead.' *James 2:17*

QUOTATIONS

Holiness has to do with very ordinary things. *(Ruth Burrow)*

As the flower is before the fruit, so is faith before good works.
(Richard Whately)

You can do very little with faith, but you can do nothing
without it. *(Nicholas Murray Butler)*

Faith is the root of works. A root that produces nothing is dead.
(Thomas Wilson)

All work that is worth anything is done in faith.
(Albert Schweitzer)

We do the works, but God works in us the doing of the works.
(St Augustine of Hippo)

For faith without works cannot please, nor can good works
without faith. *(St Bede the Venerable)*

A work is then truly excellent, when the intention of the
workman is struck out from the love of God, and returns again
and again to rest in charity. *(St Augustine of Hippo)*

He who would obey the Gospel must first be purged of all
defilement of the flesh and the spirit that so he may be
acceptable to God in the good works of holiness. *(St Basil)*

Think not that pleasing God lies so much in performing good works as in performing them with good will, and without attachment and respect to persons. *(St John of the Cross)*

To be active in works and unfaithful in heart is like raising a beautiful and lofty building on an unsound foundation. The higher the building, the greater the fall. Without the support of faith, good works cannot stand. *(St Ambrose)*

God chose that man should seek salvation by faith rather than by works, lest anyone should glory in his deeds and thereby incur sin. *(St Ambrose)*

PROVERB
Faith sees by the ears. *(English proverb)*

HUMOUR
Two priests were driving in a cab to the station, and were in some anxiety lest they should miss their train. One of them pulled out his watch and discovered it had stopped

'How annoying!' he exclaimed. 'And I always put such faith in that watch!'

'In a case like this,' answered the other, 'good works would evidently have answered the purpose better.'

WORD PICTURES
A famous heiress keeps her priceless collection of jewels in the vault of a large bank. One of her prize possessions is a very valuable string of pearls. It is a scientific fact that pearls lose their original lustre if not worn once in a while in contact with the human body. So, once a week, a bank secretary, guarded by two plainclothesmen, wears these priceless pearls to lunch. This brief contact with the human body keeps them beautiful and in good condition.

Our faith is a lot like the pearl. It must be used in order to be useful. It must be worn out among the masses of mankind where faith and hope are needed. *(Uplift)*

A people that grazes on junk music, junk books, junk art, junk newspapers, lives in junk houses on junk estates, and spends its leisure on junk entertainment, is a poor soil for the seed of religious faith. They fall prey to junk religion as easily as to junk politics. Yet in all the talk about and proposals for, the renewal of the Church and of religious faith, how often is the issue of culture renewal raised? Or when was there last an encyclical or pastoral letter on cultural deprivation?
(John F X Harriot)

St Frances Cabrini, the first US citizen to be canonised, had her own ways of supporting the many charitable institutions she founded. When bills for upkeep came, for example, she was known to stamp them PAID and send them back – explaining gently that she knew the senders really wished to contribute to God's work, so she was saving them a lot of time and trouble. No one ever complained. *(Adela Rogers St Johns)*

Faith is not merely praying
Upon our knees at night;
Faith is not merely straying
Through darkness into light;
Faith is not merely waiting
For glory that may be.
Faith is the brave endeavour,
The splendid enterprise,
The strength to serve,
whatever conditions may arise.
(Anon)

USEFUL TEXTS

Faith:
    Gift of God, *Eph. 2:8*
    Condition of salvation, *Acts 16:31*

Works:
    Encouraged, *Matt. 5:16; Titus 2:7; 1 Pet. 2:12*

See also: C22 The Light of Faith
           C30 Increase our Faith

B34

HUMAN RIGHTS

'Wherever you find jealousy and ambition, you find
disharmony and wicked things of every kind being done.'
James 3:16

QUOTATIONS

'All human beings are born free and equal in dignity and rights.'
(Adopted by UNO 10th December 1948)

Every man bears the whole stamp of the human condition.
(Michael de Montaigne)

Rights that do not flow from duty well performed are not worth
having. *(Mohandas Gandhi)*

I am the inferior of any man whose rights I trample under foot.
(Robert Ingersoll)

They have rights who dare maintain them.
(James Russell Lowell)

Wherever there is a human being, I see God-given rights
inherent in that being, whatever may be the sex or complexion.
(William Lloyd Garrison)

A right is worth fighting for only when it can be put into
operation. *(Woodrow Wilson)*

But the world *can* be different. Human society is not more than
the people of that society. And nothing makes its progress more
inevitable than people who decide that it is. *(Thomas Cullinan)*

No one can be perfectly free till all are free; no one can be
perfectly moral till all are moral; no one can be perfectly happy
till all are happy. *(Herbert Spencer)*

To shelter or give medical aid to a man on the run, from a police force which will torture and perhaps kill him, is an act of Christian love demanded by Christ in the Gospel and is no more a political act than giving first aid and a cup of tea to a member of parliament who has a car smash outside your door.
(Sheila Cassidy)

STATEMENT

At the same time, however, there is a growing awareness of the exalted dignity proper to the human person, since he stands above all things, and his rights and duties are universal and inviolable. Therefore, there must be made available to all men everything necessary for leading a life truly human, such as food, clothing and shelter; the right to education, to employment, to a good reputation, to respect, to appropriate information, to activity in accord with the upright norm of one's own conscience, to protection of privacy and to rightful freedom in matters religious too.
(Second Vatican Council – 'The Church Today')

WORD PICTURES

To those who find it difficult to believe stories of torture and ask (not unreasonably) for medical evidence, it is important to explain that a good deal of care is taken by torturers to see that no lashing marks are made on the subject.

Electric shock, the most commonly used torture in many countries, leaves no mark at all, as anyone who likes to touch a live wire can verify.

Likewise, immersion of the head in a bucket of water contaminated by excrement, unless it causes death by drowning, cannot be proved. I could go on, but the point is simple: modern torture is designed to leave no scars.

To those people who believe that people who become 'involved in politics' deserve what they get, it is worth pointing out that Article 5 of the Universal Declaration on Human Rights states clearly, 'No one shall be submitted to torture or cruel, inhuman or degrading treatment or punishment.'
(Sheila Cassidy)

A big landowner invited me to celebrate Mass at his establishment. All his workers were there, hundreds of them. If I preach and say, for example, that one must obey one's employer, that one must work with patience and goodwill and do one's duty, for this landowner I am 'a tremendous bishop', 'a holy bishop'. I can expect to be invited again to preach. But if, while speaking of the worker's duty and the landowner's rights, I have the audacity, yes the audacity, to mention the worker's rights and the landowner's duty, then it is quite a different matter. 'This is a revolutionary, a progressive, he is pro-communist . . .' *(Dom Helder Camara)*

The great mass murderers of our time have accounted for no more than a few hundred victims. In contrast, states that have chosen to murder their own citizens can usually count their victims by the carload. As for motive, the state has no peers, for it will kill its victim for a careless word, a fleeting thought, or even a poem.

But the homicidal state shares one trait with the solitary killer – like all murderers, it trips on its own egotism and drops a trail of clues which, when properly collected, preserved and analysed are as damning as a signed confession left in the grave. *(Dr Clyde Snow, forensic anthropologist, has analysed skeletal remains to expose atrocities committed by state agents in a number of countries including Argentina, Bolivia, Chile and Guatemala.)*

Jesus is stripped of his garments
I remember once talking to the last Lady Abbess of Stanbrook, who said of my Chilean captors, 'I knew they'd strip you. They always do.' She was right, of course. Somewhere in the vaults at Ampleforth is a box of my Chilean relics, containing, among other things, the shirt in which I was arrested. Half-way down the front is a small three-cornered tear which happened when, exasperated at my modesty, they started to rip it off me.

I have often reflected on nakedness since then. We are so very vulnerable without our clothes: not just physically more available to the rod, the lash or the wandering electrode but somehow stripped of our emotional defences as well. I try to be very conscious of this in my work because doctors get so used to seeing people unclothed that they forget how they can humiliate and reduce the most articulate of them to an anxious heap.

The second thing about nakedness is that when people are stripped they are somehow distanced, different from those with clothes. I believe this is one of the things that makes it possible for one person to torture another. A woman in her jeans may look like the torturer's sister; unclothed she is just another woman, a subject to be interrogated or an object to satisfy those animal desires that rise unbidden in the heart and override the strongest discipline.

One New Year's night (before my time) the guards at the Villa Grimaldi got drunk and raped all the women in their charge. Father forgive them. Such memories fade but they never go away. Fifteen years on I bear the scars of what was done to me. Others have suffered so much more than I. They still need help. And the government has announced that it is going to withdraw the funding for the accommodation of a medical group for the treatment of victims of torture in London. Father forgive them . . . because I am not able. *(Sheila Cassidy)*

They thought that by kidnapping that man
They have won, and have defeated him

But that's not what happened,
He has won;
He has beaten them
Because he gave himself body and soul to the
people.

They thought that by kidnapping that man
They would silence many.

But that's not what happened;
Now there's more voices that cry out
And demand justice and freedom for all.

They thought that by kidnapping him
And leaving him in a secret prison
Or in a clandestine cemetery
They'd be rid of him.

But that's not what happened;
His example
Is the struggle of the people.

Don't forget that there's always someone
Who can pick up the banner
Of the fallen and say,
'We carry on the struggle'.
(*Quiché Indian Rosa Pu, Guatemala.*
Her first husband 'disappeared' in 1981.
Her second husband 'disappeared' in 1990.)

THE RIGHT:
To affection, love and understanding.
To adequate nutrition and medical care.
To free education.
To full opportunity for play and recreation.
To a name and nationality.
To special care, if handicapped.
To be among the first to receive relief in times of disaster.

To learn to be a useful member of society and to develop
  individual abilities.
To be brought up in a spirit of peace and universal
  brotherhood.
To enjoy these rights, regardless of race, colour, sex, religion,
  national, or social origin.
(UN Declaration of the Rights of The Child)

See also: A21 Feeding the hungry
           A40 The equality of women
           B44 The dignity of the individual
           C1 Liberation from fear
           C33 Equality

B35

THE GRACE OF GOD

'The Lord spoke with Moses, but took some of the Spirit that was on him and put it on the 70 elders. When the Spirit came on them, they prophesied.' *Numbers 11:25*

QUOTATIONS

Grace does not destroy nature, it perfects it.
(St Thomas Aquinas)

They travel lightly whom God's grace carries.
(Thomas à Kempis)

Grace is not sought nor bought nor wrought. It is a free gift of Almighty God to needy mankind. *(Billy Graham)*

Grace is God himself, his loving energy at work within his church and within our souls. *(Evelyn Underhill)*

A state of mind that sees God in everything is evidence of growth in grace and a thankful heart. *(Charles G. Finney)*

There is no such way to attain to a greater measure of grace as for a man to live up to the little grace he has. *(Phillips Brooks)*

The law detects, grace alone conquers sin.
(St Augustine of Hippo)

Every holy thought is the gift of God, the inspiration of God, the grace of God. *(St Ambrose)*

Let grace be the beginning, grace the consummation, grace the crown. *(St Bede the Venerable)*

The burden of life is from ourselves, its lightness from the grace of Christ and the love of God. *(Archbishop Ullathorne)*

The private and personal blessings we enjoy, the blessings of immunity, safeguard, liberty and integrity, deserve the thanksgiving of a whole life. *(Jeremy Taylor)*

It would seem that grace has a certain power, accumulating through the centuries, of saturating even physical objects with its force, however men may rebel. *(R. H. Benson)*

Proverbs

In space comes grace. *(English proverb)*

God does not refuse grace to one who does what he can. *(Latin proverb)*

Word pictures

'There, but for the grace of God, goes . . .'
Who used these famous words? They have been attributed to several saintly men, including John Bunyan, but the story is rightly told of John Bradford, the Protestant martyr, who was burnt at Smithfield on Sunday 30th June, 1555. The story is that once, on seeing some criminals being taken to execution, he exclaimed, 'There, but for the grace of God, goes John Bradford.' *(Anon)*

When I want to move my hand, it moves. I don't have to stop and think, 'How shall I move it?' It happens. But if I find myself to be a selfish kind of person and want to be unselfish, it doesn't happen. Therefore, something has got to take hold of us from outside. *(William Temple)*

If grace perfects nature, it must expand all our natures into the full richness of the diversity which God intended when he made them, and heaven will display far more variety than hell. 'One fold' doesn't mean 'one pool'. Cultivated roses and daffodils are no more alike than wild roses and daffodils. *(C. S. Lewis)*

At Tara today in this fateful hour
I place all Heaven with its power,
    and the sun with its brightness,
    and the snow with its whiteness,
    and the fire with all the strength it hath,
    and lightning with its rapid wrath,
    and the winds with their swiftness along their path,
    and the sea with its deepness,
    and the rocks with their steepness,
    and the earth with its starkness:
all these I place,
by God's almighty help and grace,
between myself and the powers of darkness.
(*'Rune of St Patrick' (Anon)*)

USEFUL TEXTS

Grace of God:
    Source of salvation, *Acts 15:11*
            forgiveness, *Eph. 1:7*
            faith, *Acts 18:27*
            justification, *Rom. 3:24*

See also: B51 One with Christ
            B52 God is Love
            C47 The indwelling Spirit

B36

THE FAMILY OF GOD

'The one who sanctifies, and the ones who are sanctified, are of the same stock; that is why he openly calls them brothers.'
Hebrews 2:11

QUOTATIONS

We are one, after all, you and I; together we suffer, together exist, and forever will we recreate each other. *(Teilhard de Chardin)*

Men become what they are, sons of God, by becoming what they are, brothers of their brothers. *(Martin Buber)*

In all my travels, the thing that has impressed me most is the universal brotherhood of man – what there is of it. *(Mark Twain)*

Let us be like the lines that lead to the centre of a circle – uniting there, and not like parallel lines, which never join. *(Hasidic saying)*

Perfect virtue is when you behave to everyone as if you were receiving a great guest. Not to do to others as you would not have them do to you. Within the four seas all are brothers. *(Confucius)*

The supreme reality of our time is our indivisibility as children of God and the common vulnerability of this planet.
(John F. Kennedy)

Our true nationality is mankind. *(H. G. Wells)*

While there is a lower class, I am in it,
While there is a criminal element, I am of it,
While there is a soul in prison, I am not free. *(Eugene V. Debs)*

The great door sighs. It opens, and a child
Enters the church and kneels in the front pew.
The Maker of the Universe has smiled:
He made the church for this one interview.
(Daniel Sargent)

WORD PICTURES

The word *Church* used in most of the North European
languages comes from the Greek *Kyriakè oikia,* 'The Family of
the Lord'. It is significant that when people sought a word to
describe the reality of what it means to be Church, the word
they chose meant 'family of the Lord'. *(Leonard Doohan)*

Mankind is a single nation. One of God's signs is the creation of
the heavens and the earth and the diversity of your tongues and
your colours. Surely there are signs in this for the learned. O
mankind, surely we have created you from a male and a female
and made you nations and families that you may know each
other. Surely the noblest of you with God is the most dutiful of
you. Surely God is knowing awareness. *(The Qur'an)*

Recognise all mankind, whether Hindu or Muslim, as one:
The same Lord is the Creator and Nourisher of all;
Recognise no distinctions among them.
The monastery and the mosque are the same;
So the Hindu worship and the Muslim prayer;
Men are all one. *(Guru Gobind Singh)*

So the world is not one, its peoples are more divided now, and
also more conscious of their divisions, than they have ever been
before. They are divided between those who are satisfied and
those who are hungry; they are divided between those with
power and those without power; they are divided between those
who dominate and those who are dominated, between those
who exploit and those who are exploited. And it is the minority
which is well fed and the minority which has secured control of
the world's wealth and over their fellow men. Further, in

general, that minority is distinguished by the colour of their skin, and by their race. And the nations in which most of the minority of the world's people live have a further distinguishing characteristic – their adoption of the Christian religion.
(*Julius K. Nyerere*)

Perhaps few among you have so many dealings with men of different races, different religions, different beliefs and different cultures as I – unworthily – have. In all these dealings, I have always found a great love, a wide-open heart, always opens the heart of others. This great love must be not mere diplomacy but the result of a sincere conviction that, as I have already said, we are all the children of God, who has created mankind, who has created each one of us, and whose children we all are.
(*Cardinal Bea*)

The Church is not a clean well-lighted place where everything runs smoothly and actions automatically match ideals. It is, in the words of the Gospel, a field of cockle and wheat growing up together and beyond human power to separate.

The enthusiast will always be running up against rigidity of mind, narrowness of vision, stoniness of heart; no great development in the Church has ever received a fair wind from the start. The lover of good order, of uniformity and discipline will always be confounded by a spirit that blows where it will, by the sheer complexity of human situations and individuals, by prophets and visionaries and nonconformists who cannot be regulated like alarm-clocks.

Whether one aches for a Church of inspired wholehearted enthusiasts or a Church where everyone sings perfectly in tune, one aches in vain. It will always be untidy and riddled with contradictions. It will always have a dark side as well as a bright. Its hidden life will always be more enriching and reassuring than its public demeanour. It is, after all, the People of God. And people are imperfect and contradictory. To know it we have only to look at ourselves. (*John F. X. Harriott*)

During a battle between Muslims and Sikhs, a Sikh water carrier called Ghanaya was seen giving water to wounded Muslim soldiers as they lay suffering from thirst under the hot sun. He was brought to Guru Gobind Singh and accused of being a traitor. The Guru heard the charges and asked Ghanaya to answer them. 'When I walked through the battlefields I saw no Muslims and no Sikhs, only your face in every man,' said Ghanaya. 'You are a true Sikh,' replied the Guru. 'Continue the work; and here is some ointment to put on the wounds. You shall be known as Bhai Ghanaya from now on.' Bhai means brother; it is a term of honour among Sikhs, reserved for the best of men. *(W. Owen Cole)*

USEFUL TEXTS
Family of God – the Church:
  Loved by Christ, *Eph. 5:25*
  Head of, *Eph. 1:22*
  Persecuted by Paul, *Gal. 1:13*
  Pillar of truth, *1 Tim. 3:15*
  Gifts of, *1 Cor. 12:27-30*

See also: B34 Human rights
          C12 The Church for all men
          C17 International peace
          C24 Lord of all nations

B37

TRUE WISDOM

'I prayed, and understanding was given me; I entreated, and the Spirit of Wisdom came to me.' *Wisdom 7:7*

QUOTATIONS

The wise man reads both books and life itself. *(Lin Yutang)*

Knowledge comes, but wisdom lingers.
(Alfred, Lord Tennyson)

The art of being wise is the art of knowing what to overlook. *(William James)*

The highest wisdom has but one science – the science of the whole – the science explaining the whole creation and man's place in it. *(Leo Tolstoy)*

Wisdom is oftentimes nearer when we stoop than when we soar. *(William Wordsworth)*

He is truly wise who gains wisdom from another's mishap. *(Publius Syrus)*

Fruitless is the wisdom of him who has no knowledge of himself. *(Erasmus)*

It is great folly to wish to be wise with an impossible wisdom. *(St Francis de Sales)*

A knife of the keenest steel requires the whetstone, and the wisest man needs advice. *(Zoroaster)*

Wisdom is the foundation, and justice the work without which a foundation cannot stand. *(St Ambrose)*

The first key to wisdom is assiduous and frequent questioning. For by doubting we come to inquiry and by inquiry we arrive at truth. *(Peter Abelard)*

Common sense, in an uncommon degree, is what the world calls wisdom. *(Coleridge)*

Wisdom is the ability to use knowledge so as to meet successfully the emergencies of life. Men may acquire knowledge, but wisdom is a gift direct from God. *(Dr Bob Jones)*

To have a low opinion of our own merits, and to think highly of others, is an evidence of wisdom. All men are frail, but thou shouldst reckon none as frail as thyself. *(Thomas à Kempis)*

We learn wisdom from failure more than from success. We often discover what will do, by finding out what will not do. Great thoughts, discoveries, inventions have very generally been nurtured in hardship, often pondered over in sorrow and established with difficulty. *(Paxton Hood)*

PROVERBS
Wisdom comes by suffering. *(Greek proverb)*

There is often wisdom under a shabby cloak. *(Latin proverb)*

The great wisdom in man consists in knowing his follies
(French proverb)

HUMOUR
Fools make feasts and wise men eat them;
Wise men make jests and fools repeat them. *(Traditional)*

Some men are wise,
And some are otherwise.
(Traditional)

Wisdom is a hen, whose cackling we must value and consider because it is attended with an egg; but, then, lastly, it is a nut, which, unless you choose with judgement, may cost you a tooth, and pay you with nothing but a worm. *(Jonathan Swift)*

WORD PICTURES

It is an ironic fact that in this nuclear age,
when the horizon of human knowledge
and human experience
has passed far beyond any
that any age has ever known,
we turn back at this time
to the older source of wisdom and strength,
to the words of the prophets and the saints,
who tell us that faith is more powerful than doubt,
that hope is more potent than despair,
and that only through the love
that is sometimes called charity
can we conquer those forces
within ourselves
and throughout all the world
that threaten the very existence of mankind.
(John F. Kennedy)

Who knows not, and knows not that he knows not, is foolish;
   shun him.
Who knows not, and knows that he knows not, is humble;
   teach him.
Who knows, but knows not that he knows, is asleep;
   wake him.
Who knows, and knows that he knows, is wise;
   follow him
(Anon)

I remember the story of the old Scot on his deathbed. He was being taken through his baptismal vows, to renew them, and was asked, did he renounce the Devil and all his works? To which he answered, 'At the present very delicate juncture in my affairs, I can have no wish to give unnecessary offence in any quarter.' *(Douglas Woodruff)*

Perfect wisdom hath four parts, viz., wisdom, the principle of doing things aright; justice, the principle of doing things equally in public and private; fortitude, the principle of not flying danger but meeting it; and temperance, the principle of subduing desires and living moderately. *(Plato)*

A wise old owl sat on an oak
The more he saw the less he spoke;
The less he spoke the more he heard;
Why aren't we like that wise old bird?
(Edward Hersey Richards)

Professor Albert Einstein, the mathematical genius, was travelling by train in the United States. The dinner-gong sounded, so he left his seat in the carriage and walked down the corridor to the dining-car, taking with him a book he was reading.

When he had sat down at a table, he found that he had left his reading glasses in his compartment, but as he could manage to read the book without them he decided not to go back. As he read on, he came to a footnote which was printed in very small type which he could not decipher.

He called to Sam, one of the dining-car attendants, and pointed to the footnote.

'Would you be good enough to read that for me?' he asked.

'Ah sho' am sorry, sir,' said Sam, 'but Ah ain't educated either.' *(Peter Hargreaves)*

USEFUL TEXTS

Wisdom:
    Value of, *Job 28:12-28; Prov. 8:11; Eccles. 7:19*
    Given by God, *Eccles. 2:26; James 1:5*
    Prayers for, *2 Chron. 1:10;Ps. 90:12; Eph. 1:17*
    Personified, *Prov. 8:1*

See also: A2 Integrity
           B19 Conscience
           B20 Growth to maturity
           B26 The whole man

B38

THE SUFFERING SERVANT

'By his sufferings shall my servant justify many, taking their faults on himself.' *Isaiah 53:11*

QUOTATIONS

Unearned suffering is redemptive. *(Martin Luther King)*

Humanity's extremity is God's opportunity. *(John Flavel)*

Take the cross *he* sends, as it is, and not as *you* imagine it to be. *(Mother Cornelia Connelly)*

One ounce of patient suffering is worth far more than a pound of action. *(Jean P. Camus)*

Suffering passes, but the fact of having suffered never leaves us. *(Leon Bloy)*

It is a glorious thing to be indifferent to suffering, but only to one's own suffering. *(Robert Lynd)*

The chief pang of most trials is not so much the actual suffering itself as our own spirit of resistance to it. *(Jean Nicholas Grou)*

The hardest heart and grossest ignorance must disappear before the fire of suffering without anger and malice. *(Mohandas Gandhi)*

There is nothing that we suffer for the honour of God, however little it may be, that is not more serviceable to us than if we possessed the dominion of the world. *(Archbishop Ullathorne)*

Torture us, rack us, condemn us, crush us; your cruelty only proves our innocence. That is why God suffers us to suffer all this. *(Tertullian)*

He who knoweth how to suffer will enjoy much peace. Such a one is a conqueror of himself and lord of the world, a friend of Christ, and an heir of heaven. *(Thomas à Kempis)*

The highest privilege there is, is the privilege of being allowed to share another's pain. You talk about your pleasures to your acquaintances: you talk about your troubles to your friends. *(Fr Andrew SDC)*

PROVERBS

He who suffers much will know much. *(Greek proverb)*

Of suffering comes ease. *(English proverb)*

STATEMENT

By suffering for us He not only provided us with an example for our imitation. He blazed a trail and if we follow it, life and death are made holy and take on a new meaning. *(Second Vatican Council – 'The Church Today')*

WORD PICTURES

Let nothing disturb thee,
Nothing affright thee;
All things are passing;
God never changeth;
Patient endurance
Attaineth to all things;
Who God possesseth
In nothing is wanting;
Alone God sufficeth.
(St Teresa of Avila)

From the Will of Count Schwerin von Schwanenfeld, who was executed on 8 September, 1944, for his part in the plot against Hitler . . . Further it is my desire that in that part of the gravel bed in my forest of Sartowitz where the victims of the massacres of the late autumn of 1939 are laid to rest, a very high oaken cross be erected as soon as the conditions of the time permit, with the following inscription: Here lie from 1,400 to 1,500 Christians and Jews. May God have mercy on their souls and on their murderers. *(Kathe Kuhn – 'Dying We Live')*

The following story is from Ernest Gordon's account of life and death in a Japanese POW camp on the River Kwai:
One story that went the rounds soon after, concerned another soldier of the Argyll regiment, who was in a work detail on the railway.

The day's work had ended; the tools were being counted, as usual. As the party was about to be dismissed, the Japanese guard shouted that a shovel was missing. He insisted that someone had stolen it to sell to the Thais. Striding up and down before the men, he ranted and denounced them for their wickedness and their ingratitude to the Emperor. As he raved, he worked himself up into a paranoid fury. Screaming in broken English, he demanded that the guilty one step forward to take his punishment. No one moved; the guard's rage reached new heights of violence. 'All die! All die!' he shrieked.

To show that he meant what he said, he cocked his rifle, put it on his shoulder and looked down the sights, ready to fire at the first man at the end of them. At that moment the Argyll stepped forward, stood stiffly to attention, and said calmly, 'I did it.'

The guard unleashed all his whipped-up hate; he kicked the helpless prisoner and beat him with his fists. Still the Argyll stood rigidly to attention, with the blood streaming down his face. His silence goaded the guard to an excess of rage. Seizing his rifle by the barrel, he lifted it high over his head and, with a final howl, brought it down on the skull of the Argyll, who sank limply to the ground and did not move. Although it was perfectly clear that he was dead, the guard continued to beat him and stopped only when he was exhausted.

The men of the work detail picked up their comrade's body, shouldered their tools and marched back to camp. When the tools were counted again at the guard-house, no shovel was missing. *(Ernest Gordon – 'Miracle on the River Kwai')*

We do well to remember that Christianity did not invent suffering. Suffering was already in the world since time began. Christianity worked out a creative way of handling it: to fight against it when it is unnecessary, but to accept it lovingly when it is the way to do Christ's will. Christianity thus gave a meaning to suffering. This meaning is not that suffering is good in itself but that, in God's providence, it is an opportunity to love – the supreme test in many instances. *(John Dalrymple)*

Suffering by itself is nothing; it's useless. But suffering shared with Christ in his passion is a wonderful gift to human life. It is the most beautiful gift for us to share in the passion of Christ, yes, and a sign of love, because His Father proved that He loved the world by giving His Son to die for us, and so in Christ's own life it was proved that suffering was the gift, the greatest gift. As Our Lord has said, 'Greater love than this no man has, that he gives his life for his friends.' And so when we suffer for Jesus, this is the greatest love, the undivided love. *(Mother Teresa)*

Archbishop Romero said in words that make us shiver to this day: 'I am glad, brothers and sisters, that they have murdered priests in this country, because it would be very sad if in a country where they are murdering the people so horrifically there were no priests among the victims. It is a sign that the Church has become truly incarnate in the problems of the people.'

These words, so brutal at first sight, are far seeing. There can be neither faith nor Gospel without incarnation. And with a crucified people there can be no incarnation without the cross. Ignacio Ellacuria said many times that the specifically Christian task is to fight to eradicate sin by bearing its burden. This sin brings death, but taking it on gives credibility. By sharing in the cross of the Salvadoreans the Church becomes Salvadorean and thus credible. And although in the short term this murder is a great loss, in the long term it is a great gain: we are building a Church that is really Christian and really Salvadorean. Christians have shown truly that they are Salvadoreans and thus that Salvadoreans can really be Christians. This is no small fruit of so much bloodshed in El Salvador . . . *(Jon Sobrino SJ)*

for useful texts see overleaf

USEFUL TEXTS

Suffering Servant:
  Isa. 42:1, 49:3-6, 42:19

See also: B15 Jesus, friend of outcasts
           B49 Coping with doubt
           C13 Coping with grief

B39

CREATION

'What marvels the Lord worked for us. Indeed we were glad.'
Psalm 126:3

QUOTATIONS

Wonder is the basis of worship. *(Thomas Carlyle)*

To be surprised, to wonder, is to begin to understand.
(José Ortega y Gasset)

Quality is never an accident. It is always the result of intelligent effort. There must be the will to produce a superior thing.
(John Ruskin)

You will find something far greater in the woods than you will in books. Stones and trees will teach you what you can never learn from masters. *(St Bernard)*

A monk asks: 'Is there anything more miraculous than the wonders of nature?' The Master answers: 'Yes, your awareness of the wonders of nature.' *(Anon)*

Day after day, O Lord of my life, shall I stand before thee face to face. With folded hands, O Lord of all worlds, shall I stand before thee face to face . . . And when my work shall be done in this world, King of kings, alone and speechless shall I stand before thee face to face. *(Rabindranath Tagore)*

Humankind, full of all creative possibilities, is God's work. Humankind alone is called to assist God. Humankind is called to co-create. With nature's help, humankind can set into creation all that is necessary and life-sustaining.
(Hildegarde of Bingen)

I feel that a man may be happy in this world and I know that this world is a world of imagination and vision. I see everything I paint in this world, but everybody does not see alike. To the eye of a miser, a guinea is far more beautiful than the sun, and a bag worn with the use of money has more beautiful proportions than a vine filled with grapes. The tree which moves some to tears of joy is, in the eyes of others, only a green thing which stands in the way. As a man is, so he sees. *(William Blake)*

PROVERBS

No rain, no mushrooms – No God, no world. *(African proverb)*

A wonder lasts but nine days. *(English proverb)*

God made us and we wonder at it. *(Spanish proverb)*

HUMOUR

'Can you tell me, Johnny, who made you?'
'God made part of me.'
'What do you mean?'
'I mean he made me little. I grow'd the rest myself.'
(Anon)

A Sunday school teacher was examining her pupils after a series of lessons on God's omnipotence. She asked, 'Is there anything God can't do?'

There was silence. Finally, one lad held up his hand. The teacher, disappointed that the lesson's point had been missed, asked resignedly, 'Well, just what is it that God can't do?'

'Well,' replied the boy, 'He can't please everybody.' *(Anon)*

WORD PICTURES

In a little church in the far South of Ireland, every window but one is of stained glass, representing Christ and his saints. Through the one window which is plain glass may be seen a breathtaking view: a lake of deepest blue, studded with green islets, and backed by range after range of purple hills. Under the window is the inscription: The heavens declare the glory of God, and the firmament showeth His handiwork.'
(Robert Gibbings)

On the morning of 14 October 1991 Fr Lito Satur was murdered near the town of Valencia in the province of Bukidnon in the southern Philippines. Three masked men shot him as he was returning to the parish house on his motorcycle after offering Mass at an outstation. Most local people feel they know why he was killed. He had been very active in local efforts to protect what remains of the tropical forest on the hills of Bukidnon. In recent years the Department of Energy and Natural Resources in the Philippines, alarmed at its inability to stop the cutting has authorised citizens to arrest illegal loggers on behalf and seize the illegal timber. It is thought that Fr Satur ran foul of logging barons who paid to have him murdered.

One hopes that Fr Satur's death is not in vain and that it inspires others to commit themselves to protecting and healing the environment. If the destruction of the forest is not stopped immediately and bald hills not replanted, the Philippines can expect floods like the one which devastated Leyte to continue and to intensify.

Fr Satur is not the first priest to be murdered for endeavouring to protect the environment in Mindanao. In 1988 Fr Mario Estorba SVD, who was active in an anti-logging campaign in the nearby province of Agusan del Sur, was also gunned down. Many fear that, given the ongoing war in the Philippines between the loggers and miners who are plundering the environment and Christians who are fighting to protect what is left, Fr Satur will not be the last religious leader to die in defence of God's creation. *(Sean McDonagh)*

And I dream that these garden closes
With their glades and their sun-flecked sod
And their lilies and bowers of roses
Were laid by the hand of God.
The kiss of the sun for pardon,
The song of birds for mirth,
One is nearer God's heart in a garden
Than anywhere else on Earth.
(Dorothy Frances Gurney)

A little girl who lived in a remote part of the country was receiving her first Bible instruction at the hands of her elderly grandmother, and the old lady was reading the child the story of the creation. After the story had been finished the little girl seemed lost in thought.

'Well, dear,' said the grandmother, 'what do you think of it?'

'Oh, I love it. It's so exciting,' exclaimed the youngster. 'You never know what God is going to do next!' *(Anon)*

One of the popular poems that came to us after the First World War was *Trees* by Joyce Kilmer, sergeant in the 165th infantry (69th New York) AEF who was killed in action near Ourcy, 30 July 1918.

I think that I shall never see
A poem lovely as a tree.
A tree whose hungry mouth is prest
Against the earth's sweet flowing breast;
A tree that looks at God all day,
And lifts her leafy arms to pray;
A tree that may in Summer wear
A nest of robins in her hair;
Upon whose bosom snow has lain;
Who intimately lives with rain.
Poems are made by fools like me,
But only God can make a tree.

In his book *Confessions*, St Augustine describes his search:

'What is this God?' I asked the earth, and it answered, 'I am not He,' and all things that are in the earth made the same confession. I asked the sea and the deeps and the creeping things, and they answered, 'We are not your God; seek higher. . .'

I asked the heavens, the sun, the moon, the stars, and they answered, 'Neither are we the God whom you seek.' And I said to all the things that throng about the gateways of the senses, 'Tell me something of Him.' And they cried out in a great voice, 'He made us.' My question was my gazing upon them, and their answer was their beauty . . . I asked the whole frame of the universe about my God and it answered me, 'I am not He, but He made me.'

USEFUL TEXTS

Creation:
    Account of, *Gen. 1:1-2;25*
    Work of the Lord, *Ps. 104:1-35*
    Work of the Word, *John 1:1-14*
    Work of the Son, *Col. 1:13-17; Heb. 1:1-3*

See also: A18 Balance in Nature
           B32 The Wonders of God

B40
ONE GOD

'Listen, Israel: The Lord our God is the one Lord.'
Deuteronomy 6:4

QUOTATIONS

A comprehended God is no God. (*St John Chrysostom*)

He who knows about depth knows about God. (*Paul Tillich*)

After this I saw God in a Point, that is to say, in mine understanding, – by which sight I saw that he is in all things. (*Julian of Norwich*)

If God did not exist, it would be necessary to invent him. (*Voltaire*)

God and other artists are always a little obscure. (*Oscar Wilde*)

Do not seek God in outer space – your heart is the only place in which to meet Him face to face. (*Angelus Silesius*)

Mysterious Being, infinitely far from me, who yet in every beating of this heart must be. (*Angelus Silesius*)

The God to whom little boys say their prayers has a face very like their mothers. (*James M. Barrie*)

Now nobody denies what nobody is ignorant of – for nature herself is teacher of it – that God is the Maker of the universe, and that it is good, and that it is man's by free gift of its Maker. (*Tertullian*)

The world is so empty if one thinks only of mountains, rivers and cities, but to know someone here and there who thinks and feels with us and who, though distant, is close to us in spirit, this makes the earth for us an inhabited garden. (*Goethe*)

God as the ground of being infinitely transcends that of which he is the ground. He stands 'against' the world, in so far as the world stands against him, and he stands 'for' the world, thereby causing it to stand for him. *(Paul Tillich)*

Of course God is the 'wholly Other', but He is also the wholly Same, the wholly Present. Of course He is the *Mysterium Tremendum* that appears and overthrows; but He is also the mystery of the self-evident, nearer to me than my I.
(Martin Buber)

God is present everywhere, he hears and sees all, he penetrates even hidden and secret places. For so it is written, 'I am a God at hand, and not a God far off. If a man hides himself in secret places, will I therefore not see him? Do I not fill heaven and earth?' And again; 'The eyes of the Lord are in every place: keeping watch on the evil and the good.' *(Cyprian)*

PROVERBS

God is one; what he does, sees none. *(Yiddish proverb)*

God often visits us, but most of the time we are not at home.
(French proverb)

God has more than he has given away. *(Czech proverb)*

HUMOUR

Johnny, aged five, was told by his mother that he must finish his breakfast porridge. He said he didn't want to.

His mother replied, 'You must finish it. If you don't, God will be very angry.'

She went into the kitchen to wash up, leaving Johnny looking with a sullen determination at the porridge. Outside it was raining, and suddenly there was a heavy roll of thunder.

Johnny's mother came back into the room and found him eating his porridge as quickly as he could, and meanwhile muttering to himself, 'All that fuss for a small plate of porridge!'
(Redemptorist Record)

WORD PICTURES

Voltaire, as everyone knows, had little use for religion. He was one day walking with a friend when they passed a church. Voltaire raised his hat as they passed. 'I thought', said the friend, 'that you did not believe in God.' 'Oh,' said Voltaire, 'we nod, but we do not speak.' *(William Barclay)*

Augustus Toplady was one day overtaken by a severe thunderstorm in Burrington Combe, a rocky glen running into the heart of the Mendip Hills. There was no habitation anywhere near, and no place to which he could turn for shelter from the storm.

Looking about him, he saw two massive pillars of rock, a deep fissure in the centre of a precipitous crag of limestone, and took refuge there. Standing there in safety, he escaped the storm. Finding a piece of paper lying near, he picked it up and with his pencil wrote the famous familiar hymn, first published in 1775, 'Rock of Ages, cleft for me, Let me hide myself in Thee.' *(Anon)*

Four Hebrew letters, YHVH (which appear 6,823 times in the Old Testament) form the Hebrew name for God. 'Adonai' is a substitute for these sacred letters. The title 'Adonai' is never pronounced by pious Jews except during solemn prayer and with the head covered. *(Anon)*

It is in this hard chapter of *An Evil Cradling*, this dark sonnet, that we stumble almost unawares upon one of the most beautiful passages in a superbly crafted work. The theme is timeless: the impact of the beautiful upon those starved of it. Like Irina Ratushinskaya, who saw the eternal in the frost-covered window of her Siberian prison, Brian Keenan glimpses the back parts of God in an orange:

But wait. My eyes are almost burned by what I see. There's a bowl in front of me that wasn't there before. A brown button bowl and in it some apricots, some small oranges, some nuts cherries, a banana. The fruits, the colours mesmerise me in a quiet rapture that spins through my head. I am entranced by colour. I lift an orange into the flat filthy palm of my hand and feel and smell and lick it. The colour orange, the colour, the colour, my God the colour orange . . .

I cannot, I will not eat this fruit. I sit in quiet joy, so complete, beyond the meaning of joy. My soul finds its own completeness in that bowl of colour . . . I am drunk with something that I understand but cannot explain. I am filled with a sense of love. I am filled and satiated by it. What I have waited and longed for has without my knowing come to me, and taken all of me. *(Sheila Cassidy)*

According to Thomas Merton, man's capacity for perfect freedom and for pure love is what constitutes, in the human person, the image of God. 'At the very core of our essence we are constituted in God's likeness by our freedom, and the exercise of that freedom is nothing else but the exercise of disinterested love.' He writes in an unpublished work, 'The freedom that is in our nature is our ability to love something, someone besides ourselves, and for the sake, not of ourselves, but of the one we love. There is in the human will an innate tendency, an inborn capacity for disinterested love. This power to love another for his own sake is one of the things that make us like God, because this power is the one thing in us that is free from all determination. It is a power which transcends and escapes the inevitability of self-love.'

USEFUL TEXTS
Characteristics of God:
    Omnipotence, *Jer. 32:17, 27*
    Omnipresence, *Ps. 139:7-12*
    Omniscience, *Amos 9:2-3*
    Foreknowledge, *Isa. 48:3-5*

See also: B28 The Father who draws us to Himself
           B54 The Trinity
           C27 The Father who receives us back

B41

GENEROSITY

'I tell you solemnly, this poor widow has put more in than all who have contributed to the treasury.' *Mark 12:43*

QUOTATIONS

A man can do a great deal in this world if he doesn't mind who takes the credit. *(P. P. Parker)*

One of the most difficult things to give away is kindness – it is usually returned. *(C. Flint)*

Too many people have decided to do without generosity in order to practise charity. *(Albert Camus)*

He who gives when he is asked has waited too long. *(Anon)*

You do not have to be rich to be generous. If he has the spirit of true generosity, a pauper can give like a prince.
(Corinne V. Wells)

The truly generous is the truly wise. *(Anon)*

It is possible to give without loving, but it is impossible to love without giving. *(Richard Braunstein)*

Generosity is not in giving me that which I need more than you do, but it is in giving me that which you need more than I do.
(Kahlil Gibran)

Giving money is a very good criterion, in a way, of a person's mental health. Generous people are rarely mentally ill people.
(Karl Menninger)

Humour cannot be learnt. Besides wit and keenness of mind, it presupposes a large measure of goodness of heart, of patience, of tolerance and of human kindness. *(Curt Goetz)*

PROVERBS

No one is so generous as he who has nothing to give. *(French Proverb)*

When the hand ceases to scatter, the mouth ceases to praise. *(Irish proverb)*

The man who gives little with a smile gives more than the man who gives much with a frown. *(Jewish proverb)*

Give with a warm hand, not a cold one. *(Jewish proverb)*

HUMOUR

A pig was lamenting his lack of popularity. He complained to the cow that people were always talking about the cow's gentleness and kind eyes, whereas his name was used as an insult. The pig admitted that the cow gave milk and cream, but maintained that pigs gave more. 'Why,' the animal complained, 'we pigs give bacon and ham and bristles and people even pickle our feet. I don't see why you cows are esteemed so much more.'

The cow thought awhile and said gently, 'Maybe it's because we give while we're still living.' *(Anon)*

A small boy observed his mother put a ten pence piece in the offering plate at the morning service. On the way home from church, she freely criticised the poor sermon they had heard. 'But, mother,' said the boy, 'what could you expect for ten pence?' *(Anon)*

I enjoyed the tale of the elderly money-lender and the Salvation Army lass. She accosted him in Bond Street in Self-Denial Week, and said, 'Will you give a pound to the Lord?'

'How old are you?' said he, and she answered, 'Nineteen.'

'Well,' said the money-lender, 'I am seventy-five, so I shall be seeing him before you do, so I'll give it to him.' *(Anon)*

WORD PICTURES

Alexander the Great had a famous but poor philosopher in his court. Being pressed for money, the philosopher made application to his patron for relief. Alexander had commissioned him to draw whatever cash he needed from the Treasury, so the philosopher presented a request for a very large sum. The Treasurer refused to honour the draft until he consulted his royal master, adding that he thought the amount exorbitant. Alexander replied, 'Pay the money at once. The philosopher has done me a singular honour. By the largeness of his request he shows the idea he has conceived both of my wealth and my generosity.' *(Anon)*

The best thing to give . . .
   to your enemy is *forgiveness*;
   to an opponent, *tolerance*;
   to a friend, *your heart*;
   to your child, *a good example*;
   to a father, *deference*;
   to your mother, *conduct that will make her proud of you*;
   to yourself, *respect*;
   to all men, *charity*.
(Lord Balfour)

If ever I am rich enough to make generous gestures, let me hide my hand. Let me give freely and my giving take freedom with it. *(Joyce Grenfell, of whom Clive James wrote: 'She was one of the few who actually did good by stealth.')*

A report from an elementary school near Chicago tells about a Christmas pageant held in the school. A third grader was the innkeeper. He had only one line to say: 'Sorry. There is no room in the inn.' But the little boy entered into the spirit of the play and said his part with real feeling. And then, as Mary and Joseph turned away to leave, the little fellow called out, 'Come back, Joseph. I will give you my room!' (Didn't the Lord say something about becoming like little children?) *(Anon)*

There is a fable well known in India of a poor beggar who lived in a State ruled by a Maharaja. The beggar had no home but put up every night in a free lodging-house, sleeping on a mat on the floor, and covering himself in the cooler nights with old rags. His clothing was tattered and old and, having no means of earning a livelihood other than begging, he used to go out in the morning after a meal of cold rice left over from the previous day and sit by the wayside with his beggar's bowl. For 'punyam' (merit), passers-by used to throw some grains of rice or copper coins his way, so he usually had enough rice for two meals a day, and enough money to buy sticks for a fire and a few vegetables, fish or dhal for curry, which he ate at the choultry.

One day he heard that on the morrow, the Maharaja himself was coming that way in his chariot. That raised his hopes, as he said to himself, 'The Maharaja will not give me a handful of rice or a copper coin, or even a few annas, but nothing less than a golden Varaha.' The next day he took up his usual position by the side of the road, and patiently awaited the Maharaja's coming. The sun stood overhead and still he waited in the noonday heat, but no sign of the ruler. Patiently he waited, still full of hope, until almost sunset, and then he heard the welcome sound of the horses' hooves and the chariot wheels. Stepping into the road, he brought the chariot to a standstill, approached the Maharaja and begged for alms. Instead of giving him anything, the Maharaja extended his hands and asked the beggar to give him something. Extremely disappointed and disgusted at a wealthy ruler begging from a poor beggar, he counted out five grains of rice from his bowl and placed them angrily in the hands of the Maharaja. 'Namasthe,' said the Maharaja, and continued his journey.

With a sore heart and very disappointed, the beggar went that evening to his choultry, took out his winnowing fan and began to clean his rice for his meal. As he did so, a small glittering object attracted his attention. Picking it up, he saw that it was a grain of gold. Laying it carefully on one side, he went on winnowing till he found another glittering golden grain, then another. Now the search began in real earnest, and a fourth was found among the rice. After another search he saw a fifth and put it with the others. But no matter how long he searched after that, he found not another grain of gold.

Then the truth dawned on him. Five grains of rice given to the Maharaja had brought him in return five grains of gold. 'What a fool I was!' he exclaimed regretfully. 'If I'd known, I'd have given him it all.' *(Anon)*

USEFUL TEXTS

Generosity:
  Of God, *Ps. 103:3-12*
  Example of, *Prov. 31:20*
  Command regarding, *Matt. 5:42*

See also: A5 Man for others – unselfishness
           C18 Compassion
           C46 Loving kindness

B42

SIGNS OF THE TIMES

'Take the fig tree as a parable: as soon as its twigs grow supple
and its leaves come out, you know that summer is near.'
Mark 13:28

QUOTATIONS

I am in difficulty both summer and winter about my salary.
(Egyptian letter 256 BC)

Politicians have strained their ingenuity to discover new sources
of public revenue. *(Socrates, 50 BC)*

Philosophy has struggled to find some substitute for the divine
commandments and the surveillance of God. *(Socrates)*

Who has not seen with his own eyes the present spirit . . . which
forces up the price of commodities to such a degree that human
language cannot find words to express the transaction?
(Diocletian, AD 301)

Even though a god, I have learned to obey the times.
(Palladas, AD 400)

The golden age was the age in which gold did not reign. The
golden calf is still made of mud. *(Graffiti written during French
Student Revolt, May 1968)*

Every age has its pleasures, its style of wit, and its own ways.
(Nicolas Boileau 1674)

Future ages will wonder at us, as the present age wonders at us
now . . . our love of what is beautiful does not lead to
extravagance . . . mighty indeed are the marks and monuments
we have left. *(Pericles of Athens, Fifth century BC)*

PROVERB

The golden age was never the present age. *(English proverb)*

WORD PICTURES

Two tablets dating back to 2800 BC were unearthed in Babylon not long ago. They both commented on the trends of the day. One reads: 'Times are not what they used to be.'
The other tablet reflected a major concern of many people living 28 centuries ago. Their complaint: 'The world must be coming to an end. Children no longer obey their parents and every man wants to write a book.' *(Anon)*

Aristotle, the great Greek philosopher who lived more than 2,000 years ago, wrote this about the young people of his time: 'Their faults are nearly all errors of exaggeration. They overdo in cases of love and in all other things. They imagine that they know everything, and stubbornly stand on their point. They like to crack jokes for joking is the bad–manneredness of the well mannered.' *(Anon)*

General William Booth once said, 'I consider the greatest dangers of the twentieth century to be:
1.   Religion without the Holy Ghost;
2.   Christianity without Christ;
3.   Forgiveness without regeneration;
4.   Morality without God;
5.   Heaven without Hell.'

Buttes, in *Dyets Dry Dinner* (1599) gives the following:
Heresie and beere came hopping into England both in a yeere.

The world is passing through troublous times. The young people of today think of nothing but themselves. They have no reverence for parents or old age. They are impatient of all restraint. They talk as if they knew everything, and what passes for wisdom with us is foolishness to them. As for the girls, they are immodest and unwomanly in speech, behaviour and dress. *(Peter the Monk in AD 1274)*

The *Anglo-Saxon Chronicle* for the year 1137 says:
'Every powerful man built his castles and when the castles were built, they filled them with devils and wicked men. But by night and day, they took those people that they thought had any goods – men and women – and put them in prison and tortured them with indescribable torture to extort gold and silver. Many thousands they killed by starvation.

They levied taxes on the villages every so often and called it protection money. When the wretched people had no more to give, they robbed and burned all the villages, so that you could easily go a whole day's journey and never find anyone occupying a village, nor land tilled.

Then corn was dear, and meat and butter, and cheese, because there was none in the country. Wretched people died of starvation; some lived by begging for alms who had once been rich men; some fled the country.

There had never been till then greater misery in the country, nor had heathens done worse than they did. Men said openly that Christ and the saints were asleep.'

See also: A18 Balance in nature
B34 Human rights
C17 International Peace

B43

FORTY DAYS OF LENT

'The Spirit drove Jesus out into the wilderness and he remained there for forty days.' *Mark 1:12*

QUOTATIONS

Fasting is more effective than charity, for the latter is done with money, but the former can be done only by one's own person. *(Talmud)*

As to the repugnance felt by our (modern) Catholics for fasting, it is not without some interest to note that it is occurring in the very time when disciples of Gandhi have demonstrated the virtues of fasting on the level of natural mystique and non-violent resistance. *(Jacques Maritain)*

In these days, therefore, let us add something beyond the wonted measure of our service, such as private prayers and abstinence in food and drink. Let each one, over and above the measure prescribed for him, offer God something of his own free will in the joy of the Holy Spirit. *(St Benedict)*

If any bishop, or presbyter, or deacon, or reader, or singer, does not fast the fast of forty days, or the fourth day of the week, and the day of the Preparation (Friday), let him be deprived, except he be hindered by weakness of body. But if he be one of the laity, let him be suspended.
(Ecclesiastical Canons of the Holy Apostles)

PROVERBS

A fast is better than a bad meal. *(Irish proverb)*

Who fasts, but does no other good, saves his bread but goes to Hell. *(Italian proverb)*

STATEMENT

The Lenten season has a twofold character:

1. It recalls baptism or prepares for it;
2. It stresses a penitential spirit.

By these means especially, Lent readies the faithful for celebrating the paschal mystery, after a period of closer attention to the Word of God, and more ardent prayer. In the liturgy itself, and in liturgy-centred instructions, these baptismal and penitential themes should be more pronounced.
(Second Vatican Council – 'Liturgy')

WORD PICTURES

Lent is:

A time for a change of heart. A time for a new and closer look at the way our lives are lived, for repentance and reconciliation.

A time for concern for others. Caring for others is a valuable weapon in our fight against selfishness. Almsgiving has always been a part of Lent.

A time for prayer which costs. That means in terms of time and personal effort.

When any 'giving-up' or mortification is spoken of at the outset of Lent these three things must be kept in mind: our need for a change of heart, an outward and genuine concern for others and, underlying everything, a need to pray much more.

Each of these three parts to Lent must be present if the season is to have any real and lasting value. To go into Lent with a resolution to give up sugar in our tea, for example, is only of any value if it is part of our 'change of heart' campaign. The money saved should go to our deprived brothers and sisters and the action supported by an increased effort at prayer.
(Paul Frost)

As Ash Wednesday approaches each year, Catholics are brought into touch with what is, perhaps, the oldest kind of soap. Some scholars connect the cleansing symbolism of ashes with fire, saying that the Parsees and the Brahmins have used ashes for purification on this basis. More practical men say it comes from countries where water is scarce, and sand and ashes are used instead. Tertullian talks about sackcloth and ashes, and they seem to be one of the Jewish symbols which the Church continued. But they were kept originally for public penitents, people whom we do not see in our churches nowadays, which seems, perhaps, odd, unless it be thought that we all, on Ash Wednesday, achieve that status.

In the Middle Ages, public penitents used to be expelled from a church, being cast out by the Bishop, as Adam, the first man, had been cast out of Paradise, and Urban II, the Pope of the Crusades, decreed ashes for everybody. The English, at any rate, were already by then firmly fixed in the Ash Wednesday ritual. *(Douglas Woodruff)*

The Saxons called March 'lencten monath' because in this month, the days noticeably lengthen. As the chief part of the great fast, from Ash Wednesday to Easter, falls in March, it received the name Lencten-faesten or Lent.

The fast of 36 days was introduced in the fourth century AD, but it did not become fixed at 40 days until the early seventh century, thus corresponding with Our Lord's fast in the wilderness. *(Anon)*

USEFUL TEXTS

Forty Days:
  Gen 7: 4; Exod. 24:18; 1 Kgs. 19:8; Matt. 4:2

See also: B47 Dying to self
           C37 Temptation
           C40 Reconciliation
           C41 Starting afresh

THE DIGNITY OF THE INDIVIDUAL

'He not only died for us – he rose from the dead, and there at God's right hand he stands and pleads for us.' *Romans 8:34*

QUOTATIONS

What is dignity without honesty? *(Cicero)*

When people begin to ignore human dignity, it will not be long before they begin to ignore human rights. *(G. K. Chesterton)*

Men are born equal but they are also born different.
(Erich Fromm)

Perhaps the only true dignity of man is his capacity to despise himself. *(George Santayana)*

You can't expect a person to see eye to eye with you when you're looking down on him. *(Anon)*

Even one ear of corn is not exactly like another. *(Talmud)*

Man is more interesting than men. God made him and not them in his image. Each one is more precious than all. *(André Gide)*

A whole bushel of wheat is made up of single grains.
(Thomas Fuller)

Let not a man guard his dignity, but let his dignity guard him.
(Emerson)

First, it is imperative in the name of the Gospel to make the underdeveloped masses aware of their human dignity, of their rights to a better life, one which is worthy of the human person. The second point is to stir the consciousness of the rich at home and abroad. *(Dom Helda Camera)*

PROVERBS

The easiest way to dignity is humility. *(English proverb)*

Not all horses enjoy the same thing. *(Jewish proverb)*

HUMOUR

The two things that a healthy person hates most between heaven and hell are a woman who is not dignified and a man who is. *(G. K Chesterton)*

The butler entered the room, a solemn procession of one. *(P. G. Wodehouse)*

It is only people of small moral stature who have to stand on their dignity. *(Arnold Bennett)*

STATEMENT

Coming down to practical and particularly urgent consequence, this Council lays stress on reverence for man; everyone must consider his every neighbour without exception as another self, taking into account first of all his life and the means necessary to living it with dignity, so as not to imitate the rich man who had no concern for the poor man Lazarus. *(Second Vatican Council – 'The Church Today')*

WORD PICTURES

A quarter of a century ago, amidst the great hopes of all mankind, the United Nations Organisation was born. Alas, in an immoral world, it too grew up immoral. It is not a United Nations Organisation but a United Governments Organisation, which equates those governments which were freely elected, those which were imposed by force and those which seized power by force of arms. Thanks to the venal prejudice of the majority of its members, the United Nations jealously guards the liberty of certain nations and neglects the liberty of others. It obsequiously voted against investigating private grievances – the groans, cries and entreaties of simple, humble individuals, insects too tiny for such a large organisation to concern itself with. The best document it put out in all its 25 years was the Declaration of Human Rights, yet the United Nations did not endeavour to make endorsement of it an obligatory condition of membership, and thus it left ordinary people at the mercy of governments not of their choosing. *(Alexander Solzhenitsyn)*

I cannot bear the universal categorisation of human beings: 'bourgeois,' 'bolshevist,' 'capitalist,' 'nigger,' 'hippie,' 'pig,' 'imperialist.' The one so labelled may be reviled, imprisoned, tortured, killed or exiled because he is no longer a human being, but a symbol. He does not bleed when pricked; his heart does not cry in the night. By this conjuring trick, conscience is made to disappear. It is, perhaps, the profoundest corruption of our time. *(Eric Sevareid)*

Maurice Baring used to tell the following story:
    One doctor said to another doctor:
    'About the termination of a pregnancy, I want your opinion. The father was a syphilitic. The mother was tuberculous. Of the four children born, the first was blind, the second died, the third was deaf and dumb, the fourth also tuberculous. What would you have done?'
    'I would have ended the pregnancy.'
    'Then you would have murdered Beethoven.'

The Sunday school teacher had ended her Bible story and was asking questions of her primary tots. 'Why, do you think, does God love us all so very much?' she asked. There was a momentary silence as the children wrinkled their little brows and 'thought hard' for the proper answer. 'Why does God love us – so very much?'
    Suddenly little Kristin's hand shot up. And without the slightest doubt about the correctness of her answer she blurted: 'Because he has only one of each of us.'
    Only one of each of us! *(Anon)*

Have you not heard how a bird from the sea
Was blown inshore and landed
Outside the capital of Lu?

The Prince ordered a solemn reception,
Offered the sea bird wine in the sacred precinct,
Called for musicians
To play the compositions of Shun,
Slaughtered cattle to nourish it:
Dazed with symphonies, the unhappy sea bird
Died of despair.

How should you treat a bird?
As yourself
Or as a bird?
(Thomas Merton)

See also: B26 The whole man
B34 Human rights
B45 Free will
C47 The indwelling Spirit

B45
FREE WILL

'Jesus never needed evidence about any man; he could tell what a man had in him.' *John 2:25*

QUOTATIONS

No one can rob us of our free will. *(Epictetus)*

God presses us but does not oppress our liberty.
(St Francis de Sales)

He who has a firm will moulds the world to himself. *(Goethe)*

People do not lack strength; they lack will. *(Hugo)*

To deny the freedom of the will is to make morality impossible.
(Froude)

We have to believe in free will. We've got no choice.
(Isaac Singer)

We are not constrained by servile necessity, but act with free will, whether we are disposed to virtue or incline to vice.
(St Ambrose)

Not only in works, but also in faith, God has given man freedom of the will. *(St Irenaeus)*

The freedom of the will is then true freedom, when it does not serve vices and sins. *(St Augustine of Hippo)*

If man does not have the free faculty to shun evil and to choose good, then, whatever his actions may be, he is not responsible for them. *(St Justin Martyr)*

There are no galley slaves in the royal vessel of divine love – every man works his oar voluntarily. *(Jean Pierre Camus)*

For free will to exist, evil had to exist, in order that man's choice might be his own. God could not thereafter permit Himself to interfere in man's actions, for then there would be an end to free will and an end to the ascending revelation of life . . . For man to become truly free, God had to put man's will beyond even divine intervention. *(Meyer Levin)*

PROVERBS

When the will is ready, the feet are light. *(French proverb)*

Where there's a will, there's a way. *(English proverb)*

There is nothing good or evil save in the will. *(Greek proverb)*

Our eyes and ears are not subject to our will – but our tongues are. *(Jewish proverb)*

STATEMENT

It is in accordance with their dignity as persons – that is, beings endowed with reason and free will and therefore privileged to bear personal responsibility – that all men should be at once impelled by nature and also bound by a moral obligation to seek the truth, especially religious truth.
(Second Vatican Council – 'Religious Freedom')

WORD PICTURES

We who lived in concentration camps can remember the men who walked through the huts comforting others, giving away their last piece of bread. They may have been few in number, but they offer sufficient proof that everything can be taken from a man but one thing: the last of the human freedoms to choose one's attitude in any given circumstances, to choose one's own way. *(Viktor Frankl)*

A tourist standing by Niagara Falls saw an eagle swoop upon a frozen lamb encased in a piece of floating ice. The eagle stood upon it as it drifted towards the rapids. Every now and then, the eagle would proudly lift its head into the air to look around him, as much as to say, 'I am drifting on towards danger. I know what I am doing. I shall fly away and make good my escape before it is too late.'

When he reached the edge, he stooped, spread his powerful wings, and leaped for flight; but alas, while he was feeding on the carcase, his feet had frozen to its fleece. He leaped and shrieked, and beat upon the air with his wings until he went over into the chasm and darkness below. *(Anon)*

USEFUL TEXTS

Will of Man:
  Free to choose, *Josh. 24:15; Deut. 30:19*
  Set free from Christ, *2 Tim. 2:26*
  In bondage to sin, *Prov. 5:22; Rom. 6:16*

See also: A2 Integrity
          B26 The whole man
          B44 The dignity of the individual

B46

CHRIST THE SACRAMENT OF GOD

'The Son of Man must be lifted up as Moses lifted up the serpent in the desert, so that everyone who believes may have eternal life in him.' *John 3:14-15*

QUOTATIONS

He changed sunset into sunshine. *(Clement of Alexandria)*

Jesus alone is able to offer himself as the sufficient illustration of his own doctrine. *(Hensley Henson)*

Something fiery and star-like gleamed from his eyes and the majesty of Godhead shone from his countenance. *(St Jerome)*

Our faith is sound if we believe that no man, old or young, is delivered from the contagion of death and the bonds of sin, except by one Mediator of God and men, Jesus Christ.
(St Augustine of Hippo)

Whenever Christianity has struck out a new path on her journey, it has been because the personality of Jesus has again become living, and a ray from His Being has once more illuminated the world. *(Anon)*

WORD PICTURES

To think God learned to walk,
in Nazareth.
Later there'd be hard
walking to do,
with heavier falls.
And talking: in Nazareth
God played Adam's game –
naming things,
bringing out words:

and saw His own begetting
imaged, in the word's spring
from the intent regard.
A grave infant world
studied for Calvary,
studied for Gennesaret,
prepared to say thrice;
Simon Peter, lovest thou me?
Mary was never asked
if she loved God.
(Robert Farren)

A group of women teachers from a Christian school had fled to an outlying village in another part of Burma, when their town was invaded. It was during the disastrous days of our retreat. Stragglers from our forces came staggering in, British lads, with blistered feet and torn clothing. Famished, parched and sleepless, they were done. These women, both Burmese and Karen, took them in . . . There were some in the neighbourhood ready to inform against the women. Armed men surrounded the house. 'You have been helping the enemy,' they said. 'You shall die.' They asked for mercy, tried to buy it, offering all they had. Then they said, 'If we must die, give us a moment to get ready.' The company of them knelt in prayer, and were cut to pieces. One of them was a girl of 17. When the Japanese were gone, the bishop held his first confirmation. In the front row of those to be confirmed, he recognised a Burmese who had been a prominent anti-Christian leader.

'My friend,' said the bishop, 'how did you come to be baptised?' 'It was the way those girls in that village died two years ago,' he said. 'I knew they had something which I had not.' *(John Foster)*

Christ is all-sufficient. For the:
ARTIST, He is the altogether lovely – *(Song of Solomon 5:16)*
ARCHITECT, He is the chief cornerstone – *(1 Peter 2:6)*
ASTRONOMER, He is the sun of righteousness – *(Malachi 4:2)*

BAKER, He is the living bread – *(John 6:51)*

BANKER, He is the unsearchable riches – *(Ephesians 3:8)*

BUILDER, He is the sure foundation –
(Isaiah 28:16; 1 Corinthians 3:11)

CARPENTER, He is the door – *(John 10:9)*

EDITOR, He is good tidings of great joy – *(Luke 2:10)*

ELECTRICIAN, He is the light of the world – *(John 8:12)*

FARMER, He is sower and the Lord of the harvest –
(Matthew 13:37; Luke 10:2)

FLORIST, He is the rose of Sharon and the lily of the valley –
(Song of Solomon 2:1)

JEWELLER, He is the living precious stone – *(1 Peter 2:4)*

LAWYER, He is the counsellor, lawgiver and advocate –
(Isaiah 9:6; 1 John 2:1)

LABOURER, He is the giver of rest – *(Matthew 11:28)*
(Anon)

See also: A44 Meeting Christ in the sacraments
B4 Mary – Handmaid of God
B16 Christ heals and forgives
B51 One with Christ

B47

DYING TO SELF

'I tell you, most solemnly, unless a wheat grain falls on the ground and dies, it remains only a single grain, but if it dies it yields a rich harvest.' *John 12:24*

QUOTATIONS

They that deny themselves for Christ shall enjoy themselves in Christ *(John Mason)*

Self-centredness completely vitiates communication – with either God or man. *(Hubert Van Zeller)*

Love is like death – it kills the self-willed me, it breaks its stranglehold and sets the Spirit free. *(Angelus Silesius)*

Let our praise be with God, and not from ourselves, for God hates those who praise themselves. *(Pope St Clement I)*

Self-love is cunning, it pushes and insinuates itself into everything, while making us believe it is not there at all. *(St Francis de Sales)*

No death has greatness but that from which new life can spring. No life more vital than that which from the death of self takes wing. *(Angelus Silesius)*

Man's highest life does not consist in self-expression, but in self-sacrifice. *(R. H. Benson)*

He who lives to benefit himself confers on the world a benefit when he dies. *(Tertullian)*

Make it thy business to know thyself, which is the most difficult lesson in the world. *(Cervantes)*

When a man is wrapped up in himself, he makes a pretty small package. *(John Ruskin)*

You give but little when you give of your possessions. It is when you give of yourself that you truly give. *(Kahlil Gibran)*

Your life is without a foundation, if in any matter, you choose on your own behalf. *(Dag Hammarskjöld)*

PROVERBS

He is unworthy to live who lives only for himself.
(English proverb)

He who wants to know himself should offend two or three of his neighbours. *(Chinese proverb)*

WORD PICTURES

A. J. Cronin tells of his days as medical officer to a Welsh mining company in his book *Adventures in Two Worlds.*

I have told you of Olwen Davies, the middle-aged district nurse who for more than 20 years, with fortitude and patience, calmness and cheerfulness, served the people of Tregenny. This unconscious selflessness, which above all seemed the keynote of her character, was so poorly rewarded, it worried me. Although she was much beloved by the people, her salary was most inadequate. And late one night after a particularly strenuous case, I ventured to protest to her as we drank a cup of tea together. 'Nurse,' I said, 'Why don't you make them pay you more? It's ridiculous that you should work for so little.'

She raised her eyebrows slightly. But she smiled. 'I have enough to get along.'

'No, really,' I persisted, 'you ought to have an extra pound a week at least. God knows you're worth it.'

There was a pause. Her smile remained, but her gaze held a gravity, an intensity which startled me. 'Doctor,' she said, 'if God knows I'm worth it, that's all that matters to me.'
(A. J. Cronin)

Ira Dutton (as his name was) was born on a farm in Vermont, and was made to go to school though he hated it. He was 17 when the Civil War broke out. He enlisted in the Northern army and soon became an officer. When the war ended, he was 22, and says he allowed the demon of drink to get him into its clutches. For years he led a kind of double life, sober in daytime, but at night associating with disreputable acquaintances. However, somehow he came to a better mind, and was received into the Church when he was 40. He changed his first name to Joseph. Two years later he read about Damien, and determined to go and help him with the lepers, partly to begin a new life and partly to make reparation for his sins. He sailed (in the roughest and most uncomfortable way) to the South Seas and met Damien on the beach of Molokai (1886). He told him he asked for no special treatment or consideration: 'I just want to consider myself a servant to my fellow men.' Damien already had leprosy, and in another year or two was dead. Brother Joseph lived for another 40 years on Molokai, devoting himself to the lepers. *(F. H. Drinkwater)*

Mr Griffiths – 'old Griff', of Harrow Weald in Middlesex – was having a day out by himself in Southend.

Rather a lonely figure since the death last year of his wife, the mother of his two children, he had stopped to watch a carnival procession when suddenly his attention was distracted.

Toddler Danny Brooke, just 20-months old and wide-eyed at the big parade, was wandering into the path of a motorcycle skidding out of control near Marine Parade.

Without a moment's hesitation, Mr Griffiths threw himself in front of the boy as the motorbike hurtled into them. He took the full force of the blow and suffered multiple injuries. Danny, taken to the same hospital where Mr Griffiths died, was being treated for cuts and bruises.

A police spokesman said, 'Mr Griffiths saved the baby's life.'

Danny's mother 21-year-old Mrs Wendy Brooke, said: 'If it had not been for Mr Griffiths, my son would not be here today.'

Mr Griffiths, said his neighbours, was 'one of those who would do anything to help someone.'

Even lay down his life. *(Evening Echo)*

Are you willing to be sponged out, erased, cancelled,
made nothing?
Are you willing to be made nothing,
dipped into oblivion?
If not, you will never really change.
The phoenix renews her youth
only when she is burnt, burnt alive, burnt down
to hot and flocculent ash.
Then the small stirring of a new small bub in the nest
with strands of down like floating ash
Shows that she is renewing her youth like an eagle,
Immortal bird.
(D. H. Lawrence)

USEFUL TEXTS

Unselfishness:
> In living, *Matt. 16:24-25; 1 Cor. 10:24*
> In true love, *1 Cor. 13:4-5*
> Examples of;
>> David, *1 Chron. 21:17*
>> Paul, *1 Cor. 9:12-22; 10:33*
>> Christ, *Mark 6:30-34*

See also: A5 Man for others – unselfishness
         A7 Poor in spirit
         A10 Seeking perfection
         B26 The whole man

B48

CHRISTIAN UNITY

'The whole group of believers was united, heart and soul.'
Acts 4:32

QUOTATIONS

In order to be united we must love one another, to love one another we must know one another, to know one another we must meet one another. *(Cardinal Mercier)*

Putting all the ecclesiastical corpses into one graveyard will not bring about a resurrection. *(David M. Lloyd-Jones)*

Some of us worked long enough in a shipbuilding district to know that welding is impossible except the materials to be joined are at white heat temperature; and none of our denominational convictions is at white heat. When you try to weld them, they only fall apart. *(George F. MacLeod)*

It is not enough for the whole *oikoumene* both Rome and the World Council of Churches, to address fine speeches to the 'outer world', to society at large, and 'inside' between the Churches, merely to set up everlasting mixed commissions, arrange polite mutual visits, indulge in endless academic dialogue without practical consequences. There must be genuine, increasing integration of the different Churches. *(Hans Küng)*

Form all together one choir, so that, with the symphony of your feelings and having all taken the tone of God, you may sing with one voice to the Father through Jesus Christ, that he may listen to you and know you from your chant as the canticle of his only Son. *(St Ignatius of Antioch)*

PROVERBS

Union gives strength to the humble. *(Latin proverb)*

Strength united is greater. *(Latin proverb)*

HUMOUR

The tale is told of two Irish labourers, new to traffic lights. Having watched the transient amber and the more enduring green, one said to the other, 'they don't allow the Protestants much time to get across.' *(Anon)*

One Sunday in an Irish village, three Protestant women visited a Roman Catholic church. Recognising them and wishing to show respect, the priest whispered to his server, 'Three chairs for the Protestant ladies.'

The server jumped to his feet and shouted, 'Three cheers for the Protestant ladies.' The congregation rose, responded heartily, and the service continued. *(The Sign)*

STATEMENTS

We do not ask that any one Communion should consent to be absorbed in another. We do ask that all should unite in a new and great endeavour to recover and to manifest to the world the unity of the Body of Christ for which he prayed.
(Lambeth Conference, letter 'To All Christian People' (1920))

The World Council of Churches has come into existence because we have already recognised a responsibility to one another's churches . . . We cannot rest content with our present divisions. *(World Council of Churches, report of the first Assembly, Amsterdam (1948))*

There can be no ecumenism worthy of the name without a change of heart. For it is newness of attitudes *(cf Eph. 4:23)* from self–denial and unstinted love, that yearnings for unity take their rise and grow toward maturity. We should therefore pray to the divine Spirit for the grace to be genuinely self–denying, humble, gentle in the service of others, and to have an attitude of brotherly generosity toward them.
(Second Vatican Council – 'Ecumenism')

WORD PICTURES

The lesson must surely be that true collaboration does not mean merely working alongside one another but genuine sharing. Even where there is a difference in calling and some quite profound differences in belief, there may still be sharing. Christian partners do not have to be identical. Sharing can itself add a dimension to combined activity.

The criterion we follow in responding to a call for joint action, or for 'the double act' at a meeting or religious service (is): 'Where one plus one can add up to more than two.' To achieve that sort of sharing, it often happens that other things may be shared as well. Perhaps the most important of all is shared prayer. Sharing does not always mean possession in common. The sharing of minds is at least as important as the sharing of resources. That will come only through knowledge and trust, which result from habitual sharing.
(David Sheppard and Derek Worlock)

Speaking from the moon, the astronaut Frank Borman said, 'We are one hunk of ground, water, air, clouds, floating around in space. From here it really is one world.' *(Frank Borman)*

There is in South India a story of a wealthy landowner who had some very quarrelsome sons, always jealous of one another and always arguing among themselves. On his deathbed he called them and divided his property among them. Then he called for some sticks to be brought, nicely tied into a bundle, and asked them one by one, beginning at the eldest, to break the bundle. So long as they were thus closely bound together, they could not break any of the sticks. 'Now,' he said to the eldest, 'untie the bundle, and try to break the sticks singly.' This was not difficult, and soon each of the sticks, broken one by one, lay before them in two pieces.

The father thus taught them that: united they stood; divided they fell. *(Anon)*

for useful texts see overleaf

USEFUL TEXTS

Unity:

In Christ, *John 15:4-7; 1 Cor. 3:23; Gal. 2:20*
In Church, *Gal. 3:28*
In mind and spirit, *1 Cor. 1:10; Phil. 1:27; 1 Pet. 3; 8*

See also: A20 The Kingdom of God
B17 The Church – Bride of Christ
B36 The Family of God
B51 One with Christ

B49

COPING WITH DOUBT

'Why are you so agitated, and why are these doubts
rising in your hearts?' *Luke 24:38*

QUOTATIONS

Faith which does not doubt is dead faith. *(Miguel de Unamuno)*

Time trieth truth in every doubt. *(John Heywood)*

Cleave ever to the sunnier side of doubts. *(Anon)*

Feed your faith, and your doubts will starve to death. *(Anon)*

Doubt charms me no less than knowledge. *(Dante)*

He is a dull man who is always sure, and a sure man who is
always dull. *(H. L. Mencken)*

Ten thousand difficulties do not make one doubt, as I understand
the subject; difficulty and doubt are incommensurate.
(Cardinal Newman)

Faith keeps many doubts in her pay. If I could not doubt, I should
not believe. *(Henry David Thoreau)*

Our doubts are traitors
And make us lose the good we oft might win
By fearing to attempt.
(Shakespeare)

Who can determine when it is, that the scales in the balance of
opinion begin to turn, and what was a greater probability in
behalf of a belief becomes a positive doubt against it?
(Cardinal Newman)

There lives more faith in honest doubt, believe me, than in half the creeds. *(Alfred Lord Tennyson)*

PROVERBS

To believe with certainty we must begin with doubting. *(Polish proverb)*

The wise are prone to doubt. *(Greek proverb)*

Who knows nothing doubts nothing. *(French proverb)*

WORD PICTURES

Seeing the immense design of the world, one image of wonder mirrored by another image of wonder – the pattern of fern and of feather echoed by the frost of the window-pane, the six rays of the snowflake mirrored by the rock crystal's six-rayed eternity – I ask myself, 'Were those shapes moulded by blindness? Who, then, shall teach me doubt?'
(Dame Edith Sitwell)

The faith of Rosalyn Carter, former President Carter's wife
Rosalyn Carter was seriously shaken after enduring the sorrow that accompanied her father's death, soon followed by the death of her grandmother. 'I had prayed and prayed for him to get better, and because of those prayers, I'd expected him to get better. But he hadn't. And now my grandmother had died too. I felt very sorry for myself and didn't understand why this had to happen to me. Had I been so bad? Didn't God love me anymore? I had doubts about God, and I was afraid because I doubted.

'That was long before I knew that God is a loving God who cares for us and loves us, who suffers when we suffer and who knows that we are going to have doubts and that we're not always going to do what is right, but he loves us anyway. At that time I thought he was going to punish me more for my thoughts . . . I believed my doubts were shortcomings, and I didn't want anyone to know about them.' *(Houghton Mifflin)*

A man went to stay with a friend in Cornwall, in a part where there was a large number of deep holes in the ground. These were disused mine-shafts, some of which had no rails round them. He went for a walk one day and got lost. Darkness came and he realised that he was near these holes and it was dangerous to walk in the dark. But it was too cold to sit down and wait till morning, so he walked on with great care. In spite of this, his feet slipped and he started to slide down a mine-shaft. He managed to grasp a rock that was sticking out of the side of the shaft.

There he hung, terrified, with his feet dangling. He managed to hang on for about 20 minutes, but the agony in his arms got so great that he knew he would soon have to let go and plunge to his death. He was about to let go when he saw, to his immense relief, a little light in the distance which began to grow greater and he knew that help was coming. He shouted loud with all the energy he had left. When the rescuers arrived and shone their light down on him the first thing they saw was that his feet were dangling within a foot of solid earth. This mine-shaft had been filled in! All his agony and fears had been for nothing. *(M. Nassan)*

USEFUL TEXTS

Doubt:
> Mixed with faith, *James 1:6-8*
> In belief, *John 20:25-29*
> In trials, *Mark 4:40; 1 Pet. 1:6*

See also: C13 Coping with grief
              C22 The Light of faith
              C30 Increase our faith
              C41 Starting afresh

B50

THE GOOD SHEPHERD

'I am the good shepherd: the good shepherd is one who lays down his life for his sheep.' *John 10:11*

QUOTATIONS

The Saviour of our souls and helmsman of our bodies, the Shepherd of the Catholic Church throughout the world. *(Martyrdom of St Polycarp)*

He is the Good Shepherd, who gives his life for the sheep – his life for them, his flesh to them, the one for their redemption, the other for their food. O mighty marvel! He is himself the Shepherd of the sheep, their pasturage and their redemption's price. *(St Bernard)*

PROVERBS

The death of the wolf is the health of the sheep. *(Italian proverb)*

It is a foolish sheep that makes the wolf his confessor. *(English proverb)*

Good pastures make fat sheep. *(English proverb)*

STATEMENT

Thus the Church is a sheepfold whose one and necessary door is Christ *(John. 10:1-10)*. She is a flock which God Himself foretold that He would be the Shepherd *(cf Isa. 40:11; Ez. 34:11 ff)*. Although guided by human shepherds, her sheep are nevertheless ceaselessly led and nourished by Christ himself, the Good Shepherd and the Prince of Shepherds *(cf John. 10:11;1 Pet. 5:4)* who gave his life for the sheep *(cf John. 10:11-15)*. *(Second Vatican Council – 'The Church')*

WORD PICTURES

When a shepherd in Scotland was asked if his sheep would follow the voice of a stranger, he replied: 'Yes, when they are sick; but never when they are well. A sick sheep will follow anybody.' *(Anon)*

Raised a non-conformist, Frank Bruno became a Roman Catholic after going to what he now describes as his boarding school. It was tough and believed in boxing as a remedial subject for young men whose energies might otherwise remain misdirected.

'I've read the Bible ever since,' said Frank 'Take one everywhere I go. Read it every night. Not much. Just some. Makes me feel okay.'

I asked him if he had a favourite passage. 'Yeah' he said without a second's hesitation. 'Though I walk through the valley of the shadow of death, I will fear no evil for You are with me.'

An accurate paraphrasing of the fourth verse of the 23rd Psalm is not exactly what you expect in the way of quotes when you drop into a fighter's training camp these days. Nor, on the way to a possible holocaust of a meeting with the boxer who dismantled Michael Spinks in 91 seconds, was the selected quotation without ironic significance. *(Daily Mail)*

One night, a tall American doctor told me a story of Commissioner Lord, of the Salvation Army, also a prisoner of the Chinese in Korea.

'We were dead beat. Another terrible day's march lay ahead. The men were lying cold and half-starved in the lousy shacks waiting for the command to get going. A lot of those guys thought they couldn't make it – they felt they'd had it.

Suddenly old Commissioner Lord appeared in the doorway of our shack. He seemed very confidential about something. 'Boys,' he said, 'boys, I've got news for you – great news – listen.' We all took notice. We all thought, 'What's with this guy?'

That old Commissioner, why he just stood among us and said, 'The Lord is my shepherd; I shall not want,' and he went right through that psalm, like it was God's personal message to us.

Chaplain, I'm telling you, you could hear the silence. I never felt so moved in all my life. Then the guards came – it was get going or die. Those men rose like they had new strength. Can't tell you where they got it from. They marched and they stuck it out.' *(S. J. Davies)*

Some years ago a great actor was asked at a drawing-room function to recite for the pleasure of his fellow guests. He consented and asked if there was anything they specially wanted to hear. After a minute's pause, an old minister asked for Psalm 23. A strange look came over the actor's face. He paused for a moment, then said, 'I will, on one condition – that after I have recited it, you, my friend, will do the same.'

'I!' said the preacher, in surprise, 'I am not an elocutionist, but, if you wish it, I shall do so.'

Impressively, the actor began the psalm. His voice and intonation were perfect. He held his audience spellbound, and, as he finished, a great burst of applause broke from his guests. As it died away, the old man rose and began to declaim the same psalm. His voice was not remarkable, his tone was not faultless, but, when he finished, there was not a dry eye in the room.

The actor rose and his voice quivered as he said, 'Ladies and gentlemen, I reached your eyes and ears; he has reached your hearts. The difference is just this: I know the psalm but he knows the Shepherd.' *(Anon)*

USEFUL TEXTS

Shepherd, figurative of:
God's provision, *Pss. 23, 78:52, 80:1*
Prophets and priests, *Ezek. 34*
Jesus, *John 10:11; 1 Pet. 2:25*

See also: B15 Jesus, friend of outcasts
B38 The Suffering Servant
C44 Feed my sheep

B51

ONE WITH CHRIST

'As a branch cannot bear fruit all by itself, but must remain part of the vine, neither can you unless you remain in me.'
John 15:4

QUOTATIONS

The greatness of contemplation can be given to none but them that love. *(Pope St Gregory I)*

We become contemplatives when God discovers Himself in us. *(Thomas Merton)*

The perfect soul desires to be rapt by contemplation in the chaste embraces of her Spouse. *(St Bernard)*

How many there must be who have smothered the first sparks of contemplation by piling wood on the fire before it was well lit. *(Thomas Merton)*

The acts of contemplation are four: to seek after God, to find Him, to feel His sacred touch in the soul, and to be united with Him and to enjoy Him. *(Archbishop Ullathorne)*

Seek in reading and thou shalt find in meditation; knock in prayer and it shall be opened to thee in contemplation. *(St John of the Cross)*

To live according to the spirit is to think, speak and act according to the virtues that are in the spirit, and not according to the sense and sentiments which are in the flesh. *(St Francis de Sales)*

Holiness consists not in doing uncommon things, but in doing all common things with an uncommon fervour. *(Cardinal Manning)*

Though Christ a thousand times
In Bethlehem be born.
If he's not born in thee,
Thy soul is still forlorn.

The cross on Golgotha
Will never save thy soul,
The cross in thine own heart
Alone can make thee whole.
(Angelus Silesius)

Too late I loved you, O beauty so ancient yet ever new! Too late
I loved you! And, behold, you were within me, and I out of
myself and there I searched for you. *(St Augustine of Hippo)*

Contemplative prayer is a deep and simplified spiritual activity in
which the mind and will are fused into one. They rest in a unified
and simple concentration upon God, turned to him and intent
upon him and absorbed in his own light, with a simple gaze which
is perfect adoration because it silently tells God that we have left
everything else and desire even to leave our own selves for his
sake, and that he alone is important to us, he alone is our desire
and consumed with love and enveloped in spiritual light, worthy
to be called and to be the spouse of Christ. *(Walter Hilton)*

STATEMENT

Since Christ in his mission from the Father is the fountain and
source of the whole apostolate of the Church, the success of the
lay apostolate depends upon the laity's living union with Christ.
For the Lord has said, 'He who abides in me, and I in him, he
bears much fruit: for without me you can do nothing.'
(John 15:5) (Second Vatican Council – 'Laity')

WORD PICTURES

Jesus said: 'Cleave the wood and thou shalt find me; lift the
stone and I am there. Let him-who-seeks not cease seeking until
he finds; and when he finds he will be troubled and when he has
been troubled, he will marvel and he will reign over the All.'
(The Gospel according to St Thomas)

As Brother Lawrence had found such comfort and blessing in walking in the presence of God, it was natural for him to recommend it earnestly to others; but his example was a stronger inducement than any arguments he could use. His very countenance was a lesson in itself; such a sweet and calm devotion appearing in it, as could not but affect all beholders. And it was noticed that in the greatest hurry of business in the kitchen, he still preserved his recollection and his heavenly-mindedness. He was never hasty nor loitering, but did each thing at its right time, with a steady, uninterrupted composure and tranquillity of spirit.

'The time of business,' said he, 'does not with me differ from the time of prayer, and in the noise and clatter of my kitchen, while several persons are at the same time calling for different things, I possess God in as great tranquillity as if I were upon my knees at the Blessed Sacrament.'

Brother Lawrence said that the most excellent method which he had found of going to God was that of doing our ordinary work without any idea of pleasing men, and (as far as we are capable) purely for the love of God. *(Peter Hargreaves)*

Who sees his lord
Within every creature
Deathlessly dwelling
Amidst the mortal:
That man sees truly . . .
Who sees the separate
Lives of all creatures
United in Brahman,
Brought forth from Brahman,
Himself finds Brahman.
(The Bhagavad-Gita)

See also: B25 Quiet – time for prayer
          C47 The indwelling spirit
          C48 One in us

B52

GOD IS LOVE

'Anyone who fails to love can never have known God, because God is love.' *1 John 4:8*

QUOTATIONS

Stop trying to love God and let God love you. *(Eric Doyle)*

Love can deny nothing to love. *(Andreas Capellanus)*

There is no living in love without suffering. *(Thomas à Kempis)*

To love is to wish the other's highest good. *(R. H. Benson)*

It is only the souls that do not love that go empty in this world. *(R. H. Benson)*

Love is the movement, effusion and advancement of the heart toward the good. *(St Francis de Sales)*

It is always springtime in the heart that loves God. *(St John Vianney)*

Give me such love for God and men, as will blot out all hatred and bitterness. *(Dietrich Bonhoeffer)*

People today are hungry for love, for understanding love, which is much greater and which is the only answer to loneliness and great poverty. *(Mother Teresa)*

I beg You to stamp everything with the seal of love, nothing else will last. *(Elizabeth of the Trinity)*

PROVERBS

Whom God loves, he punishes *(Yiddish proverb)*

Love is a glass which shatters if you hold it too tightly or too loosely. *(Russian proverb)*

HUMOUR
God wants spiritual fruit, not religious nuts. *(Ethel Wilcox)*

STATEMENT
What does the most to reveal God's presence, however, is the brotherly charity of the faithful who are united in spirit as they work together for the faith of the Gospel and who prove themselves a sign of unity.
(Second Vatican Council – 'The Church Today')

WORD PICTURES
Some people want to see God with their eyes as they see a cow, and to love him as they love their cow for the milk and cheese and profit it brings them. This is how it is with people who love God for the sake of outward wealth or inward comfort. They do not rightly love God, when they love him for their own advantage. Indeed, I tell you the truth, any object you have in your mind, however good, will be a barrier between you and the inmost Truth. *(Meister Eckhart)*

An eminent baby specialist had a standard treatment for frail newborn infants who failed to gain weight.

When he came to the baby's chart during his rounds in the hospital, he invariably scrawled the following direction to the nurse in attendance:

'This baby to be loved every three hours.' *(Anon)*

Just outside Wakefield Jail is a wall and written on it in huge childish letters is the word 'MICK'. It is repeated two or three times in different places.

Mick has started up a number of questions in my mind, although I have no idea who Mick might be. Who is he anyway? Why does he have to write his name where everyone can see it? What is he trying to say? Will he go on for the rest of his life writing his name where everyone can see it?

In trying to answer these questions I have built up a picture in my imagination – a sort of 'Mick, this is your life'. It is an interesting exercise.

I imagine Mick is 13 years old and is the second in a family of three. Both parents work full time. Mick is a little fellow and feels insecure. With few people to talk to him, he gets lost in groups. Every morning the Mick household is in a state of frantic haste. Everyone grabs something to eat – there is no time for chat. Mick sets off for his big school.

There, he is known only by his surname. He is an average fellow, not outstanding in good or bad. Four o'clock and Mick rushes out to have bread and jam and telly before his parents come in.

He does some homework while the tea is being prepared, then it is telly till bed. Mick has got through another day and nobody has taken much notice.

Frustration gradually builds up and Mick takes his brush to speak to his fellow men. His message is desperate. I am Mick . . . I am myself . . . I matter. Recognise me . . . Look at me . . . Listen to me . . . Do not ignore me . . . I am a real person . . . a unique individual.

In my flight of imagination I look out for a further message soon – MICK LOVES SUE. Then I will know that he has at last found one to take him seriously, to reassure him, to comfort him and make him grow. Then at last he will be able to throw his brush away, for he will have found God's greatest gift to the world, a real person who really loves.

But I only wish that he would find someone to love him soon – and then he wouldn't have to go on spoiling that wall.
(Fr Andy Daly)

A father complained to the Besht that his son had forsaken God.
    'What, Rabbi, shall I do?'
    'Love him more than ever,' was the Besht's reply.
(Jewish saying)

Love has a hem to its garment
That touches the very dust;
It can reach the stains of the streets and lanes,
And because it can, it must.
(Anon)

God lies in wait for us with nothing so much as love.

Now love is like a fishhook.

A fisher cannot catch a fish unless the fish first picks up the hook. If the fish swallows the hook, no matter how it may squirm and turn the fisher is certain of the fish. Love is the same way. Whoever it captured by love takes up his hook in such a fashion that foot and hand, mouth and eyes, heart and all that is in that person must always belong to God. Therefore, look only for this fishhook, and you will be happily caught. The more you are caught, the more you will be liberated. *(Meister Eckhart)*

A great American storyteller wrote about two young people who were very much in love. Christmas Eve was coming and they wanted to give presents to each other. But they were very poor and had no money for presents. So each one, without telling the other, decided to sell his or her most precious possession. The girl's most precious possession was her long golden hair and she went to a hairdresser and had it cut off. She sold it then to buy a lovely watch chain for her lover's watch. He, meanwhile, had gone to a jeweller and sold his watch to buy two beautiful combs for his beloved's hair. Then they made their gifts. There were tears at first and then laughter. There was no hair for the combs and no watch for the watch chain. But there was something more precious and that was their self-sacrificing love for each other. *(Anon)*

Useful Texts

Love:

> Towards God, *Deut. 6:5*
> Towards Neighbour, *Matt. 22:39*
> Exemplified by Christ, *John 15:12*
> Obedience as proof of, *John 14:15*
> Importance of, *1 Cor. 13:1-3, 8-13*

See also: A9 Relationships
> A33 Love your neighbour
> B30 Married love
> C10 Love your enemies

B53
CONSECRATED IN TRUTH

'I have sent them into the world,
and for their sake I consecrate myself so that they too
may be consecrated in truth.' *John 17:19*

QUOTATIONS

All human beings by nature have an urge to know. *(Aristotle)*

Let us rejoice in the Truth, wherever we find its lamp burning. *(Albert Schweitzer)*

If God were able to backslide from truth, I would fain cling to truth and let God go. *(Meister Eckhart)*

Truth which is merely told is quick to be forgotten: truth which is discovered lasts a lifetime. *(William Barclay)*

If the world goes against truth, then Athanasius goes against the world. *(Athanasius)*

Any human being can penetrate to the kingdom of truth, if only he longs for truth and perpetually concentrates all his attention upon its attainment. *(Simone Weil)*

Error is none the better for being common, nor truth the worse for having lain neglected. *(John Locke)*

He who asks a question is a fool for five minutes. He who does not, remains a fool forever. *(Confucius)*

A truth that's told with bad intent
Beats all the lies you can invent.
(William Blake)

Facts that are not frankly faced have a habit of stabbing us in the back. *(Sir Harold Bowden)*

Sit down before the facts as a little child; be prepared to give up every preconceived notion, follow humbly and to whatever abysses nature leads, or you shall learn nothing.
(Thomas Huxley)

Truth is the perfect correlation of mind and reality; and this is actualised in the Lord's person. If the Gospel is true and God is, as the Bible declares, a living God, the ultimate truth is not a system of propositions grasped by a perfect intelligence, but is a personal being apprehended in the only way in which persons are ever fully apprehended, that is, by love. *(William Temple)*

Let us begin by committing ourselves to the truth, to see it like it is and to tell it like it is, to find the truth, to speak the truth and live with the truth. That's what we'll do.
(Richard Nixon: Nomination on acceptance speech, 1968)

PROVERBS
A half truth is a whole lie. *(Yiddish proverb)*

Truth is heavy; few therefore can bear it. *(Hebrew proverb)*

Truth is God's daughter. *(Spanish proverb)*

Speak the truth but leave immediately after. *(Yugoslav proverb)*

HUMOUR
Father 'I want an explanation and I want the truth.'
Son 'Make up your mind, Dad, you can't have both.'
(Anon)

It is always the best policy to speak the truth, unless of course you are an exceptionally good liar. *(Jerome K. Jerome)*

The English are always degrading truth into facts. When a truth becomes a fact, it loses all its intellectual value.
(Oscar Wilde)

WORD PICTURES

A lecturer in a theological college informed his class that the subject of his next lecture would be the sin of deceit and that, by way of preparation, he wished them all to read the seventeenth chapter of Mark's Gospel. When the time came he asked how many members of his class had complied with his instructions. Every one of them raised a hand. 'Thank you,' said the lecturer. 'It is to people like you that today's lecture is especially addressed. There is no seventeenth chapter of Mark!'
(K. Edwards)

One can tell lies without literal mis-statement. During a lull in the cold war, a Russian diplomat was explaining to an English one the difference between Russian and British newspapers.

'Suppose you and I had a race, and you came in first. Your newspapers would report: "The Soviet and British ambassadors yesterday had a race. The British Ambassador won." In *Pravda* the report would be: "A race took place yesterday between diplomats. The Soviet Ambassador came in second. The British Ambassador finished only just in front of the last man".'
(F. H. Drinkwater)

In a village in India, five blind men lived together. One day, they happened to come near an animal which someone told them was an elephant. 'What is an elephant like?' they asked. They were invited to feel its body.

'Why, an elephant is like a pillar,' said the first. He had felt only its leg.

'No, no, it is like a barrel,' said another, who had felt only the belly.

A third said, 'It is like a rope,' for he had felt the tail;

A fourth said, 'It is like a hose,' – he had felt the trunk.

'It is like a winnowing-fan,' said the last man, who had felt only the ear.

So they began to argue among themselves. Each said that his description of the elephant was the true one.

It is the same with Truth, says the Hindu, who loves telling this story. His ancient books, the Vedas, say, 'The Truth is One;

people call it by various names.' All of us, like the blind men, find a part of the truth and think we have grasped it all. But truth itself must always be One and the same.
(Swami Yogeshananda)

A six-year-old daughter gave her mother a real shock when she came home from school and announced that her class was going to see 'the handsome gorilla.'

The startled parent decided to check with the school officials without delay. She gave a sigh of relief when she learned that what the first graders were due to see was the play 'Hansel and Gretel.'

When little children confuse fantasy with reality, they do so harmlessly and therefore due allowance is usually made.

But when those who know better distort the truth that God has entrusted to them, whether deliberately or through negligence, far-reaching damage can result.

Make sure that under all circumstances you are a transmitter of 'the truth and nothing but the truth.' Be a stickler for accuracy. Check and double check information that you pass on, especially if it is detrimental to others. *(Anon)*

USEFUL TEXTS

Truth:
  Attribute of God, *Isa. 65:16*
  Spirit of, *John 15:26*
  Christ is , *John 14:6*
  Word of God is, *John 17:17*

See also: A47 The spirit of Truth
          C11 Talk
          C23 Zeal for what is right

B54

THE TRINITY

'Baptise them in the name of the Father and of the Son and of the Holy Spirit, and teach them to observe all the commands I gave you.' *Matthew 28:19-20*

QUOTATIONS

Among all things called one, the Unity of the Divine Trinity holds the first place. *(St Bernard)*

How can plurality consist with unity, or unity with plurality? To examine the fact closely is rashness, to believe it is piety, to know it is life, and life eternal. *(St Bernard)*

Tell me how it is that in this room there are three candles and but one light, and I will explain to you the mode of the divine existence. *(John Wesley)*

Though the word 'Trinity', first used in its Greek form τριαδ by Theophilus of Antioch *(c. AD 180)*, is not found in Scripture, the conception is there both implicitly and explicitly. *(F. L. Cross)*

The *monotheistic faith* taken over from Israel and held in common with Islam must never be abandoned in any doctrine of the Trinity. There is no God but God *(Hans Küng)*

The Father is my trust, the Son is my refuge, the Holy Ghost is my protection. O Holy Trinity, glory to Thee. *(Byzantine Horologion, Troparion at Nocturns. c. sixth to eighth centuries)*

The divine nature is really and entirely identical with each of the three persons, all of whom can therefore be called one: I and the Father are one. *(St Thomas Aquinas)*

It is not easy to find a term which appropriately defines such great excellence, unless it is better to say that this Trinity is one

God from whom, through whom, and in whom all things exist. *(cf Rom. 11:36) (St Augustine of Hippo)*

In the Father resides unity, in the Son equality, and in the Holy Ghost the perfect union of unity and equality. These three qualities are all one because of the Father, all equal because of the Son, and all united because of the Holy Ghost. *(St Augustine of Hippo)*

God dwells in our heart by faith, and Christ by his Spirit, and the holy Spirit by his purities; so that we are also cabinets of the mysterious Trinity; and what is this short of heaven itself, but as infancy is short of manhood, and letters of words? *(Jeremy Taylor)*

We are enclosed in the Father, and we are enclosed in the Son, and we are enclosed in the Holy Ghost. And the Father is enclosed in us, and the Son is enclosed in us, and the Holy Ghost is enclosed in us: Almightiness, All Wisdom, All Goodness: one God, one Lord. *(Julian of Norwich)*

STATEMENT
Now the Catholic faith is this; that we worship one God in Trinity, and Trinity in Unity, neither confounding the Persons, nor dividing the substance, for there is one Person of the Father, another of the Son, and another of the Holy Ghost; but the godhead of the Father, of the Son, and of the Holy Ghost is one, the glory equal, the majesty co-eternal . . . *(Athanasian Creed)*

WORD PICTURES
In their prayers orthodox Christians often make the sign of the Cross. This they do by joining the tips of the index finger, the second finger and the thumb of the right hand. This gesture symbolises our belief in God the Most Holy Trinity, Father, Son and Holy Spirit equally worshipped and glorified. The ring finger and the little finger are folded into the palm, signifying our belief that the Son of God condescended to become a man, and he is worshipped as truly God and truly man, having two

natures, divine and human. With the hand held thus, the Orthodox Christian then makes the sign of the cross over himself by touching in turn his forehead, stomach, his right shoulder and his left. He then bows slightly. In this way he dedicates his whole being to Christ in fulfilment of the commandment to 'love the Lord thy God with all thy heart, with all thy soul, with all thy strength and with all thy mind'. In bowing he remembers the Publican who was so aware of his unworthiness before God that he would not raise his eyes to heaven. *(Anon)*

So until Ascensiontide Bede worked with his pupils to conclude his translation of John's Gospel into the English tongue: but the Tuesday before Ascensiontide his sickness increased upon him. Nevertheless, he taught and bade his scholars work, saying cheerfully, 'Write with speed now, for I cannot tell how long I may last.'

The day broke (that is, Wednesday), and about the third hour the scribe said, 'There is yet a chapter wanting: it is hard for thee to continue vexing thyself.'

'That is easily done,' said he: 'take thy pen again and write quickly', and joyfully he dictated until the evening at the ninth hour.

'Dear Master,' said the boy, 'there is yet one sentence to be written.'

He answered, 'Write it quickly.' Soon after the boy said, 'It is finished now.'

'Thou has well said. It is finished. Raise my head in thy arms and turn my face towards the holy spot where I was wont to pray, for I desire to sit facing it and call upon my Father.'

So they held him up on the pavement, and he chanted, 'Glory be to the Father, and to the Son and to the Holy Spirit.' Then, as he named the Holy Spirit, his spirit took leave, and departed to the heavenly Kingdom. *(Cuthbert (seventh century) 'The Passing of the Venerable Bede')*

Think of the Father as a spring of life begetting the Son like a river and the Holy Ghost like a sea, for the spring and the river and the sea are all one nature. Think of the Father as a root, of the Son as a branch, and of the Spirit as a fruit, for the substance in these three is one. The Father is a sun with the Son as rays and the Holy Ghost as heat.

The Holy Trinity transcends by far every similitude and figure. So when you hear of an offspring of the Father, do not think of a corporeal offspring. And when you hear that there is a Word, do not suppose him to be a corporeal word. And when you hear of the Spirit of God, do not think of wind and breath. Rather, hold your persuasion with a simple faith alone. For the concept of the Creator is arrived at by analogy from his creatures. *(John of Damascus)*

Christopher Columbus had a tremendous devotion to the Blessed Trinity. He invoked the Trinity at the beginning of every enterprise, and everything he wrote began with the words: 'In the Name of the Most Holy Trinity.'

When he presented to the Council of Salamanca (that assembly of all the learned of science and theology) his theory of the New World to be discovered, he began: 'I come before you in the Name of the Most Holy Trinity, because our sovereigns have commanded me to submit to your wisdom a project which has certainly come to me inspired by the same Holy Spirit.'

On his third voyage in 1598, he vowed to consecrate to the Trinity the first land that he would discover, and hence the island he reached was called Trinidad. *(F. H. Drinkwater)*

USEFUL TEXTS

Trinity:
> Revealed at Jesus' baptism, *Matt. 3:16-17*
> Baptise in the name of, *Matt. 28:19*

See also: A37 Christ the King
A47 The Spirit of Truth
B28 The Father who draws us to Himself
B40 One God
C47 The indwelling spirit

C1

LIBERATION FROM FEAR

'When these things begin to take place, stand erect, hold your heads high, because your liberation is near at hand.'
Luke 21:28

QUOTATIONS

Nothing in life is to be feared. It is only to be understood.
(Marie Curie)

Fear is the foundation of safety. *(Tertullian)*

It will be quite enough to receive the evils which come upon us from time to time, without anticipating them by the imagination. *(St Francis de Sales)*

Half the things that people do not succeed in, are through fear of making the attempt. *(James Northcote)*

The weight of fear is the anchor of the heart.
(Pope St Gregory I)

The free man is he who does not fear to go to the end of his thought. *(Leon Blum)*

Dodgers often dodge into the danger they would avert. Don't dodge anything except sin, sir, and you will be all right. *(Stonewall Jackson)*

A good scare is worth more to a man than good advice.
(E. W. Howe)

Those who love to be feared, fear to be loved; they themselves are of all people the most abject; some fear them, but they fear everyone. *(Jean Pierre Camus)*

Let me assert my firm belief that the only thing we have to fear is fear itself – nameless, unreasoning terror which paralyses needed efforts to convert retreat into advance.
(Franklin D. Roosevelt)

If you have a fearful thought, share it not with a weakling, whisper it to your saddle-bow, and ride forth singing.
(King Alfred)

PROVERBS

Keep your fears to yourself but share your courage.
(English proverb)

Fear makes men ready to believe the worst. *(Latin proverb)*

He who fears something gives it power over him.
(Moorish proverb)

STATEMENT

In the use of all freedoms, the moral principle of personal and social responsibility is to be observed. In the exercise of their rights, individual men and social groups are bound by the moral law to have respect both for the rights of others and for their own duties toward others and for the common welfare of all. Men are to deal with their fellows in justice and civility.
(Second Vatican Council – 'Religious Freedom')

WORD PICTURES

Hildegard, a late-mediaeval German mystic, claimed that she was guided by a divine light that directed her writing and teaching. She recorded the messages and then disseminated them publicly in order that others could benefit from God's direction. Frequently these messages were ones that conjured up fear of the afterlife. Indeed, she pleaded with sinners to repent, lest they suffer the agony that she saw in her visionary revelations. 'I saw a well deep and broad, full of boiling pitch and sulphur, and around it were wasps and scorpions . . . Near a pond of clear water I saw a great fire. In this some souls were burned and others were girdled with snakes . . . And I saw a great fire, black, red, and white, and in it horrible vipers spitting flame; and there the vipers tortured the souls of those who had been slaves of the sin of uncharitableness . . . And I saw a thickest darkness, in which the souls of the disobedient lay on a fiery pavement and were bitten by sharp-toothed worms.' Her visions did generate fear, and people came from far away to speak with her and receive her counsel on spiritual matters. *(Henry Osborn Taylor)*

Fear is one of the passions of human nature of which it is impossible to divest it. You remember the Emperor Charles V, when he read upon the tombstone of a Spanish nobleman, 'Here lies one who never knew fear,' wittily said, 'Then he never snuffed a candle with his fingers.' *(Samuel Johnson)*

The tragic loss of life that resulted from the sinking of the liner Titanic more than fifty years ago brought about at least one good effect.

After the British ship struck an iceberg in the North Atlantic and sank with a loss of 1,500 lives, the International Ice Patrol was formed to prevent similar tragedies.

Almost 50 nations are now members of this safety agency. Its planes and ships are constantly on patrol during the ice season to warn other vessels of danger from icebergs.

Four reasons were given for the incredibly high toll of life in this accident:
1. There were too few lifeboats;
2. The crew was unfamiliar with the ship;
3. The ship was travelling too fast;
4. The liner's officers were overconfident. *(Anon)*

The Grey Dawn
He knows not Advent's meaning who has never sat
By twilight in a dreary cell, its window dim;
Even by day comes little light into the narrow space.
Evening falls, slowly steals away the sun.

Night throws her gloomy mantle round the room,
Terrifying, impenetrable.
Will it always be night?
Will ne'er a ray of sunshine pierce the gloom?
And a new day lead on to joy?

A faint light glimmers through the narrow rift, a witness
That the sun sets never and soon will rise again,
Yes, that the light on which men turned their backs.
The Lord will bring again, with power and glory,
And found his everlasting kingdom!

I believe in Advent!
(Max Josef Metzger,
Catholic Priest martyred in prison, 1944)

USEFUL TEXTS

Fear:
    Commanded of all, *Ps. 33:8*
    As beginning of wisdom, *Job 28:28*
    Reverential, in worship, *Heb. 12:28*

See also: B3 Joy in Christ
            B14 Freedom to serve
            C2 Joy of salvation

C2

THE JOY OF SALVATION

'God will guide Israel in joy by the light of his glory with his mercy and integrity for escort.' *Baruch 5:9*

QUOTATIONS

Joy is the echo of God's life within us. *(Joseph Marmion)*

Joy is the most infallible sign of the presence of God. *(Leon Bloy)*

The surest mark of a Christian is not faith, or even love, but joy. *(Samuel Shoemaker)*

Divine care supplies everybody with the means necessary for salvation, so long as he on his part does not put up obstacles. *(St Thomas Aquinas)*

God wills all men to be saved that are saved, not because there is no man whom He does not wish saved, but because there is no man saved whose salvation He does not will. *(St Augustine of Hippo)*

Salvation is seeing that the universe is good, and becoming a part of that goodness. *(Clutton Brock)*

The terms for 'salvation' in many languages are derived from roots like salvus, saos, whole, heil, which all designate health, the opposite of disintegration and disruption. Salvation is healing in the ultimate sense; it is final cosmic and individual healing. *(Paul Tillich)*

Salvation is free for you because someone else paid. *(Anon)*

The way to be saved is not to delay, but to come and take. *(Dwight L. Moody)*

No man has the right to abandon the care of his salvation to another. *(Thomas Jefferson)*

If you have no joy in your religion, there's a leak in your Christianity somewhere. *(W. A. Sunday)*

PROVERBS

Salvation is from God only. *(Latin proverb)*

The knowledge of sin is the beginning of salvation. *(Latin proverb)*

WORD PICTURES

There is no expeditious road
To pack and label men for God,
And save them by the barrel-load.
(Francis Thompson)

A woman dreamed she walked into a brand new shop in the marketplace and, to her surprise, found God behind the counter.

'What do you sell here?' she asked.

'Everything your heart desires,' said God.

Hardly daring to believe what she was hearing, the woman decided to ask for the best things a human being could wish for. 'I want peace of mind and love and happiness and wisdom and freedom from fear,' she said. Then, as an afterthought, she added, 'Not just for me. For everyone on earth.'

God smiled, 'I think you've got me wrong, my dear,' he said. 'We don't sell fruits here. Only seeds.' *(Anthony De Mello)*

Joy is distinctly a Christian word and a Christian thing. It is the reverse of happiness. Happiness is the result of what happens of an agreeable sort. Joy has its springs deep down inside, and that spring never runs dry, no matter what happens. Only Jesus gives that joy. He had joy, singing its music within, even under the shadow of the cross. It is an unknown word and thing except as He has sway within. *(Samuel Gordon)*

See also: B3 Joy in Christ

C3

SHARING POSSESSIONS

'If anyone has two tunics he must share with the man
who has none.' *Luke 3:10*

QUOTATIONS

When we can share – that is poetry in the prose of life.
(Sigmund Freud)

Those who have much are often greedy; those who have little
always share. *(Oscar Wilde)*

Be not anxious about what you have, but about what you are.
(Pope St Gregory)

Goods which are not shared are not goods.
(Fernando de Rojas)

In a shared fish, there are no bones. *(Democritus of Abdera)*

Man should not consider his material possessions as his own,
but as common to all, so as to share them without hesitation
when others are in need. Whence the apostle says: 'Command
the rich, of this world . . . to offer with no stint, to apportion
largely.' *(St Thomas Aquinas)*

There is no savour like that of bread shared among men.
(Antoine de Saint-Exupery)

For well you know that not life nor health nor riches nor honour
nor dignity nor lordship is your own. Were they yours, you
could possess them in your own way. But in such an hour a man
wishes to be well, he is ill; or living, and he is dead; or rich, and
he is poor; or a lord, and he is made a servant and vassal. All this
is because these things are not his own, and he can only hold
them in so far as may please him who has lent them to him.
(St Catherine of Siena)

PROVERBS

All possessions of mortals are mortal. *(Latin proverb)*

Everything goes to him who wants nothing. *(French proverb)*

He who shares honey with the bear has the least part. *(English proverb)*

HUMOUR

'Grandma,' asked a youngster, 'were you once a little girl like me?'

'Yes, dear.'

'Then,' continued the child, 'I suppose you know how it feels to get an ice-cream cone when you don't expect it!'

One child said to another, 'If one of us would get off this tricycle, I could ride it much better.'

Teacher asked Peter how he would divide 10 potatoes equally among 20 people. Peter promptly replied, 'I'd mash them.'

Two children at a Sunday School picnic found a third who had no lunch. Remembering the lesson on the loaves and fishes in the Bible, Ronny said to his friend Timmy, 'We are going to share our lunch with our new friend, aren't you, Timmy?'

The postman stared doubtfully at the formidable looking animal lying on the doorstep. 'What kind of dog is that?' he asked the little old lady.

'I don't rightly know,' she said. 'My brother sent it from Africa.' 'Well,' the postman hesitated, 'it's the oddest looking dog I've ever seen.'

The prim lady nodded her head. 'You should have seen it before I cut its mane off.'

STATEMENT

The distribution of goods should be directed toward providing employment and sufficient income for the people of today and of the future. Whether individuals, groups or public authorities make the decisions concerning this distribution and the planning of the economy, they are bound to keep these objectives in mind. They must realise their serious obligation of seeing to it that provision is made for the necessities of a decent life on the part of individuals and of the whole community. *(Second Vatican Council – 'The Church Today')*

WORD PICTURES

I heard recently of a Christian speaker in Hyde Park who declared rhetorically, expecting the answer 'Yes': 'If you had two houses, you would give one to the poor, wouldn't you?'

'Yes,' said the man to whom the question was directed, 'indeed I would.'

'And if you had two motor cars,' went on the orator, 'you would keep one and give the other away?'

'Yes, of course,' said the man.

'And if you had two shirts, you would give one away?'

'Hey, wait a minute,' said the man, 'I've got two shirts.' *(Douglas Woodruff)*

The Holy Supper is kept, indeed,
In whatso we share with another's need;
Not what we give, but what we share.
For the gift without the giver is bare.
(James Russell Lowell)

See also: A7 Poor in Spirit
A21 Feeding the hungry
A33 Love your neighbour
B41 Generosity

C4

PERSONAL PEACE

'They will live secure, for from then on he will extend his power to the ends of the land. He himself will be peace.'
Micah 5:4

QUOTATIONS

Peace of heart – without it no good can make us happy; with it, every trial, even the approach of death, can be borne. *(Frederic Ozanam)*

We should have much peace if we would not busy ourselves with the sayings and doing of others. *(Thomas à Kempis)*

The springs of human conflict cannot be eradicated through institutions, but only through the reform of the individual human being. *(General Douglas MacArthur)*

Peace is liberty in tranquillity. *(Cicero)*

Where there is peace, God is. *(George Herbert)*

If we will have peace without a worm in it, lay we the foundations of justice and good will. *(Oliver Cromwell)*

Thinking about interior peace destroys interior peace. The patient who constantly feels his pulse is not getting any better. *(Hubert Van Zeller)*

Peace is not made at the council tables, or by treaties, but in the hearts of men. *(Herbert Hoover)*

Peace is not an absence of war, it is a virtue, a state of mind, a disposition for benevolence, confidence, justice.
(Baruch Spinoza)

My religion is based on truth and non-violence. Truth is my God and non-violence is the means to reach Him. *(Mohandas Gandhi)*

We have to make peace without limitations. *(Harold Lindsell)*

Peace demands a mentality and a spirit which, before turning to others, must first permeate him who wishes to bring peace. Peace is first and foremost personal, before it is social. And it is precisely this spirit of peace which it is the duty of every true follower of Christ to cultivate. *(Pope Paul VI)*

Scrawled on the back of a van: 'Make love not war; ask driver for details.' *(Anon)*

PROVERBS

Peace within makes beauty without. *(English proverb)*

Peace without truth is poison. *(German proverb)*

STATEMENT

Peace cannot be obtained on earth unless personal values are safeguarded and men freely and trustingly share with one another the riches of their inner spirits and their talents. A firm determination to respect other men and peoples and their dignity, as well as the studied practice of brotherhood, are absolutely necessary for the establishment of peace. Hence peace is likewise the fruit of love, which goes beyond what justice can provide.

For this reason, all Christians are urgently summoned 'to practice the truth in love' *(Eph. 4:15)* and to join with all true peacemakers in pleading for peace and bringing it about. *(Second Vatican Council – 'The Church Today')*

WORD PICTURES

Henri Nouwen, a widely acclaimed author, educator, and Roman Catholic priest, tells how he came to a deeper understanding of peace – especially that peace which comes from God. In the 1980s, after having lived and taught at Harvard University, he moved to a community near Toronto called Daybreak – a 'family' comprising of six mentally handicapped individuals and four who were not, all seeking to live by the beatitudes of Jesus.

In this life of mutual sharing, it has been Adam who has had the deepest impact on Nouwen. 'He is a 25-year-old man who cannot speak, cannot dress or undress himself, cannot walk alone, cannot eat without much help. He does not cry or laugh . . . . He suffers from severe epilepsy and, despite heavy medication, sees few days without grand mal seizures.'

To many people Adam is a virtual 'vegetable,' but not to Nouwen. 'As my fears gradually lessened, a love emerged in me so full of tender affection that most of my other tasks seemed boring and superficial compared with the hours spent with Adam. Out of his broken body and broken mind emerged a most beautiful human being offering me a greater gift than I would ever offer him.'

Adam gave him the gift of peace – 'a peace rooted in being.' Nouwen had been caught up in his prestigious career – one 'so marked by rivalry and competition, so pervaded with compulsion and obsession, so spotted with moments of suspicion, jealousy, resentment and revenge.' But with Adam he discovered there was more to life and ministry. 'Adam's peace, while rooted more in being than in doing, and more in the heart than in the mind, is a peace that calls forth community . . . Adam in his total vulnerability calls us together as a family.'
(Anon)

I had a paintbox
But it didn't have the colour red
For the blood of the wounded,
Nor white
For the hearts and faces of the dead

It didn't have yellow either
For the burning sands
Of the desert.

Instead it had orange
For the dawn and the sunset
And blue
For new skies
And pink
For the dreams of young people.

I sat down and painted peace.
(Latin American Child, aged 10)

Peace is not won
By man's eternal strife,
Peace is the power of God
In human life.
It dwells with joy and love,
Is manifest in grace;
The star above His crib,
The light that is His face.
(Anon)

Give us, O God, the vision which can see thy love in the world in spite of human failure. Give us the faith, the trust, the goodness in spite of our ignorance and weakness. Give us the knowledge that we may continue to pray with understanding hearts, and show us what each one of us can do to set forth the coming of the day of universal peace. *(Frank Bormann, Apollo 8, Christmas Eve 1968)*

USEFUL TEXTS

Peace:
Fruit of the Spirit, *Gal. 5:22*
Of God, *Phil. 4:7*
Of Christ, *John 14:27*
With one another, *Mark 9:50*

See also: A2 Integrity
B19 Conscience
C17 International peace

C5

THE INSTITUTION OF MARRIAGE

'There was a wedding at Cana in Galilee. The mother of Jesus was there and Jesus and his disciples had also been invited.'
John 2:1

QUOTATIONS

And when will there be an end of marrying? I suppose, when there is an end of living! *(Tertullian)*

Marriage is an order in which the profession must be made before the noviciate. *(Jean Pierre Camus)*

Marriage is our last, best chance to grow up. *(Joseph Barth)*

Marriage is not like the hill of Olympus, wholly clear, without clouds. *(Thomas Fuller)*

Marriage is like twirling a baton, turning handsprings, or eating with chopsticks; it looks so easy till you try it. *(Helen Rowland)*

The form of matrimony consists in an inseparable union of minds; a couple pledged to each other in faithful friendship. The end is the begetting and upbringing of children, through marriage intercourse and shared duties in which each helps the other to rear children. *(St Thomas Aquinas)*

When men and women marry, the union should be made with the consent of the bishop, so that the marriage may be according to the Lord and not merely out of lust. Let all be done to the glory of God. *(St Ignatius of Antioch)*

It is clear that marriage, even in the state of nature and certainly long before it was raised to the dignity of a sacrament, was divinely instituted in such a way that it should be a perpetual and indissoluble bond, which cannot therefore be dissolved by any civil law. *(Pope Pius VI)*

How shall we ever be able adequately to describe the happiness of that marriage which the Church arranges, the Sacrifice strengthens, upon which the blessing sets a seal, at which the angels are present as witnesses, and to which the Father gives his consent? *(Tertullian)*

PROVERBS

Marriage is a covered dish. *(Swiss proverb)*

Marriage is Heaven and Hell. *(German proverb)*

Don't praise marriage on the third day, but after the third year. *(Russian proverb)*

HUMOUR

All marriages are happy. It's the living together afterwards that causes all the trouble. *(Farmer's Almanac)*

Falsely your Church seven sacraments does frame: Penance and Matrimony are the same! *(Richard Duke)*

Nowadays two can live as cheaply as one large family used to! *(J. Adams)*

Student   'To whom was Minerva married?'

Professor   'My boy, when will you learn that Minerva was the Goddess of Wisdom? She wasn't married.'

A neighbour's four-year-old daughter confided to me one day, 'When I grow up, I'm going to marry Danny.'

I asked her why she was going to marry the boy next door and she replied seriously, 'I have to, I'm not allowed to cross the street where the other boys live.'

An old Negro accused of deserting his wife was brought before the judge. After the judge had lectured him severely on the sin and serious character of desertion, he asked the old Negro: 'What have you to say?'

'Judge,' solemnly answered the old Negro: 'you done git me wrong. I ain't no deserter. I is a refugee.'

'Tis easy enough to be twenty-one:
'Tis easy enough to marry;
But when you try both games at once
'Tis a bloody big load to carry.
(The Midlands: Traditional)

STATEMENTS

Since the Creator of all things has established the conjugal partnership as the beginning and basis of human society, and by His grace, has made it a great mystery in Christ and the Church *(cf Eph. 5:32)* the apostolate of married persons and of families is of unique importance for the Church and civil society.
(Second Vatican Council – 'Laity')

Thus a man and a woman, who by the marriage covenant of conjugal love 'are no longer two, but one flesh' *(Matt. 19:6)* render mutual help and service to each other through an intimate union of their persons and of their actions. Through this union they experience the meaning of their oneness and attain to it with growing perfection day by day. As a mutual gift of two persons, this intimate union, as well as the good of the children, imposes total fidelity on the spouses and argues for an unbreakable oneness between them.

Authentic married love is caught up into divine love and is governed and enriched by Christ's redeeming power and the saving activity of the Church. Thus this love can lead the spouses to God with powerful effect and can aid and strengthen them in the sublime office of being a father or a mother.
(Second Vatican Council – 'The Church Today')

WORD PICTURES

Wedding customs differ significantly from culture to culture and from century to century. Christians who look back to the Reformation as a high point in their church tradition might be shocked to discover how different morals and marriage customs really were during the time of the great Reformers. It is well known that Martin Luther married Katherine von Bora, a former nun, but the details of the wedding are less well known.

Katie was forced to endure the ritual of having several of Luther's friends observe the sexual consummation of their marriage – one of the many indignities a sixteenth-century female had to cope with between infancy and death. Luther's biographer describes the ordeal:

'On the evening of 13 June 1525, according to the custom of the day, he appeared with his bride before a number of his friends as witnesses. The Pomeranian (Johann) Bugenhagen blessed the couple, who consummated the marriage in front of the witnesses, as (Justus) Jonas reported the next day: "Luther has taken Katharina von Bora to wife. I was present yesterday and saw the couple on their marriage bed. As I watched this spectacle I could not hold back my tears." '
(Richard Friedenthal)

When a man whose marriage was in trouble sought his advice, the Master said 'You must learn to listen to your wife.' The man took this advice to heart and returned after a month to say that he had learnt to listen to every word his wife was saying. Said the Master, with a smile, 'Now go home and listen to every word she isn't saying.' *(Anthony De Mello)*

The writer finds a wheelbarrow containing two very clean looking pillows parked outside a remote dispensary . . .

In due time the dispensary door opened and out came a woman limping very painfully, helped along by her husband. He led her gently towards the wheelbarrow. I got up and smoothed the pillows and held the wheelbarrow steady while he lifted her in. It was a tender, moving sight to see this gaunt African slowly lifting his sick wife into the wheelbarrow where she curled up in comfort on the pillow. Then proudly lifting the handles of the wheelbarrow he looked all round, at the doctor in the dispensary, at me and the waiting crowd, and wheeled away his homemade ambulance into the bush. 'That's a miracle for you,' said the doctor as we watched them disappear, 'that man cares enough for his sick wife to wheel her in his barrow for 20 miles. He's been here before. He will come again and again until she's better.' *(Cecil Northcott)*

A group of cinema engineers classified the following as the ten most dramatic sounds in the movies: a baby's first cry; the blast of a siren; the thunder of breakers on rocks; the roar of a forest fire; a fog-horn; the slow drip of water; the galloping of horses; the sound of a distant train whistle; the howl of a dog; the wedding march.

And one of these sounds causes more emotional response and upheaval than any other, has the power to bring forth almost every human emotion: sadness, envy, regret, sorrow, tears, as well as supreme joy. It is the sound of the wedding march. *(James Florn)*

We speak traditionally of the marriage knot or the bond of marriage. The Latin phrase is *nodus Herculeus*, and part of the marriage service was for the bridegroom to loosen *(solvere)* the bride's girdle, not to tie it. In the Hindu marriage ceremony, the bridegroom knots a ribbon round the bride's neck. Before the knot is tied, the bride's father may refuse consent, but immediately it is tied, the marriage is indissoluble. The Parsees bind the hands of the bridegroom with a sevenfold cord, seven being a sacred number. The ancient Carthaginians tied the thumbs of the betrothed with a leather lace. *(Anon)*

See also: B6 The family
          B30 Married love

C6
THE OLD TESTAMENT LAW

'The precepts of the Lord are right, they gladden the heart.
The command of the Lord is clear, it gives light to the eyes.'
Psalm 19:8

QUOTATIONS

Men of most renowned virtue have sometimes by transgressing most truly kept the law. *(John Milton)*

Probably all laws are useless; for good men do not need laws at all, and bad men are made no better by them.
(Demonax the Cynic)

What is hateful to you, do not to your fellow: that is the whole Law: all the rest is interpretation. *(Rabbi Hillel)*

There are 70 ways of studying Torah; one is in silence.
(Rabbi Tcharkover)

The Torah is truth, and the purpose of knowing it is to live by it. *(Maimonides)*

The Torah lives – even in a hovel, up to its neck in dirt. *(Anon)*

PROVERBS

The beginning and the end of the law is kindness.
(Jewish proverb)

Without Law, civilisation dies. *(Jewish proverb)*

WORD PICTURES

Alice   While you talk, he's gone.

More   And go he should, if he were the Devil himself, until he broke the law!

Roper So now you'd give the Devil benefit of law?

More Yes. What would you do? Cut a great road through the law to get after the Devil?

Roper I'd cut down every law in England to do that.

More Oh? And when the last law was down, and the Devil turned round on you – where would you hide, Roper, the laws all being flat? This country's planted thick with laws from coast to coast – Man's laws, not God's – and if you cut them down – and you are just the man to do it – d'you really think you could stand upright in the winds that would blow then? Yes, I'd give the Devil benefit of law, for my own safety's sake.

(Robert Bolt, 'A Man for all Seasons')

When rabbis of Judaism used the word 'Torah' or Law, a complicated concept was involved.
1. Technically the Torah refers to the Pentateuch or 'the Five Books of Moses'
2. In another sense 'the Torah' designates the actual scroll containing the Five Books of Moses
3. In a general sense, Torah is all of Jewish Law
4. In the widest use of the word, 'Torah' refers to Judaism as a religion or philosophy

USEFUL TEXTS

Law:
  Given through Moses, *Exod. 20*
  All to be obeyed, *Gal. 3:10*
  No one justified by it, *Rom. 3:20*
  Saved from, *Gal. 3:13*
  Christ is end of, *Rom. 10:4*

See also: A29 True obedience
           B4 Mary – Handmaid of God
           B31 The commandments of life

C7
The Humanity of Christ

They said, 'This is Joseph's son, surely?'
Luke 4:22

Quotations

By a carpenter, mankind was created and made, and by a carpenter, meet it was that man should be repaired. *(Erasmus)*

To know Jesus and him crucified is my philosophy, and there is none higher. *(St Bernard)*

I see His blood upon the rose
And in the stars the glory of His eyes,
His body gleams amid eternal snows,
His tears fall from the skies.
(Joseph M. Plunkett)

'Gentle Jesus, meek and mild' is a snivelling modern invention, with no warrant in the Gospels.
(George Bernard Shaw)

Theologians who are in danger of losing the sense of a living God, under the pressure of abstractions, might profitably meditate upon the eternal significance of the Second Person of the Blessed Trinity enjoying a good bowel movement among the Judean hills. *(Brendan Francis)*

He became what we are that he might make us what he is. *(St Athanasius of Alexandria)*

Tell me the picture of Jesus you have reached and I will tell you some important traits about your nature. *(Oscar Pfister)*

Poor creature though I be, I am the hand and foot of Christ. I move my hand and my hand is wholly Christ's hand, for deity is become inseparably one with me. I move my foot, and it is aglow with God. *(Symeon the New Theologian)*

PROVERBS

It is a man who counts; I call upon gold, it answers not; I call upon cloth, it answers not; it is man who counts. *(Ghanaian proverb)*

He is a man who acts like a man. *(Danish proverb)*

STATEMENT

The truth is that only in the mystery of the incarnate Word does the mystery of man take on light. For Adam, the first man, was a figure of him who was to come, namely, Christ the Lord. Christ, the final Adam, by the revelation of the mystery of the Father and his love, fully reveals man to man himself and makes his supreme calling clear. *(Second Vatican Council – 'The Church Today')*

WORD PICTURES

It was at that time that a man appeared – if 'man' is the right word – who had all the attributes of a man but seemed to be something greater. His actions were superhuman, for he worked such wonderful and amazing miracles that I for one cannot regard him as a man; yet in view of his likeness to ourselves I cannot regard him as an angel either. *(Josephus)*

One solitary life
He was born in a stable,
in an obscure village,
the child of a peasant woman.
He worked in a carpenter's shop
until he was thirty.
From there he travelled
less than 200 miles.

He never wrote a book.
He never held office.
He never had a family or owned a home.
He did none of the things one
usually associates with greatness.

He became a nomadic preacher.
He was only thirty-three when the tide of
popular opinion turned against him.
He was betrayed by a close friend,
and his other friends ran away.
He was turned over to his enemies
and went through the mockery of a trial.
He was unjustly condemned to death,
crucified on a cross between two thieves,
on a hill overlooking the town dump,
And, when dead, was laid in a borrowed grave,
through the pity of a friend.

Nineteen centuries have come and gone,
all the armies that ever marched,
all the navies that ever sailed,
all the parliaments that ever sat,
and all the kings that ever reigned
have not affected the life of man on this earth
as that One Solitary Life.

He is the central figure of the human race,
He is the Messiah, the Son of God,
JESUS CHRIST.
(*Anon*)

Consider Jesus of Nazareth, the most generous-hearted person who ever lived. He never refused a request for help. Great multitudes followed him, and he healed them all. He went out of his way to cross racial and religious barriers. He compassed the whole world in his love.

Jesus Christ alone stands at the absolute centre of humanity, the one completed, harmonious man. He is the absolute and perfect truth, the highest that humanity can reach; at once its perfect image and supreme Lord. *(Charles W. French)*

A little known religious poet of early New England, Edward Taylor, put into words the main point of incarnation-theology in this way: 'God's only Son doth hug humanity into his very Person.' *(Anon)*

St John Fisher, on the way out of the Tower of London to the scaffold where he was to be beheaded, opened his New Testament at random with the prayer: 'Lord, show me some comforting thought this day.' When he looked at the page, his eye fell on the words in St John: 'This is eternal life, that they may know thee the only true God and Jesus Christ whom thou hast sent.' He closed the book gently. 'Here is wisdom enough for me unto my life's end,' he said. *(F. H. Drinkwater)*

USEFUL TEXTS
Humanity of Christ:
  Birth, *Matt 1:18; Luke 2:2*
  Lost at 12, *Luke 4:21*
  Tempted, *Luke 4:1-13; Matt. 4:1-11*
  Angry, *Luke 19:45; Matt. 21:12*
  Tired, *Luke 8:23*
  Grieved, *John 11:35*
  Like us, except for sin, *Heb. 4:15*

See also: A37 Christ the King
          B3 Joy in Christ
          B16 Christ heals and forgives
          C45 The Divinity of Christ

C8

GOD'S MESSENGERS

'Then I heard the voice of the Lord saying:
"Whom shall I send? Who will be our messenger?"
I answered, "Here I am, send me." ' *Isaiah 6:8*

QUOTATIONS

But not everyone who speaks in the spirit is a prophet, but only if he follows the conduct of the Lord.
(Teaching of the Twelve Apostles)

The prophet is to be no mere announcer, he is rather God's agent who by the 'word' accomplishes what he foretells, whether good or bad. *(Fleming James)*

The prophet is primarily the man, not to whom God has communicated certain divine thoughts, but whose mind is illuminated by the divine spirit to intercept aright the divine acts; and the act is primary. *(William Temple)*

Prophets were twice stoned – first in anger, then, after their death, with a handsome slab in the graveyard.
(Christopher Morley)

We have made this memorial to commemorate those who have fought already, and to train those who shall fight hereafter. *(Inscription in the Chapel of Modern Martyrs, St Paul's Cathedral)*

Leave it to the people, if they are not prophets, they are the sons of prophets. *(Talmud)*

The wisest prophets make sure of the event first.
(Horace Walpole)

HUMOUR

St Jerome in his study kept a great big cat,
It's always in his pictures, with its feet upon the mat.
Did he give it milk to drink, in a little dish?
When it comes to Fridays, did he give it fish?
If I lost my little cat, I'd be sad without it;
I should ask St Jerome what to do about it;
I should ask St Jerome, just because of that,
For he's the only saint I know who kept a pussy cat.
(Anon)

WORD PICTURES

We teachers must be prophets, for prophets are men who speak forth God's Word. The word *prophet* means 'forthteller,' not *foreteller*. A prophet was known not primarily for his *hind*sight or *fore*sight but for his *in*sight. He saw God's plan. He was a *seer*, one who penetrated by insight into the mysteries of God. He knew the covenant God had made with His people, and he knew of the gap between God's call and His people's response. *(Interaction)*

St Albert (called 'the Great') was a young German who went to the University of Padua and in 1223 joined the Dominicans, drawn by the preaching of their Master-General, Jordan of Saxony. Albert became one of the greatest minds of his time, a scientist as well as a theologian, bringing Aristotle into harmony with the Faith. He started a new university in Cologne. One of his students was a silent young Dominican named Thomas of Aquino, of whom he hoped great things. They worked together at Paris and elsewhere. Albert was elected Provincial for Germany in 1254, but resigned three years later; he felt his job was research and teaching.

In 1260, he was made Bishop of Ratisbon, where there were many difficulties and troubles; once again he realised he was no administrator; he resigned in 1262 and went back to teach at Cologne. St Thomas was now in Paris, but Albert kept in close touch with him; and it was a sad blow to Albert when St Thomas died, still under 50, in 1274. 'The Light of the Church is extinguished,' said Albert and often shed tears when people spoke about his great pupil. Sometimes he had to defend St Thomas's writings against those who criticised them as untraditional. But meanwhile old age had come upon him, and he died at Cologne in 1280. He was beatified in 1622 and declared a Doctor of the Church in 1931. *(F. H. Drinkwater)*

See also: B2 The Good News
    B9 Revelation
    B24 Go tell everyone

C9

THE BEATITUDES

'A blessing on the man who puts his trust in the Lord,
with the Lord for his hope.' *Jeremiah 17:7*

QUOTATIONS

Innocence and knowledge make a man blessed. *(St Ambrose)*

A blessed life may be defined as consisting simply and solely in
the possession of goodness and truth. *(St Ambrose)*

Never undertake anything for which you wouldn't have the
courage to ask the blessings of heaven.
(Georg Christian Lichtenberg)

Blessed is the man who is too busy to worry in the daytime and
too sleepy to worry at night. *(Anon)*

It is not written, blessed is he that feedeth the poor, but he that
considereth the poor. A little thought and a little kindness are
often worth more than a great deal of money. *(John Ruskin)*

Blessed is he who expects nothing, for he shall never be
disappointed. *(Alexander Pope)*

Blessed are the simple, for they shall have much peace.
(Thomas à Kempis)

Blessed is the man who has a skin of the right thickness. He can
work happily in spite of enemies and friends. *(Henry T. Bailey)*

Reflect upon your present blessings, of which every man has
many; not on your past misfortunes, of which all men have
some. *(Charles Dickens)*

PROVERB

Blessings ever wait on virtuous deeds. *(English proverb)*

STATEMENT

Christians who take an active part in modern socioeconomic development and defend justice and charity should be convinced that they can make a great contribution to the prosperity of mankind and the peace of the world. Whether they do so as individuals or in association, let their example be a shining one. After acquiring whatever skills and experience are absolutely necessary, they should in faithfulness to Christ and his Gospel observe the right order of values in their earthly activities. Thus their whole lives, both individual and social, will be permeated with the spirit of the beatitudes, notably with the spirit of poverty. *(Second Vatican Council – 'The Church Today')*

WORD PICTURES

Blessed are they who have the gift of making friends, for it is one of God's best gifts. It involves many things, but above all, the power of going out of one's self, and appreciating whatever is noble and loving in another. *(Thomas Hughes)*

It is manifest that men are made blessed by the obtaining of divinity. And as men are made just by the obtaining of justice, and wise by the obtaining of wisdom, so they who obtain divinity must needs in like manner become gods. Wherefore everyone that is blessed is a god, but by nature there is only one God; but there may be many by participation. *(Boethius)*

The pursuit of God is the desire of beatitude, the attainment of God is beatitude. We pursue after him by loving him, we attain to him, not indeed by becoming what he is, but by coming close to him, as it were, in some marvellous intellectual fashion, wholly illumined and wholly embraced by his holiness. For he is Light itself and by that Light are we permitted to be illumined. *(St Augustine of Hippo)*

Blessings we enjoy daily, and for the most of them, because they be so common, men forget to pay their praises. But let not us, because it is a sacrifice so pleasing to him who still protects us, and gives us flowers, and showers, and meat and content.
(Izaak Walton)

See also: B2 The Good News
B3 Joy in Christ
C2 Joy of salvation

C10
LOVE YOUR ENEMIES

'Love your enemies, do good to those who hate you,
bless those who curse you.' *Luke 6:27*

QUOTATIONS
Love is all we have, the only way that each can help the other.
(Euripides)

The first duty of love is to listen. *(Paul Tillich)*

Where there is no love, pour love in, and you will draw out love.
(St John of the Cross)

Love will conquer hate. *(Mohandas Gandhi)*

Love with no condition. *(Paul Tournier)*

Love your enemies, for they tell you your faults.
(Benjamin Franklin)

Never cease loving a person, and never give up hope for him,
for even the Prodigal Son, who had fallen most low, could still
be saved. The bitterest enemy and also he who was your friend
could again be your friend; Love that has grown cold can kindle
again. *(Soren Kierkegaard)*

If we are bound to forgive an enemy, we are not bound to trust
him. *(Thomas Fuller)*

PROVERBS
There is no little enemy. *(French proverb)*

Charity gives itself rich; covetousness hoards itself poor.
(German proverb)

He who plants trees loves others besides himself.
(English proverb)

HUMOUR

Love your enemy – it will drive him nuts. *(Eleanor Doan)*

I choose my friends for their good looks, my acquaintances for their good characters, and my enemies for their intellects. A man cannot be too careful in the choice of his enemies.
(Oscar Wilde)

One day, little Jane was seated alone at a small table while her parents sat with their guests at the large table. This greatly displeased Jane. Before eating, Jane's parents thought it would be nice for Jane to be included in the group although she was seated separately, so father asked her to say the blessing. This was her prayer: 'Lord, I thank Thee for this table in the presence of mine enemies. Amen.'

A magician was sailing the Pacific, right after the Second World War, entertaining the passengers. With each amazing feat of magic, a parrot, who perched on his shoulder would squawk, 'Faker, faker.' No matter what the magician did, rabbits out of hats, vanishing bird cage and all, he would repeatedly cry, 'Faker, faker.' The magician and parrot became bitter enemies. Finally the magician promised that he would do a trick that would out-Houdini Houdini. The night came, the wand was waved, the 'woofle dust' was sprinkled. At that minute the ship hit a floating mine, which blew the ship to pieces. The next morning on a make-shift life raft, the parrot was perched at one end, the magician at the other. Finally the parrot hopped over and said, 'OK Buddy, you win, but what did you do with the ship?'

STATEMENT

Respect and love ought to be extended also to those who think or act differently than we do in social, political, and religious matters, too. In fact, the more deeply we come to understand their ways of thinking through such courtesy and love, the more easily will we be able to enter into dialogue with them. *(Second Vatican Council – 'The Church Today')*

WORD PICTURES

The Rabbi Hillel was a renowned scribe in Jerusalem about the time of Christ's birth; he seems to have died about AD 10, aged eighty. He was called 'the Great' or 'the Elder', and his interpretations of the Law were less severe than others. He is said to have been the grandfather of Gamaliel *(Acts 22:3)* who taught Paul. Our Lord must have heard often of Hillel, and could possibly have spoken with him during the three days before the finding in the Temple.

Here is one of the tales our Lord might have heard. A certain gentile came to Shammai (Shammai was the leader of the more strict school of interpretation) and said that he would like to become a proselyte, but could not stay long in Jerusalem. 'Can you teach me the whole Torah while I am standing on one foot?' Shammai sent him away angrily. So the gentile went to Hillel with the same question. Hillel admitted him as a convert, and said, 'Whatever is hateful to thee, do not do to thy fellow-man. This is the whole Law: all the rest is interpretation. Now go and study.' (*F. H. Drinkwater*)

The following story is from Ernest Gordon 's account of life and death in a Japanese pow camp on the River Kwai:
Farther on, we were shunted on to a siding for a lengthy stay. We found ourselves on the same track with several carloads of Japanese wounded. They were on their own and without medical care. No longer fit for action, they had been packed into railway trucks which were being returned to Bangkok. Whenever one of them died en route, he was thrown off into the jungle. The ones who survived to reach Bangkok would presumably receive some form of medical treatment there. But they were given none on the way.

They were in a shocking state; I have never seen men filthier. Their uniforms were encrusted with mud, blood and excrement. Their wounds, sorely inflamed and full of pus, crawled with maggots . . . Without a word, most of the officers in my section unbuckled their packs, took out part of their ration and a rag or two, and with water canteens in their hands went over to the Japanese train to help them. Our guards tried to prevent us, bawling, 'No goodka! No goodka!' But we ignored them and knelt by the side of the enemy to give them food and water, to clean and bind their wounds, to smile and say a kind word. Grateful cries of 'Aragatto!' (thank you) followed us when we left.

An allied officer from another section of the train had been taking it all in. 'What bloody fools you all are!' he said to me. 'Don't you realise that those are the enemy?'
(Ernest Gordon – 'Miracle on the River Kwai')

A former inmate of a Nazi concentration camp was visiting a friend who had shared the ordeal with him. 'Have you forgiven the Nazis?' he asked his friend

'Yes.'

'Well I haven't. I'm still consumed with hatred for them.'

'In that case ' said his friend gently, 'they still have you in prison.' (Our enemies are not those who hate us but those whom we hate) *(Anthony De Mello)*

Tolstoy's story of *The Two Pilgrims* tells of two Russians who set out on a pilgrimage to Jerusalem intent on being present at the solemn Easter festivities. One had his mind so set on the journey's end and object that he would stop for nothing and take thought for nothing but the journey. The other, passing through, found people to be helped at every turn and actually spent so much time and money along the way that he never reached the Holy City. But something came to him from God which the other missed: and something came through him from God into the lives of men which the other failed to find in the great Easter celebration. *(William P. Merrill)*

In 1941, Mama took me back to Moscow. There I saw our enemy for the first time. If my memory is right, nearly 20,000 German war prisoners were to be marched in a single column through the streets of Moscow.

The pavements swarmed with onlookers, cordoned off by soldiers and police. The crowd were mostly women. Russian women with hands roughened by hard work, lips untouched by lipstick and thin hunched shoulders which had borne half the burden of the war. Every one of them must have had a father or a husband or brother or a son killed by the Germans.

They gazed with hatred in the direction from which the column was to appear. At last we saw it.

The generals marched at the head, massive chins stuck out, lips folded disdainfully, their whole demeanour meant to show superiority over their plebeian victors . . .

The women were clenching their fists. The soldiers and policemen had all they could do to hold them back.

All at once something happened to them.

They saw German soldiers, thin, unshaven, wearing dirty, bloodstained bandages, hobbling on crutches or leaning on the shoulders of their comrades; the soldiers walked with their heads down.

The street became dead silent – the only sound was the shuffling of boots and the thumping of crutches.

Then I saw an elderly women in broken-down boots push herself forward and touch a policeman's shoulder, saying: 'Let me through.' There must have been something about her that made him step aside.

She went up to the column, took from inside her coat something wrapped in a coloured handkerchief and unfolded it. It was a crust of black bread. She pushed it awkwardly into the pocket of a soldier, so exhausted that he was tottering on his feet. And now suddenly from every side women were running towards the soldiers, pushing into their hands bread, cigarettes, whatever they had.

The soldiers were no longer enemies. They were people. (Yevtushenko)

USEFUL TEXTS

Enemy:

Help when in trouble, *Exod. 23:4-5*
Do good to and love, *Luke 6:35*
Pray for, *Matt. 5:44*
Last to be destroyed, *1 Cor. 15:26*
Of the cross, *Phil. 3:18-19*

See also: A9 Relationships
A33 Love your neighbour
B15 Jesus, friend of outcasts
B52 God is Love

C11
TALK

'For a man's words flow out of what fills his heart.'
Luke 6:45

QUOTATIONS

Many a man's tongue broke his nose. *(Seumas MacManus)*

A sharp tongue is the only edge tool that grows sharper with constant use. *(Washington Irving)*

Gossip, unlike river water, flows both ways. *(Michael Korda)*

Some people talk like the watch which ticks away the minutes but never strikes the hour. *(Samuel Johnson)*

Don't say all you'd like to say lest you hear something you wouldn't like to hear. *(Seumas MacManus)*

Much talkativeness is the sign of a feeble mind, and an undisciplined will. *(Archbishop Ullathorne)*

Conversation is the image of the mind. As the man is, so is his talk. *(Publius Syrus)*

Speaking without thinking is shooting without aiming.
(W. G. Benham)

There are few wild beasts more to be dreaded than a talking man having nothing to say. *(Jonathan Swift)*

The wise hand does not all that the foolish mouth speaks.
(George Herbert)

Think twice before you speak and then say it to yourself.
(Elbert Hubbard)

PROVERBS

Who brings a tale takes two away. *(Irish proverb)*

Man is caught by his tongue, and an ox by his horns.
(Russian proverb)

Don't let your tongue cut off your head. *(Persian proverb)*

He who talks much is sometimes right. *(Spanish proverb)*

It is better to keep your mouth
shut and be thought a fool,
than to open it and remove all
possible doubt.
(Chinese proverb)

HUMOUR

Why is the word 'tongue' feminine in Greek, Latin, Italian, Spanish, French and German? *(Austin O'Malley)*

A small boy on his way to church for the first time, was being briefed by his elder sister. 'They won't allow you to talk,' she warned him. 'Who won't?' asked the boy. 'The Hushers.' *(Sign)*

A little boy was saying his go-to-bed prayers in a very low voice. 'I can't hear you, dear,' his mother whispered. 'Wasn't talking to you,' said the small one firmly.

Charles Lamb was giving a talk at a mixed gathering and someone in the crowd hissed. Finally Lamb calmly said, 'There are only three things that hiss, a goose, a snake and a fool. Come forth and be identified.'

WORD PICTURES

Gossip is one of the so-called 'little' sins that even Christians are often unable or unwilling to avoid. It is, to be sure, a common sin, but can it truly be called 'little'? Gossip can destroy reputations, disrupt families, divide neighbours, and cause widespread heartbreak, and all to no purpose except the satisfaction that some find in passing on idle or malicious tales. *(William McElroy)*

Aesop, the philosopher of the Fables, was asked one day what was the most useful thing in the world. 'The tongue,' he replied. And what (they asked), is the most harmful thing in the world? 'The tongue,' he replied once more. *(Anon)*

Aesop has a fable of three bulls that fed in a field together in the greatest peace and safety. A lion had long watched them in the hope of making prey of them, but found little chance so long as they kept together. He therefore began secretly to spread evil and slanderous reports of one against another till he fomented jealousy and distrust among them. Soon they began to avoid one another and each took to feeding alone. This gave the lion the opportunity it had been wanting. He fell on them singly and made an easy prey of them all.

Anyone who would cultivate the art of conversation should learn that listening to others is often more important than talking to them. These words of wisdom deserve reflection:
1. Nature has given to man one tongue, but two ears, that we may hear from others as much as we speak. *(Epictetus)*
2. It takes a great man to make a good listener. *(Helps)*
3. A good listener is not only popular everywhere, but after a while he knows something. *(Mizner)*
4. To be a judicious and sympathetic listener will go far toward making you an agreeable companion, self-forgetful, self-possessed, but not selfish enough to monopolise the conversation. *(Jack)*

On one occasion when Mohamet and his friend Ali were together, they met a man who, imagining some ill-treatment, began abusing Ali.
Ali bore the insults for a long while, but at last lost patience and returned railing for railing. When Mohamet heard this, he

walked away, and left the two disputants to settle their differences as best they could. When, later on, Ali met Mohamet, he asked reproachfully, 'Why did you go away like that and leave me to bear such insults alone?' Mohamet replied, 'My friend, while that rude man was insulting you so cruelly and you kept silent there were ten angels guarding you and answering him; but as soon as you began returning his insults they left you, and I also came away.' *(Anonymous)*

In ancient Sparta, the citizens were stoical, military-minded and noted for their economy of speech. Legend has it that when Philip of Macedon was storming the gates of Sparta, he sent a message to the besieged king saying, 'If we capture your city we will burn it to the ground.' A one-word answer came back: 'If'. *(Norman Lewis)*

USEFUL TEXTS

Gossip:
>   Consequences of, *Prov. 16:28*
>   Forbidden under the law, *Lev. 19:16*
>   Result of idleness, *1 Tim. 5:13*

See also: A2 Integrity
>   A9 Relationships
>   A47 The Spirit of Truth
>   B53 Consecrated in Truth

C12

THE CHURCH FOR ALL MEN

'Grant all the foreigner asks so that all the peoples of the earth may come to know your name.' *1 Kings 8:43*

QUOTATIONS

The religion of Jesus begins with the verb 'follow' and ends with the word 'go'. *(Anon)*

But the brightness of the Catholic and only true Church proceeded to increase in greatness, for it ever held to the same points in the same way, and radiated forth to all the race of Greeks and barbarians the reverent, sincere, and free nature, and the sobriety and purity of the divine teaching as to conduct and thought. *(Eusebius of Caesarea)*

It seems to me, as I have been saying, that catholicity is not only one of the notes of the Church, but, according to the divine purposes, one of its securities. *(Cardinal Newman)*

The Church of Jesus Christ is neither Latin nor Greek nor Slav, but Catholic. Accordingly, she makes no difference between her children, and Greek, Latins, Slavs and members of all other nations are equal in the eyes of the Apostolic See.
(Pope Benedict XV)

The Church is catholic, that is, universal:
1. First with regard to place . . . The Church has three parts, one on earth, a second in heaven, a third in purgatory:
2. The Church is universal with regard to all conditions of human beings; nobody is rejected whether they be masters or slaves, men or women . . .
3. It is universal in time, and those are wrong who allow it a limited span of time, for it began with Abel and will last even to the end of the world. *(St Thomas Aquinas)*

There is no geography for the Catholic as a Catholic. *(Archbishop Hughes)*

The Church of Christ is the world's only social hope and the sole promise of world peace. *(Sir Douglas Haig)*

PROVERBS

He who is near the Church is often far from God. *(French proverb)*

In the visible Church the true Christians are invisible. *(German proverb)*

STATEMENT

So it is that this messianic people, although it does not actually include all men, and may more than once look like a small flock, is nonetheless a lasting and sure seed of unity, hope and salvation for the whole human race. Established by Christ as a fellowship of life, charity, and truth, it is also used by him as an instrument for the redemption of all, and is sent forth into the whole world as the light of the world and the salt of the earth. *(cf Matt. 5:13-16). (Second Vatican Council 'The Church')*

WORD PICTURES

The Church is composed of people built into, and held together by, Jesus Christ.

That picture of the Church reminds us of the saying of the Spartan king. He had boasted that no nation in the world had walls like Sparta. But when a visitor came to visit Sparta he saw no walls at all, and asked the Spartan king where the walls were. The Spartan king pointed at his body-guard of magnificent Spartan soldiers: 'These', he said, 'are the walls of Sparta, and every man of them a brick.' In exactly the same way, the Christian is the living stone built into the structure of the Church. *(William Barclay)*

In the misty highlands of north-western Guatemala there thrives a strange and wondrous Church. Most of its members are illiterate Indian peasants who earn a subsistence living from farming the grudging hillsides and by weaving palm hats. Once a week they gather to celebrate the Word of God – sometimes in hidden forest glades, depending on the extent of military persecution . . .

Every village in this region of El Quiché has a bloody story to tell. During an eight-year reign of terror that did not begin to subside until a civilian president took office in 1986, thousands of Indians were killed or relocated to concentration camps . . . Persecution against the Catholic Church was so ferocious that not a single priest or nun remained in the Quiché diocese . . . In order to celebrate Communion, undercover catechists travelled hours on foot, carrying consecrated Hosts hidden among ears of corn or in baskets of beans or tortillas. Anyone caught with such 'subversive material' could expect a slow death by torture.

Typical of Quiché's 'church of the catacombs' were the five catechists of Santa Cruz El Quiché . . . One day in 1982, Santa Cruz, a small market town north of Chichicastenango, was taken over by the army. The villagers were assembled and told that the catechists were 'subversives' whom their relatives must kill that very night. Otherwise, the army would raze Santa Cruz and neighbouring villages.

The army then withdrew, and the villagers discussed the brutal choice, unanimously concluding that 'we won't do it'. The catechists were loved and valued for their religious work and for the instruction they had given to promote co-operatives . . . The villagers had refused to do the deed, but the five catechists insisted that they must: 'It is better for us to die than for thousands to die.' At 4 a.m. a weeping procession, led by the catechists, arrived at the cemetery. Graves were dug, the people formed a circle around the kneeling men, and relatives of the five drew their machetes. Many could not watch the scene; some fainted as the blades fell, and the executioners' tears mingled with the blood of the catechists . . .

Next day the army captain in charge of the area was informed that his orders had been carried out. Another source of subversion had been eliminated. Or had it? Forcing the catechists' relatives to kill them was part of an army policy aimed at alienating Indian recruits from the village origins by demeaning their race, religion and traditions. But it failed to work in Santa Cruz or elsewhere in Quiché because the people honoured such martyrdom. 'We remember them with holy reverence', said a witness to the catechists' death, 'because it is thanks to them that we are alive today.' *(Penny Lernoux)*

The universality of the Church is very well illustrated by the way the European countries (the French always excepted) are quite content that their national patron saints should be foreigners. The English are content with St George of Cappadocia, and do not mind sharing him with Russians and Genoese and Catalans: the Spaniards long ago settled for St James, the Germans for St Boniface from Devon, the Dutch for St Willobrod, also from South England, and the Irish for glorious St Patrick, a Romano-British character from somewhere this side of St George's Channel. As for the Scots, they have accepted an Anglo-Saxon princess, side by side with the Galilean St Andrew.
(Douglas Woodruff)

See also: A6 Light of the world
A13 The Church is for sinners
A43 Believing community
B17 The Church – Bride of Christ

C13

COPING WITH GRIEF

'When the Lord saw her, he felt sorry for her.
"Do not cry," he said.' *Luke 7:13*

QUOTATIONS

There is no grief which time does not lessen and soften.
(Cicero)

Grief and death were born of sin, and devour sin.
(St John Chrysostom)

There is no greater grief than, in misery, to recall happier times.
(Dante)

To weep is to make less the depth of grief. *(William Shakespeare)*

Sorrow makes us all children again, destroys all differences in intellect. The wisest knows nothing. *(Ralph Waldo Emerson)*

Happiness is beneficial for the body but it is grief that develops the powers of the mind. *(Marcel Proust)*

Grief knits two hearts in closer bonds than happiness ever can, and common suffering is a far stronger link than common joy. *(Alphonse De Lamartine)*

The true way to mourn the dead is to take care of the living who belong to them. *(Edmund Burke)*

The young man who has not wept is a savage, and the old man who will not laugh is a fool. *(Santayana)*

Sorrow is a fruit; God does not make it grow on limbs too weak to bear it. *(Victor Hugo)*

Every man is a solitary in his griefs. One soon finds that out.
(Norman Douglas)

Facing and accepting a loss is the first step of managing bereavement. Only life which deliberately picks up and starts again is victorious. *(James Gordon Gilkey)*

PROVERBS

He that conceals his grief finds no remedy for it.
(Turkish proverb)

You cannot prevent the birds of sorrow from flying over your head, but you can prevent them from building nests in your hair. *(Chinese proverb)*

He who would have no trouble in this world must not be born in it. *(Italian proverb)*

WORD PICTURES

A little girl came home from a neighbour's house where her little friend had died. 'Why did you go?' questioned her father.

'To comfort her mother,' replied the child.

'What could you do to comfort her?' the father continued.

'I climbed into her lap and cried with her,' answered the child. *(Anon)*

How one handles his grief is a personal matter. Let the one who has suffered the loss take the lead. If he feels like talking, encourage him to talk. If he prefers to sit in silence, don't intrude on his silence. Friends should call, bring food, offer to run errands, and do what needs to be done. A hug, a squeeze of the hand, a look which says, 'I'm here, if you need me,' conveys more than a thousand words. *(Abigail Van Buren)*

Is it proper to cry
For a baby too small
For a coffin?
Yes, I think it is.
Does Jesus have
My too-small baby
In his tender arms?
Yes, I think He does.
There is so much I do not know
About you, my child –
He, she? quiet or restless?
Will I recognise
Someone I knew so little about
Yet loved so much?
Yes, I think I will.
Can we say
Your life was worth nothing
Because your stay was so short?
Can we say
We loved you any less
Because we never held you?
No, I think not.
Ah, sweet, small child.
Can I say
That loving you is like loving God?
    Loving – yet not seeing
    Holding – yet not touching
    Caressing – yet separated by the chasm of time.
No tombstone marks your sojourn
And only God recorded your name.
I had neither opportunity
Nor capability
To say goodbye.
Not saying goodbye
Is just as hard
As saying goodbye.
The preparations are halted,
The royal guest was called away.

The banquet was cancelled.
Just moved. Just moved.
Yet a tear remains
Where baby should have been.
   Dedicated to my baby
   this September 17, 1983
   Age: 6 months
   Sex: unknown
   Weight: unknown
   Colour of eyes: unknown
   Loved: by the Father, Son and
      Holy Spirit and by Mommy
      and Daddy *(Bob Neudorf)*

A missionary translator, labouring amongst a tribe in the mountains of Mexico, found it hard to get the right word for 'comfort'. One day his helper asked for a week's leave, and explained that his uncle had died and he wanted some days off to visit his bereaved aunt 'to help her heart around the corner.' That was just the expression the missionary needed. *(Anon)*

Power is the reward of sadness. It was after the Christ had wept over Jerusalem that he uttered some of his most august words; it was when his soul had been sorrowful even unto death that his enemies fell prostrate before his voice. Who suffers, conquers. The bruised is the breaker. *(Francis Thompson)*

USEFUL TEXTS

Grief:
Results from;
Hardness of heart, *Mark 3:5*
Disease, *Job 2:11-13*
Death, *2 Sam. 19:1-2*
Rebelliousness, *Isa. 63:10*

See also: A25 Courage
          B38 The Suffering Servant
          B49 Coping with doubt
          C18 Compassion

C14

FORGIVENESS

'I tell you that her sins, her many sins, must have been forgiven her, or she would not have shown such great love.'
Luke 7:47

QUOTATIONS:

When God pardons, he consigns the offence to everlasting forgetfulness. *(Mary Rosell)*

To err is human, to forgive divine. *(Alexander Pope)*

And you will say to life; Forgive. *(Yevtushenko)*

Humanity is never so beautiful as when praying for forgiveness or else forgiving another. *(Jean Paul Richter)*

No one true penitent forgets or forgives himself; an unforgiving spirit towards himself is the very price of God's forgiving him. *(Cardinal Newman)*

There are many kinds of alms, the giving of which helps us to obtain pardon for our sins; but none is greater than that by which we forgive from our heart a sin that some one has committed against us. *(St Augustine of Hippo)*

He who cannot forgive others breaks the bridge over which he must pass himself. *(George Herbert)*

Forgiveness is man's deepest need and highest achievement. *(Horace Bushnell)*

It is easier for the generous to forgive, than for the offender to ask forgiveness. *(J. Thomson)*

PROVERBS

Know all and you will pardon all. *(Greek proverb)*

They who forgive most shall be most forgiven. *(English proverb)*

WORD PICTURES

During the times of persecution in the early Church, Sulpicius, a presbyter of Antioch, was arrested and brought before the Imperial Legate, who asked him, 'Of what family art thou?'

'I am a Christian.'

'Know that all who call themselves Christians will be put to the torture unless they sacrifice to the immortal gods.'

'We Christians', answered Sulpicius, 'have for our King Christ, who is also God.'

He was then tortured and led away to be beheaded. As he was on his way to execution a Christian called Nicephorus rushed forward and fell at his feet. Between him and Sulpicius there had been a bitter quarrel, and Nicephorus felt that he must win his forgiveness while there was yet time.

'Martyr of Christ,' he cried, 'forgive me for I have wronged thee.'

Sulpicius did not reply, and even at the place of execution maintained the same silence. Then followed a scene which struck the beholders with astonishment and the Christians with awe.

Sulpicius, who had not flinched under torture, was seen to be growing paler as he was told to kneel down under the sword of the executioner.

'Do not strike me,' he cried. 'I will obey the Emperor, I *will* sacrifice to the gods.'

Once more Nicephorus rushed forward, but this time it was to implore Sulpicius not to forfeit the martyr's crown which he had well-nigh won, but it was in vain.

'Then', said Nicephorus, 'tell the Legate I will take his place, I am a Christian,' and he was forthwith taken at his words.

The fall of Sulpicius was quoted by the early Church to show that the sacrifice of life itself is not accepted on high when offered by those who have not learnt from their Saviour to pardon injuries. *(Anon)*

In German, the verb is 'vergeben', meaning to give over or to grant. Derived from the Old English 'forgiefan', to forgive is defined as 'to give up resentment; to cease to feel resentment against on account of a wrong committed.'

To say 'I forgive you' is to free yourself from the shackles of holding a grudge that weighs on the mind and burdens the soul. Telling someone you forgive them does not condone the wrong, nor is it weak. One must be strong to forgive.

When their only son was struck and killed by a drunk driver, Frank and Elizabeth Morris of Kentucky were consumed with the Idea of revenge. 'We wanted him dead,' Mrs Morris admitted.

They soon realised, though, that their reluctance to forgive was eating away at them. They decided to visit the youth in jail. Then Mrs Morris began helping him in his struggle against alcohol abuse. 'The accident had already wiped out one very special life. I didn't want to see it waste this young man's life, too,' she said.

Since the Morrises made the decision to speak words of forgiveness, the young man has quit alcohol, become an active church member and lectures for Mothers Against Drunk Driving. (Christopher News)

Written about a group of people who had survived massacre in South Africa:
We prayed so that all bitterness could be taken from us and we could start the life for our people again without hatred. We knew out of our own suffering that life cannot begin for the better except by us all forgiving one another. For if one does not forgive, one does not understand; and if one does not understand, one is afraid; and if one is afraid, one hates; and if one hates, one cannot love. And no new beginning on earth is possible without love, particularly in a world where men increasingly not only do not know how to love but cannot even recognise it when it comes searching for them. The first step towards this love then must be forgiveness.
(Laurens van der Post)

Rabbi Leo Beck, a German scholar who took on the leadership of German Jews in Hitler's time, is a fine example of forgiveness. He was five times arrested, and finally sent to a concentration camp, where he served on the convicts' committee of management. On the very day he was to have been shot, the Russian troops arrived. Beck could have escaped at once, but stayed behind to argue with the Russians, to persuade them to spare the lives of the German camp-guards. The Russians decided that the camp-guards should be handed over to the inmates. Beck then argued with the inmates and managed to persuade them not to take the vengeance that they were thirsting for. Later on he went to the USA and worked hard for the Council of Christians and Jews. He died in 1957, aged 80. *(F. H. Drinkwater)*

USEFUL TEXTS

Forgiveness:
>   Of man's sin;
>   By God, *Ps. 130:4*
>   By Christ, *Acts 10:43*
>   Among believers, *Eph. 4:32*
>   Of enemies, *Luke 6:27*

See also: A26 The Sacrament of Penance
>   A27 As we forgive those
>   B16 Christ heals and forgives
>   C27 The Father who receives us back
>   C40 Reconciliation

C15

PREJUDICE

'There are no more distinctions between Jew and Greek, slave and free, male and female, but all of you are one in Christ Jesus.' *Galatians 3:28*

QUOTATIONS

Dogs bark at every one they do not know. *(Heraclitus)*

Prejudices are what rule the vulgar crowd. *(Voltaire)*

Ignorance is less remote from the truth than prejudice. *(Denis Diderot)*

Prejudice is the child of ignorance. *(William Hazlitt)*

It is never too late to give up your prejudices. *(Henry David Thoreau)*

The man who never alters his opinion is like standing water, and breeds reptiles of the mind. *(William Blake)*

A prejudice is a vagrant opinion without visible means of support. *(Ambrose Bierce)*

To be prejudiced is always to be weak. *(Samuel Johnson)*

Never try to reason the prejudice out of a man. It was not reasoned into him and cannot be reasoned out. *(Sydney Smith)*

Prejudice is never easy unless it can pass itself off for reason. *(William Hazlitt)*

I pray every day that God make me like a child, that is to say that he will let me see nature and interpret it as a child does, without prejudice. *(Jean Baptiste Camille Corot)*

PROVERBS

Drive out prejudices by the door, they will come back by the window. *French proverb)*

No physician can cure the blind in mind. *(Jewish proverb)*

HUMOUR

. . . Being a star has made it possible for me to get insulted in places where the average Negro could never hope to go and get insulted. *(Sammy Davis Jr)*

I read a joke in one of the columns that said you were playing golf on Long Island and the pro asked you for your handicap and you told him, 'I'm a coloured, one-eyed Jew, do I need anything else,' *(Sammy Davis Jr)*

STATEMENT

As a consequence, the Church rejects, as foreign to the mind of Christ, any discrimination against men or harassment of them because of their race, colour, condition of life, or religion. *(Second Vatican Council – 'Non-Christians')*

WORD PICTURES

If you do not like me because I am ignorant, I can be sent to school and educated. If you do not like me because I am dirty, I can be taught to wash and be clean. If you do not like me because of my unsocial habits, I can be taught how to live in society. But if you do not like me because of the colour of my skin, I can only refer you to the God who made me.
(A negro priest in 1958)

First they came for the Jews
and I did not speak out –
because I was not a Jew.

Then they came for the Communists
and I did not speak out –
because I was not a Communist.

Then they came for the trade unionists
and I did not speak out –
because I was not a trade unionist.

Then they came for me –
and there was no one left
to speak out for me.
(Pastor Niemoeller, victim of the Nazis)

Robert was born at Aldershot; his mother was Japanese and father English. When Robert started school, he was tormented by the other children. One Christmas, his parents bought him a watch, but this was taken from him by some other older children and thrown against the school wall. The school crossing warden asked Robert one day why he was walking over a mile to school and crossing a busy road instead of using the school bus. His parents had wanted him to use the bus but Robert had refused. He told the traffic warden he was frightened of the other children because they called him a 'wog', a 'chink' and a 'bloody Jap'! He walked to school for three weeks until one day, when crossing the road he was knocked down by a car and killed. *(A. P. Castle)*

A little black boy was watching the balloon man at the country fair. The man was evidently a good salesman because he allowed a red balloon to break loose and soar high up in the air, thereby attracting a crowd of prospective young customers.

Then he released a blue balloon, then a yellow one and a white one. They all went soaring up into the sky until they disappeared. The little black boy stood looking at the black balloon for a long time, then asked, 'Sir, if you sent the black one up would it go as high as the others?'

The balloon man gave the kid an understanding smile. He snapped the string that held the black balloon in place and, as it soared upwards, said, 'It isn't the colour, son. It's what's inside that makes it rise.' *(Anthony de Mello, S. J.)*

See also: A40 The equality of women
A41 Spiritual blindness
B15 Jesus, friend of outcasts
C1 Liberation from fear

C16

COME FOLLOW ME

'Another to whom he said 'Follow me', replied,
'Let me go and bury my father first.' But he answered,
'Leave the dead to bury their dead.' *Luke 9:59-60*

QUOTATIONS

On account of him there have come to be many Christs in the world, even all who, like him, loved righteousness and hated iniquity. *(Origin of Alexandria)*

Happy are they who know that discipleship simply means the life which springs from grace, and that grace simply means discipleship. *(Dietrich Bonhoeffer)*

He who stops being better stops being good. *(Oliver Cromwell)*

There's but the twinkling of a star between a man of peace and war. *(Nicholas Butler)*

You can't be the salt of the earth without smarting someone. *(Anon)*

The attempts of Christians to be Christians now are almost as ridiculous as the attempts of the first men to be human. *(G. A. Studdert-Kennedy)*

There are two words used a great deal by Jesus in the Gospels. One is 'Come' and the other is 'Go'. It's no use coming unless you go, and it's no use going unless you come. *(Anon)*

When we have travelled all ways, we shall come to the End of all ways, who says, 'I am the way'. *(St Ambrose)*

To love God is to will what he wills. *(Charles de Foucauld)*

Notice outside a North London Church: 'Wanted – Workers
for God. Plenty of Overtime.'
('Peterborough' in the Daily Telegraph)

WORD PICTURES

He comes to us as One unknown, without a name, as of old, by
the lakeside, he came to those men who knew him not. He
speaks to us the same word 'Follow thou me!' and sets us to the
tasks which he has to fulfil for our time. He commands. And to
those who obey him, whether they be wise or simple, he will
reveal himself in the toils, the conflicts, the sufferings which
they shall pass through in his fellowship, and as an ineffable
mystery, they shall learn in their own experience Who he is.
(Albert Schweitzer: The Quest of the Historical Jesus)

It was on a Monday morning in January 1982 that the
Thunderbirds – the US Air Force's spectacular stunt-flying
team – suffered their most crushing disaster.

They were practising the 'Line Abreast Loop.' Four planes
flying side by side, wing tips as little as 18 inches apart, soar
heavenward, then gracefully arch backwards until all four
planes are upside down, then plunge towards earth in a
vertiginous dive.

As in all such manoeuvres, only one of the four pilots – 'the
boss' – pays attention to where he is relative to the ground. The
other three keep their eyes fixed on the boss's wing tip. When
he goes up, they go up. When he turns, they turn. When he goes
down, they go down.

'He's my world,' says one pilot of the Boss's leadership role.
'It makes no difference where the ground is, because my eyes
are on him.'

On this particular Monday morning, something went wrong
with the Boss's controls. He couldn't pull out of the dive. So he
continued hurtling earthward, and the other three pilots did
too: eyes fixed on their leader, waiting for him to level off. They
hit the floor of the Nevada desert, in perfect formation, at 490
miles per hour. All were killed instantly. *(Anon)*

Someone once observed that disciples come in three varieties: tugboats, sailboats, and rafts.

Tugboats follow Jesus not only in sunny weather, but also in stormy weather. They follow him not only when the wind and the waves serve them but also when they oppose them. They are people who love not when they feel like it, but always, day in, day out.

Sailboat disciples follow Jesus only in sunny weather. They go in his direction only when the wind and the waves serve them. When stormy weather comes, they tend to go in the direction that they are blown. They follow the crowd more than they follow Jesus.

Finally, there are *Raft* disciples. They are not really followers of Jesus at all. They won't even follow him when the wind and the waves serve them. They go in his direction only when they are pulled or pushed. They act like Christians because they have to, or because it is to their personal advantage to do so. *(Mark Link)*

Near the southern shore of Lake Tanganyika stands a church and on its pulpit is a brass plate commemorating the life of James Lawson. Born in the midlands in the early part of this century, he offered himself as a missionary and after training was appointed to Africa. Despite his training, he would still have been very much of a novice during his first months overseas. There were local customs to be learnt and language to be mastered so he had very little time to fulfil his calling, for, going to an unhealthy spot, within a year he was dead. Such waste! Such futility! Yet that isn't altogether how the Christian sees it. On the memorial plate with his name are the words 'Not what I did, but what I strove to do.' Perhaps in the long run that is the measure by which all of us are judged. *(Anon)*

I have spent a good part of the month visiting the schools that remain open here in Muelle de Bueyes, Nicaragua. The children are remarkably resilient, even those who have witnessed rape, torture and assassination They expect me to say Mass for an end to hostilities and give encouragement and hope . . . I had hoped to finish this letter in a major key of optimism. However, a friend, Sandra Price, a nun from California, gave me the following report, yesterday.

'On March 25 a group of the terrorists took one of our Catholic teachers, Donato Mendoza, from his home. Two kilometres further on they castrated him, gorged out his eyes, pulled out his finger nails, cut the flesh from his legs, broke every bone in his body, and shot him . . .

'Three days later, on Good Friday, his naked, mutilated body was found. Donato has always worn a chain and cross, as a distinctive mark of his position in the Church. He said he had lost the cross a few days before, while working. It was this chain without a cross that identified his dead body. He no longer wore a cross of metal; his life had taken on the passion and death of Jesus.

'On Easter Sunday we celebrated Mass with Donato's family; on the altar was the chain, matted with blood and dirt. There was no cross. As Christ's life did not terminate on the cross but in the victory of the resurrection, so too we believe that Donato has conquered death and suffering and lives on by the power of this same God whom he served faithfully during the 40 years of his life.' *(John Medcalf)*

USEFUL TEXTS

Discipleship:
    The cost of, *Luke 14:25-33*
    Responsibility, *2 Tim. 2:2-8*
    Characterised by love, *John 21:15-18*

See also: A22 Seeking God
          B11 Vocation
          B24 Go tell everyone
          C41 Starting afresh

C17

INTERNATIONAL PEACE

'Now towards her I send flowing peace, like a river,
and like a stream in spate the glory of the nations.'
Isaiah 66:12

QUOTATIONS

Yes, we love peace, but we are not willing to take wounds for it, as we are for war. *(John Andrew Holmes)*

The purpose of all war is peace. *(St Augustine of Hippo)*

The most disadvantageous peace is better than most just war. *(Erasmus)*

Peace cannot be kept by force. It can only be achieved by understanding. *(Albert Einstein)*

War is much too serious a matter to be entrusted to the military. *(Georges Clemenceau)*

Peace is better than war, because in peace the sons bury their fathers, but in war fathers bury their sons. *(Croesus)*

In War: Resolution. In Defeat: Defiance. In Victory: Magnanimity. In Peace: Good Will. *(Winston Churchill)*

I hate war as only a soldier who has lived it can, only as one who has seen its brutality, its futility, its stupidity. *(Dwight D. Eisenhower)*

If man does find the solution for world peace, it will be the most revolutionary reversal of his record we have ever known. *(George C. Marshall)*

There are two world powers, the sword and the spirit, but the spirit has always vanquished the sword. *(Napoleon)*

In modern warfare there are no victors; there are only survivors. *(Lyndon B. Johnson)*

PROVERBS

Better a bad peace than a good war. *(Jewish proverb)*

No one can have peace longer than his neighbour pleases. *(Dutch proverb)*

STATEMENT

It is our clear duty, then, to strain every muscle as we work for the time when all war can be completely outlawed by international consent. This goal undoubtedly requires the establishment of some universal public authority acknowledged as such by all, and endowed with effective power to safeguard, on the behalf of all, security, regard for justice, and respect for rights.

Peace must be born of mutual trust between nations rather than imposed on them through fear of one another's weapons. Hence everyone must labour to put an end at last to the arms race, and to make a true beginning of disarmament, not indeed a unilateral disarmament, but one proceeding at an equal pace according to agreement and backed up by authentic and workable safeguards.

(Second Vatican Council – 'The Church Today')

WORD PICTURES

The peace concluded on 24 June 1502 between England and Scotland was called 'Perpetual Peace'. In the agreement Margaret, daughter of Henry VII, was betrothed to James IV of Scotland. However, the Scots invaded England in 1513! The name has been given to other treaties, as that between Austria and Switzerland in 1471 and between France and Switzerland in 1516. *(Anon)*

We utterly deny all outward wars and strife and fightings with outward weapons for any end, or under any pretence whatever; this is our testimony to the whole world. The Spirit of Christ by which we are guided is not changeable, so as once to command us from a thing as evil, and again to move unto it; and we certainly know, and testify to the world, that the Spirit of Christ, which leads us into all truth, will never move us to fight and war against any man with outward weapons, neither for the kingdom of Christ, nor for the kingdoms of this world.
(An extract from A Declaration from the Harmless and Innocent People of God, Called Ouakers, presented to Charles II in 1660.)

'Tell me the weight of a snowflake,' a coaltit asked a wild dove. 'Nothing more than nothing,' was the answer.

'In that case I must tell you a story,' the coaltit said. 'I sat on the bench of a fir, close to its trunk when it began to snow heavily, without a sound and without any violence. I counted the snowflakes settling on the twigs and needles of my branch. Their number was exactly 3,741,952. When the 3,741,953rd dropped onto the branch, nothing more than nothing as you say, the branch broke.'

The dove thought about the story for a while and finally said to himself, 'Perhaps there is only one person's voice lacking for peace to come to the world.' Make sure it's not *your* voice that's lacking. *(Anon)*

Waste of Muscle, waste of Brain,
Waste of Patience, waste of Pain,
Waste of Manhood, waste of Health,
Waste of Beauty, waste of Wealth,
Waste of Blood, and waste of Tears,
Waste of Youth's most precious years,
Waste of ways the Saints have trod,
Waste of Glory, waste of God – War!
(G. A. Studdert-Kennedy)

There is a huge statue of Christ holding a cross standing on the Andes, between the countries of the Argentine and Chile. The story of that statue is worth knowing. Once the Argentine and Chile were about to go to war with one another. They were quarrelling over some land which each said belonged to them. So both countries started to prepare for war. Then on Easter Sunday, bishops in Argentine and Chile began to urge peace. They went round their countries crying out for peace in the name of Christ. The people did not want war and in the end they made their governments talk peace with one another, instead of war. The big guns, instead of being used for fighting, were melted down and made into the great big bronze statue of Christ. It now stands on the mountains between the two countries. Written on it are the words 'These mountains shall fall and crumble to dust before the people of Chile and the Argentine shall forget their solemn convenant sworn at the feet of Christ'. *(M. Nassan)*

See also: A33 Love your neighbour
B34 Human rights
C4 Personal peace
C10 Love your enemies

C18

COMPASSION

'A Samaritan traveller who came upon him was moved with compassion when he saw him.' *Luke 10:33*

QUOTATIONS

The purpose of human life is to serve and to show compassion and the will to help others. *(Albert Schweitzer)*

Man is never nearer the Divine than in his compassionate moments. *(Joseph H. Hertz)*

The compassion that you see in the kindhearted is God's compassion: he has given it to them to protect the helpless. *(Sri Ramakrishna)*

A tear dries quickly, especially when it is shed for the troubles of others. *(Cicero)*

We must learn to regard people less in the light of what they do or omit to do, and more in the light of what they suffer. *(Dietrich Bonhoeffer)*

Compassion is the basis of all morality. *(Arthur Schopenhauer)*

If we do not help a man in trouble, it is as if we caused the trouble. *(Nachman of Bratslav)*

When a man has compassion for others, God has compassion for him. *(Talmud)*

Compassion is not a sloppy, sentimental feeling for people who are underprivileged or sick . . . it is an absolutely practical belief that, regardless of a person's background ability or ability to pay he should be provided with the best that society has to offer. *(Neil Kinnock)*

PROVERBS

One heart is mirror to another. *(Jewish proverb)*

The comforter's head never aches. *(Italian proverb)*

WORD PICTURES

The root of the matter, if we want a stable world, is a very simple and old fashioned thing, a thing so simple that I am almost ashamed to mention it for fear of the derisive smile with which wise cynics will greet my words. The thing I mean is love, Christian love, or compassion. If you feel this, you have a motive for existence, a reason for courage, an imperative necessity for intellectual honesty. *(Bertrand Russell)*

Compassion is a word full of meaning.
It means:
sharing the same passion,
sharing the same suffering,
sharing the same agony,
accepting into my heart
the misery in yours.

Your pain calls out to me.
It touches my heart.
It awakens something within me,
and I become one with you in your pain.

I may not be able to relieve your pain,
but by understanding it and sharing it
I make it possible for you to bear it
in a way that enhances your dignity
and helps you to grow.
(Jean Vanier)

In a letter he wrote to a Christian woman Carl Jung said something very important. There was something very beautiful about what she believed, he said. When Christians saw somebody hungry and thirsty, they saw Christ. When they saw somebody naked in the street and clothed him, they saw Christ.

When they visited somebody in prison or in hospital, they saw Christ. When they welcomed a stranger, they welcomed Christ. But, he went on, what he did not understand was that they did not seem to see the poor wounded part inside themselves. Could they not see Jesus there? Why did they always have to see Jesus outside themselves?

How was it that they could not welcome the darkness that was in them so as to let the light come into the darkness and shine in it? Did they not see that inside them there was somebody hungry and thirsty, imprisoned in their own fears, a stranger who reacted in unexpected ways, an unforeseen source of anger or depression? Did they not see that there was somebody sick inside them, somebody hated, poor, broken and needing to be clothed? Did they not see that Christ was hidden in their own brokenness?

I am beginning to discover that we can only enter into compassion with those who are wounded if we enter into compassion for ourselves. *(Jean Vanier)*

USEFUL TEXTS

Compassion:
Of Jesus, *Matt 9:36*
Of God, *Deut. 13:17; Ps. 78:38*
Of Good Samaritan, *Luke 10:33-34*
As a mark of believers, *1 Pet. 3:8*

See also: A17 Gentleness
A23 Mercy
A33 Love your neighbour
C46 Loving kindness

C19

FRIENDSHIP

'Jesus came to a village, and a woman named Martha welcomed him into her house.' *Luke 10:38*

QUOTATIONS

Friendship needs no words – it is solitude delivered from the anguish of loneliness. *(Dag Hammarskjöld)*

The friend who understands you, creates you. *(Romain Rolland)*

Of all things which wisdom provides to make life entirely happy, much the greatest is the possession of friendship. *(Epicurus)*

Friendship is a disinterested commerce between equals. *(Oliver Goldsmith)*

A friend is someone who can see through you and still enjoys the show. *(Anon)*

A friend is the one who comes in when the whole world has gone out. *(Anon)*

Friendship is like money, easier made than kept. *(Samuel Butler)*

Every man should keep a fair-sized cemetery, in which to bury the faults of his friends. *(Henry Ward Beecher)*

True friendship is a plant of slow growth, and must undergo and withstand the shocks of adversity before it is entitled to the appellation. *(George Washington)*

To know someone here or there with whom you feel there is understanding in spite of distances or thoughts unexpressed – that can make of this earth a garden.
(Johann Wolfgang Von Goethe)

PROVERBS

A friend is a poem. *(Persian proverb)*

Give and take makes good friends. *(Scotch proverb)*

None is so rich as to throw away a friend. *(Turkish proverb)*

Friendship is honey – but don't eat it all. *(Moroccan proverb)*

HUMOUR

You, sir, are a foul-weather friend. *(Harpo Marx)*

A friend married is a friend lost. *(Henrik Ibsen)*

Friendship is far more tragic than love. It lasts longer.
(Oscar Wilde)

WORD PICTURES

Oh the comfort – the inexpressible comfort – of feeling
    safe with a person,
Having neither to weigh thoughts
Nor measure words –
    but pour them all right out – just as they are,
Chaff and grain together – certain that a faithful hand
Will take and sift them –
Keep what is worth keeping –
And then, with the breath of kindness,
Blow the rest away.
(Dinah Maria Mulock Craik)

I want to love you without clutching,
Appreciate you without judging,
Join you without invading,
Invite you without demanding,
Leave you without guilt,
Criticise you without blaming,
    and help you without insulting.
If I can have the same from YOU
then we can truly meet and enrich each other.
(Virginia Satir)

All kinds of things rejoiced my soul in their company –
to talk and laugh and do each other kindnesses;
pass from lightest jesting to talk of the deepest things
and back again; differ without rancour, as a man might differ
    with himself,
and when most rarely dissension arose find our normal
agreement all the sweeter for it;
teach each other or learn from each other;
be impatient for the return of the absent,
and welcome them with joy on their home-coming.
(St Augustine)

An Evil Cradling, by Brian Keenan

This is a book of staggering beauty, a book for which trees may be justly sacrificed. It is first and foremost a love story, the tale of two human beings who, while not lovers in the carnal sense, found in each other, in unspeakable desolation, a source of joy, comfort and strength; How lucky were Brian Keenan and John McCarthy to have each other for the greater part of those dark years as hostages: roped together like climbers, they were able to prevent first one and then the other from pitching headlong down into the abyss of madness.

Having myself found imprisonment a time of such spiritual encounter, I was curious to know about these two men's experience of God in their much longer and harder detention. Keenan writes in a delightfully low-key and matter-of-fact way of their simple but constant faith. There is a particularly moving description of a time when he was very ill with dysentery:

'During one of those long afternoons I lay, pain twisting and turning in my gut. I said nothing and hoped John would continue reading his book. I lay trying to sleep, to relieve this pain, but still it twisted and knotted. Through the mangle I went, and was stretched and pulled. I believed John thought I was sleeping, then I felt his hand lie gently on my stomach, and it remained there. He was praying. I was overcome. I was lost for words again. I wanted to join him in prayer, I wanted to thank him for this huge and tender gesture. It revealed more courage than my battling with the guards.'

As I said at the beginning, this is a love story. It is a tale of two strangers who find themselves journeying together to the gates of hell and beyond. Hand in terrified hand they stumble, blindfolded, chained, incontinent and ashamed, yet paradoxically secure in the knowledge that it is their captors who are prisoners and they who walk free. *(Sheila Cassidy)*

The following story is from Ernest Gordon's account of life and death in a Japanese POW camp on the River Kwai.
It was the custom among prisoners from the Argyll regiment for every man to have a 'mucker' – that is, a pal or friend with whom he shared or 'mucked in' everything he had.

'It seemed pretty certain to everyone,' Dusty continued, 'that the mucker was going to die. Certain, that is, to everyone but Angus. He had made up his mind that his mucker would live. Someone had stolen his mucker's blanket. Angus gave him his own. Every mealtime, Angus would show up to draw his ration. But he didn't eat it. He would bring it round to give to his friend. Stood over him, he did, and made him eat it. Going hungry was hard on Angus, mind you, because he was a "big man" ' As Dusty talked on, I could see it all happening – Angus drawing on his own strength, through his will, and depleting his own body to make his friend live.

'His mates noticed that Angus had taken to slipping out of the camp at night,' Dusty went on. 'These excursions could only have one purpose. He was visiting the Thai villages; it was taken for granted that he had joined the black marketeers! Angus, of all people! This shocked the others for he was known as a man of high principles!

'As the men died in the camp, it became possible for others to come into possession of objects of some value – watches, shorts, knives and so on. These were highly prized by the Thais, who would gladly pay for them in the paper money known as "Bahts", worth about one-and-sixpence each. Or they would barter for the goods, offering medicine or duck eggs.

'Although Angus' mates thought that he was trying to make a bit of money for himself, they didn't begrudge it to him,' said Dusty. 'Perhaps you can guess the end of the story. The mucker got better. Then Angus collapsed. Just pitched on his face and died.'

'And what did the docs say caused it?, I asked.

'Starvation', answered Dusty, 'complicated by exhaustion, and all for his friend.'

(Ernest Gordon, 'Miracle on the River Kwai)

USEFUL TEXTS

Friendship:

    With God, *Ps. 25:14*

    With the angry, *Prov. 22:24*

    With the world, *James 4:4*

    A continuing relationship, *Prov. 17:17*

    Betrayal in, *Ps. 41:9*

    With Jesus, *John 15:14*

See also: A9 Relationships

             A33 Love your neighbour

             B15 Jesus, friend of outcasts

C20

OUR FATHER IN HEAVEN

'Father, may your name be held holy, your kingdom come.'
Luke 11:2

QUOTATIONS

God's love for us is not greater in heaven than it is now.
(St Thomas Aquinas)

Our Heavenly Father never takes anything from his children unless he means to give them something better.
(George Mueller)

He is not to be gotten or holden by thought, but only by love.
(Julian of Norwich)

Whoever falls from God's right hand, is caught into his left.
(Edward Markham)

Beware of the man whose god is in the skies. *(Bernard Shaw)*

I am always humbled by the infinite ingenuity of the Lord, who can make a red barn cast a blue shadow. *(E. B. White)*

It is the heart which experiences God and not the reason.
(B. Pascal)

Short arm needs man to reach to Heaven, so ready is Heaven to stoop to him. *(Francis Thompson)*

Our love for God is tested by the question of whether we seek Him or His gifts. *(Ralph W. Sockman)*

PROVERBS

God puts a good root in the little pig's way. *(French proverb)*

God is a good worker, but he loves to be helped. *(Spanish proverb)*

God punishes with one hand and blesses with the other. *(Yiddish proverb)*

WORD PICTURES

God and the soldier we alike adore,
When on the brink of danger, not before;
The danger past, both are alike requited,
God is forgotten and the soldier slighted.
(Euricius Cordus)

Thou madest man, he knows not why,
He thinks he was not made to die,
And Thou hast made him: Thou art just.
(Alfred Lord Tennyson)

Cyril was a young man who became a Christian at Caesarea in Cappadocia, in the third century. His rich pagan father reviled him, beat him, and at last turned him out of the house; but nothing could quench the joy in his heart, and he won many other boys to a Christian life also.

Soon he was brought before the tribunal as a Christian. Threats failed to move him. Then the magistrate offered to release him if he would return to his home and inheritance.

'Leaving home did not trouble me,' he answered, 'there is a real home waiting for me, much grander and more beautiful, where my Father in heaven lives.'

They took him to the fire as if for execution, then back to the tribunal. 'Why don't you get on with it?' he asked. As nothing could shake his firmness, he was led forth again to die. Some Christians around were weeping, but Cyril said: 'You ought to be a joyful escort for me. Evidently you do not know the City where I am going to live!' He watched the fire being kindled, and died in it brave to the last, with his mind fixed on his heavenly home. *(F. H. Drinkwater)*

St John Chrysostom, summoned before the Roman Emperor Arcadius, and threatened with banishment, is said to have replied: 'Thou canst not banish me, for the world is my Father's house.'

'Then I will slay thee,' exclaimed the emperor, wrathfully.

'Nay, but thou canst, for my life is hid with Christ in God.'

'Your treasures shall be confiscated,' was the grim reply.

'Sire, that cannot be. My treasures are in heaven, as my heart is there.'

'But I will drive thee from men and thou shalt have no friends left.'

'That you cannot do either, sire, for I have a Friend in heaven who has said, "I will never leave thee nor forsake thee".'

The following lines were found scratched on the wall of a bomb-blasted air-raid shelter in Germany after the Second World War.

I believe in the light,
even when the sun doesn't shine.
I believe in love,
even when it isn't given.
I believe in God,
even when his voice is silent.
(Anon)

USEFUL TEXTS

Fatherhood:
Of God to all he created, *Deut. 32:6*
Of God to all who believe, *Gal. 4:4-6*
Of God to Jesus Christ, *Col. 1:3*

See also: A22 Seeking God
B28 The Father who draws us to Himself
C27 The Father who receives us back

C21

RISE ABOVE MATERIALISM

'A man's life is not made secure by what he owns, even when he has more than he needs.' *Luke 12:15*

QUOTATIONS

Theirs an endless road, a hopeless maze, who seek for goods before they seek for God. *(St Bernard of Clairvaux)*

Seek to hold and not to cling, enjoy and not possess. *(The Nomad)*

Riches are not forbidden, but the pride of them is. *(St John Chrysostom)*

The most grievous kind of destitution is to want money in the midst of wealth. *(Seneca)*

He who seeks only the glory of God finds it in poverty and in abundance. *(St Francis de Sales)*

He is rich enough who is poor with Christ. *(St Jerome)*

He is rich in spirit who has his riches in his spirit or his spirit in his riches; he is poor in spirit who has no riches in his spirit, nor his spirit in his riches. *(St Francis de Sales)*

Unless our civilisation is redeemed spiritually, it cannot endure materially. *(Woodrow Wilson)*

The poor man, rich in faith, who toils for the love of God and is generous of the little fruit of his labours, is much nearer to heaven than the rich man who spends a fortune in good works from no higher motive than his natural inclination to benevolence. *(Archbishop Ullathorne)*

Be sure, as long as worldly fancies you pursue, you are a hollow man – a pauper lives in you. *(Angelus Silesius)*

What horror has the world come to when it uses profit as the prime incentive in human progress, and competition as the supreme law of economics! *(Dom Helder Camara)*

The most terrible thing about materialism, even more terrible than its proneness to violence, is its boredom, from which sex, alcohol, drugs, all devices for putting out the accusing light of reason and suppressing the unrealisable aspirations of love, offer a prospect of deliverance. *(Malcolm Muggeridge)*

PROVERBS
Spend less than you earn and you'll never be in debt. *(Yiddish proverb)*

When money speaks, the truth is silent. *(Russian proverb)*

HUMOUR
One reason why it's hard to save money is that our neighbours are always buying something we can't afford. *(Anon)*

Money is made round to slip through your fingers. *(Edwin L. Brooks)*

The Scotsman sent an indignant letter to the editor of the newspaper. He said that if any more stories about stingy Scotsmen appeared in the columns, he was going to stop borrowing the paper. *(Anon)*

A burglar had entered a poor minister's house at midnight, but was disturbed by the awakening of the occupant of the room he was in.

Drawing his weapon, he said, 'If you stir you are a dead man. I'm hunting for your money.'

'Let me get up and turn on the light,' said the minister, 'and I'll hunt with you.'

A six-year-old went into a bank and asked to see the manager. A courteous clerk showed her into his private office. She explained that her girl's club was raising money for a new clubroom and would he please contribute?

The banker laid a five pound note and a ten pence piece on the desk and said, 'Take your choice, Miss.'

She picked up the ten pence piece and said, 'My mother always taught me to take the smallest piece.' Picking up the five pound note also, she added, 'But so I won't lose this ten pence piece, I'll wrap it in this piece of paper.' *(Anon)*

STATEMENTS

Wealth which is constantly being augmented by social and economic progress, must be so distributed amongst the various individuals and classes of society that the common good of all . . . be thereby promoted. *(Pope Pius XI – 'Quadragesimo Anno')*

What we have already said and the experience of our people lead to the rejection of capitalism, both in its economic aspects as well as in its ideological foundation which favours individualism, profit, and the exploitation of man by man himself. Thus we must strive to create a qualitatively different society. *(Catholic Bishops of Peru)*

Since in our times, variations of materialism are rampant everywhere, even among Catholics, the laity should not only learn doctrine more carefully, especially those main points which are the subjects of controversy, but should also provide the witness of an evangelical life in contrast to all forms of materialism. *(Second Vatican Council – 'Laity')*

WORD PICTURES

Is this material progress? A recent report reveals that there are 7,000 pieces of metal, of all shapes and sizes from a complete satellite to a lost screwdriver, floating in space and continually circulating planet Earth! *(Anon)*

Jesus, on whom peace, has said:
The world is a bridge,
Pass over it,
But build not your dwelling there.
*(Inscription on the Great Mosque in
Fateh-pur-Sikri, Delhi)*

A London newspaper offered a prize for the best definition of money. This was the winning answer:

'Money is an instrument that can buy you everything but happiness and pay your fare to every place but heaven.'

One has risen from the dead, and the rich confess this at their table, and yet poor Lazarus, in millions, continues to hunger at their door. The point of this parable is not as is often suspected, the consoling pipedream of heaven for poor Lazarus. It is addressed exclusively to the rich man. It is not meant to console the poor with hope of recompense beyond the grave, but to warn the rich of damnation and to incite them to hear and act in the world. *(Helmut Gollwitzer)*

To any man worth his salt, the desire for personal gain is not his chief reason for working. It is the desire to achieve, to be a success, to make his job something worthy of his mettle and self-respect. Money plays an important part in this – it is stupid to deny it – but it is not the most important part . . . It is no regret to me that I was not the son of a rich man. My father indeed had riches, but of the mind, not of the pocket. The least valuable thing a parent can endow a strong, healthy son with is money. Counsel, correction and example should count far more in equipping him for the battle of life. *(Lord Nuffield)*

Nobody is more parochial than the materialist, for it is the essence of parochialism to assume that nothing exists outside one's own parish. The materialist, like John Wesley, takes the world for his parish. Unlike Wesley, he does not realise that there are other parishes. *(Arnold Lunn)*

for useful texts see overleaf

USEFUL TEXTS

Money:

Love of, a root of evil, *1 Tim. 6:10*

Associated with greed, *2 Kgs. 5:19-27*

Not to be loaned for interest, *Lev. 25:37; Deut. 23:19*

See also: A7 Poor in Spirit

A21 Feeding the hungry

C29 Not through luxury

C22

THE LIGHT OF FAITH

'It was for faith that our ancestors were commended.'
Hebrews 11:2

QUOTATIONS

Things unseen have a light of their own. *(Raoul Plus)*

Never doubt in the dark what God told you in the light.
(V. Raymond Edman)

Faith declares what the senses do not see, but not the contrary
of what they see. It is above them, not contrary to them. *(Pascal)*

Faith is illuminative, not operative; it does not force obedience,
though it increases responsibility; it heightens guilt, it does not
prevent sin; the will is the source of action. *(Cardinal Newman)*

Ultimately, faith is the only key to the universe. The final
meaning of human existence, and the answers to the questions
on which all our happiness depends cannot be found in any
other way. *(Thomas Merton)*

Faith, like light, should always be simple, and unbending; while
love, like warmth, should beam forth on every side, and bend to
every necessity of our brethren. *(Martin Luther)*

Faith depends not on intellectual, but on moral conditions.
(R. H. Benson)

There is no love without hope, no hope without love, and
neither hope nor love without faith. *(St Augustine of Hippo)*

'I am wanting in faith . . . because I keep my eyes too much on myself, and not enough on God; I look too much on my unworthiness instead of fixing them on His goodness, His love, His Sacred Heart open to receive me.' *(Charles de Foucauld)*

The remarkable thing about faith is that it's not a sudden flash from heaven or a sudden insight of the kind. It's just something that quietly sustains. *(Terry Waite)*

PROVERBS

A person consists of his faith. Whatever is his faith, even so is he. *(Hindu proverb)*

It is by believing in roses that one brings them to bloom. *(French proverb)*

STATEMENTS

The People of God believes that it is led by the Spirit of the Lord, who fills the earth. Motivated by this faith, it labours to decipher authentic signs of God's presence and purpose in the happenings, needs and desires in which this People has a part along with other men of our age. For faith throws a new light on everything, manifests God's design for man's total vocation, and thus directs the mind to solutions which are fully human. *(Second Vatican Council – 'The Church Today')*

WORD PICTURES

The most celebrated lighthouse of antiquity was the one erected by Ptolemy Soter in the island of Pharos, opposite Alexandria. Josephus says it could be seen at a distance of 42 miles. It was one of the seven wonders of the ancient world.

Of modern lighthouses, the most famous are the Eddystone, 14 miles southwest of Plymouth, the Cordouan lighthouse, at the entrance of the Gironde in France, and the Bell Rock, which is opposite the Firth of Tay. The Bartholdi Statue of Liberty, in New York harbour, is 305 feet high. Eddystone light is 133 feet high and lights a radius of approximately 13 miles. *(Anon)*

Sometimes you will see an old house built with window spaces bricked up in the wall. This is a relic of the days of Queen Anne or the Georges, when there was a tax on windows, and people could not afford to have much lighting. When building the house, they would make the space in the hope that later on they could afford to replace the brickwork with glass, and have better lighting.

If we are always letting our time and attention be given to the things of this life only, we are bricking up the windows of the soul just as surely, and preventing the light getting through. (*Anon*)

I imagine most people think that, as soon as Henry VIII secured the title 'Defender of the Faith' from Leo X, he put it on the coins of the realm, where it has remained ever since. He was extremely eager for some special title from the Holy See to match what the Kings of France and Spain had – 'Most Christian' or 'Catholic'. In fact, while he used it in the Great Seal, it did not appear on the coins of himself or any of his successors until, as the Vicar of Bray sings, 'George in pudding-time came o'er'. Putting *Fid Def* on the coinage was a clever idea of the Whigs who imported him, for the sake of the Protestant succession, and the faith he was brought in to defend against the Catholic Stuarts was the Protestantism, for writing against which the title had been conferred nearly 200 years before. (*Douglas Woodfuff*)

USEFUL TEXTS

Faith:
    Condition of salvation, *Acts 16:31*
    Way of life, *Eph. 6:16*
    Object of, *John 14:1*
    Gift of God, *Eph. 2:8*

See also: B33 Faith and good works
             C30 Increase our faith

C23

ZEAL FOR WHAT IS RIGHT

'Jesus said to his disciples, "I have come to bring fire to the earth, and how I wish it were blazing already." ' *Luke 12:49*

QUOTATIONS

No sacrifice is more acceptable to God than zeal for souls. *(Pope St Gregory)*

We are often moved with passion, and we think it to be zeal. *(Thomas à Kempis)*

There are few catastrophes so great and irremediable as those that follow an excess of zeal. *(R. H. Benson)*

Zeal without knowledge is always less useful and effective than regulated zeal, and very often it is highly dangerous. *(St Bernard)*

Dear Crito, your zeal is invaluable, if a right one; but if wrong, the greater zeal, the greater the danger. *(Socrates)*

I prefer to do right and get no thanks rather than to do wrong and get no punishment. *(Marcus Cato)*

There is only one way of seeing things rightly, and that is seeing the whole of them. *(John Ruskin)*

Zeal dropped in charity is good; without it, good for nothing; for it devours all it comes near. *(William Penn)*

Always do right. This will gratify some people and astonish the rest. *(Mark Twain)*

I don't know about having too much zeal; but I think it is better the pot should boil over than not boil at all. *(An American Indian)*

Zeal is fit only for wise men but is found mostly in fools.
(*Anon*)

Do not act as if you had 10,000 years to throw away. Be good for
something while you live, and it is in your power.
(*Marcus Aurelius*)

PROVERBS

To perfect diligence nothing is difficult. (*Chinese proverb*)

Zeal without knowledge is fire without light,
Zeal without prudence is frenzy. (*English proverb*)

HUMOUR

'Ethics,' the man told his son, 'is vital to everyday living. For
example, today an old friend paid me back a loan with a new
£20 note. As he was leaving, I discovered he'd given me two
notes stuck together. Immediately a question of ethics arose:
Should I tell your mother?'

Here lies the body of Joshua Gray
Who died defending his right of way.
His right was clear,
His will was strong,
But he's just as dead as if he'd been wrong.
(*Anon*)

WORD PICTURES

In 1956, the Vicar-general of the Singapore diocese discovered
that it included a small island 750 miles away, far off in the
ocean south of Java. (It is called Christmas Island; not the only
one.) It is about 16 miles by 12 miles, no harbour, cliffs rising
straight up 1,000 feet out of the sea; visitors are hauled up in a
small boat by a buoy.

The island was uninhabited until phosphate deposits were
found some years ago; now there are over 2,000 people, of
whom a number are Catholics – Chinese, Malayan and a few
Australians.

The Vicar-general went by the phosphate company's ship and said Mass on the island for the first time: later he sent another priest to prepare the children for their first communion.

Before this time some of the Catholic families had a custom of going to Singapore once a year to get to the sacraments: this meant a round trip of 1,500 miles. *(Catholic Herald)*

One of the stories told of a persecution in China in the old days is about a Chinese Christian lad named Paul Moy. He was dragged before the local mandarin, who tried to induce him to renounce the Christian faith. Other persuasions having failed, the mandarin tried bribery, and promised the boy a purse of silver.

'I thank your Excellency, but a purse of silver is not enough.'

'Very well: I will give you a purse of gold.'

'Excellency, that is still not enough.'

The magistrate had not expected such obstinate bargaining on the part of one so young and was rather annoyed.

'Well, what do you want, then?'

'Most noble, Excellency, if you ask me to renounce the Faith you will have to give me enough to buy a new soul.'

He completed his glorious witness when he was beheaded a few days later. *(F. H. Drinkwater)*

The word for sincerity in the Greek original of the New Testament means 'judged in the sunlight'; and the English word is derived from the Latin 'sine cera', which means 'without wax'. In the days when art flourished in ancient Greece, it was the common practice to repair with 'invisible' wax any vase or statue that had, as a result of carelessness or misadventure, been damaged.

A rich man or a person of high rank might employ a sculptor to chisel his bust in marble. Sometimes, if the chisel slipped, the end of the nose would be chipped off. Rather than go to all the trouble of making a new bust, the sculptor would so mend the features with wax that the flaw could not be detected unless by very close scrutiny. He would then palm off on the customer his defective workmanship. If the client happened to be a knowing person, he would carry the finished statuette out of the studio into the open before paying for it, and examine it carefully in the sunlight: otherwise, in course of time, he would have the chagrin of seeing the nose drop off his statuette in the heated room of his house. The statue was not 'sincere', not 'without wax', and could not bear careful scrutiny in the sunlight.

USEFUL TEXTS

Zeal:
　Of God, *2 Kings 19:31; Isa. 26:31*
　Encouraged, *1 Thess. 2:11-12*
　For Law, *Acts 21:20*
　Misguided, *Rom. 10:2*

See also:　A2 Integrity
　　　　　C8 God's messengers
　　　　　C39 Doing God's will

C24
LORD OF ALL NATIONS

'I am coming to gather the nations of every language.
They shall come to witness my glory.' *Isaiah 66:18*

QUOTATIONS

For the whole Church which is throughout the whole world
possesses one and the same faith. *(St Irenaeus)*

Catholicism is a deep matter, you cannot take it up in a tea-cup.
(Cardinal Newman)

Catholicism is the sum of all religions and the queen of them.
(R. H. Benson)

The Catholic Church alone teaches as matters of faith those
things which the thoroughly sincere person of every sect
discovers, more or less obscurely for himself, but dares not
believe for want of external sanction. *(Coventry Patmore)*

True Catholicity is commensurate with the wants of the human
mind; but persons are often to be found who are surprised that
they cannot persuade all men to follow them, and cannot
destroy dissent, by preaching a portion of the divine system,
instead of the whole of it. *(Cardinal Newman)*

Science can make a neighbourhood of the nations, but only
Christ can make the nations into a Brotherhood. *(John Holland)*

STATEMENTS

It is our will that all the peoples who are ruled by the
administration of our clemency shall practice that religion
which the divine Peter the apostle transmitted to the Romans,
for the religion which he introduced is clear even to this day. It
is evident that this is the religion that is followed by the pontiff

Damasus and by Peter, bishop of Alexandria, a man of apostolic sanctity. We command that those persons who follow this rule shall embrace the name of Catholic Christians. The rest, however, who we adjudge demented and insane, shall sustain the infamy of heretical dogmas, their meeting places shall not receive the name of churches, and they shall be smitten first by divine vengeance and secondly by the retribution of our own initiative, which we shall assume in accordance with the divine judgement. *(Edict of the Emperors Gratian, Valentinian, and Theodosius to the People of Constantinople. 28 Feb, 380)*

While she transcends all limits of time and of race, the Church is destined to extend to all regions of the earth and so to enter into the history of mankind. Moving forward through trial and tribulation, the Church is strengthened by the power of God's grace promised to her by the Lord, so that in the weakness of the flesh she may not waver from perfect fidelity, but remain a bride worthy of her Lord; that moved by the Holy Spirit she may never cease to renew herself, until through the cross she arrives at the light which knows no setting.
(Second Vatican Council – 'The Church')

WORD PICTURES

This our European structure, built upon the noble foundations of classical antiquity, was formed through, exists by, is consonant to, and will stand only in the mould of, the Catholic Church. Europe will return to the faith, or she will perish. The faith is Europe. And Europe is the faith.
(H. Belloc: Europe and the Faith)

If Mr Hilaire Belloc means that Europe would be nothing without the faith and that its raison d'être has been and remains to dispense the faith to the world, Mr Belloc is right in saying that Europe is the faith. But speaking absolutely, no! Europe is not the faith and the faith is not Europe: Europe is not the Church and the Church is not Europe. Rome is not the capital of the Latin world. Rome is the capital of the world. *Urbs caput orbis.* The Church is universal because she is born of God, all

nations are at home in her, the arms of her crucified Master are stretched above all races, above all civilisations. She does not bring nations the 'benefits of civilisation', but the blood of Christ and supernatural beatitude.
(*J. Maritain: The Things That Are Not Caesar's*)

The Church is of her nature apostolic, mindful of the commission to go out into all the world with the Gospel, and it shows a reasonable largeness of mind to treat the moon as part of the world, since it originally was part of it. So we must commend the parish priest of Buxton, in Derbyshire, who has bought a plot of land on the moon, to erect the first Catholic Church there. He has paid for it with a dollar bill which he found in the plate, from a sound feeling that the moon is in the dollar area. We can be quite sure that those who travel in rockets and space ships will be in urgent need of spiritual consolation at the end of their journey. It is of course a little uncertain who has the power to sell space on the moon, and the lawyers have not yet got busy verifying titles. But that is no reason for delaying public manifestations of sympathetic interest in a satellite, or for not trying to influence the moon, seeing for how long and how profoundly lunar influences have played upon the human intelligence. (*Douglas Woodruff*)

USEFUL TEXTS

Nation:
Gospel preached to every, *Matt. 24:14; Rev. 14:6*
Believers from every, *Rev. 15:9*
All organically connected, *Acts 17:26*
Abraham father of many, *Gen 17:4-5*

See also: A6 Light of the world
B8 The Word
B28 The Father who draws us to Himself
C12 The Church for all men

C25

HUMILITY

'For everyone who exalts himself will be humbled and the man who humbles himself will be exalted.' *Luke 14:16*

QUOTATIONS

The only wisdom we can hope to acquire is the wisdom of humility – humility is endless. *(T. S. Eliot)*

Humility is the mother of salvation. *(St Bernard)*

The science of humility rests upon the knowledge of God and of oneself. *(Archbishop Ullathorne)*

For he is less in need who is without a garment, than he who is without humility. *(Pope St Gregory I)*

There is something in humility which strangely exalts the heart. *(St Augustine of Hippo)*

Humility in oneself is not attractive, though it is attractive in others. *(Dom Chapman)*

True humility makes no pretence of being humble, and scarcely ever utters words of humility. *(St Francis de Sales)*

To feel extraordinarily small and unimportant is always a wholesome feeling. *(R. H. Benson)*

Golden deeds kept out of sight are most laudable. *(B. Pascal)*

Humility like darkness reveals the heavenly lights.
(Henry D. Thoreau)

You grow up the day you have your first real laugh at yourself.
(Ethel Barrymore)

An able yet humble man is a jewel worth a kingdom.
(William Penn)

Instead of wasting energy in being disgusted with yourself,
accept your own failure, and just say to God, 'Well, in spite of
all I may say or fancy, this is what I am really like - so please help
my weakness.' This, not self-disgust, is the real and fruitful
humility. *(Euelyn Underhill)*

I believe that the first test of a truly great man is his humility. I
do not mean by humility, doubt of his own power. But really
great men have a curious feeling that the greatness is not in
them, but through them. And they see something divine in
every other man and are endlessly, foolishly, incredibly merciful.
(John Ruskin)

PROVERB
Too humble is half proud. *(Yiddish proverb)*

The boughs that bear most hang lowest.*(English proverb)*

Don't make yourself so big. You are not so small.
(Jewish proverb)

STATEMENT
Following Jesus who was poor, the laity are neither depressed
by the lack of temporal goods nor puffed up by their
abundance. Imitating Christ who was humble, they have no
obsession for empty honours *(cf Gal. 5:26)* but seek to please
God rather than men, ever ready to leave all things for Christ's
sake *(cf Luke 14:26)* and to suffer persecution for justice' sake.
(Second Vatican Council – 'Laity')

WORD PICTURES
We have a hard time imagining the enthusiasm Francis stirred
up in a country as spiritually weakened as Italy was in those
days. Sensibility was paralysing the flow of grace. People were
often misled by a purely formal, ostentatious piety. The period

also felt – thereby resembling our own era – a void that pleasure couldn't fill, a hunger for something different, a restlessness of the heart. The Church had forgotten how to speak to the soul, because it was bogged down in the material world.

Then in the piazza or at a turn in the road, there appeared a man with bare feet, dressed like a beggar and crying in a joyful voice, *Pace e bene!* One listened to him despite onself. The fellow knew how to talk, and what he said was so simple that everything seemed new in his language, which had no hard words, those words that make thinking a muddle. No need to have studied to follow him – and they did follow him, first of all because he spoke as he went along, and especially because he believed everything he said. He believed it so strongly that they believed as he did and along with him.

Everything that makes an Italian heart beat with love pounded in each one of their hearts with great, muted strokes. It was incredible: he was in love with God – and that wasn't all, because he went much too far, this madman with the lilting voice. He said that God was in love with us all; he would suddenly weep, weep for love, and some people would begin to weep too, the women first, with the talent they have for that, then the men, starting with the young ones. He went on, apparently not noticing that a crowd was right behind him. People left their work, came out of their houses. One would think he had bewitched them and that he was going to make them leave this world to lead them straight to God . . .
(Julien Green)

I do not know what I may appear to the world; but to myself I seem to have been only a boy playing on the seashore, and diverting myself in now and then finding a smoother pebble or a prettier shell than ordinary whilst the great ocean of truth lay all undiscovered before me. *(Isaac Newton)*

Some American tourists one day visited the home of Beethoven. A young woman among them sat down at the great composer's piano and began to play his Moonlight Sonata. After she had finished, she turned to the old caretaker and said: 'I presume a great many musicians visit this place every year.'

'Yes,' he replied. 'Paderewski was here last year.'

'And did he play on Beethoven's piano?'

'No,' he said, 'he wasn't worthy.' *(Anon)*

There is a story of a rabbi and a cantor and a humble synagogue cleaner who were preparing for the Day of Atonement. The rabbi beat his breast, and said 'I am nothing, I am nothing.' The cantor beat his breast, and said 'I am nothing, I am nothing.' The cleaner beat his breast, and said 'I am nothing, I am nothing.' And the rabbi said to the cantor 'Look who thinks he's nothing.' *(Alan Paton)*

There once lived a man so godly that even the angels rejoiced at the sight of him. But, in spite of his great holiness, he had no notion that he was holy. He just went about his humdrum tasks, diffusing goodness the way flowers unselfconsciously diffuse their fragrance and streetlights their glow.

His holiness lay in this – that he forgot each person's past and looked at them as they were now, and he looked beyond each person's appearance to the very centre of their being, where they were innocent and blameless and too ignorant to know what they were doing. Thus he loved and forgave everyone he met – and he saw nothing extraordinary in this, for it was the result of his way of looking at people.

One day an angel said to him, 'I have been sent to you by God. Ask for anything you wish and it will be given to you. Would you wish to have the gift of healing?'

'No,' said the man, 'I'd rather God did the healing himself.'

'Would you want to bring sinners back to the path of righteousness?'

'No,' he said, 'it is not for me to touch human hearts. That is the work of angels.'

'Would you like to be such a model of virtue that people will be drawn to imitate you?'

'No,' said the saint, 'for that would make me the centre of attention.'

'What then do you wish for?' asked the angel.

'The grace of God,' was the man's reply. 'Having that, I have all I desire.'

'No, you must ask for some miracle,' said the angel, 'or one will be forced on you.'

'Well; then I shall ask for this: let good be done through me without my being aware of it.'

So it was decreed that the holy man's shadow would be endowed with healing properties whenever it fell behind him. So everywhere his shadow fell – provided he had his back to it – the sick were healed, the land became fertile, fountains sprang to life, and colour returned to the faces of those who were weighed down by life's sorrow.

But the saint knew nothing of this because the attention of people was so centred on the shadow that they forgot about the man. And so his wish that good be done through him and he forgotten was abundantly fulfilled. *(Anthony De Mello)*

USEFUL TEXTS

Humility:

>Of Christ, *Matt. 11:29*
>God teaches *Deut. 8:3*
>God is with those who have, *Isa. 57:15*
>Of a child, *Matt. 18:4*

See also: A2 Integrity
>A7 Poor in Spirit
>A10 Seeking perfection
>B20 Growth to maturity

C26

THE HUMAN CONDITION

'A perishable body presses down the soul, and this tent of clay weighs down the teeming mind.' *Wisdom 9:15*

QUOTATIONS

Left to itself, human nature tends to death, and utter apostasy from God, however plausible it may look externally. *(Cardinal Newman)*

The heart sometimes finds out things that reason cannot. *(R. H. Benson)*

Relying on God has to begin all over again, every day, as if nothing had yet been done. *(C. S. Lewis)*

Man is being filled with error. This error is natural, and, without grace, ineffaceable. Nothing shows him the truth; everything deceives him. *(Pascal)*

The world owes all its onward impulse to men ill at ease. The happy man inevitably confines himself within ancient limits. *(Nathaniel Hawthorne)*

We are all as God made us, and oftentimes a great deal worse. *(Miguel de Cervantes)*

The goodness of God knows how to use our disordered wishes and actions, often lovingly turning them to our advantage while always preserving the beauty of His order. *(St Bernard)*

To what shall I compare this life of ours? Even before I can say, 'It is like a lightning flash or a dewdrop,' it is no more. *(Sengai)*

So blind is our mortality, and so unaware what will fall, so unsure also what manner of mind we will have tomorrow, that

God could not lightly do man a more vengeance than in this world to grant him his own foolish wishes. *(St Thomas More)*

HUMOUR

A witty French bishop was once asked why he kept up a country home which he seldom visited. 'Do you not know,' he replied, 'that I must have some place where, though I never go to it, I can always imagine that I might be happier than where I am?' *(Anon)*

WORD-PICTURES

I was on the point of putting an end to my life – the only thing that held me back was my art. For indeed it seemed to me impossible to leave this world before I had produced all the works that I felt the urge to compose; and thus I have dragged on this miserable existence. *(Ludwig van Beethoven)*

It is a common trait of children (and adults) to deny guilt and place the blame on someone else. Miriam Neff writes of this tendency in her own household:

'There is a fifth child who lives at our house called "Nobody". I was cleaning under the basement stairs on my once-every-two-years cleaning plan. On the dark cement in a corner I found mouldy apple cores, black, brittle banana peels, and peach seeds. It looked like someone had been operating a fruit stand or collecting compost to fertilise a garden. I called our offspring to give accounts of themselves. By the time the line-up had all had his/her turn to reply, the unanimous decision was that 'Nobody' had done it. 'Great,' I wanted to scream, 'Will 'Nobody' please crawl back there and clean it up?' Within a few days I discovered that 'Nobody' also liked to eat in the attic. I stumbled across assorted containers with remains of spaghettios and chocolate pudding.

' "Nobody" breaks windows, eats the frosting off cakes before company comes, leaves gallon boxes of ice cream on the kitchen counter before we leave the house for three hours, and delights in parking bicycles behind the car. 'Nobody' puts crayons in the clothes dryer and is not even tax-deductible!'

The nothing people
Non-volunteers
They do not lie;
They just neglect to tell the truth.
They do not take;
They simply cannot bring themselves to give.
They do not steal;
They scavenge.
They will not rock the boat;
But did you ever see them pull an oar?
They will not pull you down;
They'll simply let you pull them up,
And let that pull you down.
They do not hurt you;
They merely will not help you.
They do not hate you;
They merely cannot love you.
They will not burn you;
They'll only fiddle while you burn.
They are the nothing people;
The sins-of-omission folk;
The neither-good-nor-bad-
And-therefore-worse.
Because the good, at least keep busy
trying, and the bad try just as hard.
Both have that character
that comes from caring, action, and
conviction, so give me every time an
honest sinner, or even a Saint.
But, God and Satan,
Get together, and protect me from the
nothing people.
(Anon)

To dream the impossible dream,
To fight the unbeatable foe,
To bear with unbearable sorrow,
To run where the brave dare not go.

To right the unrightable wrong,
To love, pure and chaste, from afar,
To try, when your arms are too weary,
To reach the unreachable star!

This is my Quest, to follow that star . . .

And the world will be better for this,
That one man, scorned and covered with scars,
Still strove, with his last ounce of courage,
To reach the unreachable stars!
(from Man of La Mancha)

Robert Burns was well aware of the wreckage which he so often made of life. 'My life', he said, 'reminded me of a ruined temple; what strength, what proportion in some parts, what unsightly gaps, what ruin in others.'

Studdert Kennedy describes the feelings of a soldier in the First World War. The public tried to treat him as a hero; the padre insisted on treating him as a hell-deserving sinner.

Our padre says I'm a sinner,
And John Bull says I'm a saint,
And they're both of them bound to be liars,
For I'm neither of them, I ain't.
I'm a man, and a man's a mixture,
Right down from his very birth,
For part of him comes from heaven,
And part of him comes from earth.
There's nothing in him that's perfect;
There's nothing that's all complete.
He's nobbut a great beginning
From his head to the soles of his feet.

Every man well knows that he is a mixture. We know that we are capable at one time of an almost saintly goodness, and at another time of an almost devilish evil. We know that at one time we are capable of an almost sacrificial kindness, and at another of an almost heartless callousness. We know that sometimes the vision of goodness fills our horizon, and that other times the unclean and evil desire has us at its mercy. We are part ape and part angel. *(William Barclay)*

See also: A15 Sin
A38 Original Sin
B22 Death
B49 Coping with doubt
C37 Temptation

C27

THE FATHER WHO RECEIVES US BACK

'His father saw him and was moved with pity. He ran to the
boy, clasped him in his arms and kissed him tenderly.'
Luke 15:20

QUOTATIONS

The Lord is loving unto man, and swift to pardon, but slow to
punish. Let no man therefore despair of his own salvation.
(St Cyril of Jerusalem)

For no one is redeemed except through unmerited mercy, and
no one is condemned except through merited judgement.
(St Augustine of Hippo)

How inconsistent it is to expect pardon of sins to be granted to
a repentance which they have not fulfilled. This is to hold out
your hand for merchandise, but not produce the price. For
repentance is the price at which the Lord has determined to
award pardon. *(Tertullian)*

Repeated sickness must have repeated medicine. You will show
your gratitude to the Lord by not refusing what the Lord offers
you. You have offended but still can be reconciled. You have
One whom you may satisfy, and him willing. *(Tertullian)*

Pardon, not wrath, is God's best attribute. *(Bayard Taylor)*

When thou attackest the roots of sin, fix thy thought upon the
God whom thou desirest rather than upon the sin which thou
abhorrest. *(Walter Hilton)*

Proverbs

He who forgives ends the quarrel. *(African proverb)*

Late repentance is seldom true. *(Latin proverb)*

Humour

A small boy, repeating the Lord's Prayer one evening, prayed: 'And forgive us our debts as we forgive those who are dead against us.' *(Anon)*

Word pictures

A London man claims the distinction of landing a job with the same company he was caught stealing from.

'I only stole because I had been out of work for 11 months and had no money,' the 55-year-old man explained. He was arrested for taking tea, sugar, biscuits, and sweets from a factory in the East End. When he was put on probation for two years and hired as a labourer for £56 a week by the same company, he made this comment: 'I really intend to show the management that their goodness isn't going to be abused.' *(Anon)*

Someone once asked Charles Dickens what was the best short story in the English language, and his reply was – 'The Prodigal Son'.

Oh, the comfort, the inexpressible comfort of feeling safe with a person; having neither to weigh thoughts nor measure words, but to pour them all out, just as they are, chaff and grain together, knowing that a faithful hand will take and sift them, keep what is worth keeping, and then, with the breath of kindness, blow the rest away. *(George Eliot)*

See also: A26 The sacrament of Penance
B28 The Father who draws us to Himself
C20 Our Father in heaven
C41 Starting afresh

C28

LORD OF THE OPPRESSED

'From the dust he lifts up the lowly, from the dungheap he raises the poor to set him in the company of princes.'
Psalm 112

QUOTATIONS

Loneliness and the feeling of being unwanted is the most terrible poverty. *(Mother Teresa)*

Poverty comes from God, but not dirt. *(The Talmud)*

Satan now is wiser than of yore,
And tempts by making rich,
not making poor. *(Alexander Pope)*

The rich will do everything for the poor but get off their backs. *(Karl Marx)*

The accumulation of vast wealth while so many are languishing in misery is a grave transgression of God's law, with the consequence that the greedy, avaricious man is never at ease in his mind: he is in fact a most unhappy creature. *(Pope John XXIII)*

A poor man with nothing in his belly needs hope and illusion, more than bread. *(Georges Bernanos)*

PROVERBS

Many a defect is seen in the poor man. *(Irish proverb)*

It is no disgrace to be poor – which is the only good thing you can say about it. *(Jewish proverb)*

Poverty is a blessing hated by all men. *(Italian proverb)*

God help the poor, for the rich can help themselves.
(Scottish proverb)

HUMOUR

Don't despise your poor relations; they may become suddenly rich someday, and then it will be awkward to explain things to them. *(Josh Billings)*

STATEMENT

Those who are oppressed by poverty, infirmity, sickness, or various other hardships, as well as those who suffer persecution for the sake of justice – may they all know that in a special way they are united with the suffering Christ for the salvation of the world. *(Second Vatican Council – 'The Church')*

WORD PICTURES

The poor we see with the eyes of the flesh. They are present. We can put our fingers and our hands into their wounds. The marks of the crown of thorns are plainly visible on their heads. We should fall at their feet and say to them: 'You are our masters, we should be your servants; you are the visible image of the God whom we do not see, but whom we love in loving you.'
(Frédéric Ozanam)

It is easy enough to tell the poor to accept their poverty as God's will when you yourself have warm clothes and plenty of food and medical care and a roof over your head and no worry about the rent. But if you want them to believe you – try to share some of their poverty and see if you can accept it as God's will yourself. *(Thomas Merton)*

King Oswin was troubled to think of Bishop Aidan's long journeys on foot on the rough roads and among the stony crags of Yorkshire, and he knew that the Bishop must often find it difficult to cross the rivers, for there were few bridges. So he gave him a fine horse with royal trappings, to help him on his journeys.

One day as Aidan was riding the horse over the moorlands, he met a beggar who asked for alms. At once he dismounted and gave the horse to the poor man, and went on his way on foot. This was told to the king, who felt rather hurt that Aidan should have given away the horse he had particularly chosen for him as a gift. As they were going into dinner, he said to him, 'Have I not many less valuable horses which might have been given to the beggar?' And Aidan, who was ever a friend of the poor, replied with his ready wit, 'What sayest thou, King? Is that son of a mare more precious in thy sight than the son of God?'

They went into the hall, and Aidan took his place at the table, but the king, who had been out hunting, stood warming himself at the fire with his attendants. Suddenly he ungirded his sword and threw himself at Aidan's feet, asking his forgiveness.

'I will never speak any more of this,' he said, 'nor will I ever judge what, or how much, you shall give to the sons of God.' *(Phyllis Garlick)*

Yes, the first woman I saw, I myself picked up from the street. She had been half eaten by the rats and ants. I took her to the hospital but they could not do anything for her. They only took her in because I refused to move until they accepted her. From there, I went to the municipality and I asked them to give me a place where I could bring these people, because on the same day I had found other people dying in the streets.

The health officer of the municipality took me to the temple, the Kali Temple, and showed me the 'dormashalah' where the people used to rest after they had done their worship of the Kali goddess. It was an empty building; he asked me if I would accept it. I was very happy to have that place for many reasons, but especially knowing that it was a centre of worship and devotion of the Hindus.

Within 24 hours, we had our patients there and we started the work of the home for the sick and dying who are destitute. Since then, we have picked up over 23,000 people from the streets of Calcutta of whom about 50 per cent have died. *(Mother Teresa)*

for useful texts see overleaf

USEFUL TEXTS

Oppression:
    Deliverance from, *Ps. 72:4*
    Commanded to relieve, *Isa. 1:17*
    Of poor and needy, *Amos 4:1, 5:11*
    Not to be guilty of, *Lev. 25:14*

See also: A21 Feeding the hungry
           B15 Jesus, friend of outcasts
           B38 The Suffering Servant
           B50 The Good Shepherd

C29

NOT THROUGH LUXURY

'Woe to those ensconced so smugly in Zion and to those who feel so safe on the mountain of Samaria.' *Amos 6:1*

QUOTATIONS

Avarice and luxury, those pests which have ever been the ruin of every great state. *(Livy)*

Luxury – something you don't really need and can't do without. *(Anon)*

Luxury makes a man so soft, that it is hard to please him, and easy to trouble him; so that his pleasures at last become his burden. Luxury is a nice master, hard to be pleased. *(Mackenzie)*

There has never yet been a man in our history who led a life of ease whose name is worth remembering. *(Theodore Roosevelt)*

We act as though comfort and luxury were the chief requirements of life, when all that we need to make us really happy is something to be enthusiastic about. *(Charles Kingsley)*

Comfort comes as a guest, lingers to become a host and stays to enslave. *(Lee Bickmore)*

Luxuries are what other people buy. *(David White)*

It is easier to renounce worldly possessions than it is to renounce the love of them. *(Walter Hilton)*

You must either conquer the world or the world will conquer you. You must be either master or slave. *(Cardinal Newman)*

But not all solicitude about temporal affairs is forbidden, only such as is superfluous and out of due order.
(*St Thomas Aquinas*)

Let temporal things serve thy use, but the eternal be the object of thy desire. (*Thomas à Kempis*)

We should enjoy spiritual things but only use corporal things. (*St Francis de Sales*)

PROVERBS

We would all live in luxury, if we didn't have to eat. (*Yiddish proverb*)

A full cup must be carried steadily. (*English proverb*)

WORD PICTURES

News Item: £100,000 is being bid for something special. The car number plate VIP 1 has come on to the market and the bidding is expected to begin at £100,000! (*Anon*)

A poor mother when asked why she was spending precious money to exchange her black and white television set for a colour receiver, replied, 'I don't want my children growing up not knowing what colour is!' (*Anon*)

Croesus, King of Lydia, born in 590 BC, had immense wealth and lived luxuriously. He filled his house with all manner of costly treasures. He thought he was the happiest of mortals. Solon, one of the seven wise men of Greece, paid him a visit and was received into a magnificent chamber. Solon showed no surprise or admiration. The king, angry at his indifference, asked Solon, 'Why do you not think me the most truly happy?'
Solon replied, 'No man can be esteemed truly happy but he whose happiness God continues to the end of his life.' (*Anon*)

A big spider, which lived in the roof of an old house, decided to come and live a little lower down. So he spun a thread and came sliding down it and made a new web. He then began to catch flies and make himself fat and because he became fat he also became very stupid. He was very pleased with himself one day as he was walking round his web and he looked up and saw the thread going up in the air. 'What's the use of that?' he said and he broke it. Immediately, he went crashing down with his web to the floor beneath and killed himself. *(M. Nassan)*

A miser in France used to keep all his gold and precious things in a cellar under the floor of his house. One day he went down through a secret trap-door at the top of the cellar to gloat over his treasure. Then the trap-door banged down so that he could not get out.

No one in the house knew about the cellar and the miser could not be found. People searched all over the place without finding him. After a long time, they gave up and the house was sold.

The new people who bought the house wanted some new building done and the cellar was found. When it was opened, the miser was found sitting at a table with all his gold glittering around him. The dead man had even eaten a candle before dying of hunger. *(M. Nassan)*

See also: A7 Poor in Spirit
A21 Feeding the hungry
C21 Rise above materialism

C30

INCREASE OUR FAITH

'The apostles said to the Lord, 'Increase our faith.'
Luke 17:5

QUOTATIONS

Man is capable of nothing, it is God who gives everything, who gives man faith. *(Søren Kierkegaard)*

We live in an age which asks for faith, pure faith, naked faith, mystical faith. *(William Johnston)*

Believe that you have it, and you have it. *(Erasmus)*

Faith means battles; if there are no contests, it is because there are none who desire to contend. *(St Ambrose)*

It is love makes faith, not faith love. *(Cardinal Newman)*

Human reason is weak, and may be deceived, but true faith cannot be deceived. *(Thomas à Kempis)*

The person who says, Unless I feel, I will not believe, is as narrow and foolish as the person who says, Unless I understand, I will not believe. *(R. H. Benson)*

For faith is the beginning and the end is love, and God is the two of them brought into unity. After these comes whatever else makes up a Christian gentleman. *(St Ignatius of Antioch)*

People only think a thing's worth believing in if it's hard to believe. *(Armiger Barclay)*

It is cynicism and fear that freeze life; it is faith that thaws it out, releases it, sets it free. *(Harry Emerson Fosdick)*

All the scholastic scaffolding falls, as a ruined edifice, before one single word – faith. *(Napoleon I)*

A Christian is not a man who is trying to do something, he is a man who has received something; a man to whom something has happened and who simply cannot keep it to himself. *(Peter Marshall)*

Those who have the faith of children have also the troubles of children. *(R. H. Benson)*

WORD PICTURES

As I look back over my career in the Fire Service, I am vividly reminded of the Psalmist's words: 'The Lord is close to the brokenhearted'. I began fire-fighting 34 years ago in Belfast and after the last war moved to London.

Naturally, in the course of my work I have witnessed many harrowing incidents. I am a member of the Catholic Evidence Guild and my Faith has firmly implanted within me the conviction that Our Lord is present in a very special way in times of great danger.

My most gruesome and frightening experiences are so firmly fixed in my memory that I will never be able to forget either their horrifying details or the feeling of reassurance which accompanied them. I can still see a burning wall collapse and bury three fellow firemen – it happened in 1952. I can hear the rumble of collapsing floorboards which trapped three other friends – it happened a year later. Some experiences will never fade into the past. I can forget what someone said to me a few hours ago but I always hear the voices of the 50 people who were trapped on the upper floors of the Leinster Towers Hotel. The cries are three years old, but they are just as loud to me now as they were then.

The sights, sounds and smell of the rail crashes at Harrow Weald and Lewisham will always be with me. The horror of Moorgate will live on for me, as it surely will for many others.

We were three days working in the tunnel where the temperature rose to 110 degrees Fahrenheit and the stench of decomposing bodies forced us to resort to breathing apparatus and made it impossible for us to work for more than 10 minutes at a time. One of the things that sticks most doggedly in my mind was the expression on the face of the driver when his corpse was uncovered – it was almost a smile. I had seen the same expression on the face of the Perth-Euston driver all those years before in Harrow Weald. In times of death or disaster, man is not alone. My work has brought me into contact with suffering and carnage. I know at those times He has always been with me. *(Patrick Knight)*

Was it Archimedes who said, 'Give me a lever long enough and a place to put it on, and I will move the world'? There is such a lever, and it is called 'Faith'; there is a place to put it on, and it is called 'God'; and there is a power that can swing that lever, and it is called 'man'. *(Richard M. Steiner)*

Bruce Larson tells a story in his book *Edge of Adventure*. It's about a letter found in a baking-powder tin wired to the handle of an old pump, which offered the only hope of drinking water on a very long and seldom-used trail across the Amargosa Desert in USA; the letter read as follows:

This pump is alright as of June 1932. I put the new leather sucker washer into it, and it ought to last several years. But this leather washer dries out and the pump has got to be primed. Under the white rock, I buried a bottle of water. There's enough water in it to prime the pump, but not if you drink some first. Pour in about one-quarter, and let her soak to wet the leather. Then pour in the rest, medium fast and pump like crazy. You'll get water. The well has never run dry. Have faith. When you get watered up, fill the bottle and put it back like you found it for the next feller. (Signed) Desert Pete.

p.s. – Don't go drinking up the water first. Prime the pump with it first, and you'll get all you can hold.

See also: B33 Faith and good works
          C22 The Light of faith

C31

THANKSGIVING

'Finding himself cured, one of them turned back praising God at the top of his voice and threw himself at the feet of Jesus and thanked him.' *Luke 17:15-16*

QUOTATIONS

Joy untouched by thankfulness is always suspect. *(Theodor Haecker)*

Gratitude is a duty which ought to be paid, but which none has a right to expect. *(Rousseau)*

What is gladness without gratitude? And where is gratitude without God? *(Coventry Patmore)*

One act of thanksgiving when things go wrong with us is worth a thousand thanks when things are agreeable to our inclination. *(Bl. John of Avila)*

When I find a great deal of gratitude in a poor man, I take it for granted there would be as much generosity if he were rich. *(Alexander Pope)*

Gratitude is born in hearts that take time to count up past mercies. *(Charles E. Jefferson)*

Awake with a winged heart, and give thanks for another day of loving! *(Kahlil Gibran)*

The finest test of character is seen in the amount and the power of gratitude we have. *(Milo H. Gates)*

Gratitude is the most exquisite form of courtesy. *(Jacques Maritain)*

In ordinary life we hardly realise that we receive a great deal more than we give, and that it is only with gratitude that life becomes rich. It is very easy to overestimate the importance of our own achievements in comparison with what we owe others. *(Dietrich Bonhoeffer)*

PROVERBS

Who does not thank for little will not thank for much. *(Estonian proverb)*

Gratitude is the heart's memory. *(French proverb)*

We never know all we should be grateful to God for. *(Jewish proverb)*

WORD PICTURES

A man went into a flower shop and selected a few flowers, saying: 'They are my wife's favourites.' The young lady expressed sympathy at the illness of his wife. 'Ill!' exclaimed the husband. 'My wife is as well as you are.' The assistant apologised, saying: 'I beg your pardon for my mistake; but, to tell you the truth, husbands don't usually buy flowers for their wives unless the wives are ill or dead.' Gratitude, like love, ought to express itself more frequently. *(Anon)*

The legend goes that two angels were once sent down from heaven, each with a basket. They went from place to place, to poor houses and rich houses, visiting the children saying their prayers, the people in the churches, old and young. Then at length they came flying back with their loads. The basket borne by one angel was laden, but that of the other was very light; hardly worthwhile, one would have thought, to go so far and collect so little.

'What have you in your basket?' asked one angel of the other.

'I was sent to collect the prayers of all the people who said, "I want," and "Please give me," answered the angel who carried the heavy load. 'And what have you in yours?'

'Oh,' replied the other angel sadly, 'I have been sent to collect the "Thank yous" of all the people to whom the great God had sent a blessing; but see how few have remembered to give!' *(Anon)*

In his book, *No Man Is an Island*, the late Trappist monk and noted religious writer, Thomas Merton, says this about gratitude:

'If we are not grateful to God, we cannot taste the joy of finding him in his creation.

'To be ungrateful is to admit that we do not know him, and that we love his creatures not for his sake but for our own.

'Unless we are grateful for our own existence, we do not know who we are, and we have not yet discovered what it really means to be and to live . . . The only value of our life is that it is a gift of God. Gratitude shows reverence to God in the way it makes use of his gifts.'

God is he who created the heavens and the earth and sent down water from the clouds, then brought forth with it the fruits as a sustenance for you, and he has made the ships subservient to you, that they might run their course in the sea by his command, and he has made the rivers subservient to you.

And he has made subservient to you the sun and the moon pursuing their courses, and he has made subservient to you the night and the day. And he gives you of all that you ask him, and if you count God's favours, you will not be able to number them; surely man is very unjust, very ungrateful. *(The Qur'an)*

Today upon a bus, I saw a lovely girl with golden hair;
I envied her – she seemed so gay – and wished I were as fair.
When suddenly she rose to leave, I saw
    her hobble down the aisle;
She had one foot and wore a crutch, but
    as she passed, a smile.
Oh, God, forgive me when I whine;
I have two feet – the world is mine!

And then I stopped to buy some sweets.
 The lad who sold them had
Such charm, I talked with him – he said to me
'It's nice to talk with folks like you.
You see,' he said, 'I'm blind.'
Oh, God, forgive me when I whine;
I have two eyes – the world is mine!

Then, walking down the street, I saw a
 child with eyes of blue.
He stood and watched the others play;
It seemed he knew not what to do.
I stopped for a moment, then I said:
'Why don't you join the others, dear?'
He looked ahead without a word, and then
I knew he could not hear.
Oh, God, forgive me when I whine;
I have two ears – the world is mine!

With feet to take me where I'd go,
With eyes to see the sunset's glow,
With ears to hear what I would know,
Oh, God, forgive me when I whine;
I'm blessed, indeed! The world is mine.
(Anon)

USEFUL TEXTS

Thanksgiving:
 Response of believer, *Col. 2:7*
 To accompany prayer, *Phil. 4:6*
 Offered to God, *Pss. 69:30, 100:4, 147:7*

See also: A17 Gentleness
    A39 The Glory of God
    A48 Worship
    B41 Generosity

C32

PRAYER

'Now will not God see justice done to his chosen who cry to him day and night even when he delays to help them?'
Luke 18:7

QUOTATIONS

Prayer is conversation with God. *(Clement of Alexandria)*

The daily prayers of the faithful make satisfaction for those daily, tiny, light faults from which this life cannot be free. *(St Augustine of Hippo)*

In a single day I have prayed as many as a hundred times, and in the night almost as often. *(St Patrick)*

Men by petitioning may merit to receive what almighty God arranged before the ages to give them. *(Pope St Gregory I)*

Prayer is the noblest and most exalted action of which man is capable through the Grace of God. *(Archbishop Ullathorne)*

Prayer is the most important thing in my life. If I should neglect prayer for a single day, I should lose a great deal of the fire of faith. *(Martin Luther)*

He prays best who does not know that he is praying. *(St Anthony)*

But before all things it is good to begin with prayer, as thereby giving ourselves up to and uniting ourselves with God. *(Pseudo-Dionysius)*

Prayer in itself properly is nought else but a devout intent directed unto God, for the getting of good and the removing of evil. *(Anon)*

Pray as you can and do not try to pray as you can't.
(*Dom Chapman*)

All that should be sought for in the exercise of prayer is conformity of our will and the divine will, in which consists the highest perfection. (*St Teresa of Jesus*)

I have so much to do that I must spend several hours in prayer before I am able to do it. (*John Wesley*)

Our prayers should be for blessings in general, for God knows best what is good for us. (*Socrates*)

Prayer is turning the mind and thoughts towards God. To pray means to stand before God with the mind, mentally to gaze unswervingly at him, and to converse with him in reverent fear and hope. (*St Dimitri of Rostov*)

If you do not pray, everything can disappoint you by going wrong.
If you do pray, everything can still go wrong, but not in a way that will disappoint you. (*Hubert Van Zeller OSB*)

PROVERBS

Pray as though no work would help, and work as though no prayer would help. (*German proverb*)

Prayer is the pillow of religion. (*Arab proverb*)

If you pray for another, you will be helped yourself.
(*Yiddish proverb*)

HUMOUR

Priest 'Do you say your prayers at night, little boy?'
Jimmy 'Yes, Father.'
Priest 'And do you always say them in the morning, too?'
Jimmy 'No, Father, I ain't scared in the daytime.'

Hodge's Grace
Heavenly Father bless us,
And keep us all alive;
There's ten of us for dinner
And not enough for five.
(Anon)

One evening six-year-old Bobby asked his father for a pet. 'Sorry, son,' his father said, 'not now. But if you pray real hard for two months, perhaps God will send you a baby brother.'

Bobby prayed faithfully for a month, but it seemed futile to pray longer so he gave up.

How surprised he was, when a month later, a little baby boy arrived at their home, or so Bobby thought when he saw a squirming bundle beside his mother. His proud father drew back the cover and Bobby saw another baby. Twins!

'Aren't you glad you prayed for a baby brother?' asked his father.

'I sure am,' said the boy. 'But aren't you glad I stopped praying when I did?' *(Together)*

STATEMENT

The spiritual life, however, is not confined to participation in the liturgy. The Christian is assuredly called to pray with his brethren, but he must also enter into his chamber to pray to the Father in secret *(cf Matt. 6:6)*; indeed, according to the teaching of the Apostle Paul, he should pray without ceasing.
(Second Vatican Council – 'Liturgy')

WORD PICTURES

There's something exquisitely luxurious about room service in a hotel. All you have to do is pick up a telephone and somebody is ready and waiting to bring you breakfast, lunch, dinner, chocolate milkshake, whatever your heart desires and your stomach will tolerate. Or by another languid motion of the wrist, you can telephone for someone who will get a soiled shirt quickly transformed into a clean one or a rumpled suit into a pressed one.

That's the concept that some of us have of prayer. We have created God in the image of a divine bellhop. Prayer, for us, is the ultimate in room service, wrought by direct dialling. Furthermore, no tipping, and everything charged to that great credit card in the sky. Now prayer is many things, but I'm pretty sure this is not one of the things it is. *(Kenneth L. Wilson)*

While journeying on horseback one day, St Benedict met a peasant walking along the road.

'You've got an easy job,' said the peasant, 'Why don't I become a man of prayer? Then I too would be travelling on horseback.'

'You think praying is easy,' replied the Saint. 'If you can say one "Our Father" without any distraction, you can have this horse.'

'It's a bargain,' said the surprised peasant.

Closing his eyes and folding his hands he began to say the Our Father aloud: 'Our Father, who art in heaven, hallowed be Thy name, Thy kingdom come . . .'

Suddenly he stopped and looked up.

'Shall I get the saddle and bridle too?'

Hindu literature contains some fine stories that could serve as illustrations of Jesus' doctrine. One of them tells of the sage Narada who was on his way to the temple of the Lord Vishnu. At night he stopped at a certain village where a poor villager and his wife made him welcome. When the villager learnt that Narada was on a pilgrimage to the temple of Vishnu, he said to him, 'Will you pray to the Lord that we be given children? My wife and I greatly desire children but the Lord has not yet given them to us.'

Narada promised he would intercede for them, set out again, reached the temple and placed the petition of that villager before the Lord Vishnu. The Lord was abrupt. He said, 'It is not in the destiny of that man to have children'. Narada bowed to this statement of the Lord and returned home. Five years later he set out again on pilgrimage to that temple. Once again he sought and was gladly given hospitality in the house of that simple villager. This time, however, he was surprised to see three little children playing in the courtyard. 'Whose children are those?' asked Narada.

'Mine,' said the villager.

'So the Lord did give you children after all?' 'Yes,' said the villager, 'a little after you left us, five years ago, a saint passed by this village. He gave his blessing to me and my wife and prayed over us. The Lord heard his prayer and gave us these three lovely children you see here.' Narada was dumbfounded and couldn't wait to get to the Lord's temple the next day. When he got there the first thing he said to the Lord was, 'Didn't you tell me it was not in the destiny of that man to have children? How is it then that he has three children now?' When the Lord Vishnu heard that he laughed aloud and said, 'That must be the doing of a saint. Saints have the power to change destiny!'

A quaint story, isn't it? I thought so too, until I suddenly remembered a similar story. 'Woman, my hour has not yet come.' Then, mysteriously, his hour did come and he worked the miracle of changing water into wine. Didn't Mary show there the power of petitionary prayer to change destiny?

'A good man's prayer,' says James 5:16-18, 'is powerful and effective. Elijah was a man with human frailties like our own; and when he prayed earnestly that there should be no rain, not a drop fell in the land for three years and a half; then he prayed again, and down came the rain and the land bore crops once more.' (*Anthony De Mello*)

Martin Luther, the Reformer, said, 'If I fail to spend two hours in prayer each morning, the devil gets the victory through the day. I have so much business, I cannot get on without spending three hours daily in prayer.' He had a motto: 'He that has prayed well has studied well.'

Dr Lancelot Andrews, the saintly Bishop of Winchester in the reigns of James I and Charles I, spent the greater part of five hours every day in prayer and devotion, his book of *Devotions* was his legacy to the Church.

Thomas Ken, Prebendary of Winchester Cathedral (where his name is cut in the cloister over the dates 1656-7), afterwards Bishop of Bath and Wells, rose habitually at two or three in the morning for prayer, attending Matins in the school chapel at five, or later in the Cathedral.

Nicholas Ferrar, of Little Gidding, in Huntingdonshire, lived with his family and relations a life of ordered prayer and devotion between the years 1593 and 1637. Twice a week he kept a prayer watch in the oratory from nine p.m till one a.m. On the other days he rose at one, and continued in prayer and meditation till the morning,

John Wesley, the great revivalist preacher, spent two hours daily in prayer. He lived a most strenuous, adventurous life, and once he said, 'Today I have such a busy day before me that I cannot get through it with less than two hours prayer.' *(Maud Higham)*

USEFUL TEXTS

Prayer:
    Of Christ, *John 17*
    Hindrance to, *1 Pet. 3:7*
    Continuing in, *Col. 4:2*
    Of faith, *James 5:15*
    Of the righteous, *Prov. 15:29*

See also: A22 Seeking God
             A48 Worship
             B25 Quiet – time for prayer
             B29 The Eucharist

C33

EQUALITY

'The Lord is a judge who is no respecter of personages.'
Ecclesiasticus 35:12

QUOTATIONS

Equality consists in the same treatment of similar persons.
(Aristotle)

As men, we are all equal in the presence of death.
(Publius Syrus)

All animals are equal, but some animals are more equal than
others. *(George Orwell)*

All men are born equal but the tough job is to outgrow it.
(Don Leary)

All men are equal on the turf and under it.
(Lord George Bentinck)

The equality existing among the various social members
consists only in this: that all men have their origin in God the
Creator, have been redeemed by Jesus Christ, and are to be
judged and rewarded or punished by God exactly according to
their merits or demerits. *(Pope St Pius X)*

The Lord so constituted everybody that no matter what colour
you are, you require the same amount of nourishment.
(Will Rogers)

Equality is a mortuary word. *(Christopher Fry)*

PROVERBS

Before God and the bus driver we are all equal.
(German proverb)

Equality begins in the grave. *(French proverb)*

In the public baths, all men are equal. *(Yiddish proverb)*

STATEMENT

Since all men possess a rational soul and are created in God's likeness, since they have the same nature and origin, have been redeemed by Christ, and enjoy the same divine calling and destiny, the basic equality of all must receive increasingly greater recognition. *(Second Vatican Council – 'The Church Today')*

WORD PICTURES

There is no comparison between men and women. It is like trying to compare a rose with a jasmine. Each has its own perfume. Women are not equal to men. But then men are not equal to women. *(Islamic poem)*

From the time of the first fairy-tales, men had always believed ideally in equality; they had always thought that something ought to be done, if anything could be done, to redress the balance between Cinderella and the ugly sisters. The irritating thing about the French was not that they said this ought to be done: everybody said that. The irritating thing about the French was that they did it. *(G. K Chesterton)*

USEFUL TEXTS

Equality:
  2 Cor. 8:13; Phil. 2:6; John 5:18

See also: A9 Relationships
     A40 The equality of women
     B34 Human rights
     B44 The dignity of the individual

C34
THE VALUE OF LITTLE THINGS

'In your sight, Lord, the whole world is like a grain of dust that tips the scales, like a drop of morning dew falling on the ground.' *Wisdom 11:22*

QUOTATIONS
Great acts take time. *(Cardinal Newman)*

It is marvellous how our Lord sets his seal upon all that we do, if we will but attend to his working, and not think too highly upon what we do ourselves. *(R. H. Benson)*

From a little spark may burst a mighty flame. *(Dante)*

God does not want us to do extraordinary things; He wants us to do the ordinary things extraordinarily well. *(Bishop Gore)*

The great doing of little things makes the great life. *(Eugenia Price)*

Do little things as if they were great, because of the majesty of the Lord Jesus Christ who dwells in thee. *(Blaise Pascal)*

The greatest thing for us is the perfection of our own soul; and the saints teach us that this perfection consists in doing our ordinary actions well. *(Archbishop Ullathorne)*

Never do anything that thou canst not do in the presence of all. *(St Teresa of Avila)*

Between the great things we cannot do and the little things we will not do, the danger is that we will do nothing. *(H. G. Weaver)*

He does most in God's great world who does his best in his own little world. *(Thomas Jefferson)*

If I cannot do great things, I can do small things in a great way. *(J. F. Clarke)*

Love's secret is always to be doing things for God, and not to mind because they are such very little ones. *(Frederick W. Faber)*

HUMOUR
Be grateful for little things. It's true that the world is getting crowded, but can you imagine if Noah had taken four of everything? *(Orben)*

WORD PICTURES
To illustrate to his students the power of little things, Professor Tait had a heavy iron joist suspended from the roof of his laboratory by a strong cord, and then began to throw small paper pellets at it, striking it square each time. At first there was no perceptible movement of the joist, but after a continuous barrage of paper pellets, the iron joist commenced to sway from side to side and swing like a pendulum. *(Anon)*

I shall do so much in the years to come,
But what have I done today?
I shall give out gold in princely sum,
But what did I give today?
I shall lift the heart and dry the tear,
I shall plant a hope in the place of fear,
I shall speak with words of love and cheer,
But what have I done today?

I shall be so kind in the after while,
But what have I been today?
I shall bring to each lonely life a smile,
But what have I brought today?
I shall give to truth a grander birth,
And to steadfast faith a deeper worth,
I shall feed the hungering souls of earth,
But whom have I fed today?
(Anon)

In a fabulous necklace I had to admire the anonymous string by which the whole thing was strung together.
(Helder Camara)

Do not think that love, in order to be genuine, has to be extraordinary. What we need is to love without getting tired.

How does a lamp burn? Through the continuous input of small drops of oil. If the drops of oil run out, the light of the lamp will cease and the bridegroom will say, 'I do not know you' *(see Matt. 25:1-13)*.

My daughters, what are these drops of oil in our lamps? They are the small things of daily life: faithfulness, punctuality, small words of kindness, a thought for others, our way of being silent, of looking, of speaking, and of acting. These are the true drops of love that keep your religious life burning like a lively flame.

Do not look for Jesus away from yourselves. He is not out there; he is in you. Keep your lamp burning, and you will recognise him. *(Mother Teresa)*

I long to accomplish a great and noble task, but it is my chief duty to accomplish small tasks as if they were great and noble. Green, the historian, tells us that the world is moved along, not only by the mighty shoves of its heroes, but also by the aggregate of the tiny pushes of each honest worker.
(Helen Keller)

Over 10,000 people in Provence, France, owe their homes and environment to a little known peasant shepherd. Elezard Bouffier lived alone, in 1910, in a barren region where there were very few trees. While tending his flock in the Autumn, the shepherd would pick up each acorn that he saw. In the early Spring, while watching the sheep, he would prod the earth with his staff and drop in a nut. He did this each year between 1910 and 1947. At his death, the barren countryside was covered by trees and teeming with wild life. It is now the pleasant site of a new housing development. *(A. P. Castle)*

USEFUL TEXTS

Little things:
Luke 9:17, Luke 19:17

See also: A5 Man for others – unselfishness
A18 Balance in Nature
B20 Growth to maturity
B33 Faith and good works

C35

HOPE

'Ours is the better choice, to meet death at men's hands, yet relying on God's promise that we shall be raised up by him.'
2 Maccabees 7:14

QUOTATIONS

To be a sinner is our distress, but to know it is our hope. *(Fulton Sheen)*

The word which God has written on the brow of every man is Hope. *(Victor Hugo)*

No man is able of himself to grasp the supreme good of eternal life; he needs divine help. Hence there is here a two-fold object, the eternal life we hope for, and the divine help we hope by. *(St Thomas Aquinas)*

As long as matters are really hopeful, hope is a mere flattery or platitude; it is only when everything is hopeless that hope begins to be a strength at all. Like all the Christian virtues, it is as unreasonable as it is indispensable. *(G. K Chesterton)*

We promise according to our hopes, and perform according to our fears. *(La Rochefoucauld)*

He who wants to enjoy the glory of the sunrise must live through the night. *(Anon)*

Hope is the struggle of the soul, breaking loose from what is perishable, and attesting her eternity. *(Herman Melville)*

Hope is the only good that is common to all men; those who have nothing else possess hope still. *(Thales)*

Hope is a thing with feathers
That perches in the soul,
And sings the tune without the words
And never stops at all.
(Emily Dickinson)

Hope is the best possession. None are completely wretched but those who are without hope, and few are reduced so low as that. *(William Hazlitt)*

I am really scared. How long can we restrain the people? I have just got to believe that God is around. That is the only hope. I'm human. And I hold on, and often only by the skin of my teeth, to believe that God is in charge of his world. *(Desmond Tutu)*

PROVERBS

The man who lives only by hope will die with despair. *(Italian proverb)*

Hope is the poor man's income. *(Danish proverb)*

While there is life there is hope. *(Latin proverb)*

HUMOUR

Bill   'Have you ever realised any of your childhood hopes?'

Pete   'Yes; when mother used to comb my hair,
      I often wished I didn't have any.'

WORD PICTURES

Hope is not the closing of your eyes to the difficulty,
     the risk, or the failure.
     It is a trust that if I fail now, I shall not fail for ever;
     and if I am hurt, I shall be healed.
     It is a trust that life is good, and love is powerful.
     (Anon)

It's really a wonder that I haven't dropped all my ideals because they seem so absurd and impossible to carry out. Yet I still keep them because in spite of everything I still believe that people are really good at heart.

I simply cannot build my hopes on a foundation consisting of confusion, misery and death. I see the world gradually being turned into a wilderness. I hear the ever approaching thunder which will destroy us too. I can feel the sufferings of millions and yet when I look up into the heavens I think that it will all come right; that the cruelty too will end and that peace and tranquillity will return again.

In the meantime I must uphold my ideals for perhaps the time will come when I shall be able to carry them out. *(Ann Frank)*

The Stars of the Day (A Russian Legend)
There are always stars in the sky but we cannot always see them, since the sunlight hides them. The stars of day, more brilliantly beautiful even than those of night, can only be seen, says the legend, in deep, still wells. Perched high in the sky and invisible to the eye, these stars are only reflected in the bowels of the earth, on the black mirror of the water on which they shed their rays. And if we cannot see them when we look down from the wellhead, this is either because the water isn't dark enough, or because the surface of the water isn't still enough, or because the well itself isn't deep enough. Perhaps we shouldn't even be looking down the well from outside, but from the bottom of the well . . . upwards.

You understand the drift of the parable? Our hearts one day amputated by sorrow, our lives at certain moments plunged in darkness and night, can be and are, in the world today, among our fellow men, the wells in which the day-star is reflected, where it dwells - that loveliest of all stars, called Hope. This star is invisible to normal sight, it is without apparent existence, yet it can become visible when our lives reach rock-bottom. *(Bernard Bro OP)*

Sir Walter Raleigh is believed to have written this poem in the Tower of London on the night before his execution.

Even such time, that takes in trust
Our youth, our joys, our all we have,
And pays us but with earth and dust;
Who, in the dark and silent grave,
When we have wandered all our ways,
Shuts up the story of our days,
But from this earth, this grave, this dust,
My God shall raise me up, I trust.

In 79 AD, the city of Pompeii in southern Italy was destroyed in the eruption of nearby Mount Vesuvius. Less well known is another town, Herculaneum, which suffered in the same catastrophe. This town was a popular first century resort until that day Mount Vesuvius exploded and buried it under 65 feet of solidified mud and lava.

Herculaneum is interesting in that it was not a wealthy town like Pompeii. Excavations at the site have uncovered blocks of tenements in which the poor lived. The ruins of Herculaneum speak about the lives of ordinary people.

In one old house uncovered in 1938, in a small room on the second floor of a tenement, there was found imbedded into a stucco wall panel a small cross. It is an important find because it is among the earliest evidence of the Christian religion in the Roman Empire.

The archaeologist sees this cross and knows that a Christian lived here, a Christian who was very poor, a Christian who was almost isolated from a larger pagan community. Thus this cross is of some interest. The believer sees this cross and begins to understand a great deal about this room and its occupant(s). There was hope in this tiny room, hope in the midst of what must have been a very meagre existence. There was freedom from the Fates that ruled the lives of so many people in ancient days. There was light that comes from the knowledge that one is loved. For in this room lived a Christian, one who believed in Jesus, one who believed that the ultimate meaning of the universe is life-nourishing love. Could anything destroy this hope?

USEFUL TEXTS

Hope:

Characteristics of;
  blessed, *Titus 2:13*
  sure, *Heb. 6:19*
  good, *2 Thess. 2:16*

Inspires;
  purity, *1 John 3:3*
  courage, *Rom. 5:4-5*
  joy, *Rom. 12:12*

Of Christian;
  salvation, *Rom. 5:1-5*
  Christ, *1 Cor. 15:19*

See also: A6 Light of the world
              A19 Patience
              B21 Trust in God
              C1 Liberation from fear

C36

THE DAY OF THE LORD

'The day is coming now, burning like a furnace; and all the arrogant and evildoers will be like stubble.' *Malachi 3:19*

QUOTATIONS

Judgement cannot be pronounced on a man until he has run his course. *(St Thomas Aquinas)*

God postpones the collapse and dissolution of the universe (through which the bad angels, the demons, and men would cease to exist), because of the Christian seed, which he knows to be the cause in nature of the world's preservation. *(St Justin Martyr)*

All who set not their minds on this world are accounted fools; but who will be the merrier in the world that is to come? *(R. H. Benson)*

For when the judgement is finished, this heaven and earth shall cease to be, and there will be a new heaven and a new earth. For this world shall pass away by transmutation, not by absolute destruction. *(St Augustine)*

If we judge ourselves, we will not be judged by God. *(Jean Pierre Camus)*

God himself, sir, does not propose to judge man until the end of his days. *(Samuel Johnson)*

If we have to answer for our lives after death, those people who have made other people unhappy will be the ones really in trouble with the Boss. *(Jimmy Savile OBE)*

PROVERB

Don't try to fill a sack that's full of holes. *(Jewish proverb)*

STATEMENT

For God has called man and still calls him so that with his entire being he might be joined to Him in an endless sharing of a divine life beyond all corruption. Christ won this victory when he rose to life, since by his death he freed man from death. Hence to every thoughtful man a solidly established faith provides the answer to his anxiety about what the future holds for him. *(Second Vatican Council – 'The Church Today')*

WORD PICTURES

The last judgement is not fable or allegory, but vision. Vision or imagination is a representation of what eternally exists, really and unchangeably. Fable or allegory is formed by the daughters of memory. Imagination is surrounded by the daughters of inspiration.

The Hebrew Bible and the Gospel of Jesus are not allegory, but eternal vision or imagination of all that exists.
(William Blake)

A 200-seater amphitheatre, costing £20,000, was built overlooking Sydney Harbour, Australia, in 1925, for the Second Coming of Christ. Members of 'The order of the Star of the East,' led by Hindu mystic Krishnamurti, believed that Christ would soon return to earth in human form and walk across the Pacific Ocean to the amphitheatre. When he did not arrive by 1929, the group dissolved, and a block of flats now occupies the site. *(Anon)*

One day in 1883, recorded history's most violent cataclysm came to pass. It occurred when the volcanic island of Krakatoa in the East Indies blew up. All that was left was a cavity 1,000 feet deep in the ocean floor. Nearly 36,000 persons were killed – and the resultant tidal wave encircled the Earth four times. *(Anon)*

Then one of the soldiers, without waiting for orders and without a qualm for the terrible consequences of his action but urged on by some unseen force, snatched up a blazing piece of wood, and climbing on another soldier's back, hurled the brand through a golden aperture giving access on the north side to the chambers built round the Sanctuary . . . A runner brought the news to Titus as he was resting in his tent after the battle. He leapt up as he was and ran to the Sanctuary to extinguish the blaze . . . Thus the Sanctuary, in defiance of Caesar's wishes, was set on fire. *(Josephus – 'The Jewish War')*

USEFUL TEXTS

Day of the Lord:
  Jer. 45:10; 1 Thess. 5:2

See also: A31 Heaven
  A42 Life after death
  B22 Death

C37

TEMPTATION

'Jesus was led by the Spirit through the wilderness, being tempted there by the devil for forty days.' *Luke 4:1*

QUOTATIONS

You are not tempted because you are evil; you are tempted because you are human. *(Fulton J. Sheen)*

No man is so perfect and holy as not to have sometimes temptations; and we cannot be wholly without them.
(Thomas à Kempis)

God does not punish people for what they would have done, but for what they do. *(St Thomas Aquinas)*

Inconstancy of mind, and small confidence in God, is the beginning of all evil temptations. *(Thomas à Kempis)*

It is one thing to be tempted, another thing to fall. *(Shakespeare)*

To realise God's presence is the one sovereign remedy against temptation. *(Fenelon)*

It is good to be without vices, but it is not good to be without temptations. *(Walter Bagehot)*

As the Sandwich-Islander believes that the strength and valour of the enemy he kills passes into himself, so we gain the strength of the temptations we resist. *(Ralph Waldo Emerson)*

To pray against temptations, and yet to rush into occasions, is to thrust your fingers into the fire, and then pray they might not be burnt. *(Secker)*

Following the path of least resistance makes both rivers and men crooked. *(Anon)*

No man is matriculated to the art of life till he has been well tempted. *(George Eliot)*

There are several good protections against temptation, but the surest is cowardice. *(Mark Twain)*

PROVERBS
God promises a safe landing but not a calm passage.
(Bulgarian proverb)

The heron's a saint when there are no fish in sight.
(Bengalese proverb)

HUMOUR
The Devil, having nothing else to do.
Went off, to tempt My Lady Poltagrue.
My Lady, tempted by a private whim,
To his extreme annoyance, tempted him.
(Hilaire Belloc)

Don't worry about avoiding temptation – as you grow older, it starts avoiding you. *(Farmer's Almanac)*

'I can resist everything,' said the young lady, 'except temptation.' *(Anon)*

A shopkeeper, seeing a boy hanging about outside where there was a tempting display of various fruits, went out to him and said, 'What are you trying to do, young man; steal my apples?'
'No, sir,' said the boy, 'I'm trying not to!' *(Anon)*

STATEMENT
To be sure, the disturbances which so frequently occur in the social order result in part from the natural tensions of economic, political, and social forms. But at a deeper level they flow from man's pride and selfishness, which contaminate even

the social sphere. When the structure of affairs is flawed by the consequences of sin, man, already born with a bent toward evil, finds there new inducements to sin, which cannot be overcome without strenuous efforts and the assistance of grace.
(Second Vatican Council – 'The Church Today')

WORD PICTURES

One 82-year-old Father Christmas put too much enthusiasm into his job last Christmas and found himself out of work. The pensioner was paid to sit in his red coat and white beard in a Nottingham store and speak kindly to the shy children.

When they would whisper their wishes in his ear, however, he began to melt. 'I couldn't bear to see them go away disappointed,' he said later, 'There were a lot of toys on the shelves nearby that no one seemed to be buying. So I started handing them to some of the children as an extra present.' While store officials sympathised with the sentiment, they insisted on the hard facts of commercial life. The old man was politely sacked. *(Anon)*

The film, *The Last Temptation of Christ*, stirred heated controversy because of its distorted biblical portrayal of Jesus, but it also raised old questions. Was Jesus both fully human and fully divine? Many Christians are simply uneasy with the humanity of Jesus. Ours is a faith of the supernatural, the sacred, the divine, and we want a Jesus far above anything that is human. Yes, of course, we cherish the stories of his falling asleep on the boat and driving the swindlers out of the temple. But even those stories have a divine aura about them. Jesus is God, we insist. That is a doctrine we dare not diminish.

Was Jesus truly human? Did he ever throw up? Did he ever play 'piggyback' with a child? Did he ever run a race with his friends – and lose? Did he ever have sexual fantasies? Some Christians feel it is sacrilegious to even ask such questions. One Christian who does not is Marjorie Holmes, who explores the humanity of Jesus from the viewpoint of a committed Christian. In her novel, *Three from Galilee*, she deals with such issues as sexual fantasies in a very sensitive way.

In one scene in her book Jesus is dreaming of finding 'a woman whom he could love,' a 'wife who would bear him children to nurse at her breast.' Then suddenly he awakes out of his restless sleep.

'What was it, what was it? Jesus sat up in a cold sweat. Then to his relief it came to him: Temptation. He had been wrestling with temptation . . . He lay a few moments longer, thinking. What was temptation? Had he not been tempted many times? The girls at the grape treadings, young and lovely, sometimes unsteady from the very smell of the wine. The girls who came into the shop on pretext of some tool to be mended for their fathers – their flirting eyes and sometimes casually touching hands. The matrons who walked the streets of Nazareth, hips swinging seductively . . . Was the yearning in his loins evil, or merely nature's response to the vital instinct God himself had planted in males that the race might survive?'

As a man who was fully human, Jesus can identify with the struggles and temptations that face all of mankind.

USEFUL TEXTS

Temptation:
In the garden, *Gen. 3:1-5*
Prayer to avoid, *Matt. 6:13*
Of Christ, *Luke 4:1-13*
Common to all, *1 Cor. 10:13*
Not from God, *James 1:13-14*

See also: A15 Sin
A38 Original Sin
B19 Conscience
C26 The human condition

C38

DISCERNING GOD'S WILL

'My lord, the Lord,' Abram replied, 'how am I to know that I shall inherit it?' *Genesis 15:8*

QUOTATIONS

All heaven is waiting to help those who will discover the will of God and do it. *(Robert Ashcroft)*

The principal effect of love is to unite the wills of those who love, so as to make of them but one and the same will. *(Pseudo-Dionysius)*

No one may prefer his own will to the will of God, but in everything we must seek and do the will of God. *(St Basil)*

Nothing, therefore, happens unless the Omnipotent wills it to happen: He either permits it to happen, or he brings it about himself. *(St Augustine of Hippo)*

It is not a question of who or what you are, but whether God controls you. *(J. Wilbur Chapman)*

God's will is as energetic in the bewildering rush of the current as in the quiet sheltered backwater. *(R. H. Benson)*

It is the duty of those who are zealous for God's good pleasure to make inquiry as to what it is right for them to do. *(St Basil)*

The will of God is the measure of things. *(St Ambrose)*

It needs a very pure intention, as well as great spiritual discernment, always to recognise the divine voice. *(R. H. Benson)*

God's will is as much in sickness as in health.
(St Francis de Sales)

We should fulfil the commands of God with insatiable desire, ever pressing onward towards greater achievements. *(St Basil)*

We always find it more acceptable to have God speaking to us directly rather than through our wives! But we may learn a great deal by listening to what he says to us through them.
(Paul Tournier)

STATEMENT

The intellectual nature of the human person is perfected by wisdom and needs to be. For wisdom gently attracts the mind of man to a quest and a love for what is true and good. Steeped in wisdom, man passes through visible realities to those which are unseen.

It is finally, through the gift of the Holy Spirit, that man comes by faith to the contemplation and appreciation of the divine plan. *(Second Vatican Council – 'The Church Today')*

WORD PICTURES

This I know is God's own truth, that pain and troubles and trials and sorrows and disappointments are either one thing or another. To all who love God, they are love tokens from him. To all who do not love God and do not want to love him they are merely a nuisance. Every single pain that we feel is known to God because it is the most loving touch of his hand.
(Edward Wilson (who died with Scott in the Antarctic))

I fled Him down the nights and down the days
    I fled Him, down the arches of the years;
I fled Him, down the labyrinthine ways
    Of my own mind; and in the midst of tears
I hid from Him, and under running laughter.
(Francis Thompson – 'The Hound of Heaven')

for useful texts see overleaf

USEFUL TEXTS

Will of God:
  Christ's resignation to, *Matt. 26:39; John 6:38-39*
  Asking for, *Matt. 6:10*
  Directing early missions, *Acts 18:21; Rom. 15:30-32*

See also: A41 Spiritual blindness
          B11 Vocation
          B47 Dying to self
          C39 Doing God's will

C39

DOING GOD'S WILL

'This,' God added, 'is what you must say to the sons of Israel:
'I AM has sent me to you.' *Exodus 3:14*

QUOTATIONS

As regards the will of God, even if some take scandal, we must
not let this hamper our freedom of action. *(St Basil)*

A broken heart and God's will done would be better than that
God's will should be avoided. *(R. H. Benson)*

In his will is our peace. *(Dante Alighieri)*

The greatness of a man's power is the measure of his surrender.
(William Booth)

Life is nothing but a play and a pretence, and His will must be
done, however much we rebel at it. *(R. H. Benson)*

The Lord doesn't want the first place in my life, he wants all of
my life. *(Howard Amerding)*

A man's heart is light when he wills what God wills.
(St Thomas Aquinas)

Blessed are they who do not their own will on earth, for God
will do it in heaven above. *(St Francis de Sales)*

PROVERBS

The favourite place of God is in the heart of man.
(Yiddish proverb)

If God willed it, brooms would shoot. *(Jewish proverb)*

WORD PICTURES

Our prayers do not change God's mind, elicit his pity or reverse a sentence . . . they allow God to put into operation (in me and through me) something He has willed all along.
(Hubert van Zeller)

'Nothing in the hands of God is evil; not failure, not thwarting, not the frustration of every hope or ambition, not death itself. All in his hands is success, and will bear the more fruit the more we leave it to him, having no ambitions, no preoccupations, no excessive preferences or desires of our own.'
(Archbishop Goodier)

Kari Torjesen Malcolm, a missionary herself and a daughter of missionaries, writes of her internment in a Chinese prison camp during the Second World War. She was a teenager who at times feared she had lost her identity. She was number sixteen, a nameless Westerner, who was given a small space on the bare floor and reminded every day of her lack of freedom by the wall, the moat, and the electric barbed-wire fence that came between her and the outside world. Others there were in the same predicament, and often they managed to get together for a few moments of prayer – prayer for freedom. But as time passed, the enemy loomed larger and larger, and God somehow seemed smaller. In desperation, Kari pleaded with God to reveal himself to her.

'God answered that prayer and spoke to me as I searched the Bible for answers. Gradually it dawned on me that there was just one thing the enemy could not take from me. They had bombed our home, killed my father, and put my mother, brothers and me into prison. But the one thing they could not touch was my relationship to my God.

'With this new discovery, it became more and more difficult to join the gang in prayer at noon. There was more to life than just getting out of prison. One day, I decided I could not climb the bell tower. It was the first time I had missed.

'Debbie looked for me right after the meeting. The spot where we met is riveted in my memory. I cannot even remember trying to defend myself, but Debbie must have surmised something of what had occurred in my thinking. Her reproof ended with the final taunt, 'So we aren't good enough for you anymore, eh? Getting holier than the rest of us, I can see.'

'As I walked away, I felt lonelier than I had ever felt in my life. My last bit of security was peeled off. This was the climax to the peeling process that had been going on through the war years with the loss of my father, my home, my education, my freedom. Now I no longer belonged to my peer group.

'It was only then that I was able to pray the prayer that changed my life: 'Lord, I am willing to stay in this prison for the rest of my life if only I may know You.' At that moment I was free.'

Dr Mason of Burma once wanted a teacher to visit and labour among a warlike tribe and asked his converted boatman if he would go. He told him that as a teacher he would receive only four rupees per month whereas as boatman he was then receiving fifteen rupees.

After praying over the matter, the boatman returned to the doctor and the following conversation occurred:

'Well, Shapon,' said the doctor, 'what have you decided? Will you go for four rupees a month?'

'No, teacher,' replied Shapon, 'I will not go for four rupees a month but I will go for Christ.' (Anon)

Many people would be willing to renounce worldly pleasures if they received convincing proof that the ultimate rewards would make the deal worthwhile. But if such a deal could be made, it would not be due to love, but to business discernment. The object of the training can only be achieved by a loving donation of ourselves, uncertain of reward. Christ himself put the matter exactly. 'My doctrine,' he said, 'is not mine but his that sent me. If any man will do his will, he shall know of the doctrine whether it be of God.' The abandonment of our own interests and our surrender to his guidance must be the first step. After that, our trust will grow.

Evelyn Underhill has a good illustration of the situation. She supposes someone looking at a great cathedral, a mass of grey stone with the windows showing a dark, dusty colour. It does not look very cheerful. But if we push open the doors and go in, we suddenly see that all the windows are really brightly coloured glass . . . You cannot see the glory if you stand outside, asking sneeringly what proof there is that the inside is beautiful. You have to go in yourself. *(John Bagot Glubb – 'The Way of Love')*

See also: A41 Spiritual blindness
B11 Vocation
B47 Dying to self
C38 Discerning God's will

C40

RECONCILIATION

'It was God who reconciled us to himself through Christ and gave us the work of handing on this reconciliation.'
2 Corinthians, 5:18

QUOTATIONS

It takes two sides to make a lasting peace, but it only takes one to make the first step. *(Edward M Kennedy)*

Clean your fingers before you point at my spots. *(Benjamin Franklin)*

He that accuses all mankind of corruption ought to remember that he is sure to convict only one. *(Edmund Burke)*

We must not be unjust and require from ourselves what is not in ourselves. *(St Francis de Sales)*

Our task is to work for the expression of God's reconciliation here and now. We are not required to wait for a distant 'heaven' when all problems will have been solved. What Christ has done, he has done already. We can accept his work or reject it; we can hide from it or seek to live by it. But we cannot destroy it, for it is the work of the eternal God. *(Council of African Churches)*

Reconciliation sounds a large theological term, but it simply means coming to ourselves and arising and going to our Father. *(John Oman)*

A reconciliation that does not explain that error lay on both sides is not a true reconciliation. *(Midrash: Genesis Rabbah)*

WORD PICTURES

A love of reconciliation is not weakness or cowardice. It demands courage, nobility, generosity, sometimes heroism, an overcoming of oneself rather than of one's adversary. At times it may even seem like dishonour, but it never offends against true justice or denies the rights of the poor. In reality, it is the patient, wise art of peace, of loving, of living with one's fellows, after the example of Christ, with a strength of heart and mind modelled on his. *(Pope Paul VI)*

A soldier asked a holy monk if God accepted repentance. He said, 'Tell me, if your cloak is torn, do you throw it away?' The soldier replied, 'No, I mend it and use it again.' The old man said to him, 'If you are so careful about your cloak, will not God be equally careful about his creature?' *(Anon)*

In 1914, Clayton was one of the four curates whom Portsea contributed to the forces as chaplains. After serving with the 16th Division, he was transferred in 1915 to the 6th Division in the Ypres Salient. There, men were dying at the rate of 250 a day, and the lucky ones were those who got a bullet through the brain instead of coughing out their poisoned lungs or lingering mangled in the mud. It was a unique problem that this unique man tackled at Talbot House (Toc H in the language of the army signaller), a soldier's club in a back street in Poperinghe. Men, even on a few days' leave, needed human brotherhood; Clayton gave it. Religion was not pressed on men, but more and more came to value the long garret, stretching the whole length and breadth of the house, which formed the chapel.

When peace came, Clayton recognised the need for special training for ex-servicemen seeking ordination. For some years, nothing better than a disused prison at Knutsford was available; but that did not trouble him. When Knutsford was well established, he turned to what was to become his life's work, the establishment, first in London, then in the cities of Britain and in many other lands, of branch houses of Toc H to preserve the spirit of the trenches, and, as he put it, to 'teach the younger generation class reconciliation and unselfish service'.
(The Guardian)

USEFUL TEXTS

Reconciliation:
  To God, *Rom. 5:10-11*
  To brother, *Matt. 5:23-24; 18:15-17*
  Of whole creation, *Col. 1:19-20*

See also: A26 Sacrament of penance
  A27 As we forgive those
  B16 Christ heals and forgives
  C14 Forgiveness

C41

STARTING AFRESH

'All I can say is that I forget the past and I strain ahead for
what is still to come.' *Philippians 3:14*

QUOTATIONS

It is not of much use to be entreated to turn over a new leaf,
when you see no kind of reason for doing so. (*R. H. Benson*)

The meaning of life is to see. (*Hui-Neng*)

Every exit is an entry somewhere else. (*Tom Stoppard*)

Nothing is more expensive than a start. (*Nietzsche*)

All beginnings are somewhat strange; but we must have
patience, and, little by little, we shall find things, which at first
were obscure, becoming clear. (*Saint Vincent De Paul*)

PROVERBS

The beginning and the end reach out their hands to each other.
(*Chinese proverb*)

He who is outside the door has already a good part of his
journey behind him (*Dutch proverb*)

It is better to begin in the evening than not at all.
(*English proverb*)

A good beginning makes a good ending. (*English proverb*)

WORD PICTURES

There was an old sailor my grandfather knew,
Who had so many things that he wanted to do,
That just when he thought it was time to begin,
He couldn't – because of the state he was in! (*Anon*)

Poverty was the universal way of life in the coal-mining areas of South Wales during my boyhood there. Nonetheless our community culture was rich. It was rooted in our Christian faith and therefore was uninfluenced by the scale of our possessions.

As I grew in understanding I learned to look at people in terms of their potential when God's Holy Spirit was their inspiration. There is no limit to what God can do when commitment to Him is total. Changed lives are unfailing witnesses to that truth in every generation. It will be so in tomorrow's world, for the two great permanents of history are the unchanging needs of people and the unchanging power and love of God. *(Lord Tonypandy)*

You think because you don't find prayer easy;
because attendance at Mass is not congenial;
because your record in the service of God is not a good one;
that the things of God are not for you.
Can't you see that the more inadequate you are
the more you need God's help?
(Cardinal Basil Hume)

An escaped convict from Devil's Island, the penal colony off the French Guiana coast, (now Guyane) died some time ago, after devoting 35 years to helping the sick.

The man, sentenced to life imprisonment in connection with a murder in Marseilles, was granted asylum on the pearl fishing island of Margarita.

Since he was a doctor, he devoted his remaining years to curing the ills of the islanders. Although he was never able to obtain official authorisation as a doctor, he was allowed by local authorities to practice.

When he died at 72, several hundred neighbours gathered to pay their last respects to the man who had done so much to relieve their physical ills. *(Anon)*

A young burglar fleeing across a rooftop heard the crash of glass behind him. Looking back, he saw a policeman falling through a skylight. The 26-year-old thief went back and supported the officer until help came. Then he was arrested and sentenced to 20 months in prison. Four months later, a judge reviewed the case, saluted the man's 'outstanding gallantry' and set him free. Headlines heralded the former burglar as a hero.

He soon found that public esteem was short-lived. Every attempt to get a permanent job met with failure. Three employers discharged him when they learned of his past. Nine others refused to hire him because he told the full truth at job interviews.

The embittered man complained: 'If I hadn't stayed to save that policeman's life, I would probably not be in this fix now. But I'll never go back to crime.' *(Anon)*

See also: A25 Courage
             B14 Freedom to serve
             C1 Liberation from fear

C42

THE RISEN LORD

'Three days afterwards, God raised him to life and allowed
him to be seen, not by the whole people but only
by certain witnesses.' *Acts 10:40*

QUOTATIONS

Every parting gives a foretaste of death, every reunion a hint
of the resurrection. *(Arthur Schopenhauer)*

Faith in the resurrection is really the same as faith in the saving
efficacy of the cross. *(Rudolf Bultmann)*

It is only when one loves life and the earth so much that one
may believe in the resurrection and a new world.
(Dietrich Bonhoeffer)

The root of all good works is the hope of the resurrection; for
the expectation of the reward nerves the soul to good works.
(St Cyril of Jerusalem)

Let us consider, beloved, how the Lord is continually revealing
to us the resurrection that is to be. Of this He has constituted
the Lord Jesus Christ the first-fruits, by raising Him from the
dead. *(Pope St Clement I)*

Our Lord has written the promise of the resurrection, not in
books alone, but in every leaf in springtime. *(Martin Luther)*

Easter, like all deep things, begins in mystery and it ends like all
high things, in great courage. *(Bliss Perry)*

The Gospels do not explain the resurrection; the resurrection
explains the Gospels. Belief in the resurrection is not an
appendage to the Christian faith; it *is* the Christian faith.
(J. S. Whale)

The resurrection did not result in a committee with a chairman, but in a fellowship with an experience. *(Anon)*

HUMOUR

Just before Easter one year, this item appeared in a police log: '8.26 pm, church – lights will be on throughout the village church for the rest of the weekend; vicar trying to speed up the Easter lilies.' *(H. C. R.)*

I was showing my husband an egg which was speckled rather than all white like the rest. 'The Easter Bunny must have laid this one,' I said. 'Perhaps she did,' he answered absently, and returned to his paper. 'I always thought the Easter Bunny was a he,' I reflected. 'Look,' said my husband, putting down his paper, 'it's hard enough for a rabbit to lay eggs without being a male too.' *(Mrs George Maskell)*

STATEMENT

When Jesus rose up again after suffering death on the cross for mankind, he manifested that he had been appointed Lord, Messiah, and Priest forever *(cf Acts 2:36; Heb. 5:6, 7:17-21)*, and he poured out on his disciples the Spirit promised by the Father *(cf Acts 2:33)*. The Church, consequently, equipped with the gifts of charity, humility and self-sacrifice, receives the mission to proclaim and to establish among all peoples the kingdom of Christ and of God. *(Second Vatican Council – 'The Church')*

WORD PICTURES

It is also stated that after his execution and entombment he disappeared entirely. Some people actually assert that he had risen; others retort that his friends stole him away. I for one cannot decide where the truth lies. *(Josephus)*

The very notion 'resurrection' needs to be clarified before we discuss the implications. In one sense, it refers to what happened once with Jesus when he passed through death to the new, risen life . . . a foretaste of the glorious future awaiting us in the completion of God's plan. This is the prime meaning, for it is from this aspect that the others derive. The second meaning appears when it is applied to baptism, and we speak with the apostle of going down in the waters of baptism to death and rising again in the new life. And then there is a third meaning, which can happen, and happen more than once, in the life of each and any individual. This is the resurrection which comes to the individual, waking him or her to the surrounding world in an entirely new way; it is like a sudden break and leap forward in our personal evolution. *(Michael Hollings)*

Easter's meaning for those who formerly were without hope and without a true direction in life is a source of ever-recurring wonder. Some of the effects of Christ's resurrection were eloquently described nearly 1,600 years ago by St John Chrysostom in his Easter message:
'Those who were formerly living in the shame of sin are now living in confidence and in justice.
    'They are not only free, but saints;
    'Not only saints but just men;
    'Not only just men but sons;
    'Not only sons but heirs;
    'Not only heirs, but brothers of Christ;
    'Not only brothers of Christ but his co-heirs;
    'Not only his co-heirs, but his members;
    'Not only his members, but temples;
    'Not only temples, but instruments of the Holy Spirit.'

The word Easter derives from Eostre, the pagan goddess of Spring, and to the Saxons, April was 'ostermonud' – the month of the ost-end wind (wind, that is, from the east) so that Easter became by association the April feast, which lasted eight days.
    But Easter Sunday nowadays is the first Sunday after the first full moon following 21 March, and can therefore fall as early as 22 March, or as late as 25 April. For many years in earlier times, it was quite a popular belief that the Sun danced on Easter day. Sir John Suckling (1609-1642) wrote:
    'But oh, she dances such a way,
    No sun upon an Easter day
    Is half so fine a sight.'
We do not believe that any longer, but we still have an

affection for the 'Easter Egg'. The presentation of eggs at Eastertime is a practice that goes back to Persian times, when it was held that there were two contending forces in the world – those of Germuzd and Ahriman (Good and Evil). The egg was, so to speak, the 'bone of contention' between these opposite forces. The Jews, Egyptians and Hindus also clung to the idea and made symbolic presentations of eggs to each other. In due course, Christians adopted the custom, signifying by the new life within the egg the resurrection of Christ. They also coloured the eggs they gave red, so as to represent to their friends the Blood of the Redemption. *(W. A. Dickins)*

One ancient symbol of Christian belief in the resurrection is the phoenix. This bird symbolised hope and the continuity of life after death. According to legend, only one phoenix could live at a time. The Greek poet Hesiod, writing in the eighth century BC, said it lived nine times the lifespan of the long-living raven.

When the bird felt death approaching, it built itself a pyre of wild cinnamon and died in the flames. But from the ashes there then arose a new phoenix, which tenderly encased its parent's remains in an egg of myrrh and flew with them to the Egyptian city of Heliopolis, where it laid them on the Altar of the Sun. These ashes were said to have the power of bringing a dead man back to life. Scholars now think that the germ of the legend came from the orient, and was adopted by the sun-worshipping priests of Heliopolis as an allegory of the sun's daily setting and rebirth.

In Christian art, the resurrected phoenix became a popular symbol of Christ risen from the grave. *(Anon)*

USEFUL TEXTS

Resurrection:
Of Jesus, *John 20:1-20*
Disciples witness to, *Acts 1:22*
Hope of Believers, *Rom. 6:5; 1 Cor. 15:13*

See also: A44 Meeting Christ in the sacraments
         C43 The Living One
         C45 The Divinity of Christ
         C47 The indwelling spirit

C43

THE LIVING ONE

'You believe because you can see me. Happy are they who have not seen and yet believe.' *John 20:29*

QUOTATIONS

Taking all the evidence together, it is not too much to say that there is no single historic incident better or more variously supported than the resurrection of Christ. *(B. F. Westcott)*

Christ has conquered death, not only by suppressing its evil effects, but by reversing its sting. By virtue of the Resurrection, nothing any longer kills inevitably but everything is capable of becoming the blessed touch of the divine hands, the blessed influence of the will of God upon our lives. However compromised by our faults, or however cast down by circumstances our position may be, we can at any moment, by a total redressment, wholly readjust the world around us and take up our lives again in a favourable sense. To those who love God, all things are turned to good. *(Pierre Teilhard de Chardin)*

WORD PICTURES

There is a very beautiful saying of Christ which is one of the unwritten sayings which do not appear in the New Testament at all:

'Raise the stone and you will find me;
cleave the wood and I am there.'

It means that, as the mason works at the stone, as the carpenter handles the wood, the Risen Christ is with him. The Resurrection means that every way of life can be walked hand in hand with the living Christ. The reservoir of the power of his presence is open for every Christian to draw upon.
(William Barclay)

In the time of Cuspius and Tiberius Alexander, many of the miracle-worker's followers came forward and declared to the adherents of their master that although he had died, he was now alive and would free them from slavery. *(Josephus)*

They took away what should have been my eyes
(But I remembered Milton's Paradise).
They took away what should have been my ears
(Beethoven came and wiped away my tears).

They took away what should have been my tongue
(But I had talked with God when I was young).
He would not let them take away my soul –
Possessing that, I still possess the whole.
(Helen Keller)

The weather had changed, it was like early spring, and even warm, as she walked the two miles up from the road in the late afternoon. There were aconites and celandines just pushing up through their green sheaths on the banks. Too early, Ben would say, the snow might come again yet, even in March or April. The woods and coppices were still leafless, branches open-meshed, or else pointing up, thin and dark against the blue-white sky, she could see all the way down between the wide-spaced beech trunks, to the fields below.

But there was something in the air, something, a new smell, the beginning of growth, and, as she walked, she had felt a great happiness spurt up within her, and the countryside had looked beautiful, every detail, every leaf-vein and grass-blade was clear and sharp, it was as though she had been re-born into some new world. There was a change in the light, so that the dips and hollows of the valley that she could see between the gaps in the hedges, as the track climbed higher, up to the common, had changed their shapes, and the colours changed, too, the bracken was soft moss-green and the soil gold-tinged like tobacco. Yesterday, it had been dark as peat.

She wanted to sing. Because she had all she could ever want, the whole earth belonged to her, and in the end, seeing the cottage ahead, she had to shake her head to clear it, she was giddy with this happiness. *(Susan Hill)*

An old cathedral stood on the site of the present St Paul's in London. It perished in the great fire of 1666. After the fire, the brilliant young architect, Christopher Wren, designed a new cathedral which took 35 years to erect. The first stone that Wren picked up from the ruins of the old building bore a Latin inscription whose meaning is 'I shall rise again'. *(Anon)*

Many years ago an American film, *The World in Darkness*, depicted a scene which could help us here. An archaeologist was excavating in Jerusalem, mainly in the Calvary area. One day, he announced that he had found the tomb where Jesus was laid, the tomb of Joseph of Arimathea and the tomb was not empty. He declared that he had found a mummified corpse in it, and he put it on show. People came in crowds to see this corpse. Christ had not, therefore risen from the dead.

The news was carried by press and radio to the four corners of the earth. Immediately the world was plunged into indescribable gloom. Everything which spoke of Christ, everything which lived by him, everything which bore his mark or a trace of his memory was doomed to disappear. The churches were closed, the cathedrals demolished; the pictures which portrayed him disappeared from the galleries; monasteries emptied; missionaries returned home, the cross was torn down in people's homes.

Finally, when the world, shattered by this immense seismic shock, was plunged into complete spiritual darkness, the archaeologist confessed on his deathbed that he had told a lie and that the tomb had been empty.

Whatever the value of the film, it had at least this merit: it made it clear that nothing is more essential to the world than a knowledge of what happened on Easter morning. Was the tomb empty? Did Christ rise from the dead? That is the whole question. *(Leo Suenans)*

See also: A44 Meeting Christ in the sacraments
             C42 The Risen Lord
             C45 The Divinity of Christ
             C47 The indwelling spirit

C44

FEED MY SHEEP

'Lord, you know I love you.' Jesus said to him,
'Feed my sheep.' *John 21:17*

QUOTATIONS

It takes a great person to give sound advice tactfully, but a greater to accept it graciously. *(J. C. Macaulay)*

Advice is seldom welcome; and those who want it the most always like it the least. *(Lord Chesterfield)*

To profit from good advice requires more wisdom than to give it. *(Churton Collins)*

I divide the world in three classes:
    the few who make things happen,
    the many who watch things happen,
    the overwhelming majority who have no notion
    of what happens. *(Nicholas Murray Butler)*

All that is necessary for the victory of evil is that good men do nothing. *(Edmund Burke)*

O God, thou knowest how busy I must be this day. If I forget thee, do not thou forget me. *(Sir Jacob Asterley, before the battle of Edgehill)*

I saw the shepherd fold the sheep,
With all the little lambs that leap.
O Shepherd Lord, so I would be
Folded with all my family.
(Wilfrid Meynell)

The Good Shepherd laid down his life for his sheep, that he might convert his Body and Blood in our sacrament, and satisfy the sheep whom he had redeemed with the nourishment of his own flesh. *(Pope St Gregory I)*

PROVERBS

He who builds according to every man's advice will have a crooked house. *(Danish proverb)*

It never troubles a wolf how many the sheep be.
(English proverb)

The wolf eats oft of the sheep that have been warned.
(English proverb)

WORD PICTURES

To the searching heart
   send me with Your Word . . .
To the aching heart
   send me with Your peace . . .
To the broken heart
   send me with Your love . . .
However small or wide my world,
Lord, let me warm it
   with the promise
   that You care . . .
(B. J. Hoff)

Cardinal Heenan was ordered by his doctors to rest, and was staying at a country house in Hertfordshire. He had hardly arrived, when a letter reached him from a Catholic layman so upset by the reforms of the Second Vatican Council that he had decided to leave the Church – although, he added dourly, the Cardinal would hardly be interested in the worries of such an unimportant person.

    Back went the swift reply: 'I am a shepherd, and you are one of my flock. I shall return to London immediately to meet you and discuss your difficulties.' *(Anon)*

When the archaeologists were digging in the ruins of Nineveh they came upon a library of plaques containing the laws of the realm. One of the laws reads, in effect, that anyone guilty of neglect would be held responsible for the result of his neglect . . . If you fail to teach your child to obey, if you fail to teach him to respect the property rights of others, you and not he are responsible of your neglect. *(William Tait)*

Is there any greater pathos in our world than the number of youth, miles outside our churches, who are longing for a Saviour, looking pathetically toward revolutionaries like Che Guevara, or to the student who burned himself alive in Prague? Do you know the hush that comes down when either of them are mentioned? Why no hush for Jesus! Because we have got him lost in our violent Establishment in which the Church is seen as just 'part of the show'; preaching the love of God, silent about the bestialities and obscenities. *(Lord George MacLeod)*

USEFUL TEXTS

Shepherd:
> Duties of, *Ps. 23:2; Matt. 18:12; 1 Sam. 17:34-35*
> Figurative of, *Pss. 23, 78:52, 80:1; Ezek. 34*
> Jesus, *John 10:11; 1 Pet. 2:25*

See also: A21 Feeding the hungry
　　　　　B50 The Good Shepherd

C45

THE DIVINITY OF CHRIST

'The Father who gave them to me is greater than anyone and no one can steal from the Father. The Father and I are one.'
John 10:29-30

QUOTATIONS

Just as every human being is one person, that is, a rational soul and body, so, too, is Christ one Person, the Word and Man. *(St Augustine of Hippo)*

The Son is the Image of the invisible God. All things that belong to the Father he expresses as the Image; all things that are the Father's he illumines as the splendour of his glory and manifests to us. *(St Ambrose)*

There is one Doctor active in both body and soul, begotten and yet unbegotten, God in man, true Life in death, Son of Mary, and Son of God, first able to suffer and then unable to suffer, Jesus Christ our Lord. *(St Ignatius of Antioch)*

We profess two wisdoms in Christ, the uncreated wisdom of God and the created wisdom of man. *(St Thomas Aquinas)*

One difference between Christ and other men is this: they do not choose when to be born, but he, the Lord and Maker, of history, chose his time, his birthplace, and his mother. *(St Thomas Aquinas)*

A God on the cross! That is all my theology. *(Jean Lacordaire)*

If Socrates would enter the room, we should rise and do him honour. But if Jesus Christ came into the room, we should fall down on our knees and worship Him. *(Napoleon)*

If Jesus Christ is not true God, how could *he* help us? If he is not true man, how could he help *us*? *(Dietrich Bonhoeffer)*

I consider the Gospels to be thoroughly genuine; for in them there is the effective reflection of a sublimity which emanated from the Person of Christ; and this is as Divine as ever the divine appeared on earth. *(Goethe)*

If the life and death of Socrates were those of a man, the life and death of Jesus were those of God. *(Jean Jacques Rousseau)*

He that cried in the manger, that sucked the paps of a woman, that hath exposed himself to poverty, and a world of inconveniences, is the Son of the Living God, of the same substance with his Father, begotten before all ages, before the morning-stars; he is God eternal. *(Jeremy Taylor)*

WORD PICTURE

The cell was a concrete box too narrow to sit down. One could only bend one's knees a little, so that they were thrust up against the door, and the position becomes so agonising that it is hard not to cry out. To pray in such circumstances is not easy, but it is a great and sweet solace if one can do so, and one must try with all one's strength to love more, not less. I had to struggle not to sink below the level of love and fall back into the realm of hatred, anger and revenge; to love Romulus Luca (the prison guard) not for a moment but continuously. I had to drive my soul to do this as one may push a vehicle with locked brakes.

It was now that I came to understand Luca, his blindness and narrow hatred, his reactions which were like those of a dog rendered savage by being chained too long, or of a slave put in charge of slaves, with no freedom except to torment them. And then my thoughts went to those, whom it was natural and easy to love. I found that now I loved them differently, now that I had learnt to love Romulus Luca . . . And it was in that cell, my legs sticky with filth, that I at last came to understand the divinity of Jesus Christ, the most divine of all men, the one who had most deeply and intensely loved, and who had conceived the parable of the lost sheep. *(Petru Dumitriu – 'Incognito')*

See also: A37 Christ the King
A44 Meeting Christ in the sacraments
B4 Mary – Handmaid of God
B8 The Word
B46 Christ the Sacrament of God

C46

LOVING KINDNESS

'By this love you have for one another, everyone will know that you are my disciples.' *John 13:35*

QUOTATIONS

Kindness gives birth to kindness. *(Sophocles)*

Nobody is kind only to one person at once, but to many persons in one. *(Frederick W. Faber)*

Kindness is the golden chain by which society is bound together. *(Goethe)*

Kindness has converted more sinners than zeal, eloquence and learning. *(Frederick W. Faber)*

People are lonely because they build walls instead of bridges. *(J. F. Newton)*

The art of saying appropriate words in a kindly way is one that never goes out of fashion, never ceases to please and is within the reach of the humblest. *(Frederick W. Faber)*

Charity gives peace to the soul. For whoever loves God above all things rests his heart in the eternal peace. *(Archbishop Ullathorne)*

To give pleasure to a single heart by a single kind act is better than a thousand head-bowings in prayer. *(Saadi)*

It has been said that charity is the pardoning of the unpardonable and the loving of the unlovable. *(R. H. Benson)*

To love is to admire with the heart; to admire is to love with the mind. *(Theophile Gautier)*

Love is the noblest frailty of the mind. *(John Dryden)*

That best portion of a good man's life – his little, nameless unremembered acts of kindness and of love.
(William Wordsworth)

Don't look for flaws as you go through life;
It is easy enough to find them.
It is wise to be kind, and sometimes blind,
And to look for the virtues behind them.
(Anon)

Kindness in words creates confidence, kindness in thinking creates profundity, and kindness in giving creates love.
(Lao Tzu)

PROVERBS

A kind word is like a Spring day. *(Russian proverb)*

By a sweet tongue and kindness, you can drag an elephant with a hair. *(Persian proverb)*

One can pay back the loan of gold, but one dies for ever in debt to those who are kind. *(Malayan proverb)*

Help thy brother's boat across, and lo! thine own has reached the shore. *(Old Hindu proverb)*

WORD PICTURES

Be kind and merciful. Let no one ever come to you without coming away better and happier. Be the living expression of God's kindness: kindness in your face, kindness in your eyes, kindness in your smile, kindness in your warm greeting.

In the slums we are the light of God's kindness to the poor. To children, to the poor, to all who suffer and are lonely, give always a happy smile – give them not only your care, but also your heart. *(Mother Teresa)*

Confucius is said to have asked Lao-tzu, the Chinese philosopher, 'Which is stronger, the hard or the soft?'

Lao-tzu opened his mouth and asked, 'How is my tongue?'

'Fine,' answered Confucius.

'And my teeth?' added Lao-tzu.

'They are all gone.'

There are 10 strong things. Iron is strong, but fire melts it. Fire is strong, but water quenches it. Water is strong, but the clouds evaporate it. Clouds are strong, but wind drives them away. Man is strong, but fears cast him down. Fear is strong, but sleep overcomes it. Sleep is strong, yet death is stronger. But loving kindness survives death. *(The Talmud)*

A man offered to pay a sum of money to his twelve-year-old daughter if she mowed the lawn. The girl went at the task with great zest and by evening the whole lawn had been beautifully mown – well, everything except a large uncut patch of grass in one corner.

When the man said he couldn't pay the sum agreed upon because the whole lawn hadn't been mown, the girl said she was ready to forgo the money, but would not cut the grass in the patch.

Curious to find out why, he checked the uncut patch. There, right in the centre of the patch, sat a large toad. The girl had been too tenderhearted to run over it with the lawn mower.

Where there is love, there is disorder. Perfect order would make the world a graveyard *(Anthony De Mello)*

Smith and Jones approached the news-stand. Smith greeted the newsman very courteously, but got a most discourteous service in return. Accepting the newspaper, which was shoved rudely in his direction, Smith smiled and wished the newsman a nice day.

As the two friends walked away, Jones asked: 'Does he always treat you so rudely?'

'Yes, unfortunately, he does,' Smith answered.

'Are you always that friendly to him.?'

'I try to be.'

'Tell me, why are you so kind to him when he is so rude to you?'

'Because I don't want him to decide for me how I'm going to act.' *(Anthony De Mello)*

USEFUL TEXTS

Kindness:
  Of the Lord, *1 Pet. 2:3*
  In speech, *Prov. 31:26*
  In Ministry, *2 Cor. 6:6*
  To those in need, *1 John 3:17*
  To all, *Gal. 6:10*

See also: A17 Gentleness
           A33 Love your neighbour
           B41 Generosity
           C18 Compassion

C47
THE INDWELLING SPIRIT

'If anyone loves me he will keep my word,
and my Father will love him, and we shall come to him
and make our home with him.' *John 14:23*

QUOTATIONS
I pray thee, O God, that I may be beautiful within. *(Socrates)*

As the Spirit is the loving presence between the Father and the
Son, he can be present to us only by his work of love.
(George A. Maloney)

Your treasure house is within. It contains all you will ever need.
Use it fully instead of seeking vainly outside yourself. *(Hui Hai)*

However well of Christ
you talk and preach,
unless he lives within,
He is beyond your reach.
(Angelus Silesius)

'Too few people have experienced the divine image as the
innermost possession of their own souls. Christ only meets them
from without, never from within the soul.' *(C. G. Jung)*

'The centre of the soul is God, and when the soul has attained
to him according to the whole capacity of its being, and
according to the force of its operation, it will have reached the
last and deep centre of the soul, which will be when with all its
powers it loves and understands and enjoys God.'
(St John of the Cross)

The gift of the Holy Ghost closes the last gap between the life
of God and ours . . . When we allow the love of God to move

in us, we can no longer distinguish ours and his; he becomes us, he lives us. It is the first fruits of the spirit, the beginning of our being made divine. *(Austin Farrer)*

STATEMENT

Christ is now at work in the hearts of men through the energy of his Spirit. He arouses not only a desire for the age to come, but, by that very fact, he animates, purifies, and strengthens those noble longings too by which the human family strives to make its life more human and to render the whole earth submissive to this goal.
(Second Vatican Council – 'The Church Today')

WORD PICTURES

Jesus said '. . . the Kingdom is within you and without you. If you know yourselves, then you will be known, and you will know that you are sons of the living Father. But if you do not know yourselves, then you are in poverty and you are poverty.'

Jesus said: 'Whoever knows the All but fails to know himself, lacks everything.' *(The Gospel according to Thomas)*

There is a spirit in the soul, untouched by time and flesh, flowing from the spirit, remaining in the spirit, itself wholly spiritual. In this principle is God, ever verdant, ever flowing in all the joy and glory of his actual self. Sometimes I have called that principle the Tabernacle of the soul, sometimes a spiritual light, anon I say it is a Spark. But now I say it is more exalted over this and that than the heavens are exalted above the earth. So now I name it in a nobler fashion . . . It is free of all names, and void of all forms. It is one and simple as God is one and simple, and no man can in any wise behold it. *(Meister Eckhart)*

I was in an underground train, a crowded train in which all sorts of people jostled together, sitting and strap-hanging – workers of every description going home at the end of the day. Quite suddenly I saw in my mind, but as vividly as a wonderful picture, Christ in them all. But I saw more than that: not only was Christ in every one of them, living in them, dying in them, rejoicing in them, sorrowing in them – but because he was in them and because they were here, the whole world was here too, here in this underground train: not only the world as it was at this moment, not only all the people in all the countries of the world, but all the people who had lived in the past, and all those yet to come.

I came out into the street and walked for a long time in the crowds. It was the same here, on every side, in every passer-by – Christ. *(Caryll Houselander, A Rocking-horse Catholic)*

USEFUL TEXTS

Holy Spirit:
Ps. 51:11; Isa. 63:10; Matt. 12:32

See also: B44 The dignity of the individual
B51 One with Christ
C47 The indwelling spirit
C49 Receive the Holy Spirit

C48

ONE IN US

'Father, may they be one in us, as you are in me
and I am in you.' *John 17:21*

QUOTATIONS

I pray that in them there may be a union based on the flesh and
spirit of Jesus Christ, who is our everlasting life, a union of faith
and love, to which nothing is to be preferred, but especially a
union with Jesus and the Father. *(St Ignatius of Antioch)*

Man's perfection is to be like God . . . in unity of spirit, whereby
man not only becomes one with God in the sense that he wills
the same things as God, but in the sense that he is unable to will
what God does not will. *(William of St Thierry)*

You all are fellow-travellers, God-bearers (theophoroi) and
temple bearers (naophoroi), Christ-bearers (Christophoroi).
(St Ignatius of Antioch)

Every rational soul ought with all its strength to desire to
approach God and to be united to him through the perception
of his invisible presence. *(Walter Hilton)*

The soul that is united with God is feared by the devil as though
it were God himself. *(St John of the Cross)*

The deepest prayer which I could ever say is that which makes
me One with that to which I pray. *(Angelus Silesius)*

The end of love is no other thing than the union of the lover and
the thing loved. *(St Francis de Sales)*

It is Christ that prays in every soul in whom he lives.
(R. H. Benson)

It is not only by the imitation of Christ, but by actual union with him, that love becomes and remains the driving force of the soul. *(R. H. Benson)*

None understand better the nature of real distinction than those who have entered into unity. *(John Tauler)*

WORD PICTURES

'I came here to find the Truth, Master.'

'Why wander around and neglect your precious treasure at home?' the master replied.

'What do you call my precious treasure?'

Master replied 'That which asks the question is the treasure.' *(Cheng-tao Ke)*

And after this I saw God in a point; by which sight I saw that he is in all things . . . I saw truly that God doth everything, be it never so little . . . As all that hath being in nature is of God's making, so is every thing that is done in property of God's doing . . . There is no Doer but he . . . And therefore the Blessed Trinity is ever full pleased in all his works. All this he showed fully blissfully, as if to say thus:

'See, I am God. See, I am in all things. See, I never leave my hands off my works, and never shall without end. See, I lead everything to the end I ordain it to, from without beginning, by the same mighty power, wisdom and love that I made it with. How should anything be amiss?'

(Dame Julian of Norwich – 'Revelations of Divine Love')

Your daily life is your temple and your religion.

Whenever you enter into it take with you your all.

Take the plough and the forge and the mallet and the lute,

The things you have fashioned in necessity or for delight.

For in reverie you cannot rise above your achievements, nor fall
     lower than your failures.

And take with you all men:

For in adoration you cannot fly higher than their hopes,
   nor humble
   yourself lower than their despair.
(Kahlil Gibran)

Rossini was an Italian who composed some beautiful music. He
was once given a beautiful watch by the King of France. He was
very proud of this watch because it was a royal gift.

A few years after he had been given it, he showed it to a
friend. His friend told him that although he had the watch for
years he did not know its real value.

'Impossible,' said Rossini.

'Lend it to me for a moment,' said his friend. Taking the
watch, he touched a secret spring and an inner case flew open
revealing a beautiful little painting of Rossini himself. The
composer had never known that the painting was there.
(M. Nassan)

I was dusting the bedroom when I discovered God,
I've often looked for him, or it, before,
Upstairs, downstairs, in my lady's chamber,
But never there where I found it –
   Last place you'd think to look!
Don't think I'm going to tell you right away
Where I found it!
After all, it took me 40 years,
So why should I make it easy for you?
You can damn well wait for a couple more lines at least.
Well now, where was I?
Oh, yes, in the bedroom
Discovering God.
Well, where do you think it was then?
I'll bet you'll never guess.
It was here in me all the time!
(Like Maeterlinck's Blue Bird
Poignantly sitting at home –
That was a heartbreaker film for me to see
When I was an evacuee)

Funny really
Doesn't seem to equate with housework
   Me walking round with the Godhead inside me.
I went in Woolworth's later,
   Met several friends,
But it didn't seem to show.

Just as well, really;
After all, they never show theirs to me.
(Brenda Rogers)

USEFUL TEXTS

Trinity:
   Revealed at Jesus' baptism, *Matt. 3:16-17*
   Baptise in name of, *Matt. 28:19*
   Creation, *Gen. 1:1; Ps. 104:30*
   Salvation, *2 Thess. 2:13-14; Titus 3:4-6*

See also: B44 The dignity of the individual
          B51 One with Christ
          C49 Receive the Holy Spirit

C49

RECEIVE THE HOLY SPIRIT

'As the Father sent me, so am I sending you.'
After saying this he breathed on them and said,
'Receive the Holy Spirit.'
John 20:21-22

QUOTATIONS

Those who have the gale of the Holy Spirit go forward even in sleep. *(Brother Lawrence)*

The Holy Spirit is the living interiority of God. *(Romano Guardini)*

The whole future of the human race depends on bringing the individual soul more completely and perfectly under the sway of the Holy Spirit. *(Isaac T. Hecker)*

The Holy Ghost has called me by the Gospel, and illuminated me with his gifts, and sanctified and preserved me in the true faith. *(Martin Luther)*

The Spirit of God first imparts love; he next inspires hope, and then gives liberty; and that is about the last thing we have in many of our churches. *(Dwight L. Moody)*

Every time we say 'I believe in the Holy Spirit', we mean that we believe there is a living God able and willing to enter human personality and change it. *(J. B. Phillips)*

Love can be used either as an essential name of the divine nature or as a personal name of a divine person – then it is the proper name of the Holy Ghost, as Word is the proper name of the Son. *(St Thomas Aquinas)*

The Holy Spirit Himself, which also operates in the prophets, we assert to be an effluence of God, flowing from Him and returning back again like a beam of the sun. *(Athenagoras)*

I should as soon attempt to raise flowers if there were no atmosphere, or produce fruits if there were neither light nor heat, as to regenerate men if I did not believe there was a Holy Ghost. *(Henry Ward Beecher)*

A gift is freely given, and expects no return. Its reason is love. What is first given is love; that is the first gift. The Holy Ghost comes forth as the substance of love, and Gift is His proper name. *(St Thomas Aquinas)*

Only through Jesus' death and resurrection is the Spirit poured out. Only through repentance and faith in Christ is the Spirit received. Life in the Spirit comes through the Lord of the Spirit. *(Rob Warner)*

HUMOUR

The bishop was gradually getting through a large Confirmation, and one small boy came up whom the bishop seemed to remember he had seen already. Still, he thought he must be mistaken, and confirmed the boy. When later on the same boy appeared for the third time, however, the Bishop bent down and whispered: 'I've confirmed you already, haven't I?' The boy pointed to one of the assistant clergy. 'Yes,' he said 'but that priest over there keeps wiping it off.' *(F. H. Drinkwater)*

STATEMENT

For, wherever they live, all Christians are bound to show forth, by the example of their lives and by the witness of their speech, that new man which they put on at baptism, and that power of the Holy Spirit by whom they were strengthened at Confirmation. Thus other men, observing their good works, can glorify the Father *(cf Matt. 5:16)* and can better perceive the real meaning of human life and the bond which ties the whole community of mankind together.
(Second Vatican Council – 'The Missions')

WORD PICTURES

I have a glove here in my hand. The glove cannot do anything by itself, but when my hand is in it, it can do many things. True, it is not the glove, but my hand in the glove that acts. We are gloves. It is the Holy Spirit in us who is the hand, who does the job. We have to make room for the hand so that every finger is filled.

The question on Pentecost is not whether God is blessing our own plans and programmes but whether we are open to the great opportunities to which his Spirit calls us.
(Corrie Ten Boom)

Mei was a little Chinese girl, three-years-old, dark-eyed with black hair. Her mother had been put in prison for refusing to surrender her Christian Faith (this was in the 1950s) and Mei had to go with her because there was nowhere else for her to go. The Christian prisoners were closely guarded, but the guards let Mei run about everywhere.

Amongst the prisoners was a bishop, and some priests and nuns. They could not say Mass, but there were still priests outside. They used to send in loaves to the prisoners, with consecrated hosts secretly hidden in them by arrangement, so the prisoners were able to receive communion.

Once, one Chinese woman was in solitary confinement. Nobody was allowed to visit her, but the guards did not count Mei. So the little girl took the Blessed Sacrament to her, hidden in her closed fist held demurely in her sleeves.

Later on, Mei's mother was released, and returned with Mei to her village. There was still a missionary priest there, and Mei kept asking him to give her Holy Communion. She was still only four, but she knew all about it, and the priest let her make her first Communion, and a month afterwards she was confirmed.

When the priest was expelled from China, he said goodbye sadly to Mei and her mother, and hoped they would be left alone. He never heard how they got on, but he remembers how Mei said, 'I'm not afraid: I've been confirmed.' *(F. Steels)*

Pure and genuine love always desires above all to dwell wholly in the truth, whatever it may be, unconditionally. Every other sort of love desires, before anything else, means of satisfaction, and for this reason, is a source of error and falsehood. Pure and genuine love is in itself spirit of truth. It is the Holy Spirit. The Greek word, which is translated spirit, means literally fiery breath, breath mingled with fire, and it represented, in antiquity, the notion which science represents today by the word energy. What we translate by 'spirit of truth' signifies the energy of truth, truth as an active force. Pure love is this active force, the love that will not at any price, under any condition, have anything to do with either falsehood or error.
(*Simone Weil*)

See also: A46 Priesthood of the laity
            A47 The Spirit of Truth
            C47 The indwelling spirit

APPENDICES

APPENDIX ONE

SUNDAY THEMES
ASB Lectionary of the Church of England

Before Christmas

	Theme	Sections
9th Sunday	The Creation	A18/A39/B28/B32/B39/C20
8th Sunday	The Fall	

A13/A15/A28/A38/B45/C26/C37

7th Sunday	The Election of God's people: Abraham	A30/A43/B4/B36/B40
6th Sunday	The Promise of Redemption: Moses	A29/B4/B9/B40/C6/C20/C35
5th Sunday	The Remnant of Israel	A3/A7/A22/A30/B1/B38/C1

Advent

1st Sunday	The Advent Hope	A1/A2/A4/B1/C1/C2/C35
2nd Sunday	The Word of God in the Old Testament	A12/A30/B4/B8/C6/C8
3rd Sunday	The Forerunner	A2/A5/A7/A22/C25/C29
4th Sunday	The Annunciation	A4/A40/B7/B41/B44/C7

After Christmas

1st Sunday	The Incarnation	A4/B4/B7/B46/C7
2nd Sunday	The Holy Family	A4/B6/B7/B30/C5/C7

After Epiphany

1st Sunday	Revelation: The Baptism of Jesus	B9/B10/B11/C7
2nd Sunday	Revelation: The First Disciples	A14/B2/B9/C16
3rd Sunday	Revelation: Signs of Glory	A39/B9/B32
4th Sunday	Revelation: The New Temple	A20/B4/B9/C45
5th Sunday	Revelation: The Wisdom of God	A12/B2/B9/B37/C9
6th Sunday	Revelation: Parables	A12/B9/B24

Before Easter

9th Sunday	Christ the Teacher	A6/B2/B24/B50/C9
8th Sunday	Christ the Healer	B3/B16/B23/B32/B46/C13
7th Sunday	Christ the Friend of Sinners	A13/A44/B15/B16/B50

Lent

1st Sunday	The King and the Kingdom: Temptation	A15/A38/C26/C37
2nd Sunday	The King and the Kingdom: Conflict	A15/A38/C15/C28/C37
3rd Sunday	The King and the Kingdom: Suffering	A35/B15/B38/C13/C38
4th Sunday	The King and the Kingdom: Transfiguration	A39/B8/C23/C45
5th Sunday	The King and the Kingdom: The Victory of the Cross	A29/A37/B38/C10
Palm Sunday	The Way of the Cross	A29/B15/B38/B39
Easter Sunday		A42/C42/C43/C45

After Easter

1st Sunday	The Upper Room/The Bread of Life	A44/B27/B29
2nd Sunday	The Emmaus Road/The Good Shepherd	B50/C44
3rd Sunday	The Lakeside/The Resurrection and the Life	C42/C43
4th Sunday	The Charge to Peter/The Way, the Truth and the Life	A47/C44
5th Sunday	Going to the Father	B28/C20/C27
Sunday after		
Ascension	The Ascension of Christ	A39/B51/C48
Pentecost		A47/B53/C47/C48
Trinity Sunday		B40/B54/C20/C45/C48

After Trinity

1st Sunday	The People of God/The Church's Unity and Fellowship	A43/B48/C48
2nd Sunday	The Life of the Baptised/The Church's confidence in Christ	B17/B21/C12
3rd Sunday	The Freedom of the Sons of God/The Church's mission to the individual	B14/B44/C1/C12
4th Sunday	The New Law/The Church's mission to all men	A13/A33/B12/B52/C10
5th Sunday	The New Man	A5/A10/B26/B47/C47
6th Sunday	The More Excellent Way	A10/B11/C38/C39/C47
7th Sunday	The Fruit of the Spirit	A2/A5/A17/A19/B3/B41/C46
8th Sunday	The Whole Armour of God	A3/B21/B35/C32/C35
9th Sunday	The Mind of Christ	A6/A23/A27/A33/C18/C39
10th Sunday	The Serving Community	A1/A7/A21/B14/C3/C17
11th Sunday	The Witnessing Community	A8/A32/A43/B24/B33/C21
12th Sunday	The Suffering Community	A7/A21/B15/B38/C13/C18
13th Sunday	The Family	A46/B6/B32/C5
14th Sunday	Those in Authority	A14/A32/B13
15th Sunday	The Neighbour	A9/A33/C10/C46
16th Sunday	The Proof of Faith	A29/B21/B33/C1/C22
17th Sunday	The Offering of Life	A2/A5/A39/A46/A48/B47
18th Sunday	The Life of Faith	A1/A10/C22/C30
19th Sunday	Endurance	A3/A19/A25/B21/B49/C13
20th Sunday	The Christian Hope	A20/A31/B51/C35
21st Sunday	The Two Ways	A19/A23/C18/C46
22nd Sunday	Citizens of Heaven	A16/A20/A31/B51

APPENDIX TWO

SUNDAY THEMES
For use with the Roman Catholic
three year cycle of Readings

The material is arranged in three parts, A, B and C to correspond with the three year cycle. The themes are those which are suggested by one or more of the Sunday readings.

PART A

Advent	*Theme*	*Text*	*Section*	*Related Sections*
1st Sunday	The value of time	Rom.13:11	A1	A19/B25/C34
2nd Sunday	Integrity	Isa.11:5	A2	B19/B20/B26/C23
3rd Sunday	Perseverance	Matt.11:6	A3	A19/B49/C30/C35
4th Sunday	Emmanuel Mary's Child	Isa.7:14	A4	A37/B4/B8/B46/C45

Of the Year	*(for Christmas see Year B)*			
2nd Sunday	Man for others-unselfishness	Isa.49:3	A5	A33/B41/B47/C34
3rd Sunday	Light of the world	Ps.27:1	A6	A37/B4/B8/B46
4th Sunday	Poor in spirit	Matt.5:3	A7	A11/C21/C25/C29
5th Sunday	The light of example	Matt.5:16	A8	A9/A33/B24
6th Sunday	Relationships	Matt.5:37	A9	A33/B6/B30/B52/C10/C19
7th Sunday	Seeking perfection	Matt.5:48	A10	A20/A22/B26/C47
8th Sunday	God's loving providence	Matt.6:26	A11	A7/A19/B21/C39
9th Sunday	Holy Scripture	Matt.7:24	A12	B2/B9/B24/C6
10th Sunday	The Church is for sinners	Matt.9:13	A13	B17/C12/C27
11th Sunday	The successors of the Apostles	Matt.10:1	A14	A24/A45/B13
12th Sunday	Sin	Rom.5:12	A15	A13/A38/C37
13th Sunday	The Saints	Matt.10:41	A16	A10/B26/B51/C8
14th Sunday	Gentleness	Matt.11:30	A17	A19/B41/C18/C46
15th Sunday	Balance in Nature	Rom.8:20	A18	B32/B39/B42/C34
16th Sunday	Patience	Matt.13:28	A19	A11/B21/C39
17th Sunday	The Kingdom of God	Matt.13:52	A20	A31/B17/B51/C39
18th Sunday	Feeding the hungry	Matt.14:16	A21	A33/B15/C21/C29
19th Sunday	Seeking God	I Kgs.19:12	A22	A10/B28/C16/C38
20th Sunday	Mercy	Isa.56:1	A23	A17/C14/C18/C46
21st Sunday	Papacy	Matt.16:18	A24	A14/B13/B17/C44
22nd Sunday	Courage	Matt.16:21	A25	B35/C13/C41
23rd Sunday	The Sacrament of penance	Matt.18:18	A26	A27/B16/C14/C40
24th Sunday	As we forgive those	Matt.18:22	A27	A26/B16/C14/C40
25th Sunday	Work	Matt.20:8	A28	A1/A18/A36/A39
26th Sunday	True obedience	Phil.2:7	A29	A14/A32/B13/B31/C25
27th Sunday	The Jewish People	Isa.5:7	A30	A12/B36/C8
28th Sunday	Heaven	Isa.25:7	A31	A20/B3/B51/C48
29th Sunday	Civic duty	Matt.22:21	A32	A29/B14/B33/B34

30th Sunday	Love your neighbour	Matt.22:39	A33	A9/B52/C10/C19
31st Sunday	Hypocrisy and Ambition	Matt.23:3	A34	A2/A15/B26/B44
32nd Sunday	Preparing for death	Matt.25:13	A35	A42/B21/B22/B23/B41
33rd Sunday	Using talents	Matt.25:15	A36	A1/A28/A39
34th Sunday	Christ the King	1 Cor.15:25	A37	A4/A44/B4/B8

Lent

1st Sunday	Original Sin	Rom.5:12	A38	A15/B10/C26/C37
2nd Sunday	The Glory of God	Matt.17:2	A39	A20/B40/C31/C39
3rd Sunday	The equality of women	John 4:27	A40	B34/B44/C33
4th Sunday	Spiritual blindness	John 9:26	A41	A22/B49/C26
5th Sunday	Life after death	John 11:25	A42	A31/B22/C35

Eastertide   *(for Easter Day see Year C)*

2nd Sunday	Believing community	Acts 2:42	A43	B17/B36/C12
3rd Sunday	Meeting Christ in the sacraments	Luke 24:30-31	A44	A37/B4/B46/B51/C45
4th Sunday	The Priesthood	Ps.23:1	A45	A14/A46/B13
5th Sunday	Priesthood of the laity	1 Pet.2:9	A46	B10/B44/C49
6th Sunday	The Spirit of Truth	John 14:16-17	A47	B53/C47/C48
7th Sunday	Worship	Acts 1:14	A48	B25/B29/C32

PART B

Advent	*Theme*	*Text*	*Section*	*Related Sections*
1st Sunday	Waiting on the Lord	Mark 13:35	B1	A1/A22/A35/B21/C36
2nd Sunday	The Good News	Isa.40:9	B2	B9/B12/B24/C2
3rd Sunday	Joy in Christ	1 Thess.5:16	B3	B51/C2/C47
4th Sunday	Mary – Handmaid of God	Luke 1:38	B4	A4/A40/B7

Christmas

Christmas Day	A Saviour is born for us	Luke 2:11	B5	A4/B3/C2/C7
Sunday in Octave	The family	Eccles.3:2	B6	A9/B30/C5
1st January	Mary, Mother of God	Luke.2:16	B7	A4/A40/C7/C45
2nd Sunday	The Word	John 1:1	B8	A4/A37/B4/C45
Epiphany	Revelation	Eph.3:3	B9	A12/B2/B24/C8/C38
Sunday after Epiphany	Baptism	Mark 1:8	B10	A38/B36/C26/C47/C49

Of the Year

2nd Sunday	Vocation	1 Sam.3:10	B11	A10/A22/C16/C38
3rd Sunday	On a mission	Mark 1:15	B12	B2/B24/C12/C16
4th Sunday	Authority	Mark 1:27	B13	A14/A24/A29/A32/B14
5th Sunday	Freedom to serve	1 Cor.9:22	B14	B34/B45/C1
6th Sunday	Jesus, friend of outcasts	Mark 1:40	B15	A21/A33/B38/C3
7th Sunday	Christ heals and forgives	Mark 2:5	B16	A15/A26/A27/C22/C27/C4
8th Sunday	The Church – Bride of Christ	Hos.2:21	B17	A13/B36/C12
9th Sunday	Sunday	Mark.2:27	B18	A48/B29

10th Sunday	Conscience	Mark.3:29	B19	A2/A10/A34/B45/C47
11th Sunday	Growth to maturity	Mark.4:28	B20	A2/A7/A10/B28
12th Sunday	Trust in God	Mark.4:40	B21	A11/A19/B52/C39
13th Sunday	Death	Wisd.1:13	B22	A35/A42/B47/C36
14th Sunday	Pastoral care of the sick	2 Cor.12:9	B23	A35/A52/B38
15th Sunday	Go tell everyone	Mark.6:7-13	B24	B2/B12/C8
16th Sunday	Quiet –time for prayer	Mark 6:31	B25	A1/A10/C32/C47
17th Sunday	The whole man	Eph.4:2	B26	A2/A10/B20
18th Sunday	Bread from heaven	John 6:32-33	B27	A21/A44/B29
19th Sunday	The Father who draws us to Himself	John 6:44	B28	B40/C20/C27
20th Sunday	The Eucharist	John 6:55-56	B29	A44/B18/B27
21st Sunday	Married love	Gen.2:24	B30	B8/C13
22nd Sunday	The commandments of life	Jas.1:21	B31	A29/C6/C39
23rd Sunday	The Wonders of God	Mark 7:37	B32	A18/B39
24th Sunday	Faith and good works	Jas.2:17	B33	C22/C30
25th Sunday	Human rights	Jas.3:16	B34	A21/A40/B44/C1/C33
26th Sunday	The Grace of God	Num.11:25	B35	B51/B52/C55
27th Sunday	The Family of God	Heb.2:11	B36	B10/B34/C12/C17/C24
28th Sunday	True Wisdom	Wisd.7:7	B37	A2/B20/B26
29th Sunday	The Suffering Servant	Isa.53:11	B38	B15/B19/B49/C13
30th Sunday	Creation	Ps.126:3	B39	A18/B32
31st Sunday	One God	Deut.6:4	B40	B30/B54/C27
32nd Sunday	Generosity	Mark 12:43	B41	A5/C18/C46
33rd Sunday	Signs of the times	Mark 13:28	B42	A18/B34/C17
34th Sunday	Christ the King	(see A37)		

Lent

1st Sunday	Forty days of Lent	Mark 1:12	B43	B47/C37/C40/C41
2nd Sunday	The dignity of the individual	Rom.8:34	B44	B26/B34/B45/C47
3rd Sunday	Free will	John 2:25	B45	A2/B26/B44
4th Sunday	Christ the Sacrament of God	John 3:14	B46	A44/B16/B51
5th Sunday	Dying to self	John 12:24	B47	A5/A7/A10/B26

Eastertide   *(for Easter Day see Year C)*

2nd Sunday	Christian unity	Acts 4:32	B48	A20/B17/B36/B51
3rd Sunday	Coping with doubt	Luke 24:38	B49	C13/C22/C30/C41
4th Sunday	The Good Shepherd	John 10:11	B50	B15/B38/C44
5th Sunday	One with Christ	John 15:4	B51	B25/C47/C48
6th Sunday	God is Love	1 John 4:8	B52	A9/A33/B30/C10
7th Sunday	Consecrated in Truth	John 17:19	B53	A47/C11/C23

Trinity

Sunday	The Trinity	Matt.28:19-20	B54	A37/A47/B28/B40/C47

PART C

Advent	*Theme*	*Text*	*Section*	*Related Sections*
1st Sunday	Liberation from fear	Luke 21:28	C1	B3/B14/C2
2nd Sunday	Joy of salvation	Ba. 5:9	C2	B3/B14/C1
3rd Sunday	Sharing possessions	Luke.3:10	C3	A7/A21/A33/B41
4th Sunday	Personal peace	Mic.5:4	C4	A2/B19/C17

Of the Year   *(for Christmas see Year B)*

2nd Sunday	The institution of marriage	John 2:1	C5	B6/B30
3rd Sunday	The Old Testament Law	Ps.19:8	C6	A29/B4/B31
4th Sunday	The humanity of Christ	Luke 4:22	C7	A37/B3/B16/C45
5th Sunday	God's messengers	Isa.6:8	C8	B2/B9/B24
6th Sunday	The Beatitudes	Jer.17:7	C9	B2/B3/C2
7th Sunday	Love your enemies	Luke 6:27	C10	A9/A33/B15/B52
8th Sunday	Talk	Luke 6:45	C11	A2/A9/A47/B53
9th Sunday	The Church for all men	1 Kgs.8:43	C12	A6/A13/A43/B17
10th Sunday	Coping with grief	Luke.7:13	C13	A25/B38/B49/C18
11th Sunday	Forgiveness	Luke.7:47	C14	A26/A27/B16/C27/C40
12th Sunday	Prejudice	Gal.3:28	C15	A40/A41/B15/C1
13th Sunday	Come follow me	Luke.9:59-60	C16	A22/B11/B24/C41
14th Sunday	International peace	Isa.66:12	C17	A33/B34/C4/C10
15th Sunday	Compassion	Luke 10:33	C18	A17/A23/A33/C46
16th Sunday	Friendship	Luke 10:38	C19	A9/A33/B15
17th Sunday	Our Father in heaven	Luke 11:12	C20	A22/B28/C27
18th Sunday	Rise above materialism	Luke 12:15	C21	A7/A21/C29
19th Sunday	The Light of faith	Heb.11:2	C22	B33/C30
20th Sunday	Zeal for what is right	Luke 12:49	C23	A2/C8/C39
21st Sunday	Lord of all nations	Isa.66:18	C24	A6/B8/B28/C12
22nd Sunday	Humility	Luke 14:11	C25	A2/A7/A10/B20
23rd Sunday	The human condition	Wisd.9:15	C26	A15/A38/B22/B49/C37
24th Sunday	The Father who receives us back	Luke 15:20	C27	A26/B28/C20/C41
25th Sunday	Lord of the oppressed	Ps.112	C28	A21/B15/B38/B50
26th Sunday	Not through luxury	Amos 6:1	C29	A7/A21/C21
27th Sunday	Increase our faith	Luke 17:5	C30	B33/C22
28th Sunday	Thanksgiving	Luke 17:15-16	C31	A17/A39/A48/B41
29th Sunday	Prayer	Luke 18:7	C32	A22/A48/B25/B29
30th Sunday	Equality	Eccles 35:12	C33	A9/A40/B34/B44
31st Sunday	The value of little things	Wisd.11:22	C34	A5/A18/B20/B33
32nd Sunday	Hope	2 Macc 7:14	C35	A6/A19/B21/C1
33rd Sunday	The Day of the Lord	Mal.3:19	C36	A31/A42/B22

Lent

1st Sunday	Temptation	Luke 4:1	C37	A15/A38/B19/C26
2nd Sunday	Discerning God's will	Gen.15:8	C38	A41/B11/B47/C39
3rd Sunday	Doing God's will	Exod.3:14	C39	A41/B11/B47/C38
4th Sunday	Reconciliation	2 Cor.5:18	C40	A26/A27/B16/C14
5th Sunday	Starting afresh	Phil.3:14	C41	A25/B14/C1

Eastertide

Easter

Sunday	The Risen Lord	Acts 10:40	C42	A44/C43/C45/C47
2nd Sunday	The Living One	John 20:29	C43	A44/C42/C45/C47
3rd Sunday	Feed my sheep	John 21:17	C44	A21/B52
4th Sunday	The Divinity of Christ	John 10:29-30	C45	A37/A44/B4/B8/B46
5th Sunday	Loving kindness	John 13:35	C46	A17/A33/B41/C18
6th Sunday	The indwelling spirit	John 14:23	C47	B44/B51/C48/C49
7th Sunday	One in us	John 17:21	C48	B44/B51/C47/C49
Pentecost	Receive the Holy Spirit	John 20:21-22	C49	A46/A47/C47

APPENDIX THREE

SUNDAY THEMES
For use with the Revised Common Lectionary
(Adapted for the Church of England)

YEAR A	Theme	Text	Section	Related Sections
Advent				
1st Sunday	The value of time	Rom. 13:11	A1	A19/B25/C34
2nd Sunday	Integrity	Isa. 11:5	A2	B19/B20/B26/C23
3rd Sunday	Perseverance	Matt. 11:1-6	A3	A19/B49/C30/C35
4th Sunday	Emmanuel, Mary's Child	Isa. 7:14	A4	A37/B4/B8/B46/C45
Christmas				
Christmas Day				
Sets I & II	A Saviour is born for us	Luke 2:11	B5	A4/B3/C2/C7
Set III	God Incarnate	John 1:14	B5	A4/B3/C2/C7
1st Sunday	God among the			
	marginalised	Matt. 2:18	C28	A21/B15/B38/B50
2nd Sunday	The Word	John 1:1	B8	A4/A37/B4/C45
Epiphany	Revelation	Eph. 3:3	B9	A12/B2/B24/C8/C38
1st Sunday	The baptism of Christ	Matt. 3:13	B10	A38/B36/C26/C47/C49
2nd Sunday	Man for others –			
	unselfishness	Isa. 49:3	A5	A33/B41/B47/C34
3rd Sunday	Light of the world	Ps. 27:1	A6	A37/B4/B8/B46
4th Sunday	God values the humble	1 Cor. 1:27	C34	A5/A18/B20/B33
Presentation	The Lord comes			
of Christ	to his temple	Mal. 3:1	C36	A31/A42/B22
Ordinary Time				
Proper 1	The light of example	Matt. 5:16	A8	A9/A33/B24
Proper 2	Relationships	Matt. 5:37	A9	A33/B6/B30/B52/
				C10/C19
Proper 3	Seeking perfection	Matt. 5:48	A10	A20/A22/B26/C47
2 before Lent	God's loving providence	Matt. 6:26	A11	A7/A19/B21/C39
1 before Lent	Christ reveals God's glory	2 Peter 1:17	A37	A4/A44/B4/B8
Lent				
1st Sunday	Original sin	Rom. 5:12	A38	A15/B10/C26/C37
2nd Sunday	Grace and faith	Rom. 4:16	B21	A11/A19/B52/C39
3rd Sunday	God saves us in Christ	Rom. 5:7-8	B52	A9/A33/B30/C10
4th Sunday	Spiritual blindness	John 9:26	A41	A22/B49/C26
or Mothering				
Sunday	The equality of women	John 19:25	A40	B34/B44/C33
5th Sunday	Life after death	John 11:25	A42	A31/B22/C35
Palm Sunday	Passion and glory	Phil 2:8-9	B38	B15/B19/B49/C13
Easter				
Easter Day	The risen Lord	Acts 10:40	C42	A44/C43/C45/C47
2nd Sunday	Believing community	John 20:29	A43	B17/B36/C12

3rd Sunday	Meeting Christ in the sacraments	Luke 24:30-31	A44	A37/B4/B46/B51/C45
4th Sunday	The Priesthood	Ps. 23:1	A45	A14/A46/B13
5th Sunday	Priesthood of the laity	1 Pet. 2:9	A46	B10/B44/C49
6th Sunday	The Spirit of Truth	John 14:16-17	A47	B53/C47/C48
7th Sunday	Worship	Acts 1:14	A48	B25/B29/C32
Pentecost	Receive the Holy Spirit	John 20:21-22	C49	A46/A47/C47
Trinity Sunday	The Trinity	Matt. 28:19-20	B54	A37/A47/B28/B40/C47
Proper 4	Holy Scripture	Matt. 7:24	A12	B2/B9/B24/C6
Proper 5	The Church is for sinners	Matt. 9:13	A13	B17/C12/C27
Proper 6	The successors of the Apostles	Matt. 10:1	A14	A24/A45/B13
Proper 7	Sin	Rom. 6:2b	A15	A13/A38/C37
Proper 8	The offering of life	Matt. 10:42	B41	A5/C18/C46
Proper 9	Gentleness	Matt. 11:30	A17	A19/B41/C18/C46
Proper 10	God's word bears fruit	Isa. 55:10-11	A12	B2/B9/B24/C6
Proper 11	Patience	Matt. 13:28	A19	A11/B21/C39
Proper 12	The Kingdom of God	Matt. 13:52	A20	A31/B17/B51/C39
Proper 13	Feeding the hungry	Matt. 14:16	A21	A33/B15/C21/C29
Proper 14	Seeking God	1 Kings 19:12	A22	A10/B28/C16/C38
Proper 15	Mercy	Isa. 56:1	A23	A17/C14/C18/C46
Proper 16	Discernment	Rom. 12:2	B19	A2/A10/A34/B45/C47
Proper 17	Courage	Matt. 16:21	A25	B35/C13/C41
Proper 18	Penance	Matt. 18:18	A26	A27/B16/C14/C40
Proper 19	As we forgive those	Matt. 18:22	A27	A26/B16/C14/C40
Proper 20	Work	Matt. 20:8	A28	A1/A18/A36/A39
Proper 21	True obedience	Phil. 2:7	A29	A14/A32/B13/B31/C25
Proper 22	The Jewish People	Isa. 5:4	A30	A15/A34/A38
Proper 23	Heaven	Isa. 25:7	A31	A20/B3/B51/C48
Proper 24	Civic duty	Matt. 22:21	A32	A29/B14/B33/B34
Proper 25	Love your neighbour	Matt. 22:39	A33	A9/B52/C10/C19
Bible Sunday	Holy Scripture	Matt. 24:35	A12	B2/B9/B24/C6

Before Advent				
4th Sunday	Hypocrisy and ambition	Micah 3:5	A34	A2/A15/B26/B44
3rd Sunday	Preparing for death	Matt. 25:13	A35	A42/B21/B22/B23/B41
2nd Sunday	Using talents	Matt. 25:15	A36	A1/A28/A39
Last Sunday	Christ the King	Eph. 1:22	A37	A4/A44/B4/B8

YEAR B	*Theme*	*Text*	*Section*	*Related sections*
Advent				
1st Sunday	Waiting on the Lord	Mark 13:35	B1	A1/A22/A35/B21/C36
2nd Sunday	The Good News	Isaiah 40:9	B2	B9/B12/B24/C2
3rd Sunday	Joy in Christ	1 Thess. 5:16	B3	B51/C2/C47
4th Sunday	Mary – Handmaid of God	Luke 1:38	B4	A4/A40/B7

Christmas				
Christmas Day	See Year A			
1st Sunday	Mary, Mother of God	Luke 2:16	B7	A4/A40/C7/C45
2nd Sunday	Salvation in Christ	Eph. 1:3	C2	B3/B14/C2

Epiphany

The Epiphany	Revelation	Eph. 3:3	B9	A12/B2/B24/C8/C38
1st Sunday	The Baptism of Christ	Mark 1:8	B10	A38/B36/C26/C47/C49
2nd Sunday	Vocation	1 Sam. 3:10	B11	A10/A22/C16/C38
3rd Sunday	The Church – Bride of Christ	Rev. 19:6-8	B17	A13/B36/C12
4th Sunday	Authority	Mark 1:27	B13	A14/A24/A29/A32/B14
Presentation of Christ	The Lord comes to his temple	Mal. 3:1	C36	A31/A42/B22

Ordinary Time

Proper 1	Freedom to serve	1 Cor. 9:22	B14	B34/B45/C1
Proper 2	Jesus, friend of outcasts	Mark 1:40	B15	A21/A33/B38/C3
Proper 3	Christ heals and forgives	Mark 2:5	B16	A15/A26/A27/C22/C27/C40
2 before Lent	Christ, the eternal Son	Col. 1:15-18	C45	A37/A44/B4/B8/B46
1 before Lent	The glory of God	2 Cor. 4:6	A39	A20/B40/C31/C39

Lent

1st Sunday	Forty days of Lent	Mark 1:12	B43	B47/C37/C40/C41
2nd Sunday	True faith	Rom. 4:16	C22	B33/C30
3rd Sunday	The wisdom of God	1 Cor. 1:19	B37	A2/B20/B26
4th Sunday	Christ the sacrament of God	John 3:14	B46	A44/B16/B51
or Mothering Sunday	The equality of women	John 19:25	A40	B34/B44/C33
5th Sunday	Dying to self	John 12:24	B47	A5/A7/A10/B26
Palm Sunday	Passion and glory	Phil. 2:8-9	B38	B15/B19/B49/C13

Easter

Easter Day	The risen Lord	Acts 10:40	C42	A44/C43/C45/C47
2nd Sunday	Christian unity	Acts 4:32	B48	A20/B17/B36/B51
3rd Sunday	Coping with doubt	Luke 24:38	B49	C13/C22/C30/C41
4th Sunday	The Good Shepherd	John 10:11	B50	B15/B38/C44
5th Sunday	God is love	1 John 4:8	B52	A9/A33/B30/C10
6th Sunday	One with Christ	John 15:9-10	B51	B25/C47/C48
7th Sunday	Consecrated in Truth	John 17:19	B53	A47/C11/C23
Pentecost	Receive the Holy Spirit	Acts 2:4	C49	A46/A47/C47
Trinity Sunday	The Trinity	Rom. 8:16-17	B54	A37/A47/B28/B40/C47
Proper 4	Sunday	Mark 2:27	B18	A48/B29
Proper 5	Firm in the faith	2 Cor. 4:13	C30	B33/C22
Proper 6	Growth to maturity	Mark 4:28	B20	A2/A7/A10/B28
Proper 7	Trust in God	Mark 4:40	B21	A11/A19/B52/C39
Proper 8	Death	Wisd. 1:13	B22	A35/A42/B47/C36
Proper 9	Pastoral care of the sick	2 Cor. 12:9	B23	A35/A52/B38
Proper 10	Justice and peace	Eph. 1:14	B34	A24/A40/B44/C1/C33
Proper 11	Quiet – time for prayer	Mark 6:31	B25	A1/A10/C32/C47
Proper 12	The family	Eph. 2:14	B6	A9/B30/C5
Proper 13	Bread from heaven	Ex. 16:4	B27	A21/A44/B29
Proper 14	Community	Eph. 4:32	A9	A33/B6/B30/B52/C10/C19
Proper 15	The Eucharist	John 6:55-56	B29	A44/B18/B27

Proper 16	God's faithfulness	Eph 6:10	B40	B30/B54/C27
Proper 17	The commandments of life	Jas. 1:21	B31	A29/C6/C39
Proper 18	The wonders of God	Mark 7:37	B32	A18/B39
Proper 19	A careful tongue	A2	A2	B19/B20/B26/C23
Proper 20	Human rights	Jas. 3:16	B34	A21/A40/B44/C1/C33
Proper 21	The grace of God	Num. 11:25	B35	B51/B52/C55
Proper 22	The family of God	Heb. 2:11	B36	B10/B34/C12/C17/C24
Proper 23	The greatness of God	Heb. 4:16	A39	A20/B40/C31/C39
Proper 24	The suffering servant	Isa. 53:11	B38	B15/B19/B49/C13
Proper 25	God of compassion	Jer. 31:8	C18	A17/A23/A33/C46
Bible Sunday	Holy Scripture	Isa. 55:3	A12	B2/B9/B24/C6

Before Advent

4th Sunday	Love of God and neighbour	Mark 12:29-30	A33	A9/B52/C10/C19
3rd Sunday	Following Jesus	Mark 1:17	C16	A22/B11/B24/C41
2nd Sunday	Signs of the times	Mark 13:7-8	B42	A18/B34/C17
Last Sunday	Christ the King	Rev. 1:7	A37	A4/A44/B4/B8

YEAR C	*Theme*	*Text*	*Section*	*Related Sections*
Advent				
1st Sunday	Liberation from fear	Luke 21:28	C1	B3/B14/C2
2nd Sunday	Joy of salvation	Ba. 5:9	C2	B3/B14/C1
3rd Sunday	Sharing possessions	Luke 3:10	C3	A7/A21/A33/B41
4th Sunday	God incarnate	Micah 5:2	A4	A37/B4/B8/B46/C45

Christmas

Christmas Day	See Year A			
1st Sunday	The family	Eph. 3:13	B6	A9/B30/C5
2nd Sunday	The Word	John 1:1	B8	A4/A37/B4/C45

Epiphany

The Epiphany	Revelation	Eph. 3:3	B9	A12/B2/B24/C8/C38
1st Sunday	The baptism of Christ	Luke 3:16	B10	A38/B36/C26/C47/C49
2nd Sunday	God's gracious covenant	Isa. 62:4	B35	B51/B52/C55
3rd Sunday	The Old Testament law	Psa. 19:8	C6	A29/B4/B31
4th Sunday	The law's fulfilment	1 Cor. 13:1-3	A33	A9/B52/C10/C19
Presentation of Christ	The Lord comes to his temple	Mal. 3:1	C36	A31/A42/B22

Ordinary Time

Proper 1	God's messengers	Isa. 6:8	C8	B2/B9/B24
Proper 2	The Beatitudes	Jer. 17:7	C9	B2/B3/C2
Proper 3	Love your enemies	Luke 6:27	C10	A9/A33/B15/B52
2 before Lent	Lord of creation	Rev. 4:11	B39	A18/B32
1 before Lent	The glory of God	2 Cor. 3:18	A39	A20/B40/C31/C39

Lent

1st Sunday	Temptation	Luke 4:1	C37	A15/A38/B19/C26
2nd Sunday	Discerning God's will	Gen. 15:8	C38	A41/B11/B47/C39
3rd Sunday	Doing God's will	1 Cor. 10:6	C39	A41/B11/B47/C38

4th Sunday	Reconciliation	Luke 15:24	C40	A26/A27/B16/C14
or Mothering				
Sunday	The equality of women	John 19:25	A40	B34/B44/C33
5th Sunday	Starting afresh	Phil. 3:14	C41	A25/B14/C1
Palm Sunday	Passion and glory	Phil. 2:8-9	B38	B15/B19/B49/C13

Easter

Easter Sunday	The risen Lord	Acts 10:40	C42	A44/C43/C45/C47
2nd Sunday	The Living One	John 20:29	C43	A44/C42/C45/C47
3rd Sunday	Feed my sheep	John 21:17	C44	A21/B52
4th Sunday	The divinity of Christ	John 10:29-30	C45	A37/A44/B4/B8/B46
5th Sunday	Loving kindness	John 13:35	C46	A17/A33/B41/C18
6th Sunday	The indwelling Spirit	John 14:23	C47	B44/B51/C48/C49
7th Sunday	One in us	John 17:21	C48	B44/B51/C47/C49
Pentecost	Receive the Holy Spirit	John 14:15-16	C49	A46/A47/C47
Trinity Sunday	The Trinity	John 16:15	B54	A37/A47/B28/B40/C47
Proper 4	The Church for all people	1 Kgs. 8:43	C12	A6/A13/A43/B17
Proper 5	Coping with grief	Luke 7:13	C13	A25/B38/B49/C18
Proper 6	Forgiveness	Luke 7:47	C14	A26/A27/B16/C27/C40
Proper 7	Prejudice	Gal. 3:28	C15	A40/A41/B15/C1
Proper 8	Come, follow me	Luke 9:59-60	C16	A22/B11/B24/C41
Proper 9	International peace	Isa. 66:12	C17	A33/B34/C4/C10
Proper 10	Compassion	Luke 10:33	C18	A17/A23/A33/C46
Proper 11	Friendship	Luke 10:38	C19	A9/A33/B15
Proper 12	Our Father in heaven	Luke 11:12	C20	A22/B28/C27
Proper 13	Rise above materialism	Luke 12:15	C21	A7/A21/C29
Proper 14	The light of faith	Heb. 11:2	C22	B33/C30
Proper 15	Zeal for what is right	Luke 12:49	C23	A2/C8/C39
Proper 16	Humility	Luke 14:11	C25	A2/A7/B10/B20
Proper 17	The human condition	Heb. 13:3	C26	A15/A38/B22/B49/C37
Proper 18	Choosing the good	Deut. 30:15	B19	A2/A10/A34/B45/C47
Proper 19	Saving the lost	Luke 15:7	C27	A26/B28/C20/C41
Proper 20	Lord of the oppressed	Amos 8:4-7	C28	A21/B15/B38/B50
Proper 21	Not through luxury	Amos 6:1	C29	A7/A21/C21
Proper 22	Increase our faith	Luke 17:5	C30	B33/C22
Proper 23	Thanksgiving	Luke 17:15-16	C31	A17/A39/A48/B41
Proper 24	Prayer	Luke 18:7	C32	A22/A48/B25/B29
Proper 25	Equality	Ecclus. 35:12	C33	A9/A40/B34/B44
Bible Sunday	Holy Scripture	Rom. 15:4	A12	B2/B9/B24/C6

Before Advent

4th Sunday	God of justice	Is. 1:17	B33	C22/C30
3rd Sunday	Hope	Job. 19:25-27	C35	A6/A19/B21/C1
2nd Sunday	The day of the Lord	Mal. 4:1-2	C36	A31/A42/B22
Last Sunday	Christ the King	Col. 1:15	A37	A4/A44/B4/B8

APPENDIX FOUR

SCHOOL ASSEMBLY
Theme Index

The Human Condition

Ambition	A34
Balance in nature	A18
Death	B22 & A35
Conscience	B19
Doubt	B49
Grief	C13
Human condition	C26
Hypocrisy	A34
Original Sin	A38
Pain	B38
Prejudice	C15
Seeking God	A22
Signs of the times	B42
Sin	A15
Spiritual blindness	A41
Temptation	C37
Work	A28

Relationships

Family	B6
Feeding the hungry	A21
Friendship	C19
Human rights	B34
Love your enemies	C10
Love your neighbour	A33
Married love	B30
Reconciliation	C40
Relationships	A9
Sharing	C3

God

Father who draws us to Himself	B28
Glory of God	A39
God is Love	B52
Indwelling Spirit	C47
Lord who works marvels	B39
One God	B40
Spirit of Truth	A47
Trinity	B54
Creation	B39

Communication with God

Covenant of God	B4
God's will	C38 & C39

Good News	B2
Holy Scripture	A12
Mission	B12
Prayer	C32
Providence	A11
Revelation	B9
Vocation	B11
Worship	A48

Christ

Christ the Covenant of God	B4
Christ the King	A37
Christ heals and forgives	B16
Divinity of Christ	C45
Emmanuel	A4
Humanity of Christ	C7
Jesus, friend of outcasts	B15
Light of the world	A6
Lord of all nations	C24
Risen Lord	C42
Living One	C43
Suffering Servant	B38
The Word	B8

The Church

Authority	B13
Believing community	A43
Church for all men	C12
Church triumphant	A16
Church – Bride of Christ	B17
Church for sinners	A13
The Family of God	B36
Feed my sheep	C44
Jewish people	A30
Mary, Mother of God	B7
Mary, Handmaid of God	B4
The Pope	A24
Priesthood	A45
Priesthood of laity	A46
Successors of the Apostles	A14

The Sacraments of God

Baptism	B10
Bread of Heaven	B27
Christ the Sacrament of God	B46

INDEXES

Subject Index

INDEX OF SOURCES

ACKNOWLEDGMENTS

The compiler and publishers would like to thank the following publishers and copyright holders for permission to reproduce material from the following publications.

Hodder and Stoughton Ltd, for *Through the Year with Cardinal Heenan* by Cardinal Heenan; *In Spite of Dungeons* by S.J. Davies; *The Trumpet of Conscience* by Martin Luther King; *Candles in the Darkness* by Mary Craig, and *Better Together* by Archbishop Derek Worlock and Archbishop David Sheppard.

HarperCollins Publishers for *Through the Valley of the Kwai* by Ernest Gordon; *Autobiography* by Yevtushenko; *History and Human Relations* by Herbert Butterfield; *Naught for Your Comfort* by Trevor Huddleston; *Mere Christianity* by C.S. Lewis; *Something Beautiful for God* by Malcolm Muggeridge; *Dying We Live* by Kathe Kunn; *The Plain Man Looks at the Apostles' Creed* by William Barclay; *Incognito* by Petru Dumitrui; *Journey for a Soul* by George Appleton; *Readings with William Barclay* by Anthony de Mello; *Three from Galilee* by Marjorie Holmes; *Audacity to Believe* by Sheila Cassidy; and *The Heart of the Enlightened* by Anthony de Mello.

Darton, Longman & Todd Ltd for *Benedictine Tapestry* by Felicitas Corrigan and *The Little Way* by Bernard Bro, OP.

St. Paul Publications for *Gateway to the Trinity* by Tony Castle.

Rev. John Medcalf for an extract from one of his letters from South America.

Ateliers et Presses de Taize for material from *Mary, Mother of Reconciliation* by Mother Teresa and Bro. Roger Schultz.

Amnesty International for a quotation from Salvador de Magariaga.

Victor Gollancz Ltd for a passage from *The Nine Tailors* by Dorothy Sayers and *A Year of Grace* by Victor Gollancz.

Geoffrey Chapman Ltd for extracts from *The Documents of Vatican II* edited by Walter M. Abbot SJ.

Cassell Ltd for *Lord Nuffield* by E. Gillbank.

Yorkshire Committee for Community Relations for extracts from *Religion in a Multi-Faith School*.

Franklin Watts Ltd. for *St. Francis of Assisi* by Douglas Liversidge.

Lawrence Pollinger Ltd for *Phoenix* by Complete Poems by D.H. Lawrence.

Alfred Knopf Inc. for extracts from *The Prophet* by Kahlil Gibran.

SCM Press Ltd for *Letters and Papers from Prison* by Dietrich Bonhoeffer (Enlarged edition 1971); *The Cost of Discipleship* by Dietrich Bonhoeffer and *Interpreting the Cross* by Max Warren.

George Allen & Unwin Ltd for *Lord of the Rings* by J.R.R. Tolkien.

Hulton Educational Publications Ltd for *The Way of the Hindu* by Swami Yogeshananda.

Religious Education Press for *Orders from Christ* by John Foster.

Heinemann Educational Books Ltd for *A Man for All Seasons* by Robert Bolt.

The Daily Telegraph for *Hymn and Prayer for Civil Servants*.

Sheed and Ward Ltd for *Considerations* by Hubert Van Zeller; and *A Rocking Horse Catholic* by Caryll Houselander.

Catholic Truth Society for the translation of *Divino Afflante Spiritu.*

Gabriel Communications Ltd (formerly Associated Catholic Publications Ltd) for *52 Talks for Young People.*

A.D. Peters & Co. Ltd for *An Only Child* by Frank O'Connor.

Twenty-Third Publications of Connecticut, USA, for a story by William J. Bausch from *More Telling Stories.*

Dr. Sheila Cassidy and The Tablet for material from several articles that appeared in The Tablet.

The Catholic Herald for material from articles by Ronald Rolheiser.

St. Paul Publications for *Mary for Today* by Hans-Urs von Balthasar and material from *Gateway to the Trinity* by Tony Castle.

Christian Aid for a Latin American child's poem.

The Tablet for pieces by Jon Sobrino SJ, Benedict Heron, Penny Lernoux.

William Heinemann Ltd for *The Velveteen Rabbit* by Margery Williams.

Adam & Charles Black for *The Quest for the Historical Jesus* by Albert Schweitzer.

Argus Communications of Illinois, USA, for material by Mark Link SJ.

Mr. Paul Frost for passages from an unpublished manuscript.

Darton, Longman and Todd Ltd for material by Jean Vanier.

The Guardian for the Obituary of Tubby Clayton.

Associated Catholic Publications Ltd (The Universe) for *52 Talks for Young People* by Maurice Nassan SJ and *Woodruff at Random* edited by Mary Craig.

The estate of the late Monsignor F. H. Canon Drinkwater for *The Fourth Book of Catechism Stories.*

Geoffrey Chapman (an imprint of Cassell Publishers Ltd) for *The Documents of Vatican II* edited by Walter M. Abbott SJ.

Catholic Institute for International Relations for *This is Progress* a translation of *Populorum Progressio.*

Every effort has been made to trace the owners of copyright material and we hope that no copyright has been infringed. If the contrary is shown to be the case, apology is made and the publisher will be happy to rectify the omission at the first convenient opportunity.